Pillars of Salt, Monuments of Grace

The *Commonwealth Center Studies in American Culture*
series is published in cooperation with the
Commonwealth Center for the Study of American Culture
at the College of William and Mary,
Williamsburg, Virginia,
by Oxford University Press,
New York

Pillars of Salt, Monuments of Grace

New England Crime Literature
and the Origins of American
Popular Culture, 1674–1860

DANIEL A. COHEN

New York   Oxford
OXFORD UNIVERSITY PRESS
1993

Oxford University Press

Oxford   New York   Toronto
Delhi   Bombay   Calcutta   Madras   Karachi
Kuala Lumpur   Singapore   Hong Kong   Tokyo
Nairobi   Der es Salaam   Cape Town
Melbourne   Aukland   Madrid

and associated companies in
Berlin   Ibadan

Copyright ©1993 by Daniel A. Cohen

Published by Oxford University Press, Inc.,
200 Madison Avenue, New York, New York 10016

Oxford is a registered trademark of Oxford University Press

Library of Congress Cataloging-in-Publication Data
Cohen, Daniel A.
Pillars of salt, monuments of grace : New England crime literature
and the origins of American popular culture, 1674–1860 / Daniel A. Cohen.
p. cm.   Includes bibliographical references and index.
ISBN 0-19-507584-6
1. American literature—New England—History and criticism.
2. Popular literature—New England—History and criticism.
3. United States—Popular culture—Moral and ethical aspects.
4. New England—Popular culture—Moral and ethical aspects.
5. Crime—New England—History.   6. Authority in literature.
7. Crime in literature.   I. Title.
PS243.C64   1993a810.9′355—dc20   91-48353

I am grateful to the editors of the listed journals for permission
to reprint revised versions or sections of the following articles of mine.

"In Defense of the Gallows: Justifications of Capital Punishment
in New England Execution Sermons, 1674–1825,"
American Quarterly, vol. 40, no. 2 (June 1988): 147–64. Copyright © 1988,
American Studies Association.

"A Fellowship of Thieves: Property Criminals
in Eighteenth-Century Massachusetts," *Journal of Social History,*
vol. 22, no. 1 (Fall 1988): 65–92.

"The Murder of Maria Bickford: Fashion, Passion, and the Birth
of a Consumer Culture," *American Studies,* vol. 31, no. 2 (Fall 1990): 5–30.
Copyright © 1991, Mid-America American Studies Association.

1 3 5 7 9 8 6 4 2

Printed in the United States of America
on acid-free paper

To my parents

Preface

Late one evening in December 1685, a foulmouthed, hard-drinking currier was beating his wife at a disreputable boardinghouse in Boston. When a local butcher, sitting with two companions at a nearby fireplace, heard the woman's cries of distress, he rushed into the room to intervene in the domestic quarrel. In response, the drunken man plunged an iron spit into the butcher's belly. Three months later, after being condemned in court and proselytized in prison, the chastened currier sat in a packed meetinghouse to hear the last in a series of sermons addressing his case, this one delivered by the most prominent minister in the Bay Colony. The convicted man then left the church building and trudged along a muddy road to the gallows, accompanied by the clergyman's son and junior colleague, soon to achieve an eminence nearly equal to his father's. After offering the penitent murderer some last spiritual instructions, the young minister bid him an emotional farewell, leaving him to be launched into eternity before an audience of thousands. Contemporary readers eager to learn more about the case had only one option. They could not purchase an account of the crime itself, or a report of the trial, or a ballad on the execution, or a play reenacting the tragedy, for such popular English genres were not available in the sharply constricted literary marketplace of late seventeenth-century Boston. Instead, people rushed out to buy a volume featuring sermons by three local ministers, pious statements by the condemned currier, and descriptions of his conspicuous contrition at the gallows. The book as a whole focused on the spiritual fate of the executed man and implied that he had in the end turned to Christ for life.

Some forty years later, the young boatswain on a vessel bound from Jamaica to Guinea, bitter over mistreatment by his captain, organized a mutiny among the crew. "Damn you, if you stir hand or foot, or speak a word, I'll blow your Brains out," he warned a recalcitrant sailor. The mutineers then dragged the captain and mate up from below and threw them overboard despite their pleas for mercy. The upstart captain declared himself and his crew "Gentlemen of Fortune" and embarked on a short career of piracy. But a countermutiny soon subdued the boatswain and his supporters. Several of the men, including the ringleader, were taken to Boston, tried before a special Court of Admiralty, and sentenced to die. While they were in jail awaiting execution, a local minister met with them. It was the same clergyman who had walked to the gallows with the penitent currier. Now an old man, himself not far from death, the eminent minister tried to guide the doomed felons to repentance during their last days on earth. But the former boatswain was far less malleable than the others. "We poor Men can't have Justice done us," he complained. "There is nothing said to our Commanders, let them never so much abuse us, and use us like Dogs." Similarly unchastened on the day of his death, he was nonchalant in his demeanor at the place of execution as if "ambitious to have it said, *That he died a brave fellow!*" After the hangings local ministers published a few sermons on the case, but the volumes also featured vivid accounts of the mutiny and piracies, transcripts of contentious prison interviews, and descriptions of the felon's playful banter at the gallows. Bostonians could also read about the case in local newspapers and in a published trial report. Crime coverage, an arena of pious consensus forty years earlier, was gradually becoming contested ground.

More than sixty years after the demise of the defiant pirate, on a wintry evening in January 1791, a group of at least six men, recruited by a constable and fortified by a bottle of rum, went to arrest a young man accused of stealing an iron kettle in Stephentown, New York, just west of the Massachusetts border. Trying to escape through deep snow into the woods behind his house, the suspect was surrounded and tackled by his pursuers. In the brief struggle that followed, one of the constable's deputies was fatally stabbed. After being tried, convicted of murder, and condemned to die, the young man sat in shackles at the Albany jail, recording his side of the story for posterity. He not only penned a trial account assailing his conviction as a miscarriage of justice but also appended a religious tract assaulting the fundamental doctrines of Calvinism. In dense prose and stilted verse, the jailhouse theologian articulated beliefs similar to those of the Freewill Baptists, one of several unorthodox sects that were sweeping the hinterlands of northern New England and upstate New York during the last decades of the eighteenth century. The narrative, issued by a local newspaper publisher in nearby Lansingburgh and reprinted at least a dozen times throughout the Northeast over the next several years, was one of the earliest and most popular anti-Calvinist evangelical tracts circulated in the early republic. In the cultural maelstrom of post-Revolutionary America, no book, pamphlet, or broadside was issued by the friends of authority to dispute the condemned man's unorthodox testament.

Nearly fifty years after the last printing of the murderer's polemical tract, in October 1845, the charred corpse of a young married woman from Maine was found in a burning bedroom at a house of assignation in the West End of Boston. Her throat had been cut from ear to ear. The chief suspect was the victim's paramour, a wealthy young rake from Weymouth, who had fled from the scene of the crime. He was arrested in December off the coast of Louisiana and successively tried in Boston on charges of murder and arson. His senior counsel was a renowned criminal lawyer and Whig politician just returning to the city after a term in the U.S. Senate. The flamboyant advocate mounted a defense worthy of a romantic novelist. Had the "fallen woman" cut her own throat? Had his unfortunate client killed her while in a somnambulistic trance? Or, as the prosecutor gamely insisted, had he intentionally murdered her to free himself from his own obsessive passion? Over a period of many months, the popular press flooded the city with lurid accounts of the crime, romantic biographies of the victim, detailed reports of the two trials, and editorial responses to the controversial verdicts, indulging the antebellum public's seemingly insatiable appetite for accounts of criminal passion and courtroom melodrama.

Crime and punishment were sources of endless fascination for the readers of colonial and early national New England. Between 1674 and 1860, printers of the region issued hundreds of books, pamphlets, and broadsides relating to the lives and deaths of criminals.[1] The literature consisted of a wide variety of genres, including execution sermons, conversion narratives, dying verses, last speeches, trial reports, crime novels, romantic biographies, and newspaper stories.[2] The four vignettes just sketched outline the pattern of development. During the late seventeenth century, when ministers still dominated the local print culture, the first publications served as instruments of religious authority. Over the course of the eighteenth century, the literature gradually became an arena of ideological conflict as profit-seeking printers experimented with new forms, clergymen lost their cultural monopoly, and criminals gained a literary voice. Finally, during the first half of the nineteenth century, the print culture of crime evolved into a competitive industry, dominated by lawyers, journalists, professional authors, and cheap publishers, that saturated a mass consumer market with narratives of sex and violence.

In the pages that follow, various crime publications will be referred to as "popular" or as examples of "popular culture," somewhat ambiguous designations often used in contradistinction to "elite" or "elite culture." Such characterizations of works or genres as "popular" simply indicate that they were designed to reach—and often, in fact, did reach—an extensive, in some cases massive, audience of readers, not confined to (although generally not excluding) the wealthy, the classically educated, or the professionally trained. Execution sermons were not read primarily by ministers; trial reports were not read exclusively by lawyers. Such "popular" genres were undoubtedly perused by children, servants, farmers, apprentices, artisans, mechanics, and housewives as well. Specific claims concerning readership are based on a variety of indicators, including prices, numbers of editions, sizes of editions, advertisements and choice of advertising vehicles, diary references or owner signatures, and hints or references within the texts themselves.

In fact, almost any neat distinction between "elite" and "popular" forms, whether in terms of readership, authorship, or message, is belied by the dynamic interaction of forces that shaped the literature, both as a whole and in most of its parts, over the entire period under study. Ministers, booksellers, printers, criminals, and later lawyers, journalists, and professional authors all influenced the tone and content of New England's crime publications. Even readers, through their power in the marketplace, exercised a vast if incalculable influence on the evolution of genres. Each group sought, with varying degrees of success, to shape the literature to its own purposes. Although the aims of different parties sometimes coexisted comfortably within a single genre, at other times they evidently could not, thereby encouraging the development of new forms. When the literature is examined as a whole, any simplistic split between "elite" and "popular" gives way to a more complex sense of ongoing interaction among various interested parties, not the least influential of whom were the criminals themselves.

Although a number of historiographic debates inform this study, they seldom receive more than passing mention in it. Instead, the focus is on the criminals of early New England and on the succession of literary mediators who sought to invest their lives with cultural meaning. This book is certainly about murderers, pirates, thieves, and rapists; but it is also about ministers, printers, lawyers, and novelists. The values and experiences of both groups are embodied in the published texts, on which they often collaborated. Recalling the fate of Lot's disobedient wife in the biblical story of Sodom and Gomorrah, Puritan ministers sometimes referred to capital offenders as "pillars of salt." By this they expressed the hope that frightening examples might warn others against wrongdoing. Many published responses to crime and punishment were designed to serve a similar cautionary function. However, New England's literary pillars of salt can also serve as markers of another kind. Their acccounts vividly chart the transformation of a literary tradition and the emergence of patterns of popular culture that persist to the present day.

A brief note on quotes from primary sources: Although archaic, eccentric, inconsistent, or erroneous spellings have not been altered, a few distracting irregularities in punctuation and typography (such as the interchange of the letters *u* and *v* in seventeenth-century texts) have been silently modernized. In addition, quoted passages that were completely italicized in the original have been silently switched to roman.

Acknowledging intellectual debts is both an obligation and a pleasure. This study would not have been possible without the guidance and assistance of more people than I can hope to thank here. I was generously supported by a Crown Fellowship throughout most of my time as a graduate student in the History of American Civilization program at Brandeis University. I was aided during my long years of research by countless able librarians and staff members at the University Park Library, Florida International University; Swem Library, The College of William and Mary; Goldfarb Library, Brandeis University; Houghton Library, Harvard University; Beinecke Library, Yale University; the Library of the Boston Athenaeum; the Boston Public Library; and the American Antiquarian Society, as well as other research facilities. I was guided and stimulated by my contacts with scholars at various institutions, including Paul Bischoff, David H. Flaherty, David D. Hall, James A. Henretta, David R. Kasserman, Roger Lane, and Randolph A. Roth, and by such current and former Brandeis faculty members as John Demos, Michael T. Gilmore,

Christine L. Heyrman, Morton Keller, Alexander Keyssar, James T. Kloppenberg, Marvin Meyers, and Donald E. Worster. My primary intellectual mentor at Brandeis was David H. Fischer, a scholar and teacher of unbounded energy, broad learning, brilliant insights, and masterful editorial judgments.

I am grateful to all my friends and colleagues at the Commonwealth Center and the College of William and Mary, especially Chandos Brown, Bob Gross, Richard John, Susan Mackiewicz, Thad Tate, and Sonny Walker, for helping to make my stay in Williamsburg both pleasant and productive. Two years of generous financial support from the Commonwealth Center allowed me to transform a dissertation into a book. My colleagues in the History Department at Florida International University have provided a congenial and stimulating environment within which to complete work on this volume. Sheila Post-Lauria of the FIU English Department has been a welcome source of interdisciplinary assistance and encouragement. The School of Arts and Sciences at FIU provided me with a generous Summer Research Grant that facilitated completion of the manuscript. I am indebted to Patterson Smith for sharing his marvelous knowledge of early English and American crime literature and to Pamela Blevins for offering her more specialized expertise in the case of Albert J. Tirrell. I am grateful to Karen Wolny of Oxford University Press for shepherding my manuscript through the various stages of production and India Cooper for her skill and patience as a copyeditor. I would also like to thank the editors of *American Quarterly*, *Journal of Social History*, and *American Studies* for permission to use material (from chapters 5, 6, and 9 respectively) that has been published in their journals.

Other debts are at once professional and deeply personal. My friends from Amherst College, especially Ashley Adams, David Glasser, Vern Harrington, Blair Kamin, John Lawlor, and the late Owen Kupferschmid, have stood by me through thick and thin, occasionally reading bits and pieces of my work, offering suggestions and encouragement, and proving their friendship in countless other ways. My associates in the Brandeis graduate program have also provided unstinting intellectual assistance and emotional support over a period of many years. No struggling scholar could have a more helpful, loyal, or caring group of friends and colleagues than Daniel S. Dupre, Carol A. Ely, Ruth L. Friedman, J. Matthew Gallman, Wendy E. Gamber, C. Dallett Hemphill, John S. Hill, Tamara C. Miller, June Namias, William J. Novak, David Palmer, Thomas R. Pegram, James T. Pokorny, David B. Sicilia, Eleanor A. Sparagana, David B. Starr, Susan L. Tananbaum, Alan S. Taylor, and Howard M. Wach. I owe a special debt to Jill E. Erickson; her friendship has been a source of comfort and joy. Finally, my parents, Morris and Gloria Cohen, have been with me all along, providing the emotional, intellectual, and material support without which I could not possibly have completed this study. To them, most of all, I dedicate what follows.

Miami   D.A.C.
March 1992

Contents

Pillars of Salt, Monuments of Grace

1

An Overview:
The Succession of Genres, 1674–1860

Few civic occasions aroused as much popular interest in early New England as public hangings. Even during the late seventeenth and early eighteenth centuries, crowds at local gallows reportedly numbered well into the thousands.[1] Such great occasions did not go unnoticed by the region's moral spokesmen. Public hangings were prominent among the extraordinary communal events addressed by early New England ministers.[2] Clergymen typically delivered sermons dealing with capital cases on the Sunday preceding an execution or on the day of the hanging itself, and contemporary accounts suggest that they were almost as well attended as the actual hangings. The site of one such lecture by Increase Mather had to be moved for fear that the gallery of an old church would collapse under the weight of the thousands reportedly jammed into the building. People crowded so tightly into a meetinghouse for another execution discourse by Increase's son, Cotton Mather, that the minister "could not gett unto the *Pulpit*, but by climbing over *Pues* and *Heads*."[3]

In addition to the throngs that listened in person, many others read gallows sermons when they subsequently appeared in print.[4] Published discourses not only reached a wider (though not necessarily larger) audience but were believed to leave a more lasting impression. "*Sermons Preached*, are like Showres of *Rain*, that Water for the Instant," Cotton Mather explained. "But *Sermons Printed*, are like *Snow* that lies longer on the Earth."[5] Although discourses to condemned prisoners were frequently delivered in early modern England and were often synopsized in other crime publications, they were rarely if ever published as separate books or pamphlets.[6] As an autonomous literary genre, the execution sermon thus seems to have been an innovation of the New England Puritans.[7] In contrast to the barely reputable prison chaplains who typically delivered gallows sermons in England, the authors of New England execution discourses included many of the region's leading clergymen, among them such notables as the Mathers, Benjamin Colman, and Charles Chauncy.[8]

Likewise, the printers, publishers, and booksellers who produced and marketed execution sermons included several of the most prominent and successful at their trades in New England, among them Bartholomew Green,

3

Thomas Fleet, Samuel Kneeland, and Isaiah Thomas.[9] The first execution discourse published in the region was probably Samuel Danforth's *The Cry of Sodom Enquired Into* (1674), printed in Cambridge, Massachusetts. One of the last to appear was Jonathan Going's *A Discourse Delivered at Worcester* (1825), published in Worcester, Massachusetts.[10] The first was issued at a time when Puritan ministers and magistrates still tightly supervised the only three presses operating in the Bay Colony; the last appeared at the dawn of a new era of mass communications. During the intervening years, scores of gallows discourses issued from the presses of the region, sometimes two or three to a volume, while only a handful were produced outside of New England.[11]

Early gallows sermons were effectively marketed and distributed. Although they were commonly advertised in local newspapers (after the first was established in Boston in 1704) and occasionally plugged in notices at the back of other pamphlets, the executions themselves were undoubtedly their best form of publicity.[12] In order to take full advantage, the publishers and printers would typically rush to produce the sermons as quickly as possible after the hanging. Sometimes they appeared in pamphlet form within a week or two of the execution, much less than the month or two often taken to get less newsworthy sermons into print.[13] Most were then probably sold directly to readers from one or another of Boston's many thriving printing offices or bookshops. As early as 1686, no fewer than eight booksellers vied in Boston's literary marketplace. Sixteen new dealers, many of whom also functioned as publishers, opened their doors in the provincial capital between 1700 and 1711 alone. By 1719 Boston boasted five printing presses and nineteen bookshops, representing by far the richest literary culture in colonial America.[14] Other execution sermons were doubtless distributed wholesale to booksellers and shopkeepers in smaller New England towns or peddled across the countryside by chapmen. In 1683 Cotton Mather reported that he knew of "an old *Hawker*, who will fill this Countrey with devout and useful Books, if I will direct him." More than twenty years later, a Boston newspaper reported the death of one James Gray, who "used to go up and down the Country Selling of Books."[15]

Because book prices were seldom listed on the pamphlets or in newspaper advertisements, it is impossible to determine the precise cost of most early execution sermons. However, a valuable bit of evidence is preserved in probate records. An early Boston bookseller, Michael Perry, had several dozen copies of one recent execution sermon in stock at the time of his death in 1700, along with twenty copies of another. The inventory of his estate valued bound copies of one of those sermons at five pence each and copies of the other, probably unbound (or stitched), at a mere two pence each.[16] Even if those were wholesale prices, such cheap pamphlets would almost certainly have been well within reach of all but the poorest of New England readers. Since rural laborers of that time earned between eighteen and thirty pence daily, one of Perry's execution sermons would have cost even an unskilled worker only a small fraction of a single day's wages. Remarkably, it would come to less than the cost of a cheap paperback for a minimum-wage laborer today.[17]

Many New England readers probably did not have to pay even such nominal fees for the privilege of reading and owning execution sermons. Some were circulated free of charge by their authors, who earned no cash royalties but sometimes received substantial numbers of complimentary copies from printers or publishers.[18] Consider, for example, Cotton Mather, who published more than a dozen volumes of execution sermons over a period of forty years. By far the most prolific of New England's ministers, Mather was also the most aggressive in distributing his books and pamphlets. By his own account, Mather would hand out "half a dozen books, more or less" on a typical day of pastoral visits, thrusting them into the hands of young and old, male and female alike. Over the course of a year, he would distribute hundreds of pamphlets, mostly the products of his own pen. He would also give copies to ship's officers for the benefit of their sailors and send bundles of pamphlets to friends in other towns for distribution among local families. Through such aggressive methods, Cotton Mather saw to it that his innumerable pamphlets, including execution sermons, not only saturated the Boston book market but circulated across the countryside of New England, spread to other regions of Anglo-America, and even penetrated the farthest reaches of the English-speaking world.[19]

It seems likely that execution sermons not only reached a large geographic area but also engaged readers of a wide range of social ranks and classes. Although most gallows discourses addressed the community as a whole, many included special messages to particular social groups, ranging from the bottom to the top of the social hierarchy. While young people were most commonly singled out for cautionary attention, ministers also specifically addressed servants, sailors, blacks, and Indians, along with parents, masters, and magistrates. Concerned householders undoubtedly purchased such sermons for their children or servants; they were an ideal form of family reading. Rural ministers who owned copies gladly lent them to their rustic neighbors, along with other works of practical piety.[20] Condemned criminals not only attended sermons addressing their own executions but also occasionally read others; ministers sometimes gave copies of discourses on earlier cases to jailed malefactors. One mariner convicted of piracy claimed to have already read such a gallows sermon *before* his arrest; perhaps a copy had been thrust into his gritty hands by a conscientious ship's officer who had received a bundle from Cotton Mather.[21]

One of the only serious barriers to the reading of gallows pamphlets was illiteracy—and even that may not have been a major problem. Although the ability to read was by no means universal during the colonial period, basic literacy does seem to have been unusually widespread in Puritan New England, and it was diffused at an accelerating rate during the eighteenth century. The most careful student of the subject has concluded that well over half of all adult males in the region were literate as early as 1660, two-thirds were literate by 1710, and nearly nine-tenths were literate by 1760.[22] To be sure, reading skills during the late seventeenth century were still significantly correlated to such social variables as wealth, occupation, locale, and gender. While 75 percent of all Boston men were literate by 1660, only 45 percent of all farmers, 30 percent of all laborers, and a bit more than 30 percent of all women could sign their names at that early date.[23] Yet even then no major segment of the New England population was entirely cut off from the world of print; reading aloud was a popular practice during the early modern period, and those who could not actually read execution sermons could almost certainly listen to them read by others.

While it would be impossible to reconstruct an exact profile of their audience, there can be no doubt that execution sermons of the late seventeenth and early eighteenth centuries were extraordinarily popular products in a marketplace of literary scarcity. When a Boston hanging inspired Cotton Mather's first published sermon in 1686, the young minister happily reported in his diary that it "sold exceedingly." That boast was confirmed the following year, when printer Richard Pierce informed readers that the "speedy sale" of the volume had encouraged him to produce an expanded second edition. Some thirty years later, in 1717, Mather claimed that a local bookseller had sold off nearly one thousand copies of his newest execution sermon in just five days. Later that same year, at a time when published sermons typically appeared in editions of one to five hundred, a printer in Boston reportedly produced no fewer than twelve hundred copies of yet another of Mather's scaffold orations.[24] That was approximately one for every ten inhabitants of the town, or about one for every two households.[25] While many other published sermons were by necessity financed with public or private subsidies, execution discourses seem to have more than paid their own way, turning profits both spiritual and temporal.

If execution sermons enjoyed extraordinary sales, it was because they addressed extraordinary events. Even the earliest examples were carefully fitted to the occasion of an imminent hanging. Clergymen explained how condemned criminals had been led to their fatal wickedness, warned others against the same sort of misconduct, and justified capital punishment. Although they always addressed the community at large, ministers also generally spoke directly to the doomed prisoners in attendance.[26] Preachers berated offenders for their wickedness, exhorted them to repent, and taught them how to seek salvation during their brief remaining time on earth. Not only were the criminals a crucial focus of discussion and attention, their involvement in the sermon ritual sometimes went deeper than that. Many condemned offenders reportedly asked particular ministers to deliver execution discourses, and a few even requested that they address particular texts or topics.[27] Such reports suggest that some criminals were not merely passive auditors of execution sermons but also active instigators and even collaborators in their creation.

Yet despite their peculiar themes and contexts, early execution discourses were in many respects hardly distinguishable from other Puritan sermons, which dominated the literary output of New England during the seventeenth century.[28] Much of the resemblance resulted from a shared literary structure; the first published execution sermons adhered closely to the standard format of the Puritan discourse. The preacher invariably began by introducing the sermon's "text," a passage from the Bible; drew from that text a "doctrine," the minister's thesis; and then proceeded with the doctrine's "application," a series of pertinent instructions and exhortations. In formulating their arguments, the authors of early execution sermons generally adhered to the usual "plain style," a direct and unadorned mode that was seen as particularly appropriate to the solemnity of a public hanging. "*Plainness in delivering the Truths of God*, is always to be endeavoured after," Increase Mather explained in his first execution discourse, "but more especially when such awfull occasions are presented, as caused the Preaching of this Sermon."[29]

The similarities went beyond structure and style to content. The Puritans believed in a God who actively governed his creation, controlling all worldly events from the greatest to the smallest. They believed that their own community stood in a special, covenantal relationship with God in which they would be held collectively responsible for the wrongdoing of individual members. And they believed that all men and women were naturally prone to wickedness, completely dependent for their salvation on heavenly intervention. In accordance with those basic beliefs, Puritan ministers laced their gallows sermons—like most of their others—with invocations of divine sovereignty, communal degeneracy, individual depravity, and the overriding human need for salvation through Christ. By doing so, they sought to integrate extraordinary and perhaps frightening communal events into a familiar theological framework. Like all other events of public significance, capital crimes and criminal executions were exemplars of divine providence, evidence of God's mercies and judgments upon both individuals and the community as a whole.[30] While other New Englanders may have thought about crime and punishment in different ways during the late seventeenth century, no other types of discourse had yet achieved the authority of print.

Although the first two execution sermons published in New England appeared as simple pamphlets, the format of later works became more complex.[31] Many of the twenty or so volumes of execution sermons published between 1686 and 1726 contained a variety of supplementary materials, including confessions or warnings by condemned criminals, dialogues between ministers and malefactors, and factual accounts of capital cases.[32] To a great extent, American printers and ministers were simply following the lead of contemporary English crime pamphlets.[33] Yet most of the appended materials served to reinforce doctrinal messages prominent in the actual sermons. Some stressed motifs of warning; others emphasized themes of salvation.[34] The last confessions and dying statements of condemned prisoners were especially valued. Because of their peculiar vantage point on the threshold between time and

John Dolbeare

The Wicked mans Portion.

OR,

A SERMON

(Preached at the *Lecture* in *Boston* in *New-England* the 18 th day of the 1 Moneth 1674. when two men were *executed*, who had *murthered* their Master.)

Wherein is shewed

That excesse in wickednesse doth bring untimely Death.

By *INCREASE MATHER*, Teacher of a Church of Christ.

PROV. 10. 27. *The fear of the Lord prolongeth dayes, but the years of the wicked shall be shortned.*

EPH. 6. 2, 3. *Honour thy Father and thy Mother (which is the first Commandment with promise) that it may be well with thee, and thou mayst live long on the Earth.*

Pæna ad paucos, metus ad omnes.

BOSTON,
Printed by *John Foster*. 1675

The first book printed in Boston: an execution sermon by Increase Mather. *Courtesy, American Antiquarian Society.*

8

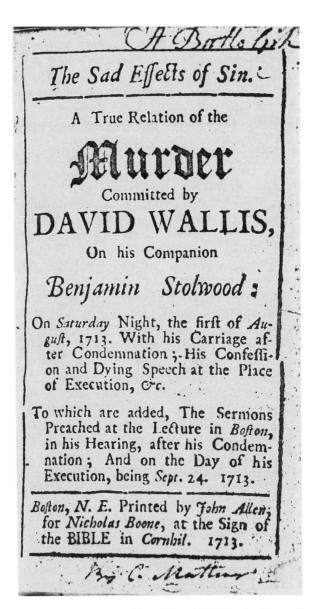

A Bottle Gift

The Sad Effects of Sin.

A True Relation of the

𝕸𝖚𝖗𝖉𝖊𝖗

Committed by

DAVID WALLIS,

On his Companion

Benjamin Stolwood :

On *Saturday* Night, the firft of *Au-guft*, 1713. With his Carriage after Condemnation; His Confeffion and Dying Speech at the Place of Execution, &c.

To which are added, The Sermons Preached at the Lecture in *Bofton*, in his Hearing, after his Condemnation; And on the Day of his Execution, being *Sept.* 24. 1713.

Bofton, N. E. Printed by *John Allen*, for *Nicholas Boone*, at the Sign of the BIBLE in *Cornhil*. 1713.

By C. Mather

Crime publication by the most prolific author of New England execution sermons, Cotton Mather. Compare the title-page typography of this volume with that of the earlier work by his father (p. 8); one enlarges the word *Sermon*, the other highlights the word *Murder*, signaling a shift in the literature as a whole from religious indoctrination to quasi-journalistic crime coverage. *Courtesy, American Antiquarian Society.*

eternity, the last statements of dying men and women were believed to be both truthful and insightful.[35] Not only were sincere confessions a "principal ingredient" of true repentance, but they were also helpful in clarifying issues of guilt or innocence and establishing the justice of courtroom verdicts.[36] Finally, capital criminals were in a particularly appropriate position to warn others against a wide variety of sins.[37] For all of those reasons, New England ministers regularly urged condemned prisoners to issue penitent confessions and gladly attached them to their published sermons.

But not all of the execution volumes were purely pious. After all, one man's providence is another's sensation. Some of the quasi-journalistic case histories attached to sermons by Cotton Mather during the early eighteenth century reflected a new interest in providing readers with factual information on capital crimes and criminals, whatever their spiritual significance. One volume of sermons included "A True Relation of the Murder Committed by David Wallis On his Companion Benjamin Stolwood, On Saturday Night, the first of August, 1713." Another featured "A Brief Relation of Remarkables in the Shipwreck of above One Hundred Pirates, Who were Cast away in the Ship *Whido*, on the Coast of New England, April 26, 1717."[38] In those two cases, the accounts actually preceded the discourses, with the words *Murder* and *Pirates* appearing on the title pages in boldface more than twice as large as the word *Sermon*.[39] A newspaper advertisement for the second work illustrated the new priorities even more baldly; the booksellers were so eager to emphasize the pirate shipwreck that they did not even bother to mention that a sermon was included in the pamphlet![40] Mather and his publishers apparently recognized that the public's fascination with the gallows extended beyond its utility in dramatizing theological doctrine. But whether their motives were spiritual or commercial, ministers and printers who attached confessions, interviews, and eyewitness accounts to published sermons established conventions of documentary reportage that would endure into the modern era.[41]

Although ministers had lost their monopoly on New England crime literature by the 1730s, execution sermons continued to appear in a persistent, if somewhat intermittent, stream well into the nineteenth century. Fluctuations in output probably had more to do with the varying incidence of criminal executions than with changes in literary vogue. Of the more than seventy-five volumes of execution sermons produced in the region between 1674 and 1825, over two-thirds appeared after 1730.[42] In fact, the execution sermon long remained a popular genre, despite the new competition from other types of crime literature. An execution discourse by the Native American minister Samson Occom appeared in about a dozen editions between 1772 and 1774 and was occasionally reprinted during the next half century.[43] Two other execution sermons of the early 1770s also appeared in at least four editions.[44] Over a period of two months during the autumn of 1773, Boston newspaper readers were confronted by a series of large, boldfaced advertisements for three different volumes of execution sermons, each written by a different minister and

Three adjacent newspaper advertisements for execution sermons on the case of
Levi Ames, each volume authored by a different minister and published by a
different bookseller. From the *Boston News-Letter,* November 11, 1773. *Courtesy,
American Antiquarian Society.*

11

sold by a different bookseller—all on the same capital case! One of those volumes was so valuable a literary property that rival editions were simultaneously produced by competing publishers.[45] While pricing information is, as usual, scarce, at least one gallows sermon of the 1770s was published at eight pence a copy, surely affordable for most readers of middling social rank and even for some of the lower sort.[46]

It might be argued that the emergence of literary alternatives to the execution sermon after 1730 actually strengthened the genre by allowing it to perform its original function with fewer distractions. By the early decades of the

Woodcut image of a minister preaching from his pulpit, originally designed as a portrait of the renowned English evangelist George Whitefield but used in 1773 to illustrate Samuel Stillman's *Two Sermons* on the execution of Levi Ames. *Courtesy, American Antiquarian Society.*

nineteenth century, the format of the gallows sermon had come full circle. Although the first published execution discourses had stood alone as topical variants of the standard Puritan sermon, printers and ministers had padded later examples with supplementary materials that in some cases overshadowed the sermons themselves. However, once New England bookmen found other genres to meet the public's demand for informative and entertaining accounts of capital cases, published execution sermons drifted back toward their original role as vehicles for the pulpit messages of local ministers. While many of the later pamphlets contained supplementary materials, the sermon itself tended to be the primary literary focus. The typography of title-pages and newspaper advertisements increasingly emphasized the word *Sermon* and the name of the minister, sometimes giving them billing equal to or greater than that of the crime or the criminal.[47] By the time the execution sermon genre expired during the early decades of the nineteenth century, other types of crime literature had long since emerged to satisfy the more worldly tastes of New England readers, allowing sermons to be sermons to the end.

While execution sermons were to remain New England's dominant form of gallows literature until the 1730s, several other crime genres were introduced to the region during the first three decades of the eighteenth century. A number of local printers and booksellers, alert to the potential of crime coverage as a literary commodity, produced a smattering of conversion narratives, execution accounts, trial reports, newspaper stories, and crime ballads. Unlike published execution sermons, those new forms were modeled on well-established British genres. That increasing resort to English literary models was consistent with general trends in provincial society and culture. After decades of Puritan autonomy and innovation, British authorities began asserting greater political and administrative control over Massachusetts (as over the other American colonies) during the last decades of the seventeenth century and the early decades of the eighteenth. At the same time, many insecure provincials increasingly looked to cosmopolitan London for cultural guidance and inspiration. The new crime publications thus reflected a much broader process of imperial tightening and cultural borrowing that was undermining Puritan culture and anglicizing New England society during the early decades of the new century.[48]

The first of the transplanted forms—one that seemed on the surface entirely consistent with the spirit of Puritan evangelism—was the "criminal conversion narrative," a genre recounting the spiritual transformation of condemned prisoners.[49] Examples published in New England were almost certainly modeled on a number of very similar accounts produced by British clergymen during the second half of the seventeenth century.[50] Those accounts were, in turn, variants of the spiritual biographies and autobiographies so popular among religious readers in early modern England.[51] Although a volume of Massachusetts gallows sermons published in 1686 implied that a condemned murderer had achieved salvation, the first fully developed criminal conversion narrative published in New England was appended to another collection of execution sermons in 1701.[52] Boston printers issued the first separate examples (unattached to sermons) in 1726 and 1738, works closely linked to a rising tide of evangelical activism that would climax with the Great Awakening.[53] Although ministers remained interested in the spiritual state of condemned men and women, few formal criminal conversion narratives appeared in New England thereafter.[54]

Another gallows genre introduced to New England during the early eighteenth century was the "execution account," recording the words of ministers and criminals at the gallows. The earliest and perhaps only surviving example was published by Nicholas Boone, a pious but shrewd Boston bookseller, in 1704.[55] As the proprietor of a local coffeehouse and a chief vendor of the recently established *Boston News-Letter* (at that time the only newspaper in the American colonies), Boone was presumably attuned to the public's demand for information on public events of note. His ephemeral broadsheet, printed on both sides of a single leaf, was a summary of the proceedings at the execution of a group of pirates near Boston Harbor, featuring the statements of both attending ministers and condemned men. The account was probably prepared by Boone in collaboration with one of the presiding ministers, very likely Cotton Mather. It was almost certainly modeled on a series of contemporary British publications regularly prepared in conjunction with executions by the chaplain (or Ordinary) of Newgate Prison in London. Hundreds of Ordinary's *Accounts* were published in England during the seventeenth and eighteenth centuries.[56] Those issued during the late seventeenth century were quite similar in format and content to Boone's broadsheet of 1704.[57] While no other examples of New England execution accounts of precisely that type are extant, at least one other similar work appeared in the region during the second decade of the eighteenth century.[58]

A third new crime genre was the "trial report," consisting of transcripts or synopses of courtroom proceedings, which had long been a staple of popular crime literature in England.[59] Probably the first trial reports published in New England were contained in a defense of the Salem witch trials produced by Cotton Mather in 1692.[60] However, Mather's legal digests were buried in a literary pastiche among excerpts from various sermons and other materials. The first separately published trial reports to appear in the region were a series of at least five accounts of piracy cases issued by Boston printers and booksellers between 1704 and 1726.[61] Those cases were part of a massive naval and judicial campaign against Anglo-American piracy, one aspect of the general tightening of imperial controls in British America during the early eighteenth century.[62] The registers of the special Courts of Admiralty that tried provincial pirates were required by law to produce summaries of the proceedings for the inspection of the High Court of Admiralty in England.[63] In 1704 Governor Dudley of Massachusetts ordered minutes of the first such case printed locally in order to quell popular opposition to the execution of men who were seen as public benefactors for bringing gold into the province.[64] Although it is not clear that subsequent prosecutions aroused similar controversy, local bookmen produced several more officially authorized reports on piracy cases, with copies sent back to administrators in London and others sold to the public in Massachusetts.[65] It seems likely that those published reports at once provided documentation for English authorities, propaganda for the provincial government, entertainment for local readers, and profits for the Boston book trade. However, the publicity received by piracy trials was exceptional; few other criminal cases evoked printed reports in New England until the early years of the nineteenth century.[66]

A fourth new type of literary response to crime was newspaper coverage, not an autonomous genre but a cluster of distinct forms within a genre. Such coverage included texts of official proclamations and advertisements for stolen goods, as well as journalistic reportage of crimes, arrests, trials, escapes, and executions. Postmaster John Campbell launched New England's first weekly newspaper, the *Boston News-Letter*, in the spring of 1704.[67] Campbell, whose office made him a direct beneficiary of imperial patronage, seems to have been an eager agent of anglicization. He called on the royal governor weekly, seeking both news and approval, adhered to the "Court" party in provincial politics, and, according to one modern scholar, "perceived or at least wanted to perceive eighteenth-century Boston as a miniature London in almost every important respect."[68] He issued his *News-Letter* as a small two-column broadsheet, closely modeled on the British newspapers that flourished in London and in various provincial towns after the expiration of the restrictive Licensing Act in 1695.[69] English newspapers had turned to crime accounts to attract readers as early as the mid-seventeenth century, and the papers that proliferated during the late 1690s and thereafter often provided extensive coverage of crimes, trials, and executions.[70] It was not surprising, then, that the new Boston paper devoted substantial space in a number of its early issues to the provincial government's proceedings against a crew of pirates and a gang of counterfeiters.[71] However, those promising forays into crime coverage were not typical. Although the *News-Letter* and other New England papers of the eighteenth century occasionally provided extensive coverage of piracy and counterfeiting—crimes likely to be of particular interest to newspaper readerships dominated by commercial and political elites—most devoted little more than an occasional stray paragraph to offenses like theft, burglary, robbery, rape, and murder.[72]

Finally, a fifth genre introduced to New England during the early eighteenth century was the "crime ballad." In 1713 Cotton Mather complained "that the Minds and Manners of many People about the Countrey are much corrupted, by foolish Songs and Ballads, which the Hawkers and Pedlars carry into all parts of the Countrey."[73] At least a few of those works probably dealt with the subjects of crime and punishment. Although no examples survive, Benjamin Franklin wrote at least one such ballad in his youth, probably in about 1719. As a teenage apprentice to his older brother, a Boston printer, Franklin composed two "occasional Ballads" at his master's urging. While one was on a local maritime tragedy, the other was "a Sailor Song on the Taking of *Teach* or Blackbeard the Pirate." Years later Franklin acknowledged that the poems were "wretched Stuff, in the Grubstreet Ballad Stile." After printing the verses, his brother sent young Benjamin out to peddle them "about the Town." Although it is impossible to know the precise format of Franklin's ballads, it seems likely that they were issued as broadsides, like many similar works in early modern England. Following the standard English practice, Franklin probably provided the name of a popular tune to which the verses might be sung near the top of the sheet. Such publications expose yet another face of cultural anglicization. Benjamin's brother, James Franklin, was a printer openly hostile to the Puritan and "Court" establishments of Boston. Trained in London and professionally committed to catering to the secular interests of an increasingly anglicized reading public, he evidently hoped that his Boston audience would be more interested in Grubstreet verses than Puritan sermons. In fact, Benjamin later recalled that one of the two ballads "sold wonderfully."[74]

The new crime genres represented at least three distinct aspects of anglicization: Conversion narratives and execution accounts sought to enrich the local religious literature of crime by imitating the contemporary popular culture of English Protestantism; trial reports and newspaper coverage reflected the increasing integration of provincial Massachusetts into an Anglo-American imperial community; and Franklin's doggerel on Blackbeard embodied the resurgence of a plebeian tradition of English popular balladry that could no longer be suppressed by the fading Puritan establishment of Boston. In producing those new genres, Boston printers and publishers variously perpetuated their traditional collaboration with local ministers, established new relationships with governmental officials, or relied on their own initiative.

However, none of the crime genres introduced to New England between 1700 and 1730 became very popular in the region during the eighteenth century. Criminal conversion narratives never proliferated as an independent form; execution accounts failed to achieve the success enjoyed by similar works in England; trial reports did not become a popular genre in New England until the first decades of the nineteenth century; newspaper coverage of crime, while gradually expanding in the context of successive regional crime waves after 1760, did not really take off until the advent of the mass-circulation "penny press" during the 1830s; and crime ballads of the type composed by Benjamin Franklin never caught on as a published form in New England (or, at least, have not survived), although execution verses of a somewhat different sort would soon become popular.[75] Puritan ministers may have slowly been losing their monopolistic grip on New England crime literature, but local printers had yet to produce a successful alternative to the execution sermon.

By the 1730s Boston was very different from the Puritan stronghold of the 1670s, when the town's first and only printer had launched his career by publishing an execution sermon. A social order still closely regulated by Puritan ministers and magistrates had gradually evolved into a more conflicted and cosmopolitan milieu. Opposition factions contested political authority; members of various religious denominations worshipped openly; clubs, coffeehouses, and taverns flourished; several local newspapers circulated freely; restrictive censorship of the press was a fading memory; and aggressive printers, publishers, and booksellers vied for the patronage of an expanded reading public.[76] In that altered social setting, local printers of the 1730s turned to execution broadsides as popular alternatives to the gallows sermon.[77] If early sermons had reflected a book culture still dominated by orthodox ministers, the new broadsides signaled the transition to a somewhat more secular and diverse literary marketplace.

The printers of New England execution broadsides ranged from obscure or disreputable artisans to the most prominent bookmen in eighteenth-century Massachusetts.[78] Several of the earliest surviving broadsides, issued during the 1730s, were produced by the prolific Boston printing house of Thomas Fleet; a few others were issued by the equally prominent Boston partnership of Kneeland & Green. The backgrounds of those two firms suggest the way in which execution broadsides mediated an important transition in the local publishing industry. As descendants of Samuel Green, who first established a press in Cambridge, Massachusetts, in 1649, both Samuel Kneeland and Timothy Green II were fitting heirs to a dynasty of Puritan printers. Throughout their careers they specialized in religious publications (as had their forbears), particularly those of Cotton Mather and Jonathan Edwards, producing a number of the most important American theological works of the eighteenth century. In death, Samuel Kneeland was eulogized as "an upright Man and a good Christian."[79]

Thomas Fleet, remembered less for his personal piety than for his wry sense of humor, had a very different background and career. He arrived in Boston from England in about 1712 and for the next two decades reportedly specialized in the production of pamphlets, ballads, and small books for children.[80] Perhaps he was the printer of the "foolish Songs and Ballads" about which Cotton Mather complained in 1713. From that humble but profitable base in plebeian culture, Fleet gradually achieved respectability and prominence, becoming the official printer for the Massachusetts House of Representatives between 1729 and 1731 and assuming control of a Boston newspaper in 1733 that he quickly transformed into the "best paper" in the region. However, during the 1730s Fleet continued to produce cheap broadsides even while taking on more dignified jobs. In large part because of his varied output, Fleet has been characterized by modern scholars as one of "the most influential and successful printers in eighteenth-century America" and has been credited with helping to complete the shift of the printing industry from a trade largely dependent on "religious pamphleteering" to a highly diversified business. As suggested by the roles of Samuel Kneeland, Timothy Green II, and Thomas Fleet, early New England execution broadsides reflected both the origins of the local printing trade in a popular culture of Protestant piety and its subsequent evolution into a more varied and secularized enterprise.[81]

Most execution broadsides published in New England belonged to one of two genres: "dying verses" and "last speeches." Both types were produced by Thomas Fleet and Kneeland & Green during the 1730s and continued to appear through the end of the century. Occasionally the two forms were combined on a single sheet. As the day of an execution drew near, printers would rush to produce broadsides quickly enough to cater to the thousands of spectators who often gathered at the gallows. They would set the text in two or more parallel columns of small type, commonly adding an illustrative wood-cut at the top of the page. They would then print the unbound sheets by hanging day, sell them directly from their shops, and probably also arrange for hawkers to peddle them among the crowds assembled at the scaffold. Because broadsides could be hurried into print for marketing at the gallows, they may have been more profitable than execution sermons, conversion narratives, and trial reports, all of which generally took at least a week or two to make their way into print.

Crime broadsides were also issued during the days or weeks immediately before or after the execution. Most were printed in the town where the hanging took place, generally a local publishing center. Some were then sold by itinerant peddlers in surrounding rural areas.[82] Although a printer in one town would occasionally reprint an execution broadside originally published in another, such borrowing rarely extended beyond the boundaries of New England.[83] Fragmentary evidence suggests that crime broadsides enjoyed a socially diverse readership, though young people were often particularly targeted.[84] Certainly the few pennies charged for the sheets could not have been much of a barrier to wide circulation.[85] One also suspects that *individual* copies of broadsides often reached a *multitude* of readers and auditors. Surely they were sometimes read aloud, passed from hand to hand, and posted for display on walls, especially at quasi-public venues like printing offices and taverns. In general, however, execution broadsides were an extremely ephem-eral literary form; evoked by the local or regional interest surrounding a particular capital case, they rarely long outlasted the criminal.

More than twenty-five dying-verse broadsides survive from the years be-tween 1732 and 1799; others continued to appear well into the nineteenth century.[86] In general format and style, New England's early execution poems resembled the other obituary verses or elegies commonly issued in the region as broadsides during the late seventeenth and eighteenth centuries.[87] They may also have been inspired by contemporary British execution verses, literary successors to the "hanging ballads" that were quite popular in seventeenth-century England.[88] However, unlike traditional English ballads, New En-gland's dying verses were never published with the names of popular tunes to which they might be fitted; most American execution poems were probably intended to be read, whether silently or aloud, not sung.[89] Finally, it should be noted that several execution verses issued as broadsides in Scotland during the

The Wages of Sin;

O R,

Robbery juſtly Rewarded:

A

POEM;

Occaſioned by the untimely Death of

Richard Wilſon,

Who was Executed on *Boſton* Neck, for Burglary,

On *Thurſday* the 19th of *October*, 1732.

THis Day from Goal muſt *Wilſon* be
    conveyed in a Cart,
By Guards unto the Gallows-Tree,
    to die as his Deſert.

For being wicked overmuch,
    there for a wicked Crime,
Muſt take his fatal Lot with ſuch
    as die before their Time.

No human Pardon he can get,
    by Interceſſion made ;
But flee he muſt unto the Pit,
    and by no Man be ſtay'd.

The fatal ſad and woful Caſe,
    this awful Sight reveals,
Of one whom Vengeance in his Chaſe
    hath taken by the Heels.

Here is a Caution in the Sight,
    to wicked Thieves, and they
Who break and rob the Houſe by Night,
    which they have mark'd by Day.

We ſee the Fall of one that caſt
    his Lot in by Decree,
With thoſe that wait the Twilight paſt,
    that ſo no Eye may ſee.

That wicked Action which be thought
    by Night would be conceal'd,
By Providence is ſtrangely brought
    thus far to be reveal'd.

By which we ſee apparantly,
    there is no Places ſure,
Where Workers of Iniquity
    can hide themſelves ſecure.

There is no Man by human Wit,
    can keep his Sin conceal'd
When he that made him thinks it fit
    the ſame ſhould be reveal'd.

He that gets Wealth in wicked Ways,
    and ſlights the Righteous Rule,
Doth leave them here amidſt his Days,
    and dies at laſt a Fool.

Here we may ſee what Men for Stealth
    and Robbing muſt endure ;
And what the Gain of ill got Wealth
    will in the End procure.

Here is a Caution high and low,
    for Warning here you have,
From one whoſe Feet are now brought to
    the Borders of the Grave.

He does bewail his miſ-ſpent Life,
    and for his Sins doth grieve,
Which is an hopeful Sign that he
    a Pardon will receive.

He ſays, ſince he forſook his God,
    God has forſaken him,
And left him to this wicked Crime
    that has his Ruine been.

He calls his Drunkenneſs a Sin,
    with his neglect of Prayer,
The leading Crimes have brought him in
    to this untimely Snare.

All you that practice curſed Theft,
    take Warning great and ſmall,
Leſt you go on, and ſo are left
    to ſuch untimely fall.

Repent of all your Errors paſt,
    and eye the Stroke of Fate,
Leſt you thus come to Shame at laſt,
    and mourn when 'tis too late.

Remember what the Scripture ſaith,
    a little honeſt Wealth,
Is better far than mighty Store
    of Riches got by Stealth.

This Warning ſoundeth in our Ear,
    this Sentence loud and Shrill,
O *Congregation*, hear and fear,
    and do no more ſo ill.

F I N I S.

BOSTON: Printed and Sold at the *Heart* and *Crown* in *Cornhill*.

The earliest surviving dying-verse broadside published in New England, printed by Thomas Fleet of Boston in 1732. *Courtesy, New-York Historical Society.*

19

late eighteenth century were very similar to their New England counterparts, suggesting the existence of a transatlantic genre.[90]

It is impossible to know just who wrote most of the execution poems of early New England. A few may have been penned by the dying criminals to whom they were conventionally attributed.[91] For example, it is conceivable that John Young, an itinerant schoolteacher convicted of raping one of his students, actually did draft the crude doggerel that was ostensibly "Corrected from his Own Manuscript."[92] At least one execution "hymn" was written by Elhanan Winchester, a young minister of unorthodox leanings.[93] However, most of the dying verses were probably written by the printers themselves or by members of their households. As already mentioned, Benjamin Franklin wrote a crime-related ballad in about 1719, while an apprentice to his brother James. Much later in the century, a "young woman" living in the family of Ezekiel Russell, a Boston printer who specialized in cheap, sensational pamphlets and broadsides, "sometimes invoked the muse, and wrote ballads on recent tragical events" that Russell "immediately printed."[94] A few other execution poems were written by freelance itinerants like Thomas Shaw, a farmer and cooper of Standish, Maine, who occasionally traveled the New England countryside selling his own broadside verses.[95]

Whether written by criminals, ministers, printers, apprentices, or literary itinerants, broadside poems conveyed many of the same messages as execution sermons. They typically warned against wickedness, explained how lesser sins led to great crimes, and emphasized the prisoner's desperate need and dying hope for salvation through Christ. As early expressions of literary sentimentalism, they also evoked the horror of hangings and pleaded for sympathy toward condemned offenders. Like many British ballads, New England's broadside verses served a quasi-journalistic function as well.[96] They often contained detailed accounts of the condemned offender's sins and crimes, sometimes based on his or her own dying statement.[97] Their journalistic tone was commonly enhanced by the convention that they had been authored, or at least authorized, by the criminal. At once pious, moralistic, sentimental, and informative, execution verses satisfied several of the increasingly varied literary cravings of New England readers.

Even more popular than dying verses were last speeches, also introduced to New England by the 1730s. Copies of more than thirty-five survive from between 1733 and 1799; others were undoubtedly issued but have been lost.[98] Most of the eighteenth-century prose broadsides conformed to a standard pattern, consisting almost entirely of first-person statements by condemned criminals, with such formulaic titles as *The Last Speech and Dying Words of John Ormsby* (1734), *The Last Words and Dying Speech of Joseph Lightly* (1765), and the *Life, Last Words and Dying Confession of Rachel Wall* (1789).[99] Despite those titles, they did not generally contain speeches actually delivered by prisoners at the gallows but rather written statements prepared collaboratively by criminals, printers, ministers, and jail officials during the days preceding an execution. Such last speeches were displaced after 1800

Pfal. LI. 14. Deliver me from Blood-Guiltiness, O God, thou God of my Salvation: and my Tongue shall sing aloud of thy Righteousness. Isa. I. 18 Come now and let us Reason together, saith the Lord: though your sins be as scarlet, they shall be as white as snow: though they be red like crimson, they shall be as wool.

The last SPEECH and dying ADVICE of
poor Julian,

Who was Executed the 22d of *March*, 1733. for the Murder of Mr. *John Rogers* of *Pembroke*. Written with his own Hand, and delivered to the Publisher the Day before his Execution.

FRom my Childhood to Twenty Years of Age, I liv'd in a Family where I was learnt to Read and say my Catechism, and had a great deal of Pains taken with me.—— And in my younger Years I was under some Convictions and Awakenings, and concern'd about the Condition of my Soul ;—— and I had many Warnings in the Providence of God to turn from my Sins——— But I have (and I desire to lament it) abused God's Patience and Goodness to me, and apostatised from God and good Beginnings, and now I have forsaken God, he has forsaken me, and I acknowledge he has been just in leaving me, so that I have gone from bad to worse, till for my Sins I am now to die.

Whereas I have been charged with and tried for burning my Master's Barn, I now declare as a dying Man that I did not do it, nor was I any way privy to it.

I acknowledge I deserve to die, and would confess especially my Drunkenness and Sabbath-breaking, which have led me to this great Sin for which I now die.

I desire therefore that all, and especially Servants, would take Warning by me ; I am a dying Man, just going to leave this World, and the Thoughts of it terrify me, knowing how unfit I am to appear before my Judge.

O beware of sinning as I have done—— Beware of Drunkenness, of Sabbath-breaking, and of running away from your Masters, and don't put away the Thoughts of Death and of Judgment : I once put these Things far away, but now they are near, and I am going to appear before my great and terrible Judge, which surprizeth me beyond what I am able to express.

If you have been instructed and catechized from your Childhood, and joined your selves to Assemblies in which the Lord Jesus Christ is most purely worshipped, then let me warn and charge you to beware of casting off the Things that are good, left God leave you to your selves, and you go on in Sin till you come to the greatest Wickedness.

O take Warning by me all of you, I intreat you—— See and fear and do no more so wickedly as I have done.

O let me once more intreat you all, especially Servants, to beware of the Sin of Drunkenness, and be obedient to your Masters ; don't run away from them, nor get Drunk, for if you do it will bring you to Ruine as it has done me.

I call to you now as one come from the Dead, to turn from your evil Ways while you have Time, and not put off your Repentance to another Day, left you then call and God will not answer you.

My Master often told me that my Sins would bring me to this, but I little thought that it would be so.

I return my hearty Thanks to the Rev. Ministers who have taken Pains to assist me in preparing for my latter End. And as I desire to be forgiven, so I forgive all Mankind.

These Things I declare freely and voluntarily, and desire Mr. *Fleet* to Print the same for the Benefit of the Living : And I do hereby utterly disown and disclaim all other Speeches, Papers or Declarations that may be printed in my Name, as Witness my Hand this 21st. of *March*, 1733.

Julian.

Witness
Zach. Trescott.

Printed and Sold by *T. Fleet*, at the *Heart* and *Crown* in *Cornhill, Boston*.

The earliest surviving last-speech broadside published in New England, printed by Thomas Fleet of Boston in 1733. Like earlier confessional statements appended to execution sermons, it contains little biographical information and is dominated by religious and didactic content. *Courtesy, The Trustees of Boston Public Library.*

by broadsides of other types and by longer autobiographical narratives issued in pamphlet form.

The last speeches of eighteenth-century New England were variations on a long literary tradition. Many of the dying confessions of condemned political prisoners were printed as broadsheets or pamphlets in Tudor and Stuart England.[100] Throughout the seventeenth century, similar statements by common criminals were featured in a variety of English or Anglo-American genres, including conversion narratives, Ordinary's *Accounts*, and execution sermons.[101] Unlike most of New England's last-speech broadsides, those earlier confessions did not typically contain much biographical information. But then, during the first two decades of the eighteenth century, printers began to issue criminals' last speeches in Edinburgh and Dublin.[102] Some of them were quite similar, both in form and content, to the broadsides that were soon to become popular in America. That close resemblance may suggest the existence of a distinctive provincial print culture of crime, independent of the metropolitan center of London. But whatever the precise path of literary transmission, New England's early last speeches were undoubtedly influenced by transatlantic models.

Despite a relatively stable literary format, the tone and content of New England's last speeches changed considerably over the course of the eighteenth century. The earliest surviving examples, published during the 1730s, featured confessional statements quite similar to those occasionally inserted into volumes of execution sermons. In fact, two of the earliest broadside confessions were also appended to published discourses.[103] Such statements consisted largely of contrite acknowledgments of guilt and solemn warnings against a familiar catalog of sins. The condemned criminals or their editors were apparently more interested in conveying pious advice than in providing factual accounts of their lives and crimes. However, later published statements tended to reverse the literary priorities of the earliest confessions. While a few pious formulas remained to frame and perhaps legitimize the narratives, most subsequent last speeches were predominantly secular in tone and autobiographical in content. Those published after midcentury routinely included such basic biographical information as dates and places of birth, as well as detailed accounts of upbringings, travels, occupations, and offenses. Although the recitals usually took the form of dry, naively empirical itineraries of names, dates, locations, and crimes, they sometimes featured recognizably picaresque motifs.[104] Accounts of sexual exploits and daring escapes highlighted the genre's gradual drift away from the realm of spiritual biography, toward a form of documentary biography that exposed New England's developing criminal subculture.[105]

The shift from pious confessions to largely secular autobiographies may have reflected a corresponding change in the literary channels by which the words of condemned criminals made their way into print. Most of the contrite confessions appended to execution sermons during the late seventeenth and early eighteenth centuries had been extracted from criminals by ministers.[106]

Such statements were valued by clergymen both as warnings to others and as tokens of the prisoner's own sincere repentance. While some of the broadside confessions were obtained by ministers as well, others seem to have been procured by enterprising printers, either directly or through cooperative prison officials.[107] Some of those more worldly literary brokers were probably less interested in conveying the religious affirmations of condemned criminals than in portraying their lives and crimes. Since ministers and printers certainly played active roles in extracting last speeches through interrogations in jail and undoubtedly often drafted such statements for the signature marks of illiterate criminals, it is not surprising that a change in literary mediators would have significantly altered the resulting statements.[108]

Slight hints of the shift from ministers to printers as the chief mediators between criminals and readers are evident even in the early output of the 1730s. Two of the three surviving last speeches produced by the pious firm of Kneeland & Green were published both as appendices to execution sermons and as separate broadsides. One of them specifically indicated that it had been extracted orally from the malefactor in the presence of four ministers. By contrast, neither of the two last speeches known to have been published by Thomas Fleet during the same decade was attached to an execution sermon. And both explicitly claimed to have been written by the criminals themselves, without indicating that local clergymen had played any role whatsoever in their production; one even included a caveat by the dying prisoner that emphasized Fleet's status as the sole legitimate link between himself and his readers. The very titles of the broadsides may have hinted at the different orientations of the two firms. Whereas two of Kneeland & Green's broadsides were designated "confessions," a term with distinct religious connotations in Puritan New England, both of Fleet's were designated "last speeches," a more secular label. If the confessions of Kneeland & Green reflected the tenacity of a regional culture of Protestant piety, the last speeches of Thomas Fleet signaled the emergence of an increasingly secular and autonomous printing industry—one more prone to allow criminals to speak to the reading public through intermediaries other than ministers.[109]

The shift in tone and content of published statements probably also reflected changes in the backgrounds and sensibilities of the prisoners themselves. Most of New England's earliest criminal confessions were made by men and women who, despite their generally low social status, were integral members of the local community. Although condemned youths, slaves, servants, artisans, and yeomen had certainly deviated sharply from communal norms, many probably accepted the conventional values of the society to which they belonged. Such integrated offenders may have simply lacked an alternative ethical code or language of defiance with which to resist the literary draftsmanship of local ministers.[110] In contrast to those domesticated deviants, many of the criminals condemned in New England after 1730 were either recent immigrants from other parts of the British empire—often former soldiers and sailors—or inhabitants of an indigenous criminal subculture that gradually developed in the region during the eighteenth century.[111] Those condemned men and women had little reason to restrict themselves in their last public expressions to the platitudes of a local religious community into which they were imperfectly integrated, at best. Their last speeches naturally reflected their more worldly backgrounds and sensibilities, despite the proddings of pious redactors. In exploring the seamy underside of New England society, several last speeches may have subtly subverted, even as they ostensibly upheld, the traditional communal values articulated by local ministers.[112]

Some New England publishers of the second half of the eighteenth century, recognizing the popular appeal of criminal autobiographies, moved beyond the ephemeral broadside format and began issuing narratives in pamphlet form. Many such pamphlets published in the region after 1760 were virtually identical in content to contemporary prose broadsides. In a few cases, last speeches were published both as broadsides and as pamphlets.[113] Often the switch to the pamphlet form seems to have been made simply to accommodate criminal statements that could not be comfortably compressed onto one side of a single sheet. Relatively concise last speeches and dying confessions had gradually developed into longer "sketches" or "narratives," sometimes with poems, letters, or execution accounts appended. By the beginning of the nineteenth century, a few of New England's criminal narratives had even developed into full-length autobiographies.[114]

Whereas execution broadsides tended to be a distinctly ephemeral genre, catering to the intense local or regional interest temporarily aroused by a particular capital case, a number of the crime pamphlets published after 1780 demonstrated a far wider and longer-lasting appeal.[115] To a certain extent, such works reflected a broad redrawing of communication patterns and cultural boundaries during the mid- to late eighteenth century. The gradual development of a cooperative network of provincial newspapers in the context of a series of imperial crises and conflicts increasingly led Americans in various sections of the country to follow events in distant colonies or states.[116] Similarly, books and pamphlets published in one region of the United States during the early republican period were frequently reprinted in other sections of the country.

That process of journalistic and literary diffusion was facilitated by a rapid proliferation of printers in many relatively small provincial towns, particularly in the Northeast, during the post-Revolutionary decades. The spread of printing across the countryside was simply one aspect of the gradual commercialization of rural America during the late eighteenth and early nineteenth centuries.[117] Works issued in such large publishing centers as Boston, New York City, and Philadelphia were now routinely reissued—often with great rapidity, but sometimes many years after their original appearance—by printers in smaller towns like Bennington, Vermont; Otsego, New York; and Carlisle, Pennsylvania. Conversely, appealing titles issued by such smaller provincial presses occasionally made their way to the larger publishing centers. Thanks to the efforts of urban and rural printers, booksellers, shopkeepers, and peddlers, criminal narratives became part of a distinctive popular literary culture that often transcended regional boundaries.[118]

An inevitable result of that process was a gradual loosening of the link between crime literature and social reality. New England's earlier gallows literature had consisted largely of local, ephemeral publications. Readers often already knew of the events being described, either through newspapers, word of mouth, or personal observation. Indeed, many purchasers of execution sermons, criminal confessions, and gallows poetry undoubtedly attended the executions of their subjects; as already noted, dying verses and last speeches were probably sold among the crowds that flocked to view local hangings. However, when crime pamphlets described events that were both geographically and temporally remote from their readers, journalistic commitments to factual accuracy were sometimes significantly weakened. In such cases, the line between truth and fiction could easily blur. For example, when a fictional British story about a man falsely accused of murder was reprinted in America during the late eighteenth century, it was repeatedly presented to readers as a factual account.[119] By the first half of the nineteenth century, such fictions were commonplace.[120]

Several of the crime narratives published in New England during the late eighteenth and early nineteenth centuries not only blurred the line between fact and fiction but also subverted the perceived moral link between crime and punishment. Indeed, virtually all of the most popular crime pamphlets published in the early republic dealt with alleged miscarriages of justice. Criminals or their editors questioned both the accuracy of verdicts and the fairness of judicial proceedings. Convictions based on dubious testimony or inadequate evidence were obvious points of attack. In at least one case, the author of a criminal autobiography even challenged the fitness of others to judge his behavior at all. Such expressions of defiance reflected a number of cultural insurgencies—sentimental, evangelical, and philosophical—that were seriously challenging traditional authority during the decades following the American Revolution.[121]

Although still popular during the 1790s, last speeches suddenly vanished as a popular genre after the turn of the century. While a handful of execution broadsides with similar titles were issued over the next few decades, they were not first-person, autobiographical narratives of the same type. During that period criminal autobiographies were invariably issued as books or pamphlets. Dying verses also petered out as a popular form, though a bit less abruptly. Their fate was sealed by the 1830s with the rise of the penny press (to be discussed shortly) and the abolition of public executions.[122] The early demise of execution broadsides in New England contrasted sharply with the situation in Britain, where they flourished beyond all precedent during the early Victorian period. Although last speeches of the old sort did disappear, as many as two and a half *million* crime broadsides of other types were reportedly issued on a single English case during the mid-nineteenth century. One reason for their persistent popularity may have been the fact that English broadsides, which sold for a penny or even half a penny, were still much cheaper than British newspapers, an obvious alternative source of information on capital cases. Another factor may have been the reluctance of the English government to abolish public executions, a prime locus for sales. An even more basic cause may have been the persistence of a traditional sort of semiliteracy among the English laboring classes, both urban and rural, to which the simple broadside ballads and accounts were particularly well suited. It was only after the repeal of the last of the taxes that had artificially inflated newspaper prices (1855), the abolition of public hangings (1868), and the gradual spread of working-class literacy, capped by the enactment of Forster's Education Act (1870), that the English execution broadside finally reached the end of its rope.[123]

While execution broadsides would continue to appear in Great Britain for several decades, a strikingly new configuration of crime literature emerged in New England after 1800. On the one hand, publishers discarded two of the dominant genres of the eighteenth century, execution sermons and last-speech broadsides. While last speeches disappeared suddenly after the turn of the century, execution sermons vanished more gradually by about 1825.[124] On the other hand, three key elements were added to the literary mix. First, trial reports began appearing with increasing regularity during the years immediately after 1800, vying in popularity with criminal biographies throughout the antebellum period. Second, newspaper coverage of crimes and trials increased dramatically, often featuring serial transcripts of judicial proceedings later issued in pamphlet form. Third, many crime publications, particularly a new flood of biographies of offenders and their victims, incorporated language and motifs derived from the sentimental and romantic fiction that revolutionized American literary culture during the early national period.[125]

Although criminal trial reports had not been a particularly popular form in New England during the seventeenth and eighteenth centuries, printers issued more than a dozen during the first ten years of the nineteenth century, at least twenty-four during the decade after that, and many more throughout the antebellum period.[126] The nineteenth-century reports generally conformed quite closely in structure to the actual order of trial proceedings, including the indictment, opening arguments, testimony of witnesses, closing arguments, judge's charge, verdict, and sentence. The reports ranged from relatively brief pamphlet-sized synopses of trial testimony and legal arguments to complete transcriptions of entire trials, sometimes running to two hundred or more pages in length. Some were published by obscure or disreputable printers who catered to a plebeian audience; others were issued by highly reputable publishers who sought the patronage of lawyers and other elites.[127] Why did such trial reports emerge as a popular form when they did? Several factors were certainly involved, including intellectual tensions generated by earlier crime publications, shifts in the legal system and the social status of lawyers, and profound changes in the very nature of New England society.

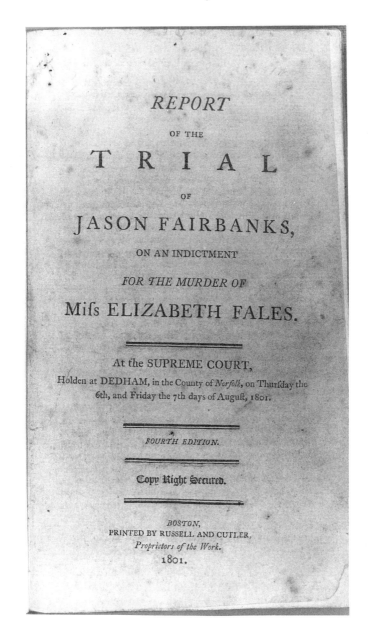

REPORT

OF THE

T R I A L

OF

JASON FAIRBANKS,

ON AN INDICTMENT

FOR THE MURDER OF

Mifs ELIZABETH FALES.

At the SUPREME COURT,

Holden at DEDHAM, in the County of *Norfolk*, on Thurfday the 6th, and Friday the 7th days of Auguft, 1801.

FOURTH EDITION.

Copy Right Secured.

BOSTON,
PRINTED BY RUSSELL AND CUTLER,
Proprietors of the Work.
1801.

Early example of a nineteenth-century trial report; note the edition number as an indication of the genre's increasing popularity in New England after 1800. For a thorough exploration of the controversial Fairbanks case, see chapter 8.

At the outset it might be noted that trial reports were a natural response to epistemological and ideological tensions within the literature itself. As already mentioned, the most popular crime narratives of the late eighteenth and early nineteenth centuries depicted alleged miscarriages of justice. Criminals or their editors, enjoying a virtual literary monopoly, presented one-sided versions of events to the public. Whether or not their claims were fully accepted by readers, such antiauthoritarian accounts suggested a troubling epistemological impasse in New England's literature of crime and punishment. How could readers seeking the truth about criminal cases rely on narratives based largely on the testimony of condemned offenders, who had an obvious personal stake in their own vindication? Trial reports provided an ideal solution to that dilemma, not by suppressing ambiguity and disagreement, but by providing a literary vehicle designed to present and fairly evaluate competing factual accounts and legal interpretations of disputed events.

Although a number of the new trial reports treated cases in which defendants were acquitted, they were not necessarily antiauthoritarian. On the contrary, the occasional triumph of accused individuals against government prosecutors tended to vindicate the adversarial system of justice as a bulwark not only of public safety but of individual liberty as well. Ironically, by highlighting the controversial character of legal inquiry, New England's trial reports may well have helped restore public confidence in the moral nexus between crime and punishment. If guilt and innocence no longer seemed as self-evident as they had often been portrayed in early execution sermons and criminal confessions, New England readers might still pride themselves on a system of justice able to resolve the formidable problems involved in distinguishing one from the other. Trial reports thus tended to reclaim crime literature as an effective instrument of authority, although they adopted an epistemological stance very different from that implicit in the earlier sermon form. The truth was no longer baldly asserted and imposed by an authoritative spokesman, whether minister or lawyer, but was mediated and accredited through the autonomous judgment of the community itself, as represented by jurors and, by extension, readers.[128]

The rise of the trial report as a genre was also encouraged by major changes in the legal system and in the position of lawyers within the broader culture. Both in New England and elsewhere, the gradual evolution of the criminal trial system over the course of the eighteenth century tended to increase the inherent drama of such proceedings, making them more attractive as both spectator events and subjects for literary treatment.[129] The rough outline of that transformation can be traced through a number of highly publicized criminal cases, all subjects of early trial reports. In the Salem witch trials of 1692, as in all criminal proceedings in seventeenth-century England, accused men and women were denied the assistance of legal counsel; as a result, the trials were largely one-sided affairs in which the prisoners were unable to construct effective defenses.[130] Although defense counsel were present at some (but not all) of the piracy trials held in New England before special Courts of Admiralty during the first three decades of the eighteenth century, the attorneys were still hampered by procedural obstacles; they were ostensibly restricted to addressing matters of law and were probably not allowed to cross-examine prosecution witnesses.[131] By contrast, attorneys for the accused soldiers at the Boston Massacre trials of 1770 enjoyed procedural parity with government lawyers; they constructed elaborate defenses, cross-examined opposing witnesses, and freely addressed issues of law and fact.[132] Although those British soldiers probably enjoyed exceptional counsel, defense lawyers were regularly appointed in capital cases by the mid-1780s, if not earlier.[133] By the beginning of the nineteenth century, New England's capital cases were typically tried in highly competitive, lawyer-dominated proceedings that were often entertaining events for both spectators and readers.[134]

Popular trial reports depended not only on legal actors to give them drama but on literary redactors to preserve the script. That task was undoubtedly facilitated by the professional stenographers and court reporters who created an American law reporting system during the post-Revolutionary decades.[135] One of the first volumes of law reports appeared in Connecticut in 1789; the first official court reporter was appointed for the Supreme Judicial Court of Massachusetts in 1804. A number of pioneer stenographic reporters not only prepared collections of court decisions for the use of legal professionals but also produced popular accounts of individual criminal trials for the edification, or entertainment, of both lawyers and laymen.[136] In 1806, for example, the controversial Boston murder trial of Thomas O. Selfridge was first jointly taken in shorthand by Thomas Lloyd, the U.S. congressional reporter, and George Caines, the former New York state reporter; checked for accuracy by Dudley Tyng, the official reporter of the Massachusetts Supreme Judicial Court, as well as by the trial lawyers themselves; and only then printed by a consortium of Boston publishers, who distributed the volume nationwide.[137] Professional reporters like Lloyd, Caines, and Tyng provided a crucial link between the courtroom and the reading public.

More broadly, the increased popularity of trial reports and the corresponding decline of execution sermons reflected a gradual shift in the balance of cultural leadership from the ministry to the bar. As both contemporary observers and subsequent scholars have often noted, the early republic was an increasingly law-oriented and lawyer-dominated society.[138] In that context, New England's early trial reports were at once products of, and testimonials to, the region's maturing legal profession.[139] Court reporters were not only often members of the bar in their own right but frequently relied on the notes of other lawyers and magistrates involved in the particular cases being reported.[140] Even more important, the trials themselves were preeminently arenas for the exercise of legal and juridical skills. The trenchant arguments of opposing counsel tended to set the tone for the proceedings—and to provide much of their drama, at least as presented in the published reports. Much as earlier criminals had been ministered to by the most prominent of Puritan clergymen, so now New England defendants were represented by the most gifted lawyers of their time. Such legal and political luminaries as Harrison Gray Otis, Prentiss Mellen, Lemuel Shaw, Daniel Webster, and Rufus Choate all served as defense counsel in one or more reported criminal cases during the course of their careers.[141] It is not surprising that defendants so ably represented were occasionally acquitted or, at least, convicted of lesser offenses.[142] Those courtroom victories may be seen as secular analogies to the spiritual victories won by ministers in earlier cases. Lawyers of the early republic saved lives where clergymen had once saved souls; each could provide a dramatic resolution to the literary enterprise.

In addition to responding to ideological tensions, legal changes, and shifting elites, trial reports also reflected a profound if gradual transformation in the underlying nature of New England society. While it had been the most ethnically homogeneous region in colonial Anglo-America, increasing numbers of cultural outsiders penetrated New England during the decades around 1800, foreshadowing the massive influx of Irish Catholics and others during the middle decades of the nineteenth century.[143] More significantly, even the core culture descended from the Puritans began to fragment, with profound and acrimonious splits between conservative Calvinists, radical anti-Calvinist evangelicals, and Arminian rationalists in religion, and between Federalist elites and Jeffersonian yeomen in politics. At the same time, the regional economy became increasingly complex and conflicted, with overcrowding in older farm areas, geographic expansion, commercializing agriculture, disruptions in international trade, and the first major strides toward industrial development. In short, despite the lingering ideal of a cohesive, covenanted community, the region was increasingly fractured during the early national period by various ethnic, religious, political, and economic differences.

In such a pluralistic setting, adversarial trials provided a natural framework for the expression of various social tensions and conflicts. In 1806, for example, the trial of two Irishmen for the murder of a young traveler in Wilbraham, Massachusetts, exposed widespread popular hostility toward one group of American immigrants.[144] That same year the case of a Federalist lawyer accused of killing the son of a prominent Republican journalist in Boston became the focus of partisan passions over many months.[145] A few years later, in 1809, the trial of seven men for the murder of a surveyor involved in a local land dispute dramatized economic conflicts dividing a frontier community in rural Maine.[146] More than two decades after that, in 1832, the alleged murder of a pregnant millworker by a Methodist minister in Rhode Island set off a prolonged public controversy that pitted powerful industrial interests against the representatives of a rising religious denomination.[147]

In each of those cases, criminal trials provided social mechanisms by which profound social tensions or divisions could be structured, expressed, and finally, perhaps, contained. If execution sermons typically embodied the traditional ideals of ideological unity and communal cohesiveness, adversarial trial reports neatly epitomized the emerging realities of social pluralism and conflict on a variety of fronts. As in the cases of Salem witchcraft, Anglo-American piracy, and the Boston Massacre, trial reports were a seemingly objective form ideally suited to occasions of public division and controversy; by the early nineteenth century, such occasions had become endemic. Trial reports exemplified "the transition from a coherent Christian culture to a competitive pluralistic one" while reaffirming crime literature's traditional commitment to social order and the rule of law.[148]

A final factor encouraging the publication of trial reports in antebellum New England was the gradual expansion of newspaper coverage of criminal cases, itself a second major development in the evolving literary treatment of crime and punishment. Most newspapers of the eighteenth and early nineteenth centuries were narrowly geared to the interests of economic and political elites, focusing on foreign news, commercial information, and later partisan politics.[149] Although they sometimes provided extensive reports on the relatively specialized crimes of piracy and counterfeiting—offenses likely to be of particular interest to a largely commercial or governmental readership—most other types of local property and violent crime tended to be treated, if at all, by little more than short isolated paragraphs.[150]

However, after 1800 coverage of crimes and trials became more extensive and sustained, particularly in sensational cases. That trend became especially dramatic after 1830, with the development of cheap urban daily newspapers, the so-called penny press, that sought to appeal to a heterogeneous mass audience by offering greater coverage of local news, especially crime. The rise of the penny press was simply one aspect of the emergence of a mass consumer culture in New England during the second quarter of the nineteenth century. For the first time, paid journalists were regularly sent out to cover local stories of human interest. As in contemporary British periodicals, the low tragicomedy of the daily police court and the high melodrama of major criminal trials were among the primary objects of journalistic attention.[151] In major cases, particularly in murders with a strong sexual component, coverage typically included not only sensationalistic crime accounts and moralistic editorials but also detailed synopses or even verbatim transcripts of criminal proceedings. Those trial reports, appearing serially in successive issues and special "extras" of the penny dailies, were sometimes reprinted in pamphlet form. Popular trial reports thus reflected not only the rise of the legal profession but the development of modern journalism as well. By the middle decades of the nineteenth century, crime broadsides and pamphlets were often little more than secondary tributaries to the surging torrent of newspaper coverage.[152]

A third major development in literary treatments of crime in nineteenth-century New England involved the transformation of criminal biographies and related genres. It will be recalled that the first such works issued in New England during the early eighteenth century had been conversion narratives, part of the extremely popular literary canon of Puritan spiritual biography. The earliest confessional broadsides had been similarly pious in tone and substance. However, much of the religious content had gradually leached out of the last speeches, resulting in dry, factual, largely secular accounts framed by brief vestigial expressions of warning, penitence, and spiritual hope. Only a few longer narratives of the late eighteenth century, mostly depicting alleged miscarriages of justice, diverged significantly from that pattern. But after 1800 criminal narratives were transformed by an influx of motifs from contemporary sentimental and romantic fiction.[153] Indeed, the new literary models had so powerful and pervasive an impact that they occasionally influenced not only the style of criminal biographies but also the tone of newspaper coverage, the packaging of trial reports, and even the content of judicial proceedings.

Anglo-American literary sentimentalism is a phenomenon more easily described than defined. Early sentimentalists intuitively valued true feelings and spontaneous emotions over cold logic and artful calculations. They also valued intimate private experiences over public events and institutions, and feminine traits and virtues over masculine ones. Sentimentalists celebrated the human capacity to respond with intense empathy to the misfortunes of others. The shedding of tears, as a visible manifestation of emotional sensitivity, was the quintessential sentimental activity. Sentimentalists were particularly fascinated by the emotions and feelings associated with romantic love. The greatest virtue for sentimentalists was sincerity; the most detestable vice was seduction, the triumph of counterfeited emotions over innocence. In American popular culture of the first half of the nineteenth century, the values and motifs of sentimentalism were gradually subsumed into the more complex literary configuration of romanticism, which depicted a greater variety of characters, situations, and plots (some drawn from the gothic and the picaresque) and evoked a correspondingly greater range of emotions and attitudes in its readers.[154]

The vogue of British sentimental fiction is conventionally dated to the appearance of Samuel Richardson's *Pamela* in 1740. Although imports and reprints began filtering into the colonies within a very few years, and although newspaper advertisements suggested an increased circulation of English novels in America after about 1770, it was not until the last two decades of the eighteenth century that the new fiction transformed New England culture. Literary magazines featuring sentimental poems, tales, and essays began sprouting up in the region during the 1780s, and the first American novel, William Hill Brown's *The Power of Sympathy*, appeared in Boston in 1789.[155] Between that year and the end of the century, more than thirty novels by American authors were published in the United States, many of those in New England. Overshadowing that early blossoming of native fiction was the dramatic growth of foreign imports from a small trickle into a veritable literary flood. During the last decade of the century, the volume of imported fiction "jumped tremendously," and the number of domestic reprints of foreign works leaped from 56 during the entire period between 1744 and 1789 to more than 350 between 1789 and 1800. The popular impact of that literary influx was multiplied many times over in New England and elsewhere by the rapid spread of local circulating libraries, which often specialized in novels.[156]

The dramatic effect of the new fiction and related genres on the reading habits of New Englanders is neatly described in Royall Tyler's *The Algerine Captive*, published at Walpole, New Hampshire, in 1797. The picaresque hero of the novel, Updike Underhill, was imprisoned abroad during a seven-year period stretching from 1788 through 1795. In the preface to his tale, Tyler described the transformation in literary culture that had occurred in New England during his protagonist's absence. When Underhill left his home region in 1788, several modern types of literature, including "books of Biography, Travels, Novels, and modern Romances," were still confined to the inhabitants of coastal towns or to ministers, doctors, and lawyers in rural districts. On the other hand, Tyler explained, the typical "farmer's library" was largely restricted to "funeral discourses, the last words and dying speeches of Bryan Shaheen, and Levi Ames, and some dreary somebody's Day of Doom."[157] However, by the time of the captive's return in 1795, that traditional regime had been demolished by an influx of new literary forms and the establishment of circulating libraries in inland towns. "No sooner was a taste for amusing literature diffused," Tyler explained, "than all orders of country life with one accord forsook the sober sermons and Practical Pieties of their fathers for the gay stories and splendid impieties of the Traveller and the Novelist."[158]

Although he may have exaggerated the speed and completeness of that transition, the general outline of Tyler's account of a literary revolution is confirmed by modern historians of American print culture.[159] The literary order of Puritan New England was essentially traditional and intensive, dominated by three kinds of works: a small number of fundamental texts, such as the Bible and the catechism; a somewhat larger pool of "steady sellers," such as *Pilgrim's Progress* and *The Day of Doom*; and a scattering of ephemeral publications, such as funeral sermons and execution discourses, designed to reinforce cultural values already embedded in the first two categories. As late as the 1780s, it seems likely that novels and related genres were indeed still largely restricted to elites in seaport towns and to their country cousins, the rural professionals mentioned by Tyler.[160] However, after 1789 even rural bastions of the old regime were decisively breached by a flood of popular sentimental fiction, widely disseminated through a growing network of country printers, booksellers, and circulating libraries. The old order was then finally overwhelmed, during the first half of the nineteenth century, by a powerful combination of changing popular tastes and cultural values, rising literacy rates among both men and women, and improved production technologies and distribution methods in the book trade.[161] By 1855 approximately 60 percent of all books published in the United States were novels.[162]

It is indicative of the great cultural distance traveled within a relatively short time that although last speeches were not introduced to New England until the 1730s and did not achieve their greatest vogue until the 1770s and

1780s, Royall Tyler already looked upon them, from the rapidly shifting cultural vantage point of the 1790s, as a traditional, hackneyed, and outdated literary form.[163] In fact, Susanna Rowson, author of *Charlotte Temple*, the early republic's most popular sentimental novel, had already offered a similar critique of the last-speech genre. In a piece of fiction first published in England in 1788 but reprinted twice in America during the 1790s, Rowson linked such works to an intellectually impoverished "lounger" who rejected the writings of modern novelists and travel writers in favor of ballads and "last dying speech[es] of people that were hanged."[164] Although Tyler linked last speeches to sermons—a traditional religious genre—while Rowson linked them to ballads—a traditional secular genre—both novelists rejected what they perceived to be a vulgar and outdated literary regime in favor of an emerging genteel culture of travel, satire, and sentiment. Significantly, the literary judgments of Tyler and Rowson were vindicated by the sudden demise of the last-speech genre after 1800 in both Great Britain and New England.[165] By contrast, many subsequent criminal biographies would closely resemble contemporary fiction. Indeed, nineteenth-century criminal narratives occasionally became fiction, taking the form of tales or novels based on highly publicized capital cases.[166]

The emergence of the trial report, the development of popular journalism, and the rise of romantic fiction were related cultural developments. Each was associated with the transition from a literary culture of piety, scarcity, and intensive reading to one of variety, abundance, and, at times, casual consumption.[167] Each form was committed to an essentially modern epistemology that conceived social reality not primarily in transcendent, universal, or typological terms (as in early execution sermons) but as an aggregate of individual worldly events or experiences, each firmly if elusively embedded in its own particular spatial and temporal setting. Each also implied a conception of truth not as the pronouncement of a single authoritative voice but as the collaborative product of a multiplicity of independent speakers and viewpoints.[168] The three literary forms were linked as well by a complex of specific influences and relationships. Scholars have noted the close connection between various news genres and the development of the novel; historians of journalism have stressed the importance of trial coverage in the rise of popular newspapers; and literary critics—both contemporary and modern—have compared early novelistic detail to courtroom testimony, an analogy obviously strengthened by the frequency with which early novels treated criminal themes.[169] Together the three developments created a popular literature of crime that was at once legalistic, journalistic, and romantic.

One of the most striking aspects of the nineteenth-century literature, cutting across the different genres, was its preoccupation with crimes of sexual deviance and violence. Such themes evoked a range of literary voices, including the sentimental, the romantic, and the pornographic. Some treatments aroused pity and sympathy for female victims of male lust; others explored the darker passions and destructive impulses of *both* sexes; still others graphically recounted the details of sexual violence, dwelling particularly on the mutilation of female bodies.[170] Sometimes all of those approaches were juxtaposed in a single work. Although the increasingly elaborate sexual content of crime publications presupposed the disintegration of Puritan social and cultural controls, authors and publishers still regularly justified their pamphlets as vehicles of moral warning. Graphic trial reports and newspaper accounts were presumably also shielded from attack by emerging conventions of judicial procedure, legal reportage, and journalistic accuracy.

It is difficult to know for certain who actually read antebellum accounts of illicit sexuality and violence.[171] One might intuitively assume that trial reports and criminal biographies were the sort of subliterary fare covertly devoured by adolescent boys and young men. In fact, the appearance in 1833 of a murder trial report with heavy gynecological content led people to quip that, given the wide availability of such prurient literature, "the next age would have no need of physicians, as every boy capable of reading would be perfectly instructed in all the secrets of the Materia Medica."[172] And yet it would be unwise to assume that young males constituted the sole, or even the primary, audience for antebellum crime literature. After all, American women of all ages reportedly flocked to attend criminal trials and public executions during the first half of the nineteenth century. Likewise, an antebellum wax museum that specialized in criminal figures and tableaux and sold related pamphlets drew patrons both urban and rural, male and female, young and old. A magazine editor claimed in 1852 that the regular readers of "shocking murder" stories in antebellum newspapers included "timid delicate women who swoon at the sight of blood." And a contemporary literary sketch suggested that the Lowell "mill girls" were avid readers of cheap novelists like Joseph Holt Ingraham and Osgood Bradbury, who specialized in sensational themes of crime and violence. Meanwhile, in early Victorian England, the street vendors of crime broadsides and pamphlets testified to the mixed readership of their wares, both urban and rural: One claimed that murder accounts were "bought by men, women, and children"; another insisted that "the ladies, bless 'em" were their "best customers." While such fragments of evidence are certainly not conclusive, they do suggest the likelihood that a great variety of Americans of both sexes enjoyed antebellum crime literature.[173]

Internal evidence can also help to clarify the issue of readership. As already mentioned, authors and editors still occasionally insisted that they were producing a cautionary literature suitable for the entire family. For example, one fictional account of the "adventures, intrigues, and dark crimes" of two beautiful twin sisters from Philadelphia, issued in 1853 by a cheap publisher with a wide distribution network, included a pretentious plug at the outset: "We aspire to making our simple narration . . . a companion book for young men, and a reference . . . for young women. We hope that it may be admitted to the domestic fireside, and that the rich tones of the father may read it aloud to his family." Should such statements be dismissed as pure tongue-in-cheek? Maybe. But a rare surviving copy of the potboiler contains a revealing owner's

Satirical illustration of Lowell "factory girls" reading in their crowded attic quarters. The figure on the far left is reading a translated French sex manual; the pair in bed are perusing a racy novel by Joseph Holt Ingraham. According to an accompanying dialogue, the young women were avid readers of the cheap fiction of J. H. Ingraham and Osgood Bradbury, who both specialized in stories of crime and violence. From the [Boston] *City Crier and Country Advertiser,* **April 1845.** *Courtesy, American Antiquarian Society.*

inscription. The crudely penciled note, dated 1854, reports that the pamphlet had been presented to thirteen-year-old Albert Peck of Great Barrington, Massachusetts, by his grandmother, Mrs. Perly Olds. One cannot help but wonder whether Granny Olds dusted off her spectacles and perused the racy tract before handing it over to little Albert.[174]

Whatever the precise mix of readers, it seems clear that antebellum accounts of illicit sexuality and sexual violence reached a genuinely mass audience. For they were part of a veritable explosion in the overall output of American presses during the middle decades of the nineteenth century, one aspect of the general expansion of American industrial capitalism during that period. On the supply side, the publishing boom was facilitated by a series of major technological innovations, including the development and diffusion of stereotyping, electrotyping, and steam-powered printing presses, along with papermaking and bookbinding machines; on the demand side, it was driven by the development of a mass urban readership.[175] As a result, between 1820 and 1850 the value of all books produced and sold in the United States increased fivefold, from $2.5 to $12.5 million.[176] Growth was particularly dramatic at the lower end of the market. One editor reported in 1846 that, aside from the output of elite publishing houses like Harper and Appleton, there were "in Boston, New York, and Philadelphia ten establishments for the publication of cheap novels which issue upwards of 200,000 volumes every week." Another observer of the mid-1840s worried about "the multiplication of books and other readable matter in the shape of newspapers and other periodical literature, *poured* in endless profusion and variety from the American press." That flood of cheap print not only provided employment for "innumerable depots and bookstalls, but to vast armies of pedlars who traverse every nook and corner of the land with their budgets of literature." American readers, one of the commentators concluded, regularly crammed their heads "with an incongruous mass of undigested rubbish."[177]

Even within the surging torrent of antebellum print, the subject sometimes referred to as "criminal knowledge" seems to have occupied a privileged position, stimulated beyond all precedent by "the spirit of enterprise and competition." As the editor of the *Boston Daily Times* noted in 1850: "Not only does it [crime] attract the attention of the ordinary press to a degree that never before was known, but there are presses regularly devoted to it, and whose business it is to discuss it at length, to publish all its statistics, and to give at full breadth the details of every horrible or loathsome affair that may chance to illustrate the history of human frailty." And so aggressive bookstore clerks behind their counters and legions of ragged newsboys on the streets urged an endless stream of crime accounts upon a receptive urban public. While some mistakenly concluded that the incidence of crime was increasing at an alarming rate, the *Times* editor insisted it was merely the coverage of crime that had gotten out of hand.[178]

Criminal knowledge was indeed a thriving industry in antebellum Boston. Individual midcentury trial reports were occasionally advertised as appearing in editions as large as twenty thousand. The most publicized cases often evoked competing editions by rival publishers, as well as multiple printings by individual firms. Similarly, the most popular of the midcentury penny dailies, such as the *Times*, which relied heavily on sensational crime coverage and trial reports, claimed daily circulation figures of as much as twenty thousand each. At a time when the total population of Boston hovered at about one hundred thousand, those figures suggest, crime pamphlets and newspaper coverage achieved an extraordinary degree of popular penetration, even allowing for a fair amount of exaggeration in circulation claims. As with the penny dailies, antebellum crime pamphlets were probably consumed by a broad spectrum of readers of the middle and working classes. If colonial execution sermons were extraordinarily popular products in a marketplace of literary scarcity, subsequent innovations in technology, distribution, and readership allowed antebellum newspaper stories, trial reports, and criminal biographies to achieve an even more pervasive presence on the cultural scene.[179]

It is reasonable to assume that authors, reporters, and publishers produced a seemingly endless stream of accounts of illicit sexuality and criminal violence because large numbers of people, most likely old and young, male and female, urban and rural, middle-class and working-class, were willing to pay for the privilege of reading them.[180] In part that demand embodied a timeless human fascination with sex and violence. In part it probably exposed frustrations inherent in an emerging regime of Victorian gender relations that celebrated romantic engagement while demanding sexual restraint.[181] Like many of the cases that they described, nineteenth-century newspaper stories, trial reports, and criminal biographies exposed some of the darker contradictions of a moralistic consumer culture that alternately mandated self-discipline and self-indulgence—and that mediated those demands by transforming human aggression and sexuality into marketable commodities.

The following chapters will more closely examine each of the major types of crime literature that appeared in New England between 1674 and 1860. Part I will discuss persistent themes of warning and salvation in execution sermons and conversion narratives, especially of the period 1674 to 1738. Part II will trace evolving explanations of crime and justifications of capital punishment in execution sermons of the late seventeenth through early nineteenth centuries. Part III will explore criminal autobiographies of the mid- to late eighteenth century, ranging from last-speech broadsides to full-length memoirs. Part IV will investigate the various crime genres, especially trial reports, romantic biographies, and newspaper stories dealing with cases of sexual violence, that became popular during the first half of the nineteenth century.

Given the very different genres under study, a range of analytical and expositional strategies is adopted in the various chapters, each intended to clarify the cultural context, literary message, and historical significance of the particular publications in question. Depending on the specific genre or cluster of genres under examination, the focus may be on devotional practices, or ministerial ideas, or criminal lives, or judicial proceedings. What ties the chapters together is the overarching relationship among the literary forms. Although execution sermons, criminal autobiographies, trial reports, and so forth were very different genres, they were all, at one time or another, popular literary responses to crime and punishment. The fact that such responses took sharply divergent forms in different periods is itself of historical significance. By examining the individual genres in detail we can learn a great deal not only about the evolution of New England culture and society between the late seventeenth and mid-nineteenth centuries, but also about the origins of our own modern preoccupation with crime and punishment.

I

Saints and Sinners:

The Literature of Protestant Piety

2

Pillars of Salt and
Monuments of Grace:
Themes of Warning and Salvation in
Seventeenth-Century Crime Literature

The complex social realities of crime and punishment inspired a rich popular literature in early modern England. Enterprising printers of the sixteenth and seventeenth centuries produced a steady stream of crime accounts, trial reports, hanging ballads, murder plays, rogue biographies, and conversion narratives, all based on actual crimes and criminals. The literature in its various forms ranged from the pious to the profane, from the bawdy to the belletristic, mirroring the diverse strands of a heterogeneous popular culture.[1] By contrast, the crime publications of late seventeenth-century New England were much more restrained in form and content, reflecting the preferences and inhibitions of a simpler and more disciplined cultural regime. After all, Puritan ministers and magistrates actively censored the few presses operating in Massachusetts, exercising a degree of control that was not matched by the authorities in London.[2]

Whether because of vigilant censors or disapproving readers, crime genres like hanging ballads, murder plays, and rogue biographies, long popular in England, seem to have been totally ignored by the printers of early Massachusetts and rarely sought as imports by the local booksellers.[3] Conversely, literary responses to crime in the region generally took the form of execution sermons, apparently unknown in England as a free-standing published genre.[4] Yet New England's cultural arbiters did not simply abandon their Old World heritage. On the contrary, in creating an almost uniformly pious literature of crime and punishment, the ministers, printers, booksellers, and criminals of Massachusetts drew on forms and practices deeply rooted in the religious culture of early modern Europe. In order to probe those cultural roots, this chapter will begin not in Puritan New England but in Catholic Italy.

One caveat: This chapter and the next will discuss criminal conversion narratives and other crime pamphlets as if they provided factually accurate records of criminal proselytization in prison and criminal behavior at the gallows. Of course, it is generally impossible to verify those accounts from sources outside the pamphlet literature. At best, they probably offer highly selective and idealized representations of what actually happened. The authors were reporting patterns of devotional conduct and spiritual transformation that they very much wanted to see; that desire undoubtedly colored their perceptions and descriptions. As in any other type of narrative, the demands of selection and compression, as mediated through the author's own values and intentions, ensured that even the most scrupulous accounts contained a fictive element. Still, the works were presented to the early modern public not as romances or allegories but as factual accounts. There is really no reason why modern scholars should read them as anything else, unless they simply assume that Christian clergymen and pious laypeople are naturally more prone to fabricate or prevaricate than other types of nonfiction writers.

In fact, there are a number of good reasons to trust the reports. Aside from their own moral inhibitions against writing falsehoods, the authors of criminal conversion narratives would presumably have been discouraged from offering blatantly inaccurate sketches by their knowledge that many readers would have themselves visited the condemned prisoner in custody or attended the execution, both popular practices during the early modern period. Further, the fact that some of the same authors occasionally reported the behavior of criminals who defied their efforts at proselytization suggests that they did not simply impose a conversionist framework on criminal narratives regardless of the circumstances of the case. If the narratives as a group seem highly repetitive and formulaic, that may simply reflect the intense application of highly formalized patterns of criminal proselytization, devotional practice, and gallows ritual. After all, literary formulas may be rooted in actual behavior, especially when that behavior is consciously modeled on the conduct of earlier literary exemplars.[5]

Criminal Conversion in Early Modern Culture

On April 18, 1592, Signor Troilo Savelli, a young nobleman just eighteen years of age, was beheaded at the Castle of Saint Angelo in Rome. The youthful baron, graced with an olive complexion, striking features, sweet voice, and ready smile, had reportedly committed both rapes and murders as a leader of one of the gangs of aristocratic banditti that terrorized the Italian countryside during the late sixteenth century. Prosecuted by Pope Clement VIII at the beginning of his pontificate, the young felon was condemned and executed despite his tender age and noble lineage as an example of impartial justice.[6]

Although his life had certainly been profane, Savelli's death was remarkably pious. Following his condemnation, the prisoner expressed great remorse and penitence, spending his last days and hours in the company of Jesuit priests and lay members of the *Confortatori della misericordia*, a religious fraternity dedicated to the spiritual comfort of condemned criminals.[7] Throughout the night prior to his execution, priests and laymen gathered in the convict's cell, praying, reading scriptures, reciting psalms, consulting devotional manuals, exchanging spiritual consolation, and weeping together in anticipation of Savelli's imminent death. Through it all the penitent murderer maintained a demeanor of unflagging bravery, piety, and humility. To observers who carefully monitored the young nobleman's spiritual progress during his final moments, Savelli seemed a marvelous exemplar of divine grace; he was a "proud rebellious worme" transformed into a "humble member of the body of Christ," a "drop of filth" transposed into a "strange image of perfection."[8]

The condemned youth's confessor, a Jesuit priest named Giuseppe Blondo, was so impressed by the dying penitent's exemplary piety that he compiled a narrative of Savelli's last hours, painstakingly recounting the various spiritual exercises undertaken by the condemned man and his religious guides during the night preceding his execution. The priest probably intended the work not only for the benefit of other condemned criminals but also as a devotional guide to all who would eventually confront the terrors of death.[9] Although Blondo wrote his account in Italian, it was eventually translated into several languages and circulated widely both in manuscript and in print. Unfortunately, surviving copies of early editions are so scarce that it is difficult to trace the precise diffusion of Blondo's narrative; however, some evidence does remain available.

The original Italian manuscript was compiled not long after Savelli's death in 1592 and reportedly circulated in Rome for many years; the first French version was published in Paris in 1596; at least four more editions had appeared in Paris by 1613, along with provincial printings at Douay in 1599 and Tournon in 1602; finally, an English translation was produced in 1620 by Sir Tobie Matthew, a prominent Catholic expatriate.[10] Although that last version was published at Saint Omer in northern France, across the channel from Dover, it was apparently intended for an English audience.[11] According to Matthew, the work had already been greeted by the readers of several countries with great avidity and many tears.[12] It should be stressed that the wide success of the narrative was not based on the sensationalism of Savelli's crimes—which were scarcely mentioned in the pamphlet—but on Blondo's success in portraying the condemned nobleman as a paradigmatic "penitent sinner," a model for all dying mortals in need of grace. As an early religious best-seller, the narrative of Troilo Savelli was part of a much broader complex of devotional practice and literary expression, the influence of which was felt throughout early modern Europe.[13]

Although the wide diffusion of Blondo's narrative certainly suggested the existence of a common cultural discourse on criminal executions, rituals associated with capital punishment varied significantly from country to country. In his preface Sir Tobie Matthew contrasted the treatment and demeanor of condemned criminals in England with those of Catholic Europe. In many of the towns of Italy and Spain, he explained, there existed confraternities of pious gentlemen who, along with priests and other religious laymen, regularly visited prisons, offering spiritual comfort and guidance to even the poorest of offenders while instructing them how to "dye well." In England, by contrast, many condemned men approached their deaths with a sort of "profane stupidity," going "drunke, or dauncing to the gallowes," as if they were only dying "in a play" and had no account to make for their sins. As an alternative to that profane gallows theater, Matthew offered his country's readers the example of Troilo Savelli, a model of "humility, patience, courtesy, magnanimity, obedience, and charity."[14]

In fact, English Protestants of the late sixteenth and early seventeenth centuries had already begun to adopt practices similar to those long found in Catholic Europe. Although there do not seem to have been formal organizations like the *Confortatori della misericordia* described in Blondo's narrative, English ministers and pious laymen increasingly gathered in prisons and at gallows to proselytize condemned men and women. One early evangelist of that sort was the great sixteenth-century Puritan divine William Perkins. At the outset of his career, Perkins had made it a regular practice to preach every Sunday to fettered prisoners in a shirehouse near the local jail. It was claimed that he had been "the happy instrument of converting many of them unto God." Perkins would also accompany condemned criminals to the gallows and try to convert them to Christ during their last moments. A particularly dramatic example of his success was recorded by Samuel Clark, the popular seventeenth-century nonconformist biographer.[15]

According to Clark's account, Master Perkins first called the despondent prisoner, a "young lusty fellow," down from the top rung of the gallows ladder. The minister then joined the condemned man at the foot of the gallows, the two kneeling "hand in hand," and addressed him with a powerful discourse. He began by berating the malefactor with so forceful an account of his aggravated sins and of the "horrible and eternal punishment" he justly faced that the "poor prisoner burst out into an abundance of tears." Having thus brought the man down to the very gates of hell, Perkins immediately reversed direction and raised the malefactor so high with hope in Christ's saving mercy that the doomed man broke into "new showres of tears for joy." Finally the prisoner "rose from his knees chearfully; and went up the Ladder again so comforted, and tooke his death with such patience, and alacrity, as if he actually saw himself delivered from the hell which he feared before, and heaven opened for the receiving of his soul, to the great rejoycing of the beholders."[16] By rushing the young prisoner through the essential spiritual stages of conviction and assurance, Perkins had transformed him into an exemplar of divine grace, much as the Italian priests and laymen had transfigured Troilo Savelli.

Not surprisingly, the labors of such English evangelists as William Perkins occasionally bore literary fruit. One early crime account, published in London in 1573, described the "spirituall comfort and councell" offered by a number of English ministers to three convicted murderers and reported that one of the offenders had died "with a marvellous apparance of heartie repentance." Another narrative, published in 1604, described the hundreds of visitors, some godly, others profane, who daily flocked to visit a penitent murderess. A third pamphlet, issued in 1612, provided a first-person narrative of "the true and hearty Repentance" of a convicted robber; a fourth, published six years later, described "the happy Conversion, contrition, and Christian preparation" of a condemned counterfeiter.[17] In addition to those crime accounts, English hanging ballads and rogue biographies of the late sixteenth and early seventeenth centuries also frequently referred to the spiritual hopes of dying malefactors.[18]

During the turbulent decades of the mid- to late seventeenth century, English criminal conversion narratives became increasingly focused and elaborate, emerging as a distinctive genre in the popular canon of Anglo-Protestant spiritual biography. Between 1640 and 1680, accounts of celebrated criminal converts like John Atherton, Freeman Sonds, Nathaniel Butler, and Thomas Savage appeared under such evocative titles as *The Penitent Death of a Woefull Sinner* (1641), *A Mirrour of Mercy and Judgement* (1655), *The Penitent Murderer* (1657), *A Murderer Punished and Pardoned* (1668), and *The Murtherer Turned True Penitent* (1680).[19] Those compilations included extensive accounts of prison conferences between capital convicts and various clergymen and laymen, along with pious criminal confessions, prayers, letters, and last speeches. The prisoners were described meditating on their sins, reading works of practical piety, and even receiving communion. Two of the compilations also included transcripts of funeral sermons delivered following executions.[20]

As literary treatments became more elaborate, so also did the devotional practices on which they were based. By the mid-1670s the entire process had become sufficiently formal to justify publication of a devotional manual intended exclusively for the spiritual cultivation of criminals. That short work, entitled *The Penitent Prisoner* (1675), prescribed appropriate prayers, meditations, sighs, and ejaculations for offenders under confinement, along with suitable devotions for malefactors on their way to the gallows. For the convict willing to make "a *Pulpit* of his Prison" and "a *Sermon* of his shackles," the anonymous author provided a ready script. Repentance did not have to be spontaneous in order to be sincere.[21]

A number of the increasingly formal and elaborate criminal conversions— and conversion narratives—were at once products of extensive collaboration and objects of intense popular interest. Freeman Sonds was the beneficiary of public prayers by all the pious ministers of an English county; an early account of Thomas Savage embodied the spiritual (and literary) labors of at least five or six nonconformist ministers; a compilation on the case of Nathaniel Butler included a statement endorsed by no fewer than eighteen clergymen of London.[22] Authors and their collaborators included orthodox churchmen and nonconformists, royalists and regicides.[23] In Ireland even Catholics reportedly flocked to the execution of John Atherton, an Anglican bishop, mixing their tears with those of local Protestants; the resulting narrative was published first in Dublin and then twice in London.[24] Other conversion accounts were even more popular: A compilation on Nathaniel Butler was printed in no fewer than five editions; a narrative on Thomas Savage appeared in as many as thirteen.[25] Although nonconformists seem to have been particularly active in the field, criminal conversions and conversion narratives were not the monopoly of any particular sect or denomination but enjoyed wide currency in the popular culture of early modern England.[26]

Yet few of the religious crime publications in late seventeenth-century England focused exclusively on conversions. Most also demonstrated the utility of the gallows as an instrument of warning. Executed criminals, however pious, were not simply "monuments of grace," but also "pillars of salt," symbols of the potentially fatal end of all wickedness. Cautionary messages of that type were prominent in such English crime accounts as *Blood for Blood, or, Justice Executed* (1670), *Hell Open'd, or, The Infernal Sin of Murther Punished* (1676), and *A Warning to Young Men* (1680).[27] John Quick's *Hell Open'd*, compiled in response to a poisoning case in Plymouth, England, was particularly urgent in tone, warning against not only great sins but little ones as well; all could lead alike to damnation. "Remember *Lot's* Wife," the minister insisted, for God had erected "*A Pillar of Salt* in *Plymouth.*"[28] As we shall now see, such messages of warning also dominated the first two crime publications to appear, during that same decade, in Puritan Massachusetts; only later did New England ministers return to the more hopeful themes of criminal conversion and salvation, drawing on traditions deeply rooted in their received culture.

Themes of Warning

By the mid-1670s more than thirty years had passed since the end of the Great Migration that had established the Bay Colony as a stronghold of Protestant piety. Although some of the original zeal of the Puritan enterprise may have faded, an effective alliance of ministers and magistrates still closely monitored the moral behavior and social practices of Massachusetts residents. Sabbath observance was mandated by law, while frivolous holidays and profane recreations were discouraged or prohibited.[29] The printing trade was also tightly regulated in the interests of civil and religious propriety. No presses were allowed to operate outside of Cambridge, and the few tolerated there were subject to the close supervision of clerical licensors appointed by the General Court.[30] Execution sermons, the earliest literary responses to crime in New England, reflected that broad pattern of Puritan cultural dominance.

In March 1674 seventeen-year-old Benjamin Goad of Roxbury, Massachusetts, was arraigned, tried, and convicted of the capital crime of bestiality for buggering a mare in an open field.[31] Goad's condemnation provided the Reverend Samuel Danforth with suitable material for a sermon. Local Christians may have thought it doubly fitting that Danforth should address the matter. Not only was his congregation located in the offender's home community, but he was a pastor known to be "particularly watchful against the inroads of immorality among the young."[32] It was perhaps a measure both of the exceptional zeal with which the preacher addressed his subject and of the popular interest aroused by Goad's unusual case that the resulting discourse was published, one of Danforth's only sermons to be so dignified.

The work, evocatively entitled *The Cry of Sodom Enquired Into*, was issued by Marmaduke Johnson, a Cambridge printer who had established the Bay Colony's first private press in 1665. Johnson was no saint. Before establishing his own shop, he had been fined and nearly deported for dallying with his employer's daughter. A few years after striking out on his own, he had been fined again by local authorities, this time for his unauthorized printing of *The Isle of Pines*, a "mildly erotic" piece of fiction. In publishing Danforth's execution sermon, Johnson was undoubtedly on safer ground.[33] The pious pamphlet began with an introductory commendation by three local ministers, all official licensors of the press. "It's surely no season for Watchmen to be silent," the clergymen declared, "when Heaven-daring sins are calling aloud for Vengeance."[34]

Much of Danforth's sermon was devoted to warning his audience against a wide range of offenses associated with Goad's capital crime. Most of the relevant sins came under the general heading of "uncleanness," a broad category of sexual wrongdoing including masturbation, fornication, adultery, incest, sodomy, and bestiality. In addition, Danforth cautioned against a variety of "inlets, occasions, incentives and provocations" to such misbehavior. He particularly described pride, gluttony, drunkenness, disobedience to parents and masters, evil company, irreligion, and profanity as dangers to be avoided. Resorting to the frightening imagery of physical infection, the pastor urged each of his sinful listeners to perform a radical surgery on his or her own moral body: "He that hath a lascivious eye, hath a Spiritual Gangrene in his eye; he that hath an unchaste ear or hand, hath a Spiritual Gangrene in his ear or hand: either cut off the gangrened part, or Soul and Body will be cast into hell fire, where the worm dieth not, and the fire is not quenched."[35]

Despite Danforth's powerful exhortation, sinful individuals continued to commit capital crimes in the Bay Colony. Less than a year after the execution of Benjamin Goad, two foreign-born servants, Robert Driver and Nicholas Faevor, killed their master, a fisherman from Piscataqua, with an axe. The two men, each claiming that the other had delivered the fatal blow, were together convicted of murder and sentenced to death.[36] Once again, an imminent public hanging provided the occasion for a sermon, this one delivered by Increase Mather, the renowned pastor of Boston's North Church. Mather's lecture was subsequently published under the title *The Wicked Man's Portion* (1675). It was issued by John Foster, a graduate of Harvard who had just purchased the first printing press in Boston from the widow of the recently deceased Marmaduke Johnson. Foster had gone into business with the active encouragement of his friend and patron Mather, a newly appointed licensor of the press. The minister's sermon, the first book of any kind printed entirely in the town of Boston, seems to have aroused considerable contemporary interest; the pamphlet was quickly reissued and was reprinted yet again a decade later.[37]

Like Samuel Danforth the previous year, Mather devoted much of his discourse to themes of warning. However, unlike Danforth, Mather directed his primary cautions not to individual sinners but to the community as a whole. In that regard, he suggested that the public execution of two servants was intended by God to rebuke and humble the entire colony for some prevailing social evil. The minister found just such an evil in the pervasive pattern of disrespect for authority that he felt existed in Massachusetts. Mather saw social insubordination all around him: in courts, churches, schools, and families. Citizens dishonored their magistrates; laypeople belittled their ministers; servants defied their masters; students despised their teachers; and children disobeyed their parents. Even in the streets, Mather complained, one could observe "the child behaving himself proudly against the antient, and the base against the Honourable."[38]

Such a pattern of insubordination was by no means characteristic of a well-ordered society. On the contrary, Mather argued, New England had "become degenerate from the good manners of the *Christian world.*" Even more to the point, it was just such misbehavior that culminated in the sort of crime committed by the two servants. That murder was both a natural outcome of pervasive social insubordination and its just punishment. The crime itself was "an awfull Providence" designed by God "to rebuke and humble" the community as a whole. Not satisfied to leave it at that, Mather added one last dramatic turn to the rhetorical screw. "If ever *New-England* be destroyed," he concluded ominously, "this very sin of disobedience . . . will be the ruine of this Land."[39]

The execution over which Increase Mather sternly presided was at once a monument to God's particular judgment against individual offenders and an emblem of far broader collective guilt. His exhortation thus transformed the spectacle of the hanging from a discrete act of communal catharsis to a symbolic demand for more general reformation. As in the days of the Old Testament prophets, a degenerate Israel was exhorted to abandon its wicked ways—or face disaster. In achieving that conceptual shift, Mather effectively integrated his execution sermon into the dominant literary and rhetorical genre of the second generation of New England ministers: the jeremiad. Most often presented as fast-day or election-day sermons, jeremiads embodied just the sort of collective threat presented by Increase Mather in his execution discourse. They generally included an extensive listing of communal offenses, a proposed plan of reformation, and a description of the terrible judgments that lay in store for society if it failed to mend its ways. While ostensibly proposing a cure for communal malaise, Perry Miller has pointed out, jeremiads reflected not only "anxiety and insecurity" but also an almost debilitating sense of collective moral decline. Both in spirit and content, jeremiads were well suited to the "awfull Providence" of a public hanging.[40]

Increase Mather was certainly not the last minister to make extensive use of jeremiadic motifs in a gallows sermon. Rather, suggestions of communal degeneration and invocations of collective punishment were common elements in many early execution discourses. Motifs of communal warning continued to find their way into such works long after the passing of the second generation.[41] One modern scholar has even traced jeremiadic themes in execution sermons delivered as late as the 1790s.[42] However, such motifs were rarely as central to later examples as they were to Increase Mather's lecture of 1675. On the contrary, individual wickedness, rather than communal guilt, tended to remain their primary focus. Early execution sermons were typically filled with warnings to sinners. Although social groups deemed particularly susceptible to wickedness (e.g., children, servants, slaves, and sailors) were often singled out, the primary focus was generally on the sinner as an individual.

In discourses published between 1674 and 1740, ministers regularly inveighed against drunkenness, Sabbath-breaking, disobedience to parents, sexual indulgence, wicked company, swearing and cursing, stealing, and lying, in approximately that order of frequency. In addition to warning against particular sins, ministers also cautioned against wickedness in general, expounding with hair-raising imagery on the wrath of God, the horrors of hell, the cruelties of the devil, and the terrors of the last judgment.[43] Those cautionary themes showed remarkable cultural resilience; although terminology certainly changed somewhat along the way, a similar mix of warnings appeared in many execution sermons published between 1741 and 1825.[44] Such motifs would be carried over into other crime genres long after the demise of the gallows discourse as a literary form.[45]

Themes of Salvation

Although themes of warning remained central to most crime publications of late seventeenth-century New England, one or two cases of the period did evoke a lively interest in the spiritual condition of a condemned offender. The criminal subject of one of those cases was James Morgan, a loutish Boston currier of about thirty years of age, who was at best an unlikely candidate for heaven. In testimony taken in connection with his trial, Morgan was described by a neighbor as a profane and malicious drunkard married to a woman of like character. Either despite or because of their shared disposition, the couple often quarreled. Morgan habitually called his wife a jade, a bitch, and a devilish whore, while his wife called him a dog, a rogue, a devil, and a whoremaster.[46]

At about ten o'clock on the evening of December 10, 1685, Joseph Johnson, a local butcher, sat by the fireside with John Buckley and Silvester Witheridge, two young seamen of Marblehead, at a disreputable boardinghouse in Boston. Suddenly the three men heard a woman's cry for help coming from another room. When Buckley and Johnson rose and went next door, they discovered James Morgan and his wife lying together in bed. The distraught woman claimed that Morgan had been beating her and had thrown one of his children into the fire. When Buckley rebuked him for abusing his wife, Morgan rose from the bed, threatening the two intruders with physical violence. Buckley and Johnson thereupon withdrew, only to hear the woman's cries renewed. As Johnson again rushed into the room, with Buckley at his heels, Morgan lunged at the butcher with an iron spit, thrusting it deep into his belly.[47]

When Joseph Johnson died of that wound three or four days later, a coroner's jury held Morgan responsible. He was tried for the murder on March 3, 1686, found guilty, and sentenced to be hanged on March 11.[48] Morgan thereupon submitted a painfully contrite petition to the colony's high court, pleading with the authorities to grant him additional time to repent his sins and make his peace with God.[49] However, the court refused Morgan's request, forcing him to condense a wicked lifetime's worth of penitence into the space of a week. During the murderer's last days, at least two or three local ministers, including Increase Mather, repeatedly met with him in prison, exhorting him to confess and repent.

Despite those able spiritual guides, Morgan proved to be a difficult pupil, mixing his contrition with several bouts of drunkenness, lying, and at least one fit of anger.[50] Still, some progress seems to have been made. Morgan eventually submitted a written confession of his sins to the local ministers and requested that two of them, Cotton Mather and Joshua Moody, address his case in sermons to be delivered on the Sunday preceding his execution. Morgan's plight was also the subject of a discourse delivered by Increase Mather on the day of the hanging itself. Following that sermon, on the afternoon of Thursday, March 11, 1686, James Morgan walked from Boston's South Church to the gallows, where he was launched into eternity before an enormous crowd of onlookers.[51]

The three sermons evoked by the execution of James Morgan became the basis for a compilation published shortly thereafter. The first discourse in the volume (actually the last delivered) was Increase Mather's *A Sermon Occasioned by the Execution of a Man Found Guilty of Murder*. It was a harsh sermon, largely devoted to justifying the capital penalty and to warning listeners against those lesser sins and passions that could lead to the crime of murder. Yet the minister also focused considerable attention on the dying thoughts and spiritual status of the condemned offender. In the middle of his exhortation, Mather broke off to present a written communication from Morgan, a contrite statement of confession and warning almost certainly prepared with the active collaboration of one or more of the local ministers who visited him in jail. After reading Morgan's statement, Mather returned to his exhortation and then concluded his sermon with a separate address to the condemned prisoner. He pressed Morgan to consider what a wicked sinner he had been and to reflect on the misery he had brought on himself. But he also urged him to realize that he might yet be saved. "Notwithstanding all that has bin spoken to you, don't *despair*," Mather assured him; "repent but do not despair." The

Portrait of Increase Mather, painted in London by Jan van der Spriett about two years after the execution of James Morgan. *Courtesy, American Antiquarian Society.*

preacher then completed his discourse by praying that God would have compassion on the condemned man.[52]

Significantly, Increase Mather's portion of the printed volume on the Morgan case did not end with his sermon. Appended to the discourse was a transcription of James Morgan's own remarks at the gallows. It is unclear whether it was inserted by Mather himself or by the publisher. The brief statement, reportedly taken in shorthand at the place of execution, consisted of a series of prayerful warnings rather similar to those contained in the written statement read earlier by Mather. Finally, Morgan's very last words, carefully distinguished from the rest of his dying speech, were transcribed by the editor: "O Lord receive my spirit, I come unto thee O Lord, I come unto thee O Lord, I come, I come, I come."[53]

Several days earlier, on the Sunday prior to the execution, Cotton Mather, Increase Mather's flamboyant twenty-three-year-old son and ministerial colleague, and Joshua Moody, a much older Boston minister, had also delivered sermons addressing the upcoming event. Cotton Mather's complete discourse was included in the volume on the Morgan case, following his father's sermon, under the separate title of *The Call of the Gospel Applyed*. It was his first published sermon. In addition, a portion of Moody's discourse that directly addressed Morgan's plight (originally inserted at the explicit request of the condemned man) was appended as well, under the title of *An Exhortation to a Condemned Malefactor*. Cotton Mather's sermon and Joshua Moody's address appeared in the Morgan volume under separate title pages but were paginated continuously with Increase Mather's opening discourse.[54]

John Dunton, an astute nonconformist bookseller from London who had just arrived in Boston at about the time of Morgan's execution, seems to have played a key role in putting together the volume of sermons.[55] Apparently sensing commercial possibilities in the highly publicized hanging, Dunton quickly arranged with another local bookseller to issue the anthology from the Boston press of Richard Pierce, a young craftsman who had married into the extended Mather family several years earlier. Dunton's partner in the project was a Dutch-born bookman named Joseph Brunning, a favorite publisher of the Mathers. The dispatch with which Dunton and his associates acted may be judged by the fact that Increase Mather's introduction was dated March 26, 1686, just two weeks after the execution itself. Brisk demand for the volume evidently vindicated Dunton's commercial instincts; a second edition was issued by Richard Pierce the following year.[56] As in the case of Blondo's narrative a century earlier, the success of Dunton's pamphlet was surely not based on "blood and guts" alone—the details of Morgan's crime were barely mentioned—but also on Morgan's dramatic embodiment of the fundamental Christian paradigm of the penitent sinner confronting death. That purpose was especially apparent in the second edition.

"The general *Usefulness & Acceptableness* of this Book," printer Richard Pierce explained of his new edition, "together with the *speedy sale of the 1st* Impression, as also some honest *gain* to my *self & good* to *others*, has enclin'd me to renew the Impression of it." But despite the notable success of the original format, Pierce was not content to leave it alone. Instead, he added another section to the volume in order to "render it more compleat." It seems that Cotton Mather had engaged Morgan in a last conversation as they walked together from Boston's South Church to the gallows. Mather later produced a transcript of his dialogue with Morgan, apparently for personal use or private circulation. Pierce then took the liberty of procuring a copy of the transcript, ostensibly without Mather's knowledge, for inclusion in the second edition of the collected volume.[57]

"I'm come hither to answer your desires which just now you exprest to me in the Church, that I would give you my company at your Execution," the minister explained to Morgan as they trudged along the muddy road. In the conversation that followed, Mather berated the condemned man for his past wickedness, explored the state of his soul, and told him how to approach his imminent death. To judge by the printed transcript, Morgan eagerly seized on Mather's extemporaneous advice. "I beseech you Sir speak to me," he begged. "Do me all the good you can: my time grows very short: your discourse *fits* me for my Death more than any thing." When they finally arrived at the foot of the gallows, the young minister took leave of Morgan with the hope that he might yet be saved by God's infinite grace. "Farewel poor heart, Fare thee well," Mather exclaimed. "The everlasting arms receive thee!"[58]

Surely the dialogue between minister and malefactor was appended to the three sermons in order to focus additional attention on the spiritual fate of the condemned man. In that regard, the revised format of the new edition, by completing the second dramatic cycle implicit in the earlier version, added significantly to the literary effectiveness of the whole. In both editions the expectant tension generated by Increase Mather's harsh sermon was dramatically shattered by Morgan's last moving words at the gallows. It was only in the revised version, however, that a second wave of anticipation, built up through Cotton Mather's discourse and Joshua Moody's exhortation, was broken with similar effect by the emotional leavetaking at the gallows. The reader of the expanded edition was thus actually dragged twice through the same vicarious ordeal. Significantly, the dramatic structure of the anthology tended to shift the reader's attention away from subtleties of ministerial doctrine, feelings of revulsion at Morgan's crime, or vindictive satisfaction at his judicial death and toward an aroused concern over the condemned man's spiritual fate.

In his introductory remarks to the reader, Increase Mather had expressed a skeptical but noncommittal attitude concerning the final disposition of Morgan's soul. Such "Secret things," he suggested, were better left with God, adding that "Late Repentance is seldom true." However, the overall content and structure of the publication in which Mather's sermon appeared suggested a more optimistic outlook. Recall that Increase Mather's sermon closed with an exhortation to the condemned prisoner. *"Betake your self to the City of Refuge,"* he urged, "go to *Christ* for life." Then Morgan's own last speech, inserted immediately after Mather's discourse, concluded with these dying words: "O Lord receive my spirit, I come unto thee O Lord, I come unto thee O Lord, I come, I come, I come."[59] Given the relatively intimate juxtaposition of Mather's demand and Morgan's dying response, contemporary readers might naturally have understood the gallows scene as the climax of a sincere conversion.

What was true of the first section of the volume was equally true of the work as a whole, particularly in its second edition. The doctrine of Cotton Mather's hopeful discourse was that Jesus Christ invited "all *the Children of men to* Look unto *Him* . . . *for* SALVATION." The sermon concluded with directions to Morgan on seeking redemption during his last days. "And now let the Everlasting Saviour LOOK down in much mercy on you," Mather declared as he neared his peroration. "O that he would give this *Murderer* and *extraordinary Sinner*, a place among the *Wonders of free Grace*." Moody's exhortation also closed on a somewhat optimistic note. "All the sins that ever thou has committed shall not damn thee," he assured Morgan, "unless thou add Unbelief to all the rest."[60] As in the case of Increase Mather's forceful demand and Morgan's dying response, the juxtaposition of those exhortations with the last dialogue between minister and malefactor could only have strengthened the reader's impression that Morgan was probably heaven-bound.

While walking with Mather to the gallows, Morgan's manner was impeccably contrite; his words, humble and penitent. In turn, the minister's attitude toward the prisoner was properly stern but at times also compassionate, even sympathetic. Mather's parting remarks were at once a climactic expression of the minister's faith in God's saving grace and an impassioned plea that it be exercised in behalf of the condemned man. "The Great GOD who is a *great forgiver*, grant thee *Repentance unto Life*; and glorify himself in the Salvation of such a *wounded* soul as thine forever," Mather exclaimed. "*With HIM, and with His free, rich, marvellous, infinite Grace, I leave you*, Farewell."[61] In light of all that had already been revealed concerning Morgan's conspicuous contrition during his last moments, how could a merciful God have refused Mather's emotional request?

A bibliographic postscript may further clarify the literary context of the Morgan volume. During the winter of 1690–91, John Dunton was back in London, reestablished as a bookseller and publisher. There he arranged to reprint Increase Mather's sermon on the Morgan execution, with its attached statement by the condemned man. The new edition was actually published as an addendum to a much longer work, *The Wonders of Free Grace* (1690), subtitled "A Compleat History of All The Remarkable Penitents That have been Executed at Tyburn, And elsewhere, For these last Thirty Years." The compilation included narratives of more than a dozen pious offenders, including such celebrated criminal penitents as John Atherton, Nathaniel Butler, and Thomas Savage, all of whose cases had already been memorialized in popular English conversion narratives.[62] That Dunton annexed Mather's sermon and Morgan's dying words to *The Wonders of Free Grace* suggests he probably conceived of his earlier Boston publication as a conversion narrative in its own right, one constructed through the suggestive juxtaposition of ministerial exhortations and statements of criminal contrition. Of course, the Morgan anthology did differ from English and European conversion narratives in that it was formally dominated by three sermons. Although that reliance on the sermon form marked it as a product of the singularly constricted literary culture of seventeenth-century New England, the work's actual focus on the spiritual transformation of a condemned criminal exposed its rootedness in the popular religious culture of early modern Europe.

Cotton Mather's *Pillars of Salt*

Between 1686 and 1726, at least twenty volumes of execution sermons were published in New England.[63] About half of them contained discourses by Cotton Mather, an immensely prolific author eager to follow up the success of his first gallows sermon. Most of his subsequent execution sermons appeared in volumes like the Morgan anthology in that they contained a variety of supplementary materials, including confessions, dialogues, last speeches, and dying prayers. Yet not all the capital criminals of early New England proved as malleable as James Morgan. Some of the resulting works offered few hints of criminal salvation and were correspondingly dominated by motifs of warning. Such, for example, were five volumes dealing with the cases of several women executed for infanticide during the last decade of the seventeenth century.[64] The somber titles accurately suggest their cautionary tone; they included Cotton Mather's *Warnings from the Dead* (1693), Samuel Willard's *Impenitent Sinners Warned of the Misery* (1698), Cotton Mather's *Pillars of Salt* (1699), Increase Mather's *The Folly of Sinning* (1699), and John Williams's *Warnings to the Unclean* (1699).[65]

By far the most interesting was Cotton Mather's *Pillars of Salt*, evoked by the execution of Sarah Threeneedles, a young woman from Boston convicted of murdering her illegitimate infant. Although Threeneedles had sexual relations with another prisoner while awaiting execution and showed little interest in the gallows theater of repentance, Mather was far too resourceful a literary publicist to be discouraged. On the contrary, he used the opportunity to compile the most ambitious piece of crime literature to appear in New England up to that time. As indicated by its subtitle, Mather's compilation featured "An History of some Criminals Executed in this Land, for Capital Crimes," along "With some of their Dying Speeches; Collected and Published, For the Warning of such as Live in Destructive Courses of Ungodliness."[66]

Mather opened his book with the first part of a discourse delivered by him on the day of Sarah Threeneedles's execution. That was followed by the main body of text, consisting of twelve case studies of capital offenders executed in New England. Several of those accounts would already have been familiar to local readers. In fact, the bulk of that section consisted of the confessions, dialogues, and last speeches of James Morgan and Hugh Stone (another penitent murderer), all lifted verbatim from earlier compilations. The remaining studies included cases already described in *The Wicked Man's Portion* (1675), *Warnings from the Dead* (1693), and *Warnings to the Unclean* (1699), along with two accounts that had been annexed to the volume on Hugh Stone. The last example was that of Sarah Threeneedles herself, represented in part by the concluding portion of the discourse with which Mather had opened the volume. In short, *Pillars of Salt* consisted of a dozen criminal case studies sandwiched between two parts of a single execution sermon.[67]

As a landmark in the development of early modern crime literature, Cotton Mather's *Pillars of Salt* may be compared to John Dunton's earlier *Wonders of Free Grace* (1690). One appears to have been the first cumulative digest of domestic capital cases published in England; the other was the first such work to appear in New England.[68] Both editors drew liberally on earlier crime publications for their case studies. Dunton's work emphasized the theme of salvation; Mather's stressed the competing, or complementary, mo-

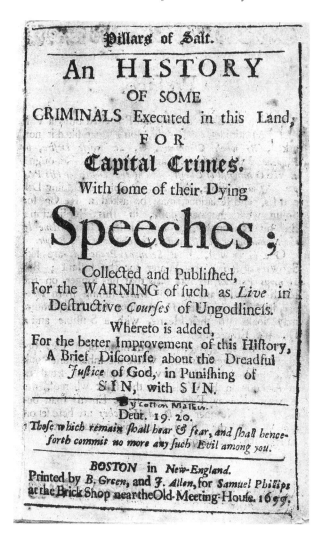

Cotton Mather's *Pillars of Salt,* consisting of an execution sermon and twelve criminal case studies. *Courtesy, American Antiquarian Society.*

tif of warning. Finally, each compilation included an execution sermon, although in both cases the sermon was described on the title page as an appendage, subordinate to the main body of case studies.[69]

In moving away from primary reliance on the sermon form, Mather may have been more of an innovator than Dunton. While England's literature of crime and punishment had never included many execution sermons, New England's gallows authors had relied on them almost exclusively. In making the literary shift, Mather was probably motivated in part by commercial considerations. Dramatic accounts of capital criminals and dying speeches were evidently more apt to catch the eye of potential readers than doctrinal discourses, even in Puritan New England. Yet the change may also have resulted from a thematic logic inherent in the literature itself. If a primary function of execution volumes was to warn survivors, perhaps that purpose was best served not by theological arguments, however cogent, but by flesh-and-blood examples, and the more, the better. At least that seems to have been the rationale for assembling *Pillars of Salt*. When Sarah Threeneedles proved reluctant to warn her fellow sinners against the "Destructive Courses of Ungodliness," Cotton Mather simply retreated to the local literary graveyard, spade in hand, and there exhumed an entire phalanx of provincial malefactors to do so in her place.

Published responses to crime in late seventeenth-century New England were typical of the region's early literary marketplace. The standard characterization of the Boston book trade was formulated more than seventy years ago by Worthington Chauncey Ford. According to Ford, the literary world of Puritan Massachusetts was very different from that of the mother country in that it was dominated by local ministers who, with the support of local magistrates, effectively excluded many of the plays, ballads, news accounts, and other profane works that proliferated in London.[70] However, David D. Hall has implicitly challenged that view in his recent study of popular religion in Puritan New England. In contrast to Ford, Hall downplays the differences between the London and Boston book markets, suggesting that the latter quickly evolved into a "provincial version" of the former. While acknowledging the existence of local censorship and the caution of local printers, he emphasizes the degree to which secular, even profane, English works made their way into Massachusetts bookshops and households.[71]

Although Hall is certainly correct to point out the gradual seepage of non-Puritan materials into New England's literary marketplace, local responses to crime tend to support Ford's conventional wisdom. Boston's book market was *not* a fragment of London's in the sense of being a smaller version of the same thing. Rather, it generally replicated only that portion of the parent trade that conformed to Puritan beliefs and sensibilities. As late as 1700, the Mathers may have continued to function as informal censors of the Boston press.[72] In any case, printers and booksellers like Marmaduke Johnson, John Foster, Richard Pierce, and Joseph Brunning were simply too dependent on the patronage of local ministers to knowingly alienate them by undertaking objectionable projects.[73] Although Johnson erred once with *The Isle of Pines*, he seems to have learned his lesson.

Unlike Johnson, most early Massachusetts printers and booksellers probably did not even need the prodding of pious censors; the religious books and pamphlets that they produced reflected their own deeply held beliefs and values. John Foster, for example, was remembered at the time of his death in 1681 as a "Pious, Learned, Ingenious, and Eminently Usefull Servant of

God." The loyal Puritan printer even went so far as to remember the two Mathers, along with another local minister, in his will. A generation later, Bartholomew Green, the printer of no fewer than ten execution sermons, was a deacon of Boston's South Church. The respected craftsman was described by those who knew him as "a very humble and exemplary Christian," devoted to strict Sabbath observance and domestic piety. Though a diligent and successful printer, he reportedly avoided publishing anything that might be construed as "offensive, light or hurtful."[74]

And so, despite the existence of popular English models, Massachusetts printers of the late seventeenth century produced no hanging ballads, no murder plays, and no rogue biographies. The few crime accounts and trial reports that they produced appeared in volumes authored by local clergymen.[75] Further, despite their purchases of thousands of copies of other English publications, Massachusetts booksellers do not seem to have imported many examples of those five popular crime genres from their colleagues in London.[76] Rather, local readers interested in the subjects of crime and punishment eagerly turned to execution sermons, pious works rarely, if ever, published separately in seventeenth-century England but regularly compiled by local ministers, produced by local printers, and sold by local booksellers.[77] The same Boston bookshop of 1700 that contained a total of eight copies of two chivalric romances (carefully noted by David Hall) also stocked more than fifty copies of an execution sermon by Increase Mather, along with scores, even hundreds, of copies of other religious works, many by local ministers.[78] While the initiatives taken by John Dunton and Richard Pierce suggest that printers and booksellers were by no means entirely passive, they tended to act, whether by choice or by necessity, through local clergymen. In the book market of late seventeenth-century Boston, and more particularly in the indigenous crime literature of early New England, Puritan ministers still held sway.[79]

In producing a crime literature that consisted almost entirely of execution sermons, New England's ministers of the late seventeenth century achieved a monopoly on that branch of cultural expression that could not be matched by their counterparts in England, who were forced to share the popular press with less pious spokesmen. Puritan clergymen like Samuel Danforth, Increase Mather, and Cotton Mather employed the gallows primarily as an instrument of warning, depicting condemned offenders as figures of caution both to individual sinners and to the community as a whole. Yet a few early execution sermons also suggested that dying criminals might serve not only as pillars of salt, but also as monuments of grace, dramatic exemplars of divine mercy. That theme of criminal salvation, deeply embedded in early modern religious culture, would achieve increasingly direct and dramatic expression in New England during the first half of the eighteenth century, even as local ministers were losing their monopolistic grip on the region's crime literature.

3

Toward a Great Awakening:
Criminal Conversion Narratives
in New England, 1701–1738

During the first four decades of the eighteenth century, New England printers, ministers, and malefactors produced at least three fully developed criminal conversion narratives, along with many other works featuring themes of
criminal penitence and redemption.[1] Those publications at once reflected a
long tradition of criminal proselytization in early modern religious culture and
prefigured, even as they promoted, a massive upsurge of popular evangelism
in New England by the early 1740s. The new pamphlets and broadsides also
suggested that ministers were gradually loosening their control over the region's crime literature, conceding a literary voice to the prisoners themselves.
Although aggressive printers and assertive offenders played key parts in that
process, the role of ministers, as the prime instigators and architects of early
criminal confessions and conversion narratives, was initially crucial. In their
eagerness to exploit the words of dying men and women for their own pious
purposes, New England clergymen helped transform the gallows into a pulpit
not only for ministers but for malefactors as well, a forum for literary messages both spiritual and profane.

Esther Rodgers: A Monument of Grace

The executions of several women for infanticide between 1693 and 1699
evoked no fewer than five volumes of gallows sermons. Yet not one of the
unclean women became as hopeful a candidate for heaven as James Morgan,
the penitent murderer. The case of Esther Rodgers, hanged for infanticide in
1701 and memorialized in a volume containing three execution sermons by
John Rogers (no relation to the criminal), reversed that disappointing trend.[2]
If Cotton Mather's *Pillars of Salt* represented a logical culmination of gallows
literature as a medium of warning, Rogers's *Death the Certain Wages of Sin*,
published just two years later, fulfilled another central purpose of the genre—
that of illustrating the marvelous efficacy of God's saving grace.

    The volume opened with a preface by William Hubbard, a venerable
colleague of John Rogers at the Congregational church in Ipswich, Massachu-

setts. He left little doubt as to the significance of the case about to be addressed, suggesting that the work would inspire readers to praise God for transforming a "heinous Sinner" into an example of "Grace and Mercy." As such, the conversion of Esther Rodgers was no mere local oddity but a worthy addition to a long tradition recorded in both ancient and modern history, including—Hubbard noted in particular—the examples described in Samuel Clark's sketch of William Perkins. A second introductory statement, by Nicholas Noyes and Joseph Gerrish, ministers from the nearby towns of Salem and Wenham, similarly stressed the value of the work as a conversion narrative. The clergymen particularly praised their worthy colleague, John Rogers, whose efforts, they claimed, had succeeded in "convincing, humbling, comforting, and (it is generally believed) converting" one who had been a "leud, and rude, and wretched . . . Sinner."[3]

Following the introductory statements of the neighboring ministers came the three discourses of John Rogers, occupying nearly 120 pages of text. The first sermon argued that the wages of sin were death; the second explained that the reward of penitence was life; and the third described the way for young people to "avoid the former, and attain the latter." The last discourse concluded with an impassioned exhortation by John Rogers to the condemned woman, setting the stage for the narrative that was to follow. That account of the conversion and execution of Esther Rodgers occupied the last thirty-five pages of the volume. It was a literary pastiche, alternating the words of various members of the local Christian community with those of the prisoner herself. Although it occupied much less space than the three sermons, it clearly was the focus of the publication as a whole, the climax toward which the opening comments of Hubbard, Noyes, and Gerrish had together pointed.[4]

The conversion narrative itself began with yet another introduction by a local clergyman. Samuel Belcher, a minister from West Newbury, explained that the two primary purposes of the account were to dramatize the conversion of Esther Rodgers and to establish the role of the broader community, particularly of the clergy, in facilitating her spiritual transformation. In his very first sentence, Belcher made explicit what had been only implicit in the earlier volume on James Morgan. "*This serves only to draw the Curtain, that thou mayst behold a Tragick Scene, strangely changed into a* Theater of Mercy," Belcher declared, "*a* Pillar of Salt *Transformed into a Monument of Free Grace.*" Eight months after entering prison "a Bloody Malefactor," Esther Rodgers had emerged "Sprinkled, Cleansed, Comforted, a Candidate of Heaven."[5]

In explaining her remarkable spiritual rebirth, Belcher scrupulously divided the credit between heavenly and earthly agents. But the minister left little doubt as to who had done most of the strenuous spadework. Of course, Esther's conversion was to be ascribed ultimately to divine grace. Yet Belcher immediately went on to explain that the spiritual change was "Instrumentally" due "to the Labours, Prayers and Endeavours of the Reverend Elders of the

Church of Ipswich, and many other good Christians there." That local community of "Sound, Serious and Praying Christians" had labored "not only for her, but with her, in their own Houses, joyning & turning their Private Meetings into whole days of Fasting and Prayer." In addition to welcoming the condemned woman into their own homes, they had also taken turns visiting her in prison, thereby "turning a Den of Thieves . . . into a House of Prayer." Finally, Belcher added, the local pastor (John Rogers) had taken "constant & unwearied pains" in encouraging her conversion, efforts that had finally been realized "through the Blessing of God."[6]

In all, the names of seven ministers appear in the little volume, each in one way or another involved in the proselytization and memorialization of Esther Rodgers. The youngest in the group was John Rogers, thirty-five years old. The eldest was William Hubbard, born in England before the founding of the Bay Colony, participant in the original Great Migration of Puritans to Massachusetts and member of the first graduating class at Harvard College. An octogenarian by 1701, Hubbard was an uncle and colleague of John Rogers at the meetinghouse in Ipswich. All of the other ministers had been born in northeastern Massachusetts, two in Roxbury, two in Ipswich, and two in Newbury. Every one of them was a graduate of Harvard College, and every one of them was settled with a congregation on the North Shore of Massachusetts. The seven seem to have belonged to a close-knit community of local clergymen. With similar backgrounds, educations, and values, the ministers preached to each other, prayed together, and socialized among themselves.[7] The Rodgers conversion and narrative were very much group efforts. In fact, there may have been a conscious division of labor among the clergy, based perhaps on seniority. Two of the younger ministers, Rogers and John Wise (still in his forties), seem to have done the bulk of the actual legwork in shepherding Esther to eternity, while the older clergymen, Hubbard, Belcher, Noyes, and Gerrish (all over fifty years of age), oversaw the efforts of their junior colleagues and later granted their imprimatur in prefatory statements.

But the ministers were not the only ones to be heard. Following all of the sermons and introductions was a series of statements by Esther Rodgers herself, including her responses to a number of religious interrogations. They were all linked by an intermittent chronological narrative that traced the young woman's spiritual progress from her initial imprisonment to her death on the gallows. The compilation began with an autobiographical confession in which Rodgers described her apprenticeship to one Joseph Woodbridge of Newbury, Massachusetts, at the age of thirteen. Although taught to read and properly catechized in her new household, Esther was little concerned about salvation. At about the age of seventeen, she had sexual intercourse with a "*Negro* Lad" living in the same household. She conceived and carried the resulting pregnancy to term in complete secrecy. Then, determined to avoid "Public Shame," Rodgers smothered the newborn infant and concealed its corpse in an upper room of the house. The next night, under cover of darkness, she secretly buried her baby in the garden.[8]

During the following half year, while she remained in the household at Newbury, Rodgers was beset by feelings of fright and spiritual conviction. Afterward, though, she went to live at a tavern in Piscataqua, where she soon abandoned her fears and returned to evil ways and wicked companions. A year later she returned to Newbury, first to her old household and then to another. There, Rodgers acknowledged, she took every opportunity to follow her old practice of "running out" at night and entertaining her "Sinful Companions in a back part of the House." As before, she had sexual intercourse with a "*Negro* man" attached to the household and carried a secret pregnancy to term. She delivered the infant in a field, where she "covered it over with Dirt and Snow, and speedily returned home again." But this time she fell under immediate suspicion: "The Child being found by some Neighbours was brought in, & laid before my Face, to my horrible Shame & Terror; under which Confusion I remained during my Confinement at *Newbury*, being about one Month, Thinking only of the punishment I was like to suffer."[9]

After being transferred to await trial at the jail in Ipswich, where she was to remain for many months, Esther was frequently visited by John Rogers and other local ministers and laypeople. At first she was "very much reserved" in her conversation with them and reluctant to attend religious services. However, Esther gradually began to show "more freedom of spirit, and liberty of speech." She expressed deep remorse over her sins, willingly attended public worship, and diligently studied the Holy Scriptures. Encouraged by strong feelings of "hope, comfort, and joy," Rodgers became convinced that she had experienced a soul-saving conversion. During a reprieve of nearly two months (provided by an adjournment of the provincial court), she frequently attended prayer meetings in private homes, finding "much sweetness" in the society of her spiritual friends.[10]

"Oh! I have had the joyfullest day to day that ever I had in my whole life," Esther declared to visitors on the night before her execution. "I bless God that ever I came into this Prison." When asked how she expected to answer for the shedding of her children's blood, Rodgers expressed her faith in the advocacy of Christ. The following morning John Wise, a minister from Essex, went to the prison to cross-examine the condemned woman on her spiritual condition. She described her conversion experience and acknowledged that it had been initiated by John Rogers's forceful discourse with her in prison. Thereupon Wise offered his "charitable Opinion of her good Estate."[11]

The sheriff had prepared a cart to carry Esther Rodgers to the gallows after the public lecture. But after earnestly requesting permission to travel there by foot, Esther was allowed to walk to the place of execution, accompanied by two or three ministers and surrounded by an armed guard. As they walked together, one of the ministers tried to terrify the condemned woman by reminding her of the gallows and pointing out the coffin that would soon receive her body. "How can you bear the sight of all those things?" he demanded. At that point, Rodgers wheeled around, smiled, looked the minister in the face, and replied: "I know I am going to the Lord Jesus Christ." One observer later recalled that the suddenness of her profound reply, along with her bravery and cheerfulness, produced surprise and astonishment. As they continued along the way, the ministers granted Rodgers "an Absolution, though not from the Temporal Punishment, yet from the Condemning Guilt of all her great Abominations."[12]

After walking for more than a mile, Rodgers faltered momentarily but then quickly pressed forward. As the gallows came into view, she declared that her "strength and joy" only increased. Bidding the ministers a tearful farewell at the foot of the gallows, Rodgers ascended the ladder without pause or trembling. There she delivered an emotional statement of warning, directed particularly to the young: "O let me beg of you all to hear me! for the Lords Sake Remember me! O let every one Remember me! Let me beg of all Young Ones, be not Disobedient, go not with bad Company, O my dear Friends—Take Warning by me." Afterward she uttered a lengthy prayer for divine mercy. Two ministers offered some last words of comfort. Esther again called on Jesus for mercy.[13]

When an officer bound the handkerchief over her face, she received it cheerfully, with her eyes and hands raised toward heaven. Asked by Mr. Wise if her faith still held, Esther thanked God that it did and leaned her head back against the ladder to receive the halter. She cried some last words of supplication: "O Lord Jesus, Now Lord Jesus, I am a Coming: O Come Lord Jesus by Thy Pardoning Mercy, to save me Now, or I Perish for ever. My Blessed Jesus,—O Lord Jesus, have Pity upon me, O Good Lord." Thus she remained, with her hands lifted toward heaven, until Mr. Wise spoke some final words: "We have Recommended you to God, and done all we can for you. . . . And so we must bid you *Fare-Well.*"[14]

It was superb gallows theater. Esther Rodgers had played her part flawlessly. The crowd of spectators, numbering at least four or five thousand by the estimate of the narrator, were reportedly amazed by the dying woman's cheerful courage, composure, and confidence, as well as by her pleasing eloquence. Indeed, her manner "melted the hearts of all that were within seeing or hearing, into Tears of affection, with greatest wonder and admiration." As the narrator himself concluded, there could be little doubt among men of faith: The good Christians of Ipswich had proudly hanged a saint.[15] But what did it all signify? More particularly, why had a number of ministers and laypeople of Ipswich and vicinity taken the trouble of collaborating to memorialize the drama? In part, of course, they were simply acting out a pattern of devotional activity and literary expression with deep roots in their received religious culture. One of the ministers explicitly cited the criminal conversions achieved during the sixteenth century by William Perkins, and at least some local readers, among them the editors of the Rodgers volume, would likely also have been familiar with one or more of the English conversion narratives of the mid- to late seventeenth century. After all, the account of Esther Rodgers bore striking similarities to those of Nathaniel Butler, Thomas Savage, and others.[16]

Yet in addition to that broader cultural context, the published account of Esther Rodgers also seems to have been a locally rooted expression of communal chauvinism. As stressed in the narrative, Esther's damning sins and capital crimes had all been committed in Newbury. Even after her confinement there she had remained in a confused state of shame and terror. It was only after her arrival at the prison in Ipswich that the ministrations of local clergy and laypeople began to take effect. By implication, the people of Newbury properly bore the stigma of Rodgers's guilt; conversely, the "Sound, Serious and Praying Christians" of Ipswich had earned a large share in the glory of her salvation. Again and again, throughout the narrative, the role of the local community and clergy in the conversion of Esther Rodgers was pointedly stressed.[17] In contrast to the collective guilt proclaimed by Increase Mather in his gallows jeremiad of 1675, the execution of a sinful penitent at Ipswich in 1701 was apparently an occasion for communal pride.

The case of Esther Rodgers had certainly demonstrated the extraordinary potential of the criminal conversion process as an extended ritual of communal self-justification. The series of prayerful meetings in prison and in private homes, all culminating in the emotional ceremony at the gallows, had affirmed social solidarity by symbolically reintegrating a formerly deviant member into the moral consensus of the community.[18] In the process, however, Esther Rodgers had also demonstrated that the gallows could serve as an effective pulpit not only for ministers but for malefactors as well. For all the self-congratulation generated among the community's pious leaders by her conversion, it was the condemned woman herself who finally emerged as the unrivaled heroine of the drama. If anything, her affecting manner and modest poise made the ministers and other townspeople seem heavy-handed by comparison. Perhaps some of the young servants and other social subordinates who read about Esther facing down her inquisitors were inspired in ways unintended by the ministers.

While the local clergy may have expected both the proceedings and the resulting narrative to illuminate their own pastoral diligence, Rodgers had, consciously or not, exploited the very structure of the drama to hold the spotlight and steal the show. The other actors could only hope to bask in the reflected glow of her glorious death. Through her tenacious adherence to the Puritan model of conversion, Esther Rodgers had forged an irreproachable spiritual identity that offered her great psychological and emotional support during her last days on earth.[19] In meeting the moral arbiters of the community on their own ground, the once lowly servant and disgraced deviant had not merely salvaged her private sense of self-worth but established a formidable public dignity as well.[20] By collaborating in the construction of her own conversion narrative, she had not only achieved a dramatic presence but also a literary voice.[21] In the process Rodgers had demonstrated just how powerfully the conventions of Puritan spirituality could destabilize long-established social hierarchies of age, rank, and especially gender. As one of the local ministers proudly noted in his introduction to the conversion narrative, Esther

Rodgers had succeeded in "out doing all the old Roman Masculine bravery . . . shewing what Grace can do, in, and for the Weaker Sex." In the eyes of such Puritan clergymen, women may have remained "the Weaker Sex," but that weakness could be magnificently transcended through the workings of Protestant evangelism.[22]

If the conversion of Esther Rodgers was a source of personal strength for herself and a cause for satisfaction among the good Christians of Ipswich, it was almost certainly an embarrassment to the people of nearby Newbury, the location of all her crimes and of her resulting confusion and despair. It is impossible to know for certain why the inhabitants of that town might have defaulted on their spiritual responsibilities after the imprisonment of Esther Rodgers. One possible answer may lie in the character of the town's original settlers, a "mixt multitude" who arrived during the Great Migration of the 1630s from a variety of regions and subregions in southern England. Unlike the founders of other Massachusetts towns, most of the early settlers of Newbury seem to have been motivated less by religious aspirations than by economic ambitions. They were a contentious lot, who left a lasting imprint on the communal life of Newbury. Over the years the town was racked by much social, economic, political, and religious conflict. As an assemblage of fragmented individuals, the citizens of Newbury were better suited to squabbling among themselves than to the delicate collaboration involved in proselytizing a social pariah.[23]

By contrast, Ipswich had been settled during the 1630s by a much more cohesive group of migrants from East Anglia. Many were motivated to leave by religious persecution in their home region and came over in congregational groups under the leadership of Puritan ministers. They were drawn together not merely by spiritual ties but by a complex if elusive web of social and economic relationships. As a result, Ipswich developed a tradition of strong local leadership, both civil and religious. Although extremely commercial in economic orientation, the "Sound, Serious and Praying Christians" of Ipswich were much better prepared than the "mixt multitude" of Newbury to come together in the pursuit of spiritual goals.[24]

Another more immediate explanation for the failure of Newbury residents to proselytize Esther Rodgers may lie in the character of Newbury's only settled minister, Christopher Toppan, whose name is conspicuously absent from the narrative on the Rodgers case. In 1701 the pastor of Newbury's First Congregational Church was a man of wide secular interests who would soon become heavily involved in land speculations on the Maine frontier. As a practicing physician and surgeon, Toppan may have been more interested in the cure of sick bodies than in the salvation of lost souls. In any case, when the Great Awakening swept through New England during the 1740s, Toppan stood in sharp opposition to the revivalists, dismissing the massive outbreak of evangelism as "a delusion of Satan."[25]

John Rogers took a very different stand. In 1743, more than forty years after his successful proselytization of a condemned sinner, the longtime minister of

Ipswich, by then quite old and frail, issued a written statement endorsing the revivalists.[26] It was a position completely consistent with his much earlier foray into evangelical activism. The neighboring ministers, Rogers and Toppan, thus seem to have represented two divergent strands in the development of New England religious culture, one determined to renew and sustain the intense piety of early modern devotional practice, the other content to settle into a more worldly Christian ministry. As a product of the more spiritual strand of regional culture, the narrative of Esther Rodgers at once echoed the strenuous evangelism of earlier English nonconformity and faintly heralded—even as it promoted—the coming revivalism of the Great Awakening. At the same time, the narrative's tearful indulgence in the plight of a dying heroine suggestively foreshadowed the spirit of early sentimental romanticism.

Excursus: Pirates Penitent and Defiant

Most of the capital criminals executed in New England during the thirty years after 1700 were not domestic deviants like Esther Rodgers or the Salem witches, but international brigands. During the early decades of the eighteenth century, swarms of pirates preyed on commercial shipping throughout the Western Hemisphere. In response the British government launched a massive campaign of suppression, resulting in the trials and executions of hundreds of offenders.[27] About half of the dozen or so volumes of execution sermons appearing in New England between 1704 and 1726 addressed the cases of such condemned pirates.[28] Most were written by Cotton Mather, who eventually became convinced that the pirates were as obsessed by him as he was by them.[29] As in other types of capital cases, the piracy sermons fluctuated between motifs of warning and salvation, a pattern suggested by such titles as *Faithful Warnings to Prevent Fearful Judgments* (1704) and *The Converted Sinner* (1724).[30]

Like earlier offenders, some of the pirates conveyed pious messages through their statements and behavior in prison and at the gallows. In 1723, for example, a group of twenty-six pirates condemned at Newport reportedly engaged in daily devotions in prison, praying together, reading Scripture, consulting books of piety, and singing psalms; several of them also warned the public against a variety of sins. The following year, two penitent pirates, John Rose Archer and William White, spent their last days in jail similarly engaged in reading and prayer; they also bewailed their sins at the gallows and were finally declared hopeful candidates for heaven.[31] As in earlier cases, printers or ministers inserted a variety of accounts, confessions, dialogues, and letters into volumes of published sermons in order to confirm the spiritual progress of the penitent offenders.[32]

However, other pirates spurned the guidance of local ministers and pious laymen, engaging in a very different form of gallows theater that had little to do with the Puritan model of conversion. When Captain John Quelch was executed in Boston with five associates in 1704, he declined to acknowledge the sins that had led to his downfall, as urged by attending ministers. Instead of striking a pose of pious humility, Quelch seemed determined to "brave it out" during his last moments on earth, acting unconcerned about his fatal predicament. After mounting the gallows, he quickly "pulled off his Hat, and bowed to the Spectators." John Brown, another pirate executed in Boston in 1717, also misbehaved at the gallows, resorting to furious language, impertinent prayers, and a defiant last speech at which "every body trembled."[33]

Perhaps the most uncooperative of all of the pirates executed in early eighteenth-century New England was William Fly, the leader of a band of mutineers who had turned to piracy before being apprehended and executed at Boston in 1726.[34] Fly's unrepentant attitude was manifested both at meetings in prison with Cotton Mather and at the gallows. In his first meeting with Mather, Fly denied committing the murder for which he was condemned to die and also refused to forgive the man who had brought him to justice. "It is a Vain Thing to ly," the pirate insisted. "If I should say, that I forgive that Man, and that I wish him well, I should ly against my Conscience, and add Sin to Sin." At a second meeting with the minister, Fly openly criticized the government's action against himself and his comrades. "I shan't own myself Guilty of any Murder," he declared defiantly. "Our Captain and his Mate used us Barbarously. We poor Men can't have Justice done us. There is nothing said to our Commanders, let them never so much abuse us, and use us like Dogs."[35]

Fly was similarly impenitent on his dying day. "He pass'd along to the place of Execution, with a *Nosegay* in his hand, and making his *Complements*, when he *thought he saw occasion*," Cotton Mather wrote in an account appended to his execution sermon. "Arriving there, he nimbly mounted the Stage, and would fain have put on a Smiling Aspect." Once on the gallows, Fly engaged in some playful banter with the hangman and adjusted the noose around his own neck. When called on to deliver a last warning to spectators, he failed to offer the standard catalog of sins, but defiantly cautioned ship captains against mistreating their men. He also persisted in his refusal to forgive the man responsible for his arrest. Only fear marred Fly's performance; Mather vindictively noted that "in the Midst of all his affected *Bravery*, a very sensible *Trembling* attended him; His hands and his *knees* were plainly seen to *Tremble*."[36]

Like James Morgan and Esther Rodgers before them, such pirates as Captain Quelch and William Fly were playing familiar roles. The difference was that Morgan and Rodgers had willingly relied on a pious script outlined for them by local ministers, while Quelch and Fly insisted on leaving the stage of life in accordance with a very different code of conduct. Much of their behavior was almost certainly modeled on the demeanor of condemned highwaymen and other capital offenders in early modern England. During the seventeenth and eighteenth centuries, such criminals (at least those who successfully resisted the guidance of English clergymen) often maintained an air of swaggering bravado during processions to the gallows. It was also traditional for them to carry flowers, as William Fly did in Boston.[37] Perhaps the pirates executed in New England had seen such British hangings or other Anglo-American imitations, heard about them from others, or even read of them in England's popular crime literature. Some British publications actually glorified notorious brigands as popular heroes.[38] In any case, Quelch and Fly were apparently trying to cast themselves in just such dashing roles. Cotton Mather struck at the heart of the matter when he noted that Fly "seem'd all along ambitious to have it said, *That he died a brave fellow!*"[39]

What was perhaps most remarkable about the cases of John Quelch, John Brown, and William Fly was not their behavior per se, but rather the degree to which Cotton Mather subsequently memorialized it in print. Of course, the minister framed their defiant words and conduct in extremely hostile terms. Mather introduced his description of Brown's distasteful conduct at the gallows with the observation that he had behaved "as one would hardly imagine that any Compos Mentis, could have done so." Similarly, Mather described Fly as "a very hardened Wretch" and a "most uncommon and amazing Instance of Impenitency and Stupidity."[40] Nonetheless, Mather's presentation of a fairly extensive record of the criminal's own words and conduct allowed the reader to reach an independent judgment.

How times had changed! Forty years earlier, a youthful Cotton Mather had launched his career as colonial America's most prolific author in a volume containing his dialogue with a flawlessly penitent murderer; in that case the words of minister and malefactor alternated smoothly in the service of Mather's evangelical agenda.[41] Although the situation may have been similar in 1726, the tone was very different as an aging Mather, himself not far from death, traded barbs with a defiant pirate who gave as good as he got. To be sure, Mather gamely sought to turn the dialogue with Fly to his own ideological ends, even incorporating the pirate's critique of maritime authority into his sermon.[42] But in that case who was really calling the ideological tune? Under the evolving conventions of New England's crime literature, the last words and actions of condemned criminals were increasingly presented to readers, even when they subtly subverted or boldly challenged the authority of ministers and magistrates.

Despite that trend, the cultural chasm between clergymen and criminals should not be exaggerated. To a degree, even Mather and the pirates still shared a common universe of discourse and values. Fly's response to the minister's demand that he forgive the man who captured him is instructive in that regard. Recall that the pirate had justified his refusal in terms of an unwillingness to "ly against" his "Conscience" and thus add "Sin to Sin." Although his rationale may well have struck Mather as impudent sophistry, it nonetheless suggested that the two men shared a common language of moral reference. When Mather offered Fly a copy of his own earlier execution sermon, *The Converted Sinner* (1724), the pirate responded that he had already read the work *before* his capture. More than twenty years earlier, Captain Quelch had confided to a local minister: "I am not afraid of Death, I

Portrait of Cotton Mather, shortly before his death in 1728. Mezzotint by Peter Pelham. *Courtesy, Massachusetts Historical Society.*

am not afraid of the Gallows, but I am afraid of what follows; I am afraid of a Great God, and a Judgment to Come."[43] In early eighteenth-century New England, not even pirates could entirely evade the pious discourse of sin and conscience, warning and salvation.

Joseph Quasson: A Prisoner of Hope

In 1726, forty years after the appearance of his first published sermon on a condemned murderer, Cotton Mather produced his last crime pamphlet, on the case of William Fly and his fellow pirates. That same year also marked the appearance of Samuel Moody's *Summary Account of the Life and Death of Joseph Quasson, Indian.* In contrast to the earlier accounts appended to sermons, Moody's relation was the first criminal conversion narrative to be published in New England as a separate work. The modest volume consisted of a short autobiography extracted from Quasson after his imprisonment, a longer third-person account of his behavior in jail and at the gallows, and a short collection of lessons and observations. After half a century of addressing capital cases in execution sermons, a New England minister had finally adopted the criminal conversion narrative as an independent form.[44]

In some respects, Joseph Quasson may have been a more promising candidate for heaven than either James Morgan or Esther Rodgers. He had been born at Monamoy (now Chatham) on Cape Cod but was raised as a servant in a religious household in Yarmouth, Massachusetts. There he was taught the catechism, acquainted with the Holy Scriptures, obliged to attend many sermons, and admonished against sin. In his youth he avoided such offenses as lying, swearing, and stealing and even reproved those who took the Lord's name in vain. However, after leaving his master's household, Quasson turned to drink, sold his Bible, and finally, while in military service in Maine during the summer of 1725, mortally wounded a kinsman and fellow soldier, probably in a drunken quarrel. Since the next local session of the superior court was not to be held until the following May, Quasson spent more than half a year awaiting trial in the jail at York, Maine. When told that the delay would allow him eight or nine months to repent, he thought to himself that he could "accomplish the Work in a quarter of that time."[45]

Quasson plunged into the work of repentance, assisted by the local minister, Samuel Moody, a passionate and widely respected frontier evangelist who would later support the Great Awakening and earn the admiring friendship of such prominent revivalists as George Whitefield and Jonathan Edwards.[46] It may be worth noting that Moody was originally from the town of Newbury, Massachusetts, and so was undoubtedly familiar with the case of Esther Rodgers, if not at firsthand then certainly by report. Quasson was also supported in his spiritual struggles by a number of local laypeople, particularly women, and by an ever expanding circle of concerned Christians throughout New England.[47]

In jail Quasson prayed seven or eight times a day and spent many hours poring through his Bible, folding over scores of leaves to mark particularly encouraging passages. He also received "personal Instructions" from his many visitors, along with a variety of "suitable Books." Quasson read some of those devotional works intensively, perusing them not just once or twice but again and again, finding them a source of blessed "Awakening." He made particular use of such pertinent literary examples as the "marvellous Conversion and triumphant Death" of Esther Rodgers. As he struggled for salvation during his last months on earth, Quasson's "natural Love" of "Reading" stood him in good stead.[48]

Quasson was also the subject of spiritual striving throughout a much broader Christian community. He was the beneficiary of "fervent and effectual Prayer, solitary and social," both within individual families and at other private religious meetings. His desire for spiritual intercession was widely conveyed throughout the region by "Word and Writing," particularly at an annual convention of clergymen that happened to meet during his imprisonment. As a result, prayers were reportedly offered for him by more than one hundred ministers and by thousands of Christians in no fewer than four provinces and colonies. Such intercolonial mobilization apparently foreshadowed the aroused and widespread evangelism of the Great Awakening. In any case, Samuel Moody later recalled that there had "seemed to be much of the Spirit of Prayer in a good number, moving them to strive together and apart for his Conversion."[49]

Yet despite his own initial confidence, subsequent diligence in prison, and many Christian benefactors, Quasson encountered serious obstacles on the road to salvation. He discovered, as an earlier minister had put it, that "Heart-work, is hard work."[50] Throughout his time in jail, he wavered uncertainly between hope and despair, painfully aware of his own "Darkness, Deadness and hardness of Heart." It was a disease that not even literacy could cure. "I have had many Books, and have read much," he confessed to a visitor in jail, "but I don't see that I'm a lot the better." His spiritual progress was also stymied for many weeks by a fellow prisoner who distracted him from prayer with constant "singing" and "profane Talk." It was only after his trial, conviction, and condemnation in May 1726 that Quasson began to progress spiritually, placing all of his hopes in "the Mercy of God" and "the Merits of Christ."[51]

During the last week of Quasson's life, "a very remarkable Alteration was observed in him" as he was carried by faith beyond all "Fear of Death." On the morning of the execution, his "Faith and Hope" increased "more and more." As he took his last walk to the gallows erected by the seashore, he was accompanied by "most of the Ministers of the County," who engaged themselves in "directing, incouraging & cautioning the Prisoner of Hope." Again and again Quasson expressed his "Hope" for salvation, but always "very modestly." At the gallows, around which thousands of spectators had gathered, "the humble Penitent chearfully ascended the Ladder," gave a last pertinent warning and prayer, and displayed a remarkable "readiness to die." Samuel Moody believed that in enacting the death of a Christian penitent, "after much Pains-taking and long Waiting," Quasson had "found Mercy at last." Sometime within the next several months, Moody compiled his account of the criminal conversion and arranged for its publication in November 1726 by Samuel Gerrish, a Boston bookseller who was at that time aggressively marketing works of popular piety and adventure. Priced at only ten pence a copy, Quasson's narrative was not the cheapest pamphlet available in Boston but was well within reach of a wide audience.[52]

Patience Boston: A Remarkable Conversion

Nearly a decade after the death of Joseph Quasson, Samuel Moody had the opportunity to compile another criminal conversion narrative, this one prepared in collaboration with his son and ministerial colleague, Joseph Moody. The new narrative treated the strange case of Patience Boston, an Indian servant with a long history of defiantly self-destructive and antisocial behavior. The pamphlet consisted of a two-page preface by the ministers; a twenty-nine-page first-person narrative by the malefactor herself, although not "exactly" in her own language; and a six-page account of Boston's behavior in jail and at the gallows, extracted from the diary of someone who had been "much Conversant" with the prisoner. Even more than in the previous narrative of Joseph Quasson, the ministers had modestly relegated themselves to the role of all but silent editors, conceding the primary literary voice to a condemned criminal.[53]

Like Quasson before her, Patience Boston had been born at Monamoy on Cape Cod.[54] Her mother died when she was only three years old, and her father soon bound her out as a servant in a religious household. There she was taught to read, thoroughly catechized, and repeatedly warned against sin. But unlike Quasson, she ignored the admonitions of her pious mistress, becoming a "mischievous and rebellious Servant." As a girl, Patience would play on the Sabbath, tell lies, mock her elders, sabotage household operations, and engage in other forms of wickedness. At about the age of twelve, she repeatedly set fire to her master's house. After her mistress died a few years later, Patience began to go out at nights, keeping "bad Company" and engaging in "lewd Practices." Having long defied the authority of her superiors, she was glad when her term of servitude expired. "I thought my self happy that I had no Body to Command me," she later recalled.[55]

After being freed from her master, Patience "grew worse and worse," turned to stealing, and all the while felt little or no remorse. Yet only a year later, despite her profound aversion to authority, Boston married a Negro servant (or slave) and bound herself for life to her husband's master. Having thus doubly subordinated herself, Patience quickly turned to alcohol and began abusing her husband; as she became "mad and furious" with drink, she took to "speaking dreadful Words, and wishing bad Wishes" upon herself and others. She became pregnant, ran away from her master while her husband was absent on a whaling voyage, continued to drink to excess, and committed adultery. When her baby was finally delivered, both of its arms were already broken, the result of her rough living during pregnancy. Although the injured child died a few weeks later, Boston felt no pangs of conscience but went on drinking, lying, swearing, and quarreling with her husband.[56]

Yet when Patience again became pregnant she was beset by feelings of religious conviction. She refrained from wicked behavior, began to pray, and consulted a minister. The clergyman gladly received, counseled, and encouraged her, supplying her with a catechism and other pious reading. Boston's description of her devotional activities during that period suggest how fluid were the lines between cultural patterns that have often been sharply distinguished by modern scholars: "I . . . loved to hear my Husband read, and would sit up to read my self after the Folks were in Bed, and loved to hear the Word

Preached, and began to pray in Secret." Boston's devotionalism thus encompassed the oral and written, collective and individual, public and private. In early eighteenth-century Massachusetts, those distinctions did not always denote sharp divisions in class practice, cultural style, or even personal sensibility, but represented complementary and widely shared spiritual strategies.[57]

Although her reformation persisted for several months, Patience eventually abandoned God, stopped praying, and resumed her wicked ways, drowning her scruples in "strong Drink" and "growing worse than ever before." She had murderous feelings toward her second child, as she had toward her first, and may even have tried to kill it. When the baby suddenly died two months later, probably of natural causes, Boston was terrified. In a later drunken quarrel with her husband, she falsely accused herself of having killed the child. Although she repeatedly confessed to her imagined crime when taken before justices of the peace, she pleaded not guilty at her trial and was acquitted. Thereafter she was shuttled from one master to another, at one point again falsely accusing herself of having delivered and murdered an illegitimate infant.[58]

The disturbed servant eventually came into the hands of a master at Falmouth, Maine, in Casco Bay, against whom she developed "some groundless Prejudice." She decided to avenge herself on him by murdering his young grandson, despite her apparent love for the boy. "I would have killed my Master himself, if I could have done it," she later recalled. But on July 9, 1734, after considering the possibility of poisoning the old man and after unsuccessfully attempting to burn down his barn, she finally lured the grandson to a well, where she drowned him by pushing him under the water with a long pole. Patience Boston had finally acted out her infanticidal impulses, simultaneously venting her rage against an older figure of domestic authority. She promptly surrendered to local officials; when a coroner's jury brought in a verdict of "wilful murder" against her, she was placed in jail to await trial.[59]

As in the earlier case of Joseph Quasson, there was a long delay until the next session of the superior court, and so the murderess spent nearly a year in confinement, with nothing to do but repent. Like Quasson, she plunged into that work with diligence, spending much of her time in reading, praying, meditating, consulting pious visitors, and listening to the sermons of local ministers. Among the books read by or to her were two sermons by Increase Mather, a number of the criminal narratives of Cotton Mather collected in his church history, and several "Examples of poor Indians converted," possibly including the published account of Joseph Quasson. But most important of all were the Holy Scriptures. "Good Books were precious to me," the prisoner declared, "but the *Bible* seemed more *delightsome* than any Book."[60]

Even more than earlier criminal converts, Patience Boston embraced a spirituality that was at once intensely textual and verbal. The erratic rhythms of her devotional striving often turned on emotional responses to a variety of passages from sermon and Scripture—and were typically expressed in extremely vocal terms.[61] Written texts and spoken words interacted in a traumatic struggle for salvation, characterized by radical fluctuations in mood and outlook. At first she was beset by such "strong Convictions and killing Terrors" that her "Conscience seem'd all on a Flame." During that period she would fly into prolonged paroxysms of self-accusation and remorse. "We went up, and found her crying out in a most terrible manner, such as I never heard the like," one witness recalled. "She smote her Hands often together, and kept continually lamenting and roaring and shrieking, for I think Hours together, with little Intermission." Throughout those episodes she would ejaculate pious words and phrases "with utmost vehemency, ten or twenty Times together." The prisoner cried in agony: "O my God, my God, my God! why hast thou forsaken me!—O *Patience! Patience!* you wicked Wretch, you first forsook God, and then he forsook you! . . . O God's Anger! God's Anger! God's Anger!—O the Wrath of God! the Wrath of God!—O my dear Soul! my dear Soul! . . . O my Soul is in Hell; my Soul is in Hell!"[62]

Tormented by feelings of guilt and despair, Boston became suicidal. "I wished I could have gone to the Water, which I saw through the Grates, to have Drowned my self," she recalled. "I wrung my Hands, and beat my Breast, and could have torn into my Vitals, if I had the strength to do it." One night, however, after receiving encouragement from local ministers and other visitors, she began to feel "some Glimmering of Hope" as "Light and Joy" again entered her life. As she lay awake, musing on her spiritual state, Boston was particularly encouraged by two sermons of Increase Mather, two verses from the Gospel of John, and some fresh "Words" of hope that she attributed to divine revelation. "When the Morning came, I looked out, and all Things seemed pleasant and smiling," she remembered. "God seemed now to accept my Prayers and Praises, which could never enter into my Heart to believe, in the Time of my Distress."[63]

Thereafter Patience fluctuated between feelings of distress and comfort, despair and hope, self-loathing and Christ-loving, between images of darkness and visions of light.[64] On June 19, 1735, she finally stood trial, pleading guilty to murder. During her remaining weeks on earth, she devoted herself to "religious Exercises," becoming "more settled" in mind. That new composure was apparently based on Boston's increasing intellectual grasp and sensual appropriation of the language of Protestant piety. Hers was an intensely linguistic spirituality, one rooted in childhood training, but only realized in preparing for death. "The *Catechism* I learnt in my Youth, is often brought to my mind, and many precious Words that I had heard and read for my seasonable Rilief and Comfort," she explained. "My Soul is carried out in Love to good experienc'd Christians that come to see me. Methinks now I can understand their Language, and sweetly relish it, which in Years past I had no Savour of; because I did not know the Meaning of it."[65]

After a lifetime of vocal defiance and rebellious rage, Patience Boston had finally reconciled herself to both superiors and dependents, expressing gratitude to her judges and loving concern for the health of her one surviving child.[66] Appropriately enough, she was ushered out of the world in a pious flurry of verbal, written, and textual communications. On the day before her execution, she was "very sorrowful" at first and uttered "some despairing Words" but, after hearing the "Discourse" of a Christian visitor, became more "calm and comfortable." The following morning Patience assured one of the attending ministers that "her Hopes were above her Fears." After hearing a sermon by "Mr. Moody," she walked to the place of execution in a "calm Temper." At the gallows Patience uttered a series of pertinent prayers and warnings; upon appearing "faint, and a little confused," she was told to sit down. As a written statement prepared by her in advance was read to the audience by someone else, Patience sat on a board in the cart, reading her Bible with admirable "composure and calmness of mind."[67]

Having already assured Patience that "her sins were all forgiven," one of the Moodys commented that "he had suffered Reproach already on the Account of the dear Child of Christ standing there, and expected to suffer more for what he was now going to say." He then urged the spectators to seek God in earnest, predicting that hundreds of them would perish forever if they failed to respond that very night. The Moodys must have realized that there were those in the community who would disapprove of both their attempt to generate a mass revival at the gallows and their solicitude for a condemned murderess. Yet their support continued at the gallows, as "Mr. Moody" gently guided Patience through the final stages of the drama. After the rope had been placed around her neck, he asked whether she believed that Christ would help her till the end; she smiled and said, "Yes." When her face had been covered, he asked whether she remembered her last words, apparently prepared in advance; she again answered in the affirmative, adding: "Lord Jesus receive my Spirit." The executioner then performed his task, dispatching the "dear Saint" to sleep "in Jesus."[68]

The written account of Patience Boston was not an afterthought to her execution but rather an intrinsic aspect of the intense devotional activity leading up to her death. That process had been highly verbal and linguistic all along; it was only natural that it would culminate in a new literary text. The bulk of the narrative was written in the first person, gradually extracted from Boston over the course of her long imprisonment; the concluding third-person account took the form of a diary, with entries as early as November 1734 and as late as July 1735. "The Account was not drawn up in haste," the editors insisted, "but Things were written down at twenty several Times—One Day Week and Month after another."[69] Yet after the execution interest in the case apparently died down; the editors were unable to obtain enough subscriptions to finance publication. Instead, a copy of the manuscript was deposited at the local courthouse, where it was shown to people doing business there. Three years after Boston's death, one such patron, identified only as a pious and well-educated gentleman, was so impressed by the narrative that he agreed to subsidize its publication.[70]

In May 1738 the account compiled by Samuel and Joseph Moody was finally published in Boston by Kneeland & Green. It was called *A Faithful*

Narrative of the Wicked Life and Remarkable Conversion of Patience Boston.[71] The similarity of that title to Jonathan Edwards's *A Faithful Narrative of the Surprising Work of God in the Conversion of Many Hundred Souls*, an immensely popular tract that appeared in no fewer than twenty printings between 1737 and 1739, suggests that the conversion and memorialization of Patience Boston was part of a much broader evangelical current that was gaining force in New England during the 1730s.[72] Not long afterward, in 1740, the great English revivalist George Whitefield arrived in New England, setting off the first Great Awakening, a massive outpouring of evangelical fervor and devotional expression. The revival was naturally supported by such provincial ministers as John Rogers of Ipswich, Massachusetts, and Samuel Moody of York, Maine, clergymen whose evangelical activism in jails and at the gallows had already embraced the most despised of their fellow sinners and transformed them into saints.[73]

Ironically, the two pamphlets of Samuel Moody that marked the first full emergence of the criminal conversion narrative in New England also signaled its virtual demise. Although themes of criminal salvation frequently appeared in subsequent crime pamphlets, they would seldom so completely dominate their form and content. Conversion narratives had emerged in New England when ministers still largely dominated the literary culture of the region. Clergymen proselytized condemned men and women in the course of their pastoral duties and produced accounts of their efforts as adjuncts to published execution sermons. The resulting narratives served readers as devotional primers in seeking salvation and confronting death, establishing penitent criminals as unlikely models for popular emulation. But by focusing attention on the offenders themselves, the ministers helped cultivate—and legitimate—a biographical interest in condemned criminals that was expressed in increasingly secular terms after the Great Awakening, as printers exercised more initiative and control over their literary output.[74]

During the second half of the eighteenth century, last speeches and longer, often largely secular, criminal autobiographies vied in popularity with execution sermons, while the criminal conversion narrative as such was essentially abandoned.[75] As suggested by the delay and difficulty involved in bringing the account of Patience Boston into print, such narratives were apparently unable to compete successfully in a changing and increasingly diversified literary marketplace. To some extent, the genre may also have been undermined by changing conceptions of salvation, as many New England ministers of the mid- to late eighteenth century embraced theories of spiritual development based on gradual, rational growth in faith and moral conduct rather than rapid, emotional illumination and transfiguration.[76] In addition, the same humanitarian feelings that prompted spectators at the Rodgers execution to burst into tears eventually led to widespread revulsion toward the gallows itself. That disillusionment was expressed during the late eighteenth and early nineteenth centuries in an increasingly powerful transatlantic movement

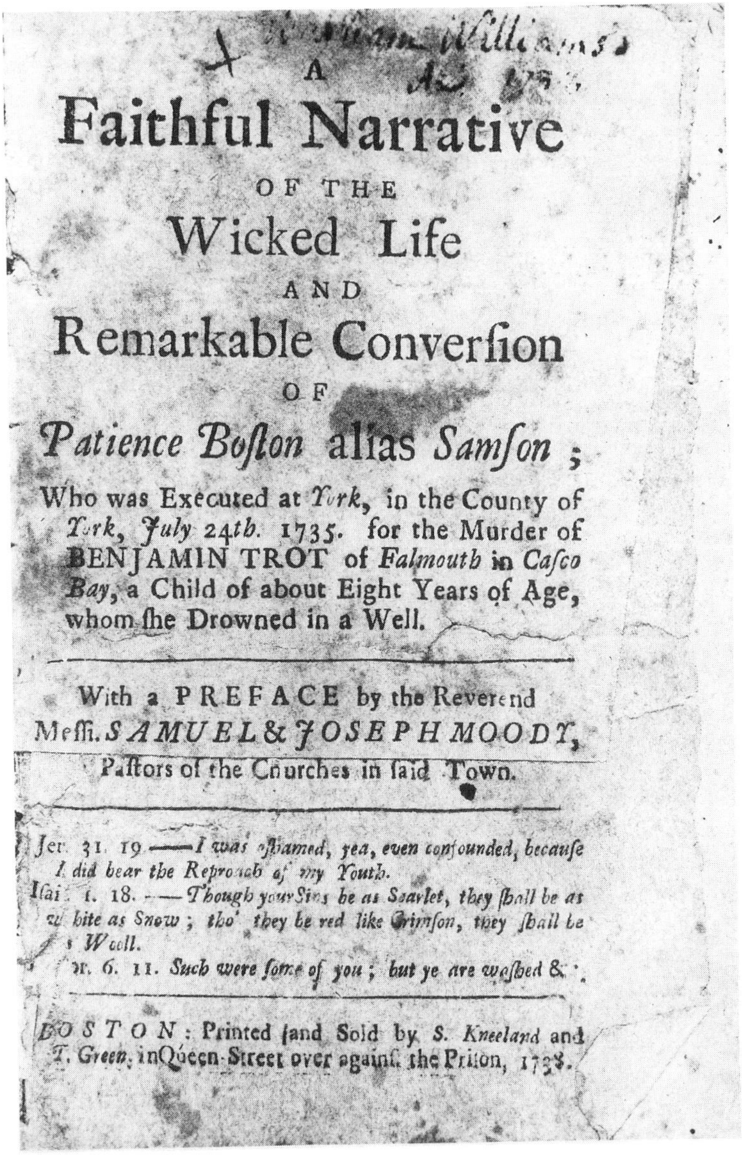

A

Faithful Narrative

OF THE

Wicked Life

AND

Remarkable Converſion

OF

Patience Boſton alias *Samſon* ;

Who was Executed at *York*, in the County of
York, *July* 24*th*. 1735. for the Murder of
BENJAMIN TROT of *Falmouth* in *Caſco
Bay*, a Child of about Eight Years of Age,
whom ſhe Drowned in a Well.

With a PREFACE by the Reverend
Meſſ. *SAMUEL* & *JOSEPH MOODY*,
Paſtors of the Churches in ſaid Town.

Jer. 31. 19 ——*I was aſhamed, yea, even confounded, becauſe
I did bear the Reproach of my Youth.*
Iſai. 1. 18. ——*Though your Sins be as Scarlet, they ſhall be as
white as Snow ; tho' they be red like Crimſon, they ſhall be
white.*
1 Cor. 6. 11. *Such were ſome of you ; but ye are waſhed &.*

BOSTON : Printed ſand Sold by *S. Kneeland* and
T. Green, in Queen-Street over againſt the Priſon, 1738.

The criminal conversion narrative of Patience Boston, drawing on traditions of devotional practice and literary expression deeply rooted in early modern religious culture. *Courtesy, American Antiquarian Society.*

against the death penalty. The new reformist outlook, linked both to sentimental humanitarianism and Enlightenment rationalism, could only have discouraged literary depictions of executions as ennobling experiences—yet another probable factor in the demise of the criminal conversion narrative.[77]

Over the years, scholars have tended to emphasize the degree to which Puritan religious activities and sensibilities diverged from those of their English and European rivals, proving their point with vivid descriptions of gutted churches, shattered stained-glass windows, and the like.[78] However, the remarkable continuity in devotional practices involving capital criminals among New England Puritans, English Protestants, and European Catholics suggests the need for a significant revision of that conventional wisdom.[79] As one manifestation of what seems to have been a broad pattern of devotional continuity, the evangelical impulse that generated early New England conversion narratives was one deeply and widely rooted in early modern religious culture. In 1738 the narrative of Patience Boston was published in provincial Massachusetts; the following year, half a world away at another periphery of European culture, the Jesuits of Vilna, a city then in northeastern Poland (now Lithuania), published a translation of the very similar narrative of Troilo Savelli, first compiled nearly 150 years earlier.[80]

Over a period of a century and a half, from the Castle of Saint Angelo in Rome, to Newgate Prison in London, to the York county jail in rural Maine, clergymen and other pious Christians gathered to proselytize condemned criminals and wrote about their success afterwards, expressing their profound faith in the transformative powers of divine grace. Although literary expressions of that belief may have dwindled after the Great Awakening, the faith itself remained very much alive within the popular religious culture of New England, reemerging at unexpected times and places. Such was the case of Edmund Fortis, an illiterate ex-slave from "the back parts of Virginia" who moved to rural Maine, where in 1794 he stalked, raped, and murdered a teenage girl walking near some woods in the vicinity of Vassalborough. In his *Last Words and Dying Speech*, Fortis described his spiritual illumination in prison, complete with visions of angels singing to him in his cell. Much like Signor Troilo Savelli, another rapist-murderer executed two centuries earlier, Fortis died a transfigured man, "cool and calm," believing in the grace of a merciful God.[81]

And yet there was a dramatic contrast in social backgrounds between the noble Savelli and the lowly American converts. The subjects of the latter narratives, vocal exemplars of piety and penitence for New England readers, included a young female servant prone to interracial sexual liaisons, an Indian soldier who murdered a kinsman in arms, an unruly Indian servant married to a black bondsman, and a runaway slave who brutally raped and murdered a white girl.[82] That attention to the lives and voices of females, blacks, and Indians is noteworthy. In a provocative study of publication and the public sphere in early America, Michael Warner has argued that colonial literary culture systematically marginalized women and excluded racial minorities. By his account, not even the radical print discourse of republicanism that emerged during the early eighteenth century allowed an active role "for women, or blacks, or Indians, or the unpropertied, or various persons classed as criminal."[83]

If Warner is right, criminal conversion narratives of that same period constitute a dramatic exception to the rule of exclusion. In fact, accounts of felons like Esther Rodgers, Joseph Quasson, Patience Boston, and Edmund Fortis boldly privileged the spiritual insights and subjective experiences of precisely those disadvantaged groups. While race, class, gender, age, and deviant conduct had certainly counted against the criminals throughout their lives, such factors had little bearing on their fundamental human need for redemption through Christ. If anything, those same traits made the criminal converts all the more valuable as religious models; if even such pariahs could achieve a glorious salvation in the shadow of the gallows, surely the humdrum readers of their narratives could aspire to heaven as well.

Of course, the ministers who edited conversion accounts tried to turn them to their own pastoral ends, both as vehicles of spiritual edification and as instruments of social control. Yet condemned criminals were actively integrated into an ongoing public discourse, not only as readers but also as authoritative speakers and even as posthumous authors. There is every indication that the criminals seized upon that discursive opportunity with passion and courage and spiritual conviction, recognizing that the printed word could provide them with both comfort and strength during their last days on earth. While remaining formally within the bounds of a traditional literature of Protestant piety, criminal conversion narratives thus subtly prefigured the rise of sentimental fiction during the late eighteenth century, a new discourse that would also publicize the subjective experiences of the socially powerless and provide marginalized groups like women and young people with a powerful literary voice. But like many of the young heroines of sentimental seduction tales, penitent criminals achieved celebrity at the cost of their lives.

The three fully developed criminal conversion narratives published in New England between 1701 and 1738 represented the culmination of a long tradition of criminal proselytization, one deeply embedded in early modern religious culture. As such, they reinforced habits of devotional practice, evangelical activism, and literary expression that would climax in the Great Awakening. At the same time, those works illustrated a gradual drift in New England crime literature away from exclusive reliance on execution sermons and toward a greater literary role for condemned criminals. In their eagerness to exploit the last words of dying offenders, ministers inadvertently eased the transition toward more secular and at times antiauthoritarian crime genres. After 1730 such new forms as the last-speech broadside largely replaced the fragile conversion narratives that had probably helped to legitimize their birth. But before examining the autobiographical literature, it may be useful to return to that persistent staple of religious crime literature, the execution sermon, tracing the evolution of certain key themes from the late seventeenth through early nineteenth centuries. For the same breakdown of Puritan cultural hegemony and disintegration of Calvinist worldview that facilitated the gradual shift from execution sermons to more secular crime genres also generated important ideological changes within the sermon form itself.

II

Paradigms and Polemics:

The Literature of Doctrinal Development

4

The Road to the Scaffold:
Explanations of Crime in New England Execution Sermons, 1674–1825

In warning against a variety of sins and urging offenders to seek salvation, local clergymen articulated values that lay at the heart of Puritan ideology. Treatments of those themes in execution sermons tended to change relatively little between the late seventeenth and early nineteenth centuries, that is, from the time of the first published discourse (1674) to that of one of the last (1825). But all was not continuity. Other ideas presented by the ministers did change significantly during the late provincial and early national periods. Social phenomena once explained or justified theologically were increasingly addressed in secular terms. Ministers may have conserved the force of orthodox theology, but only by decisively narrowing its application. In order to explore that process of theological retrenchment and intellectual transformation, the next two chapters investigate sermon themes in which conceptual continuity was challenged by ideological change. This chapter examines shifting explanations of crime; the next explores evolving justifications of capital punishment.[1]

The Theology of Crime

"The holiest man hath as vile and filthy a Nature, as the Sodomites," Samuel Danforth explained in the first gallows sermon published in New England.[2] That gloomy insight lay at the heart of the Puritan understanding of criminality. The ultimate cause of all human wickedness lay in the "original sin" of Adam's Fall. Because of that first act of disobedience, all men and women inherited a tendency toward sin. Over the years, minister after minister informed his audience of the consequences of man's corrupt nature.[3] "All of us are Born into the World, with Hearts full of Sin," Nathaniel Clap insisted in 1715, "with Corrupt Natures empty of Grace, ready to Sin, ready only to Sin, always ready to Sin."[4]

The clergymen's emphasis on universal human depravity as the wellspring of crime forced readers to recognize their kinship with the offender about to be executed.[5] A death at the gallows was an occasion not for complacency or self-righteousness but for earnest self-examination. After all, capital criminals were to be taken as living (and dying) proof of the Puritan doctrine of natural depravity. "The sorrowful Spectacle before us should make us reflect most seriously on *our own* vile Nature; which the Falls of others are but a Comment upon," Thomas Foxcroft noted in a gallows discourse of 1733, "and should excite us to humble ourselves under a sense of the Corruption of *our Hearts*, which are naturally as bad as the worst."[6] One person's particular depravity thus served as an alarming gloss on the character of the species as a whole.

The problem with universal depravity as an explanation of capital crime was that, in explaining so much, it actually explained very little. A trait shared by all human beings could hardly by itself explain the peculiarly wicked actions of a relative few. Why did some depraved men and women commit enormous crimes, while most did not? Unwilling to credit humanity or society for the restraint of the majority, New England's ministers ascribed it to the actions of God: People were inhibited from committing crimes by the influence of divine grace. Although some were fortunate enough to be withheld from sin by God's "special" or "saving" grace (the only type, according to Puritan theory, that offered ultimate salvation), most depended on God's lesser and more provisional "common" or "restraining" grace.

Those divine restraints were thoroughly explored by Cotton Mather in an execution sermon entitled *The Curbed Sinner* (1713). According to Mather, God shielded men from sin in a number of ways: He kept them out of situations in which they might be tempted to sin, restrained them from sin by providing them with other things to do, gave them a sense of their own self-interest, endowed them with a conscience, and infused them with his grace.[7] The value of those various controls could be dramatized by envisioning the horrible consequences of their absence. "A man would soon Murder his Father & Mother, Destroy his own Wife, and Debauch his Neighbors, Blaspheme God, and Fire the Town," Mather had noted in an earlier sermon, "if God should not Lay upon him *Restraints*."[8]

But if God graciously restrained men from sin, why did some nonetheless commit outrageous crimes? According to Puritan ministers, it must have been because the sinner's residual wickedness eventually caused God to withdraw his restraining grace. The theological understanding of crime as resulting from God's just abandonment of the sinner to his own corrupt impulses was present in one form or another in virtually all early execution discourses.[9] In 1675, for example, Increase Mather insisted that two servants who had murdered their masters must have "been guilty of many other Grievous sins" in order to "have provoked the Lord to leave" them to commit their last horrible crime.[10] Over the following decades ministers repeatedly employed the language of justified withdrawal and abandonment to explain the removal of divine restraints. As one minister bluntly put it: "If you leave God, God may leave you."[11] Or, as Cotton Mather explained in 1715: "The Holy GOD in His

Righteous *Providence*, withdraws His *Grace* from the Sinner . . . and then, O Sinner, what an Horrid *hardness of Heart* will soon seize upon thee!"[12]

A few early New England ministers developed the image of divine abandonment into the doctrine of "sin punished by sin." That thesis may have received its most comprehensive expression in a sermon delivered by Cotton Mather before the execution of a young woman for infanticide in 1698, a gallows lecture that would appear in *Pillars of Salt*. His doctrine on that occasion was that "the Holy God, often Punisheth many Sins of men, by Giving them up to still Blacker Sins against Him." As formulated by Mather, the doctrine consisted of three familiar propositions: (1) "The *Original Sin*, which man hath Depraved himself withal, contains in it, an hideous and hellish Disposition, to *Every Sin* whatsoever"; (2) "If God should not by His *Grace*, Restrain the Rage of *Original Sin*, in the Hearts of Men, they would soon rush upon the most Outrageous Impurities in the World"; and (3) "God, upon great provocations, *Withdraws*, or *Withholds* from Sinful men, the *Grace*, which He never owed them; and *Then*! they Sin, most horribly, enormously, prodigiously." In short, Mather's doctrine held that one of the ways in which God punished sin was by withdrawing his restraining grace and thereby abandoning men to their naturally corrupt and self-destructive impulses.[13]

The punishment of sin by sin, ultimately due to the withdrawal of God's restraining grace, was instrumentally achieved in a variety of ways. God might present additional opportunities or incentives to sin, seduce through the demoralizing examples of pious hypocrites, give up to Satanic possession, or mislead with intellectual delusions.[14] In none of those cases did God himself *instil* evil into humans or *force* them to act wickedly. Rather, he simply enabled them to follow their own naturally depraved inclinations. That, indeed, was the essence of God's withdrawal of grace. Its result was a progressive slide into depravity, largely predictable in its sordid details. "First the young Wretch, confines his Wantonness unto himself alone," Mather wrote of the typical youth seduced by unchastity, "but he goes on to Fornication, he goes on to Adultery; he goes on . . . to . . . stupendous Abominations."[15]

Mather's doctrine of "sin punished by sin" apparently served a useful theological function in helping to resolve—or at least to obscure—a troubling paradox in Puritan thought. On the one hand, New England Calvinists believed in an omniscient and omnipotent God, who exercised absolute sovereignty over all the affairs of creation. As Nathaniel Clap noted in an execution sermon of 1715: "Every thing that cometh to pass in the World, is directed by the Infinite Wisdom of God." Since earthly creatures were under God's "absolute Government," they could not so much as "stir without His Permission." On the other hand, Puritans held that men and women exercised absolute free will and were morally liable for all their actions. "Indeed He does not force the Wills of Sinners, nor compel them to Sin against himself in breaking of his Laws," Clap declared. "There is no such decree or purpose of God as lays any necessity of compulsion upon the Wills of any of his Creatures."[16]

Not surprisingly, opponents of the Puritans tried to exploit the tension between the doctrine of absolute divine sovereignty and the actual prevalence of human wickedness. Having little appreciation for the theological subtlety of their rivals, various *"Jesuites* and *Arminians"* reportedly reviled the Calvinists for "Holding that *God is the Author of Sin."* Cotton Mather sought to blunt those polemical thrusts with his fine distinction "between *Sin*, as it is a *Crime*, and as it may be the *Punishment* of a *Crime."*[17] He claimed that God was invariably the author of the latter, but never of the former. And even in imposing sin as a punishment, God always acted by indirection, never actually infringing on human free will. Mather's formulation thus tended to vindicate the absolute sovereignty of God while freeing him from any moral implication in the wickedness of his subjects.

One also suspects that the notion of a restraining grace granted to all human beings and withdrawn only as a punishment for sin may have been useful to Puritan ministers in helping to shield God from imputations of unfairness in his arbitrary and far more selective bestowal of saving grace on the chosen elect. *All* men and women were the undeserving recipients of the deity's common or restraining grace. If some of those depraved individuals drove God to withdraw that grace through their own impulsive wickedness and if their sins were then punished by still greater sins, they had only themselves to blame. Innate but willful human corruption and insubordination, rather than the arbitrariness of an omnipotent God, were both the ultimate and proximate causes of the damning wickedness of sinners. At the same time, the idea of a universally accessible common grace whose retention was conditioned only on good behavior may have served some uneasy Puritans as a conceptual way station between the redemptive exclusivity of Calvinism and the spiritual voluntarism of some of its more democratic theological successors.[18]

Finally, the doctrine of "sin punished by sin" may have helped to explain the extreme moral variability in human behavior. Only a relatively small portion of humanity was assumed by Calvinist doctrine to be among God's elect.[19] Yet relatively few of the unredeemed majority committed palpably criminal acts and fewer still were so stupendously wicked as to earn death on the gallows. The idea that God's fluid restraints on wickedness might be calibrated to the morality of each person's past worldly conduct provided a theological explanation for the wide range of behavior found even among the unredeemed. In other words, the linked concepts of restraining grace and "sin punished by sin" helped make theological sense of the vast expanse of human conduct that lay somewhere between visible sainthood and palpable damnation. A theology essentially dualistic in its conception of humanity's moral standing was thus reconciled to the far more complex and gradated realities of social experience.

The Natural Progress of Sin

Although ministers ignored the doctrine of "sin punished by sin" after 1713, they continued to refer to divine abandonment and the withdrawal of restraining grace throughout the eighteenth century and beyond.[20] Yet they also offered more secular models of degeneration alongside the explicitly theological explanations. They expressed their insights in a variety of ways. For example, Samuel Danforth, author of the first gallows discourse published in New England, addressed the subject in organic terms. In explaining how one sin led to another, the minister employed the powerful imagery of contagion and disease. Wickedness, he suggested, was a deadly infection that, unchecked, could only spread and destroy its tainted victim.[21] Other ministers would subsequently liken the progress of sin to a fall down a steep hill, a habit difficult to break, an appetite strengthened by being fed, and a spark that could lead to a conflagration.[22]

Whatever similes they employed, clergymen assumed an intimate relationship among sins and a natural progression from one to another. "See wither lesser sins will lead you, even unto *greater* till at *last* you come to the *Great Transgression*," Joshua Moody warned in 1686. "*Custom* of sin will take away *Conscience* of Sin; and when Conscience of sin is *gone*, what sin is there that you are not ready for?"[23] More than fifty years later, Eliphalet Adams offered a similar explanation. "Sinners begin with Lesser Crimes and then they grow worse & worse," he noted in 1738. "It is like the passage down some steep Hill, It will be difficult stopping till they come to the bottom."[24] The sins of the wicked were not isolated acts but links in a behavioral chain that might eventually drag a criminal to the gallows.

That view of wickedness as a coherent chain of misconduct caused ministers to fill their sermons with warnings against a wide range of attitudes and actions believed to have causal links to capital crimes. Recall, for example, that Samuel Danforth's sermon of 1674 on the case of a sexual offender not only warned its audience to refrain from all "Carnal Uncleanness," including masturbation, fornication, adultery, incest, sodomy, and bestiality, but also to "beware of the inlets, occasions, incentives and provocations thereunto." Those included pride, gluttony, drunkenness, sloth, idleness, irreligion, profanity, evil company, and disobedience to parents and masters. Filthy jests, amorous songs, and lascivious touches were also to be avoided. Similarly, in his sermon to the murderer Morgan in 1686, Increase Mather warned against such evils as unjustified anger, cursing, quarreling, and cruelty, suggesting that they all had "a tendency to, and a degree of Murder in them."[25]

Ministers typically tried to establish such causal linkages through the capital cases at hand. To that end, clergymen sought broad acknowledgments of wickedness from offenders awaiting execution. Cotton Mather, for example, sometimes tried to convince condemned criminals that they had violated *all* of the commandments of God.[26] Although doomed offenders occasionally balked, most yielded contrite confessions that ministers or printers then appended to published sermons.[27] Not surprisingly, those statements tended to confirm the causal linkages between lesser and greater sins. A condemned pirate's acknowledgment to Cotton Mather, appended to a gallows sermon of 1717, was typical: "Why, I have been guilty of all the Sins in the World! I know not where to begin. I may begin with Gaming! No, Whoring, That Led on to

Gaming; and Gaming Led on to Drinking; and Drinking to Lying, and Swearing, and Cursing, & all that is bad; and so to Thieving; And so to This!"[28]

The Dangers of Drink

While insisting that vices were all intimately connected, ministers occasionally focused on particular sins they deemed especially dangerous to moral health. One of the offenses most commonly singled out was drunkenness. In describing how excessive drink led on to greater evils, even early ministers resorted to secular analysis. For example, in his sermon on the execution of James Morgan in 1686, Increase Mather generalized from the murderer's case about the harmful effects of alcohol on human behavior and launched a broad attack on the easy availability of hard liquor in the Bay Colony. Morgan had not only confessed that he was apt to behave violently when under the influence of alcohol but also acknowledged that he had been "drinking to excess" on the night of the murder. Drawing on that sad example, Mather made his general claim: "Wicked men when they are in drink, will fall to Quarrelling; words will bring on blows, and those blows will cause wounds, and those wounds may perhaps prove *mortal*: and then, what Woe & Sorrow followes!"[29]

Mather went on to point out that many people died while under the influence of alcohol and even suggested that those who made them drunk were in a sense guilty of murder. That was particularly true of those who had "given or sold *strong liquor* to the *Indians*." But the social problem was apparently a pervasive one, especially among the lower classes. "It is an unhappy thing that of later years, a kind of Strong Drink hath been *common* amongst us, which the poorer sort of people, both in Town & Country, can make themselves drunk with, at cheap & easy rates," Mather observed. "It's a very sad thing, that so many Bodyes & Souls should be eternally ruin'd, and no help for it."[30] Although the orthodox minister would surely have affirmed that the "eternal ruining" of souls was ultimately a function of humankind's natural depravity, Mather was too astute a social observer not to recognize more proximate causes as well.

The Puritan critique of drunkenness was presented even more comprehensively in a sermon preached by Samuel Danforth (the younger) at the execution of two Indians in 1710 for a murder occasioned by the intoxication of both killers and victim. Danforth had chosen his subject in response to a direct request by the judges of the Superior Court. His sermon, entitled *The Woful Effects of Drunkenness* (1710), presented various secular insights into the evils of drink, all set within a theological context. It was part jeremiad and part temperance tract, but none the less compelling for its hybrid character. Danforth's formal doctrine introduced the theological premise that framed his more worldly arguments: "The Abounding of the Vice of Drunkenness among any People . . . doth bring down from Heaven, dreadful Woes, and desolating Judgments upon them, as a Nation or Body of People, as well as Signal Punishment on Some particular Drunkards among them."[31]

Danforth began by describing the impact of drunkenness on physical health. "The greatest part of the Sicknesses among Men may be ascribed to Intemperance," he declared. "How many Diseases do Drunkards bring upon themselves!" He then listed the various maladies in blood-curdling detail.[32] In addition to its purely physical effects, Danforth held, drunkenness stimulated personal passion and conflict, brought poverty on drunkards and their families, destroyed their reputations, and damaged their "immortal souls." On a social level, he claimed that rampant drunkenness obstructed "the Propagation of Religion," brought "Confusion and Disorder," encouraged official corruption, sapped a nation's "Martial Spirits," and provoked God to send famine or war. But perhaps most important, the minister was convinced that excessive drink, deplorable in itself, led men on to many other forms of wickedness. Danforth concluded that drunkenness "unfits men to keep any of God's Laws: and inclines and disposes them to break them all."[33] While placing his entire argument within the theological framework of human action and divine response, Danforth's critique of drunkenness made behavioral claims that would today be described as physiological, psychological, and sociological. Although those secular insights gained rhetorical force through their association with orthodox doctrine, their credibility did not really depend on pious trappings. On an abstract level, Puritan ministers conceived of sin theologically; however, their sermons often linked the actual incidence of crime to more proximate secular causes.

The Role of Education

Ministers would continue to explain the criminal's progress to the scaffold in terms of innate human depravity, God's withdrawn grace, and sin's natural progress well into the nineteenth century. But beginning in 1739 a number of execution sermons delivered by clergymen outside of the orthodox Congregational fold located the cause of crime less in the offender's nature than in his or her early social experience. Some ministers had begun to see deviance as the unfortunate product of a flawed upbringing or a bad education. They still held sinful individuals responsible for crime but now shifted much of the burden of guilt from the perpetrators themselves onto their negligent parents, teachers, or masters.

Arthur Browne, an Irish-born Anglican clergyman, first introduced the new theme in a sermon entitled *Religious Education of Children Recommended* (1739). He spoke at Portsmouth, New Hampshire, on the day of the execution of Penelope Kenny, a young Irish servant, for infanticide.[34] The text of Browne's sermon was from Proverbs: "Train up a Child in the Way he should go, and when he is old, he will not depart from it." Although the minister acknowledged that human beings were naturally prone to evil, he did not stress their intrinsic or irreversible wickedness but rather the importance of proper religious training. Given their natural inclinations, Browne argued, "the neglect of Education lays Children under a kind of Necessity" of pursuing evil. He even suggested that nurture might be more important than nature in the formation of character: "Perhaps a great deal of what we call natural Temper, is little more than that particular Frame of Heart, which was first infused in our Education."[35]

Significantly, Browne's attitude toward the young immigrant who had killed her own child was as much one of pity as of condemnation. He described her to his American audience as "a miserable poor Creature" led to the gallows by "a want of those Opportunities of Instruction, you so plentifully enjoy." The absence of religious training, he suggested, "was the Source of all her Misfortunes." Browne did not deny human depravity or the causal linkages among sins, but neither did he stress their role in the genesis of crime. People were not by necessity slaves to their own depraved inclinations; they were, rather, highly susceptible to moral guidance and training, particularly in their early years. Education could thus provide the basis for a profound social optimism. "Rebellions, Rapines, Murders, and other monstrous Impieties, are but the natural Fruits of depraved Nature, uncultivated by Education," Browne acknowledged. "But if Youth be wisely and justly managed, how happy will its Influence be upon Society, and what Blessings will it draw down from Heaven upon Men."[36]

Although Browne had already broached the subject on the eve of the Great Awakening, it was not until after the Revolution that other ministers began to express the new ideas on education in published execution sermons. In December 1786 Hannah Ocuish, a twelve-year-old girl, was executed in New London, Connecticut, for beating and choking a little child to death. Henry Channing, a young Yale tutor and licensed preacher of Unitarian leanings, was chosen to deliver the execution sermon.[37] His discourse, *God Admonishing his People of their Duty, as Parents and Masters* (1786), focused on the issue of juvenile education. Like Arthur Browne before him, Channing affirmed the concept of natural depravity, commenting on the case at hand: "We have here a striking evidence of the depravity of human nature; that we are indeed *transgressors from the womb*."[38] But also like Browne, he emphasized the critical role of upbringing in the development of personality.

To keep a child in ignorance, given his or her natural "thirst for knowledge," was simply impossible. "Since . . . the mind cannot be kept a blank until brought to maturity," Channing explained in terms suggestive of Locke, "those, who do not chuse to give virtuous principles the first possession, must, unavoidably give this advantage to those which are vicious."[39] But a proper education, one well suited to the individual child, could go a long way toward assuring a successful upbringing. "The tempers of mankind are various, and require as different modes of cultivation as the various soils under the hand of the discerning husbandman," the minister wrote. "Hasten therefore to scatter the good seed, and 'ere long it shall *yield a joyful crop*." Even the beginnings of a vicious disposition, Channing implied, could be redirected by the measured application of parental persuasion and authority. However, in the absence of proper guidance in childhood, the young man or woman would experience a nearly inevitable progress from lesser to greater sins.[40]

In Channing's view, the blame for a failed upbringing fell as much on the parents and society as on the child. He presented the fate of Hannah Ocuish, the ignorant daughter of an alcoholic Indian, as an indictment of the community as a whole. "Shameful and unpardonable, my brethren, is the almost universal neglect of family Instruction and Government," Channing insisted. "One of the truly unhappy consequences of this neglect, we behold in the ignominious end of this poor girl."[41] While earlier Puritan ministers had certainly viewed executions as symbols of communal guilt, they had not generally stressed the absence of education as a key determinant of individual criminality. For Channing, as for Browne, parental failure rather than Adam's Fall seemed to explain the moral degeneration of young criminals. Significantly, Channing's ideas did not offend the orthodox Congregationalists of New London; on the contrary, they were so impressed by his sermon that they immediately hired him as their pastor.[42]

The theme of parental culpability received even more direct expression in two subsequent execution sermons. The first of those, *The Importance of a Religious Education* (1793), was delivered by Aaron Bancroft, a Congregational minister of Arminian convictions who would later become a prominent Unitarian.[43] His sermon addressed the case of Samuel Frost, executed at Worcester, Massachusetts, in October 1793. The defendant had beaten his father's brains out with a handspike in 1783 but had been acquitted by reason of insanity. Ten years later, at the age of twenty-eight, Frost similarly murdered Captain Elisha Allen, his guardian and employer, with a garden hoe.[44] One might have expected that the case of a young man who had brutally murdered two of his elders would inspire a sermon arraigning the depravity and ingratitude of youth. Instead, Bancroft's discourse stressed the importance of juvenile education and assailed the negligence of a parent who had failed to provide it.

Samuel Frost, the minister asserted, was a person "devoid of social affection and a sense of moral obligation." Was it God who had "denied him those powers and affections, which men in common possess?" No, the minister explained; Frost had possessed "intellectual facilities to distinguish right from wrong, to comprehend the nature of moral duty." What, then, had gone wrong? Bancroft found the answer in Frost's upbringing, particularly in the conduct and character of his murdered father. The elder Frost had not only failed to instruct his children properly but had set them an example that was "impious, cruel, and barbarous." Trained in his father's school of depravity, young Samuel's "rough, malignant, and revengeful passions" took control of his mind. "Is it not highly probable," Bancroft asked rhetorically, "that his present insensibility arises from the want of early education?" Young Frost, the minister concluded, was "a striking instance of the fatal effects of the neglect of early education and good example."[45]

If the case of Samuel Frost illustrated the sad consequences of paternal malevolence, that of Horace Carter demonstrated the equally unhappy results of maternal misconduct. Carter was a young man hanged at Worcester in 1825 for raping the elderly tenant of an almshouse. Jonathan Going, a prominent

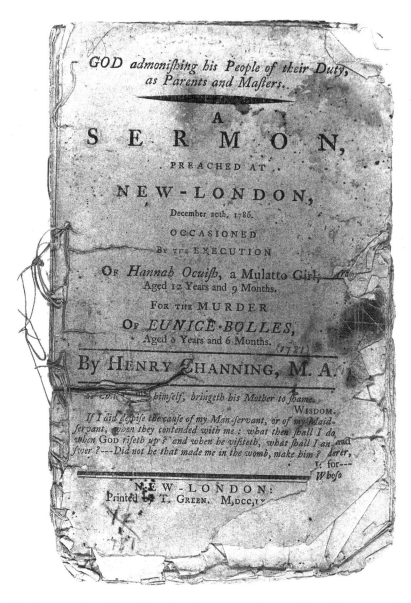

*GOD admonishing his People of their Duty,
as Parents and Masters.*

A
S E R M O N,

PREACHED AT

NEW-LONDON,

December 20th, 1786.

OCCASIONED

BY THE EXECUTION

OF *Hannah Ocuish*, a Mulatto Girl,
Aged 12 Years and 9 Months.

FOR THE MURDER

OF *EUNICE·BOLLES*,
Aged 6 Years and 6 Months.

By HENRY CHANNING, M. A.

.... himself, bringeth his Mother to shame.
WISDOM.

*If I did despise the cause of my Man-servant, or of my Maid-
servant, when they contended with me: what then shall I do
when GOD riseth up? and when he visiteth, what shall I answer?---Did not he that made me in the womb, make him?* ......

NEW-LONDON:
Printed by T. GREEN. M,DCC,LV

**The Congregationalists of New London were so impressed by this sermon that
they offered Henry Channing a job. The owners of this copy also seem to have
been impressed; they read it nearly to tatters and then mended it with thread.**

92

Calvinist Baptist minister then settled in Worcester, addressed his case in *A Discourse* (1825) delivered on the Sabbath following the execution.[46] According to Going, Carter had been the son of an ineffectual father and a "cruel" mother. From the latter, the minister suggested, Carter naturally received "the first elements and all the strong lines of his future character." Instead of properly instructing him, Carter's mother "left the mind of her child a perfect blank, open to receive the crooked lines impressed upon it by the casual hand of circumstance." Even worse, she encouraged him to commit his first petty thefts, sending him out "to pilfer the neighbours' fields, and orchards, and gardens."[47]

"With an education," Going reminded his readers, "Carter might have been a good citizen." But as a result of his mother's malfeasance, the young man was condemned "to enter life ignorant of its dangers, without experience, without education, unsupported by cultivated moral principle; and, worse than all, without the habit of self-control." Not surprisingly, he was soon caught up in the degenerative cycle of wickedness so often described in execution sermons. "We may from the history of Carter learn the natural and rapid progress of vice," Going concluded. "See Carter profane and thievish; next intemperate, and a gambler; and finally a debauchee, and the victim of unbridled lust." While not challenging the propriety of his punishment, Going left little doubt as to who was ultimately responsible for Carter's fall: "Every parent ought to be deemed a felon, and punished as such, who suffers his children to grow up in ignorance of their duty as members of civil society, and as creatures accountable to God."[48]

The ideas expressed by Browne, Channing, Bancroft, and Going certainly suggested a growing ambivalence toward "natural depravity" as the primary explanation for human wickedness, at least among ministers outside the narrow bounds of Congregational orthodoxy. On that level they illustrated the slow attrition of Calvinist theology in New England and the gradual emergence of liberal alternatives over the course of the eighteenth century.[49] But they also reflected a broad reorientation of Anglo-American attitudes toward childrearing, juvenile education, and generational relations. In fact, a major transformation in the theory and practice of pedagogy, drawing on the thought of Locke and Rousseau, was well under way in America by the middle decades of the eighteenth century. The movement gained still wider acceptance during and after the Revolution, when education became a major focus of cultural attention and concern.

Exponents of the "new education" sought to implement a "revolution against patriarchal authority," advocating the replacement of coercive norms of familial relations by those based on mutual affection. Reformers urged parents not to "break the wills" of their froward children but to guide them gently through reason and their own good example.[50] At the same time, a variety of cultural spokesmen challenged long-standing habits of veneration for old age with an emerging "cult of youth."[51] On the level of popular literature, the result was a shift in the depiction of relations between young and old; young people once typically arraigned for their headstrong disobedience were now occasionally portrayed as victims of parental injustice.[52] On the level of public policy, the new concern over childhood training eventually resulted in a widely successful antebellum movement to establish state-regulated, compulsory elementary education. The willingness of several ministers to blame the sins and misfortunes of children on the failings of their elders undoubtedly helped to create a public climate favorable to the ongoing revolution in educational practices and generational relations.

Crime, Contingency, and the Romantic Personality

Early national clergymen not only substituted defective education for natural depravity as a prime cause of crime but also began to abandon the holistic conception of the criminal character implicit in traditional paradigms. Early ministers had assumed that condemned men and women committed wicked crimes because they were themselves fundamentally wicked. That sense of inner corruption as an essential component of the criminal character was based both on the clergymen's broader belief in natural depravity and on the consistent behavioral pattern of accelerating sinful conduct that they found in their case studies of individual offenders. However, by the early national period, descriptions of criminals in a number of execution sermons indicated that the old image of the fundamentally flawed and inherently wicked deviant was occasionally being replaced by a more complex, more fragmented, and less uniformly negative sense of the criminal personality.

Those new perceptions were already evident in the sermons of Aaron Bancroft and Jonathan Going, which suggested that Samuel Frost and Horace Carter were not entirely wicked or deplorable characters. According to Bancroft, Frost was not influenced by many of the vices that frequently led men to murder. He had not been corrupted by "intemperance and dissipation"; nor was he driven by "ambition and avarice." The minister even concluded that Frost possessed some "manly and noble" qualities. Similarly, Jonathan Going insisted that Carter was not by nature defective or depraved. Rather, the convicted rapist had been well endowed in physique, appearance, intelligence, and talents. "No malignant star frowned on his birth," the minister concluded. "No special villainy appears to have been inwrought into his moral structure."[53]

While Bancroft and Going ascribed the actions of a murderer and a rapist to defects in their upbringing and education, ministers in other capital cases of the early national period focused on causes even more fortuitous and contingent. In *The Guilt of Innocent Blood Put Away* (1778), for example, Thaddeus MacCarty, an orthodox Congregational minister from Worcester, examined the case of Bathshua Spooner, a lady of "respectable" social standing who was convicted of hiring three furloughed soldiers to murder her husband.[54] The murderess explained to MacCarty that "her match with her husband" had not been "agreeable to her." Gradually "dissentions" in the Spooner household had gone from bad to worse, until Bathshua "conceived an utter aversion" to her husband and finally "meditated his destruction."[55]

Rather than dismissing Mrs. Spooner's story as the rationalization of a depraved murderess, MacCarty took it both seriously and sympathetically. After all, she was a woman of "many agreeable qualities" and "uncommon fortitude of mind," whose "behaviour to all was very polite and complaisant." At one point the minister even portrayed Mrs. Spooner less as a culpable malefactor than as a victim of unfortunate circumstance. "I was led to conceive of her, as a person naturally of a kind, obliging, generous disposition," he wrote. "But she was unhappy . . . in her first setting out in the world, and so left to a fatal capital crime." By implication, Mrs. Spooner was ruined not by natural depravity, nor by a prolonged course of vice, nor by a flawed education (she was nothing if not well bred), but by an unhappy marriage.[56]

If Bathshua Spooner was ruined by an ill-advised union, Thomas Starr was brought down some twenty years later by an unconsummated engagement. His life was described in an account appended to an execution sermon of 1797 by Enoch Huntington, a Congregational minister in Middletown, Connecticut.[57] Starr, it seems, had been an extremely promising and talented young man. He came of reputable family, performed well in school, manifested a taste for books, excelled in music and penmanship, and displayed good "manners and deportment." But the youth's bright future was shattered by an act of "ungentlemanly" behavior that caused his betrothed to break off their planned marriage. According to the appended account (probably written by Huntington), that single "unhappy step" would change "ALL THE COLOUR OF HIS FATE." The broken engagement led to a degeneration of Starr's character, so that he "sunk by degrees into the various stages of intemperance and debauchery." His doom was sealed when the embittered man fatally stabbed one of his kinsmen with a penknife. As in the case of Bathshua Spooner, Starr's admirable natural endowments and promising upbringing had been overwhelmed by an unfortunate courtship.[58]

An account of the life of Richard Doane, executed for murder in 1797, offered another variation on the same theme. The story was appended to an execution sermon by Nathan Strong, an orthodox Congregational minister.[59] Doane had been born in England of reputable parents and moved to America, where he lived "regularly and industriously" with his wife and only child. But when his spouse died, Doane was thrown "into a state of great dejection" and embraced "an intemperate life as a remedy for sorrow." Although not a "malicious" man when sober, the widower often became "abusive" under the influence of drink. Finally Doane murdered one of his friends in a "fatal affray" that "arose wholly from intoxication." Once again the unforeseen breakdown of a conjugal relationship, in this case the death of a beloved spouse, had led to further tragic consequences.[60]

While the depictions of Spooner, Starr, and Doane certainly suggested changing cultural attitudes toward love and matrimony at the dawn of the romantic era, they also reflected a new flexibility in charting the criminal's path to the gallows.[61] Most important, they suggested an emerging sense of the contingent and anomalous qualities of criminality. Lives no longer always conformed to the highly patterned models of spiritual and behavioral development postulated by Puritan theory. Wicked acts were not necessarily the product of intrinsically wicked people but could develop out of fortuitous and unforeseen developments in the lives of previously decent, even admirable, individuals. In those cases, depravity was portrayed less as the essence of the criminal's character than as the unfortunate outcome of adverse circumstances in the offender's life. Images of misused children, an unhappy wife, a jilted suitor, and a disconsolate widower all suggested a new sensibility—and an understanding of human motivation very different from that implied by earlier sermons. The stark tragedy of original sin and human depravity was gradually losing ground to newer, more varied forms of environmental determinism, psychological explanation, and social melodrama. The older ideas had by no means been discredited or overwhelmed; on the contrary, they generally remained dominant. Still, a process of infiltration was well under way by the last decades of the eighteenth century.

Crime, Society, and Public Policy

Some execution sermons of the early republic went beyond the circumstances of individual offenders to address the impact of larger social groups, practices, policies, and institutions on the incidence of crime. For example, in 1793 Aaron Bancroft not only assailed parents who failed to train their children properly but also praised New Englanders for providing a system of public education in which schools for all were supported by a proportional property tax. More than thirty years later, Jonathan Going, himself a tireless advocate of improved common schools in Worcester, reiterated the same point. "It is ascertained that by far the largest part of those who are publickly punished for the breach of the laws, are unable to read," the minister noted. "This fact speaks volumes in praise of the system of free schools existing in this Commonwealth, and several other States." Such comments implied that the incidence of crime had as much to do with public policy as with the innate character of individuals.[62]

Ministerial treatments of drunkenness also increasingly focused on broad social practices and public policies, reflecting a growing awareness of the scope of the problem. Modern social historians have noted that alcoholic consumption in America reached an all-time high during the early national period, partly in response to anxieties associated with rapid social change and economic development.[63] New England's orthodox ministers, alarmed by the rampant drunkenness around them and concerned about their own threatened social status in an increasingly egalitarian culture, played leading roles in the early temperance and prohibition movements.[64] Not surprisingly, a few also addressed the problem of drink in execution sermons, treating it more as an issue of public policy than of individual depravity.

For example, in his sermon on the execution of Richard Doane for a murder committed in 1797 during a drunken brawl, Nathan Strong linked the abuse of alcohol to the existence of "tipling houses and dram shops" and called on public officials to enforce laws against such places. In addition, he suggested that those in authority had an obligation to place "habitual drunkards" in "confinement," both for their own good and for the sake of public safety. "Had this man, in due time, received the correction of the workhouse," Strong concluded, "it might have saved him from the halter." If New England's system of free schools was an example of successful public policy in preempting the social causes of crime, official negligence in regulating taverns and confining drunkards were instances of policies that failed to protect the public.[65]

David D. Field, a Congregational minister settled in Haddam, Connecticut, offered a similar analysis of excessive drink as a problem of social mores and public policy. His formulation appeared in *Warning Against Drunkenness* (1816), a sermon delivered on the execution day of Peter Lung for beating his wife to death while under the influence of alcohol.[66] Field understood that the problem of drunkenness derived not only from the personal failings of the drunkards themselves but also from the pervasiveness of alcohol in the social life of the early republic. "Our country is nearly inundated by ardent spirits, which are offered for sale in every town, society, and village, and proclaimed by every vehicle which conveys ordinary intelligence to our doors," Field explained. "It has approached almost to a general article of faith, that the fatigues of labor, and the extremes of heat and cold, cannot be endured; that diseases of the body and mind cannot be prevented nor removed; that neither generosity, hospitality, nor politeness can be maintained, nor any common public occasion suitably attended, without a liberal use of ardent spirits."[67]

The minister then proposed a comprehensive program that the "temperate and serious part of the community" could adopt to counteract the pervasive use of alcohol. Parents should withhold liquor from their children; doctors should prescribe it "as sparingly as possible"; ministers should warn the public against it; magistrates should prevent "the unlawful sale of ardent spirits" and close all "houses of corruption"; employers should provide their workers with nonalcoholic refreshment. Field also called for the creation of voluntary "moral societies" in all localities to aid governmental officials in enforcing existing laws, adopt concerted plans for further limiting drunkenness, and distribute temperance tracts "into every village and family." According to Field, such organizations "would accomplish a degree of good, beyond the reach of private individuals." The clergyman thus proposed a solution as comprehensive in scope as the problem itself, one based on an essentially sociological understanding of the causes of drunkenness.[68]

In analyzing the social causes of crime in the early republic, ministers occasionally went beyond the familiar topics of education and drunkenness to address other issues of public policy. In a discourse treating the murder of a young traveler by two foreign highwaymen in 1805, Ezra Witter, a Congregational minister from Wilbraham, Massachusetts, raised the issue of immigration.[69] The minister first attacked the policy of allowing "so many idle vagrants" to crisscross the country, claiming that they were responsible for many "thefts and robberies." Those vagrant criminals were generally foreign immigrants, he then suggested, as were most of those who were crowded into state prisons. "We see the evil attending a continual influx of vicious and polluted foreigners into this country," Witter concluded. As the prisons of Europe and the West Indies disgorged themselves on American shores, the United States was becoming a "general asylum of convicts." In exposing the negligence of government officials who allowed America to be inundated by foreign undesirables, Witter linked a serious crime problem to flawed public policies.[70]

What Witter attributed to immigrants, another minister ascribed to African Americans. In his sermon on the execution of a young black man for rape in 1817, William Andrews, a Congregational minister then settled in Danbury, discussed the prevalence of crime among Connecticut's blacks.[71] "On them may be justly charged no small portion of the crimes and misdemeanors in our land," the minister explained. "It is a shocking fact that one third or more of the criminals sentenced . . . within the last twenty-six years, have been colored people." Of three capital verdicts during that same period, two were delivered against blacks. Andrews suggested that much of the blame for black criminality rested on the white community, both for cruelly bringing blacks to America in the first place and for subsequently keeping them in "ignorance and degradation."[72]

Having located the source of the problem in the downtrodden condition of "people of color in the neighborhood," Andrews argued that both self-interest and moral duty required the broader community to assist and enlighten its black members. "The shameful fact must be confessed that our countrymen are largely their debtors," he insisted. "The mention of their claims, so long neglected, ought to affect every heart and crimson every face." In order to right the long-standing wrong, Andrews urged the establishment of a "benevolent society" for "reforming the morals and improving the condition of our blacks." Much like David Field in his earlier *Warning Against Drunkenness*, the minister called for voluntary mobilization against an underlying social cause of crime.[73]

Discussing a variety of public problems, ministers of the early republic increasingly looked beyond issues of personal character in order to discover some of the underlying social causes of crime. Of course, colonial ministers had also recognized the social problem of drunkenness and noted that certain social groups were prone to commit crimes. But such earlier analysis was generally set in an intellectual framework still dominated by images of human depravity and divine judgment. By contrast, ministers of the early republic were more prone to view the underlying causes of crime in essentially social terms, although theological figures of speech still laced their sermons. Despite occasional invocations of natural depravity and divine justice, their discussions of public education, temperance, foreign immigration, and racial injustice, along with the public policies that they proposed, were at least as suggestive of the moral activism of antebellum reformers as it was of the theological piety of their Puritan predecessors.

Almost every execution sermon published between 1674 and 1825 contained at least a few formulaic references to the fallen nature of humanity and the natural progress of vice. Although the formal doctrine of "sin punished by sin" fell into disuse, the basic Puritan explanations of crime showed remarkable resilience in the sermons of New England ministers. A dominant theme in tracing that literature is conceptual continuity. Yet some of the later sermons, particularly those issued in the early republic, conveyed ideas that went beyond the old assumptions. Several ministers, influenced by the educational theories of Locke and others, downplayed the impact of inherited depravity and emphasized instead the importance of faulty upbringings in leading men and women to the gallows. In a sense, they tended to substitute a new environmental determinism based on education for the more traditional spiritual determinism of original sin. At the same time, a few other clergymen suggested a strong sense of the contingent quality of human experience, stressing the role of unpredictable change and chance, particularly reversals of fortune in affairs of the heart, in causing the downfalls of otherwise promising individuals. Such treatments were undoubtedly influenced by a new romantic sensibility that was infusing Anglo-American popular culture during that period. Finally, a number of early republican ministers explained crime in essentially sociological terms; their diagnoses and prescriptions sometimes sounded closer to the language of antebellum reform than to the lingering discourse of the Puritan jeremiad. In execution sermons of the early republic, ministers charted faulty pedagogy, romantic contingency, and flawed public policy as plausible routes to the scaffold, conceptual alternatives to the traditional road of natural depravity. By investing those conceptual alternatives with the status of print and with their own moral stature and intellectual prestige, New England ministers directed popular thinking about crime toward discourses in which the clergy themselves were not the sole authoritative voices. Indeed, by validating new explanations of crime, execution sermons helped usher in an era of ideological pluralism, romantic expression, and social reform.

It is important to note that the new etiologies of crime had serious implications for the administration of justice in the early republic. Although those implications were rarely explored in execution sermons, contemporary reformers eagerly drew inferences ignored by the clergymen. The new critical scrutiny of public policy led theorists and policymakers in the new post-Revolutionary state governments to formulate various alternatives to existing penal practices. The new liberal theology encouraged movement away from Calvinist concepts of divine retribution and reliance on Old Testament penal codes.[74] The new romantic sensibility fueled feelings of humanitarian revulsion toward the gallows.[75] The new environmental psychology embedded in Lockean thought raised fears about the brutalizing impact of public executions and stimulated faith in the potential of penitentiaries for reshaping the criminal character.[76] Those innovative ideas and attitudes contributed to successive waves of reform agitation and penal legislation beginning in the 1780s.[77] However, despite the shifting explanations of crime and the evolving programs of penal reformers, ministers would continue to defend capital punishment for as long as execution sermons issued from the presses of New England. The changing rationale for that defense is the subject of the following chapter.

5

In Defense of the Gallows:
Justifications of Capital Punishment in New England Execution Sermons, 1674–1825

> Rouse ye, good clergymen, servants of God;
> Stand by my side while I fight for your fun;
> Hanging preserves us from shedding of blood;
> Remedy like it there never was one.
> Rally your forces, thump pulpits and be
> Clerical guards of the good gallows-tree;
> What if our Saviour denounces the law?
> *You* go for hanging—for hanging! Hurrah!

The debate over capital punishment in antebellum America was largely a confrontation between reformers associated with liberal theological positions and supporters of the death penalty from among the Calvinist clergy. The trenchant skill with which orthodox ministers carried their side of the argument provoked some bitter attacks on men of the cloth. For example, many thousands of copies of the satiric doggerel excerpted above were reportedly printed by opponents of the death penalty.[1] In fact, the popular association of orthodox clergymen with support for the gallows long predated the antebellum struggle. For more than a century and a half, New England ministers had regularly sought to justify capital punishment in their execution sermons. Throughout that period clergymen apparently viewed themselves, and were viewed by others, as quasi-official apologists for the courts.[2] In most cases before the turn of the nineteenth century, execution sermons actually contained the *only* published vindications of judicial authority. While ministers consistently defended the death penalty between 1674 and 1825, their justifications varied significantly over the years. By examining their diverse arguments, one can trace the changing rationale for capital punishment in colonial and early national New England.

Puritan Justifications: God's Gallows

Even the earliest of New England's execution sermons sought to justify the imposition of capital punishment. That purpose was often reflected in the scriptural texts from which seventeenth-century ministers drew their doctrines and was frequently implicit in the doctrines themselves. For example, the text of Increase Mather's *Sermon Occasioned by the Execution of a Man* (1686), addressing the punishment of James Morgan for stabbing a companion to death with an iron spit, was taken from the book of Numbers: "And if he smite him with an instrument of iron (so that he die) he is a murderer, the murderer shall surely be put to death." The doctrine that Mather reasonably drew from the verse was that "Murder is a Sin so great and hainous as that whoever shall be found Guilty of it, must be put to Death by the hand of Publick Justice." The justification implicit in text and doctrine was then generally made explicit in the minister's subsequent application. Thus Mather's first use of his doctrine was to argue that it "justifieth the Authority here, in respect of the Sentence of death which has been passed on the Murderer, who is this day to be executed."[3]

It was only when the justice of the capital sentence had been firmly established on the sound authority of Scripture that ministers like Increase Mather felt themselves justified in moving on to other issues. That should not be surprising; among conscientious Puritans, there could hardly be a more effective bulwark of judicial severity than that provided by Holy Writ. By defining capital crimes largely in theological terms, as offenses against the law of Scripture and its divine author, New England's early ministers shifted the burden of ultimate responsibility for capital sentences to a magistrate far less vulnerable to popular challenge than any temporal authority. In the case of bestiality addressed by Samuel Danforth in his *Cry of Sodom* (1674), Benjamin Goad was not finally condemned by mortal jurors or earthly judges but by God himself. The young malefactor from Roxbury had become a "Monument" to the deity's "fierce Wrath and Indignation"; his judicial death would be a "Dreadful Example of Divine Vengeance."[4]

The clergy's reliance on divine decree as a warrant for judicial severity was more than mere rhetoric. Their approach was actually quite consistent with contemporary Puritan legal doctrine. Unsuccessful attempts at penal reform in seventeenth-century England had included efforts to reduce the great number of property crimes already punishable by death. Conversely, reformers sought to introduce the death penalty for a number of offenses, such as adultery, blasphemy, and sodomy, severely condemned by Scripture but not then capital under British law. Those aims of Puritan legal reformers, frustrated in England, were largely realized in the earliest criminal codes of Massachusetts. On the one hand, such crimes against property as larceny, burglary, and robbery, punishable by death in England, were not capital offenses in the Puritan colony. On the other hand, such biblically condemned sins as adultery, blasphemy, sodomy, and bestiality were made capital under the colonial codes.[5] Statutes imposing the death penalty were characterized by a closer fidelity to biblical law than almost any other category of legislation in seventeenth-century Massachusetts. Puritan lawmakers lifted some capital provisions almost verbatim from relevant biblical texts and appended scriptural citations to the actual statutes.[6]

However, not even Puritan legislators viewed scriptural precedents as binding in all cases. Rather, they were seen as justifications for capital statutes deemed otherwise socially expedient. In other words, legal theorists of the time saw biblical precedent as a necessary but not always sufficient condition for the promulgation of a capital penalty. Puritan doctrine also allowed for a significant measure of judicial discretion in dealing with specific capital cases.[7] Given that pragmatic outlook, Puritan ministers occasionally went beyond the letter of Scripture to justify particular executions in terms of the aggravated circumstances of individual cases. Samuel Danforth, for example, was not content to rationalize the execution of Benjamin Goad solely in terms of scriptural warrant but also emphasized the degree to which the youth's chronic misconduct had actually forced the hand of public justice. To that end, the minister drew up an extended biographical indictment against Goad, in which he placed the young offender's final outrage in the context of an extended career of wickedness.

According to Danforth, Benjamin Goad had been the chronically disobedient son of religious parents. Although generally "addicted to Sloth and Idleness," Goad was energetic in the field of depravity. In addition to such routine offenses as lying, stealing, and Sabbath-breaking, Goad compiled an impressive record of sexual misconduct that included numerous acts of bestiality. When taken from his father's home and placed in another household, perhaps in the hope that the discipline of a neighbor might succeed where that of his own parents had failed, Goad broke away and defied his new master. The primary instruments of communal control of the young, those exercised by parent or master in the household, had clearly failed to restrain the incorrigible Goad, who finally completed his record of depravity by openly buggering a mare.[8]

By his chronic defiance of proper authority and fundamental norms of conduct, and more particularly by his public flouting of sexual taboos, Benjamin Goad had established himself as a clear threat to the social order as conceived by Puritan ministers and magistrates. Given the limited institutional remedies available in seventeenth-century Massachusetts, such a challenge could best be met by the deviant's final excision from the community. Although the threat posed by Goad was in that sense social, Danforth insisted on presenting the issue in terms of a Christian community's obligation to God. He stressed that the public character of Goad's climactic act of depravity—the fact that he had buggered a mare in an open field and in the middle of the day—implicated the community as a whole in his wickedness and threatened to draw down "the wrath of God" upon them all. "If we will not pronounce such a Villain Accursed, we must be content to bear the Curse our selves," Danforth concluded ominously in language echoing the Puritan jeremiad. "The Land cannot be cleansed, untill it hath spued out this Unclean Beast."[9]

In addition to the general warrant provided by Scripture and the specific rationale offered by the circumstances of each case, a third justification for capital punishment suggested by seventeenth-century Puritan ministers was its value as a deterrent to others. In making that claim, preachers sometimes drew an analogy between the fate of a condemned malefactor and that of Lot's wife in the biblical story of Sodom and Gomorrah. In *The Wicked Man's Portion* (1675), for example, Increase Mather invoked the striking image of the unfortunate woman whose untimely disobedience had caused her to be "turned into a pillar of salt, that others might be seasoned thereby and preserved from the like evil." Mather, like Danforth before him, had artfully framed an essentially social rationale—deterrence—in the language of Puritan piety. "God is wise and wonderfull in his Providences, and knoweth how to order the death of two or three so as to prevent the destruction of many thereby," the minister observed. "Hence he hath appointed that Justice shall be *executed* in a solemn way, upon *Capital offenders*, that others may hear and fear, and none may do any more so wickedly."[10]

Provincial Justifications: Sacred and Secular

The justifications of capital punishment offered by New England clergymen during the first two-thirds of the eighteenth century continued to rest largely on Scripture. A few ministers drew their doctrines from biblical texts that directly condemned the capital crimes in question; many others cited such passages in the course of their analysis.[11] Further, clergymen continued to justify executions in terms of the community's obligation to an avenging God; like their seventeenth-century predecessors, they insisted that the execution of criminals was needed to "purify the land" and hence avoid divine judgments against society as a whole.[12] But despite the persistence of those theological motifs, some eighteenth-century ministers evidently sought to distinguish—and to establish a rough equilibrium—between religious and secular justifications of capital punishment. The resulting hybrid pattern, suggestive of the early Enlightenment's love of balance, may be illustrated by three execution sermons authored over a period of forty years by Boston ministers of liberal leanings: Benjamin Colman's *The Hainous Nature of the Sin of Murder* (1713), Samuel Checkley's *Murder a Great and Crying Sin* (1733), and Charles Chauncy's *The Horrid Nature and Enormous Guilt of Murder* (1754).[13]

Those similar titles were matched by similar arguments in defense of capital punishment for murder. Each author explicitly justified the penalty on both religious and secular grounds. In defending the capital punishment of a murderer in 1713, Benjamin Colman declared of the authorities: "It is their *Obedience* to the Divine Law, and their *Fidelity* and *Tenderness* to Humane Society, that constrain them to the Condemnation and Execution." Likewise, in 1733 Samuel Checkley insisted that both the "Law of God" and the "Safety of Mankind" called for "Vengeance on Murderers." Two decades later, in 1754, Charles Chauncy condemned homicide in similar terms. "It is at once a Sin against *God* and *Man*," Chauncy explained. "It virtually *usurps God's sovereign Authority* . . . and it does the *highest Injustice* to Man." Each author thus stressed the hybrid nature of the offense of murder—and of the rationale for its punishment. The two types of justification were easily distinguishable in the sermons and seemed to be granted equal validity.[14]

The specific religious arguments offered by the three ministers were virtually identical. All cited scriptural texts condemning murder, decried it as a violation of God's sovereignty (as well as a desecration of his image as embodied in human beings), and followed their seventeenth-century predecessors in suggesting that God required the community to punish murderers in order to cleanse the land.[15] The secular justifications offered were also remarkably similar. Each minister found a natural warrant for the capital punishment of killers in the fact that extreme penalties were imposed for murder by virtually all human societies, Christian and pagan.[16] But beyond the presumptive authority of universal practice with its implication of natural law, the secular argument most stressed by the clergymen was that of deterrence or, more broadly, society's right of self-defense.[17]

Much as the arguments of Mather and Danforth during the 1670s had reflected contemporary Puritan legal doctrine, so too did the approach embraced by Colman, Checkley, and Chauncy at least loosely correspond with subsequent penal developments in the province. As noted earlier, the first criminal codes introduced in Massachusetts had diverged from British practice in failing to provide capital punishment for property offenses and in imposing the death penalty for a number of biblically condemned moral and religious offenses that were not capital under English law. That break with British standards was gradually mended over the course of the seventeenth century as a number of property crimes were made capital, particularly for repeated offenses. The process of convergence was accelerated by the imperial reorganization of the government of Massachusetts in 1692.[18]

During the decades surrounding the turn of the eighteenth century, the cohesiveness and influence of Puritan leaders waned, imperial authorities intervened more frequently in legal and governmental affairs, and, according to some scholars, colonial institutions underwent a broad process of anglicization.[19] The criminal law of Massachusetts was naturally influenced by those broad transformations in an increasingly mature and complex provincial society. On the one hand, colonial administrators struck religious and moral offenses from the capital code. On the other hand, provincial legislators gradually stiffened punishments for crimes against property. While burglary and robbery were capital only on a third conviction under the revised code of 1692, robbery was made subject to the death penalty on a second conviction in 1711, and one type of burglary became capital even on a first offense in 1715.[20] Murder, the crime addressed by Colman, Checkley, and Chauncy, may not have been directly affected by the legal changes just described. But the clergy's emphasis on the protection of public order and safety as legitimate grounds for capital punishment, independent of scriptural authority, was certainly consistent with the increasingly secular, property-oriented character of the capital code.[21]

Revolutionary Justifications: For the Public Good

Hybrid justifications of capital punishment like those formulated by Colman, Checkley, and Chauncy continued to be offered by clergymen during the second half of the eighteenth century. However, some execution sermons issued during the Revolutionary decades revealed a significant shift in ministerial thought and language away from traditional religious justifications, with some even questioning the applicability of scriptural laws to their own society. Biblical citations and invocations of divine wrath continued to appear, but the balance of discussion—and the burden of justification—had apparently swung toward the secular arguments. That change was undoubtedly related to broad shifts in public attitude and discourse generated by the political upheaval of those years. In an era of republican revolution against long-established royal authority, invocations of ancient Scripture and divine sovereignty probably had less rhetorical resonance than assertions of current need and the common good. On a theological level, the new pattern reflected the gradual erosion—even among New England's orthodox clergy—of Calvinism's theocentric approach to human obligation.[22] The ministers were probably also influenced by the new social and penal theories of Enlightenment thinkers and republican ideologues, although there is scant evidence of direct borrowing in the sermons themselves.

In addition to those broad changes in the intellectual climate, more immediate considerations were also involved. The earliest of the innovative sermons were addressing executions not for murder, an offense to which Scripture repeatedly assigned the capital penalty, but for burglary, a crime for which there was no explicit biblical provision of death. At least one or two of the executions of burglars in that period generated significant popular opposition, and the ministers apparently felt constrained to update their rhetoric in order to combat it.[23] However, the revised approach was not simply an ad hoc adjustment to the increasingly hard line against property crime, or a passing response to public revulsion against the execution of burglars. On the contrary, a more secular orientation eventually infiltrated sermons addressing executions for such nonproperty offenses as rape and murder.[24]

Perhaps the earliest appearance of the new approach was in *Excessive Wickedness, the Way to an Untimely Death* (1768) by Noah Hobart, a leading clerical intellectual who has been described as "the great protagonist of eighteenth-century Connecticut Congregationalism."[25] Hobart's sermon addressed the execution of Isaac Frasier, a professional burglar responsible for an extended crime spree throughout southern New England during the

1760s.[26] The minister's defense of the execution was based primarily on deterrence and the community's right to protect itself.[27] Hobart did note, in passing, the Mosaic law that allowed for the killing of those who broke into houses at night, and he suggested that this implied a general forfeiture of life for the crime of burglary.[28]

However, in contrast to Danforth and Mather, who had carefully dressed their social justifications in theological garb, Hobart seemed eager to place even scriptural authority within a secular frame of reference. Thus he claimed that in "sins against the second table of the moral law, the comparative evil . . . may be judged of by the damage or injury done either to a particular person or to the public." And while he affirmed that "Civil Magistracy" was an "ordinance of God," Hobart insisted that its ultimate goal was social "peace" and "security."[29] In fact, the language of divine sovereignty was largely replaced in Hobart's argument by the rhetoric of governmental right and collective good. "Human laws, consider crimes in a political view," he observed, "and the scale by which the evil of them is measured and determined, is their tendency to destroy the public good, or the safety and happiness of society."[30] Hobart was recognized in his own time as a leading voice of "Connecticut orthodoxy," and his approach reveals a profound shift in the intellectual orientation of New England's Congregational clergy.[31] The minister's arguments in defense of Isaac Frasier's execution were at least as attuned to the rhetoric of John Locke and the (soon-to-be) Founding Fathers as to the sort of theological discourse employed by Hobart's clerical predecessors.

The skepticism toward purely theological rationalizations of capital punishment implicit in Hobart's discourse received more forceful expression two decades later in Peres Fobes's *The Paradise of God Opened to a Penitent Thief* (1784), an execution sermon delivered in a climate of widespread public opposition to the hanging of John Dixson for burglary in Taunton, Massachusetts. By the minister's own account, "a considerable number, chiefly of the populace, manifested their doubts and dissatisfaction concerning the lawfulness of the intended execution," some even claiming that "it would be a murderous bloody deed." Fobes's observation that opponents of the penalty attacked the "judges and jury, the sheriff and state's-attorney, the prosecutor *and the preacher*" suggests both his own and the public's perception of the minister as a quasi-official apologist for the legal authorities.[32] In fact, Fobes embraced just such a role in delivering a sermon that defended the execution and in appending to its published version an essay "On the Nature and Enormity of Burglary." His essay set out to defend the capital punishment of burglars on both religious and secular grounds but finally went even further than Hobart's sermon in discrediting Scripture as a foundation for contemporary penal codes.

The minister began his essay by laying out a number of somewhat strained scriptural arguments in defense of capital punishment for burglars.[33] But then, midway through his discussion, Fobes reversed himself and embarked on a completely different line of argument. He began by contrasting the wealth

The Paradise of God opened to a penitent Thief, in Answer to his dying Prayer to a dying Saviour, considered and improved in

A

SERMON;

THE SUBSTANCE OF WHICH WAS DELIVERED AT

TAUNTON,

NOVEMBER 11, 1784.

UPON THE DAY OF THE EXECUTION OF

JOHN DIXSON,

FOR

BURGLARY,

ÆTAT 24.

WITH AN

APPENDIX,

ON THE NATURE AND ENORMITY OF BURGLARY.

AND

A SKETCH OF DIXSON's LIFE.

By PERES FOBES, A. B. A. A. S.
PASTOR OF THE CHURCH IN RAYNHAM.

'*The way of Transgressors is hard,* PROV. xiii. 13.
'*He that pursueth Evil, pursueth it to his own Death,* xi. 19.
'*The Robbery of the Wicked shall destroy them.*' xxi. 7.
'*If a Man be found stealing—that Thief shall die.*' DEUT. xxiv. 7.

PROVIDENCE:
PRINTED BY BENNETT WHEELER.

The appendix to Fobes's execution sermon reversed a century of reliance on Scripture in justifying the death penalty. Note, however, how the last biblical citation on the title page is spliced so as to create a specious scriptural rationale for the capital punishment of property criminals.

and luxury of his own day with the austere simplicity of material life during the time of the biblical Hebrews and during the early days of American settlement. His point was that his own "advanced age" of prosperity required sanctions against theft more stringent than those of the earlier periods. It was therefore entirely appropriate—and perfectly just—that Massachusetts legislators had not made burglary a capital offense on first conviction until 1715, more than eighty years after the initial Puritan settlement.[34]

Lest readers miss the broader implications of his argument, Fobes made them all but explicit by rhetorically demanding whether it was "possible to suppose, that a body of judicial laws, though made in heaven, for a people who existed some thousand years ago, and so different from us in their manners, connexions, pursuits, situation, soil, climate, and an endless variety of other circumstances, can, or ever ought, in equity, and in particular, to bind us, or any other nation on earth, at this day?" Montesquieu himself could hardly have stated the issue, or implied the answer, more clearly. Finally, to complete his case, the minister illustrated some of the absurd penal consequences of rigid adherence to scriptural precedent, citing such biblically capital crimes as "the loss of virginity before marriage, the striking of parents, and sabbath-breaking." Fobes thus ridiculed the very enterprise of scriptural justification that had occupied him over the first half of his essay—and that had engaged the authors of New England execution sermons for more than a century.[35]

Further arguments in support of an essentially secular rationale for capital punishment were offered a few years later in Stephen West's *Sermon . . . at the Execution of John Bly, and Charles Rose* (1787). West's discourse was delivered just before the hanging of two "insurgents" convicted of burglary in 1787, following the violent suppression of Shays's Rebellion in western Massachusetts. The deployment of a sheriff's guard of about 250 men in the procession to the gallows may well suggest the threat of active popular opposition— as in the case of John Dixson three years earlier.[36] West, like Hobart and Fobes before him, began by defending the execution on scriptural grounds. But his argument quickly turned secular when he examined the rationale behind the Mosaic codes, concluding that "none of these crimes, not even murder itself, were made capital, by the Jewish law, *because they were sins against God*; but *because they were sins against society*." Crimes, considered as sins against God, could only be punished by God. Social need, rather than divine demand, provided the proper basis for earthly law. According to West, even God's own punishments of sinners, like those of "human governments," were intended not for his own glory but for "the general good" and "welfare" of the community below.[37]

Although West was himself a convert to Hopkinsianism, a relatively strict branch of contemporary Calvinism, his analysis nonetheless exemplified the broad shift in New England theology away from an earlier theocentric piety and toward an implicitly anthropocentric moralism.[38] In contrast to seventeenth-century ministers, who had viewed earthly justice as a subordinate arm of

God's unfathomable and sovereign will, West depicted divine justice as a sort of celestial auxiliary to the civil magistrate's pursuit of the common good. By implication, divine authority and scriptural law were not determinative of earthly penal codes; they were either supplementary or simply irrelevant. "Men have a right to inflict capital punishments in every case wherein the good of society requires it," West concluded, "and, *of this* men must be the judges."[39]

It should be emphasized that the changes reflected in the sermons of Hobart, Fobes, and West were more than rhetorical. Rather, the new approach corresponded with a concurrent transformation in the actual enforcement of the criminal law. In a study of penal developments in late provincial and early national Massachusetts, William E. Nelson found a radical shift in law enforcement, during the decades following the American Revolution, away from its traditional role as a regulator of religion and morality and toward its modern emphasis on the protection of property. "The aims of the criminal law had now consciously become the preservation of order in society," David H. Flaherty has likewise concluded of law enforcement in post-Revolutionary America, "without reference to the saving of souls or the building of God's kingdom on earth."[40] While Nelson implied that the change in approach occurred rather suddenly, during the decades immediately following the Revolution, Flaherty and others have suggested that it happened more gradually, as a result of longer-term shifts in attitude. Although the timing of a transformation in legal theory and practice cannot be established on the basis of changes in ministerial doctrine, the pattern of development in sermon themes depicted here—featuring the transitional, hybrid justifications of the first half of the eighteenth century—is certainly more consistent with the gradualist view. New England ministers were apparently moving in the same direction, and at approximately the same pace, as actual enforcers of the criminal law.

Republican Justifications: Patriotism at the Gallows

Several execution sermons issued in the early republic suggested a new secular rationale for capital punishment. The defense was a formalistic one, based on the presumed fairness of the laws and legal procedures under which the criminal was condemned. It was often implied rather than explicitly stated, and it was generally offered as a supplement rather than a substitute for more traditional justifications. The new procedural defense was apparently nurtured by the patriotic pride felt by many Americans of the early republic in their governmental institutions and perhaps also by a weakening of the ministers' own faith in their other lines of defense.[41] In at least two cases, it was also fostered by doubts concerning the condemned criminal's guilt.[42] The legal-procedural defense seems to have been most popular during the decade straddling 1800, when it appeared in at least four execution discourses.[43]

An early example of the new approach can be found in Enoch Huntington's *Sermon* (1797) on the execution of Thomas Starr. In his discourse Huntington reminded the condemned man, along with his broader audience, of the equity of the courtroom procedures at the murderer's trial, particularly noting the skill of the defense lawyers. "You have had, to my personal knowledge, a fair, candid trial before man," the minister informed Starr; "you have had the assistance of most able counsellors and advocates, who in managing your cause appeared to adduce every argument and motive that might possibly operate in your favor." Huntington was also careful to remind the prisoner of the provenance of the statute by which he was condemned, declaring: "You will . . . soon . . . suffer the punishment you justly deserve *from the laws of your country.*" To be sure, Huntington also defended Starr's punishment on orthodox scriptural grounds, referring to the "laws of God" that required death for the crime of murder; but the minister had deftly introduced the legal-procedural justification to his audience.[44]

A more overt appeal to the patriotic pride of Americans in their new legal system was offered the following year in an appendix to Timothy Langdon's *Sermon* (1798) on the execution of "Anthony, a Free Negro" for rape. Appended to the actual discourse was an address originally delivered at the gallows by another clergyman, Samuel Blatchford. Although he was himself a recent immigrant to the United States, his address featured a patriotic disquisition on the American form of government, in which he particularly stressed the fairness of its criminal procedures. "In most countries the life of a subject is at the will of his Lord; but here nothing is attempted against the life of a citizen, without an open and fair trial," Blatchford explained. "Evidences are required to make out the charge, and the utmost deliberation is used by those impartial judges of the fact, called jurors, before they deliver their verdict." The humanity of American law was still further demonstrated by its treatment of prisoners sentenced to death: Executions were "deferred for a considerable time" to allow the condemned ample opportunity for prayer and repentance. "You who are come hither to-day to see this sad spectacle," the minister suggested modestly, "will go away perhaps satisfied with the justice of your country."[45]

Another example of the legal-procedural defense is contained in Moses C. Welch's *The Gospel to be Preached to All Men* (1805), a sermon addressing a capital case in which the degree of the condemned man's guilt was in some doubt. Samuel Freeman had been convicted for the murder of his common-law wife in Ashford, Connecticut. While acknowledging that he had brutalized the woman, Freeman steadfastly denied having intentionally killed her. "I know not, certainly, that you are guilty of the crime for which you are to die," Welch conceded to the prisoner. "The truth is known to God and your own soul." Yet that did not prevent the minister from implicitly justifying the fatal sentence:

> Having been accused of the crime of shedding human blood, the Grand-Jury of the county, after a due investigation of the case, have indicted you for

Murder. You have been brought to the bar of the Honorable Superior
Court, and assisted in your defence by able and learned counsel. But the
evidence was so clear against you as to induce twelve sober, judicious,
disinterested jurors, on their oath, to pronounce you guilty. The sentence of
death, according to the law of the land, has been passed upon you.[46]

In the increasingly law-oriented culture of America's early republic, the
mere recitation of well-ordered judicial procedures was apparently gaining,
even for ministers, the sort of incantatory moral force traditionally reserved
for invocations of sacred Scripture.[47] Not surprisingly, it was during the first
decade of the nineteenth century that the trial report emerged in New England as a popular literary alternative to the execution sermon. Such reports
may be seen, in part, as a repackaging of the procedural justification of capital
punishment in its own distinctly legalistic literary format. When execution
sermons began to slip out of literary vogue during the following decades,
defenders of judicial authority could rely on another popular genre to continue carrying their message to a sometimes restive public.[48]

Despite an upsurge of antigallows sentiment and a flurry of penal reform,
criminal executions continued to take place during the early decades of the
nineteenth century, and gallows sermons continued to issue from the presses
of New England.[49] While ministers occasionally invoked biblical authority,
their justifications for capital punishment were largely secular, featuring references to "the good order of society," "the security of life," "the peace of
community," "the laws of the country," and "the public safety."[50] One of the
last published sermons, Jonathan Going's *A Discourse Delivered at Worcester*
(1825), offered a legalistic argument based less on procedural fairness than on
efficient deterrence. "Whatever difference of opinion may exist in respect to
the justice, or the policy of capitally punishing this offence [rape], it should
seem that there ought to be but one opinion in relation to the execution of the
laws while they are in force," the Baptist minister explained. "Every instance
of the failure of their execution, carries in it a kind of pledge of their future
infraction with impunity; and renders the whole administration of justice, of
dubious aspect."[51] The patriotic legal-procedural justification had degener-
ated into a defensive plea for administrative consistency as a bulwark of
deterrence.

In fact, the pendulum would soon swing back toward the older religious
approach. When a new wave of agitation for abolition of the death penalty
swept the country during the 1830s and 1840s, the defense of the gallows was led
by clergymen from orthodox Protestant denominations.[52] Although they employed a variety of arguments, those ministers actually spearheaded a significant revival of the traditional scriptural justifications of capital punishment.[53]
Even opponents of the death penalty increasingly relied on biblical claims.[54]
The reversion to scriptural authority was probably fostered by several decades
of widespread revivalism and reflected the increasing bibliolatry of nineteenth-
century Calvinist orthodoxy.[55] It may also have been encouraged by a gradual

narrowing of the public role of clergymen from their traditional status as authoritative communal leaders to their new function as professional specialists, expert in the circumscribed realm of scriptural interpretation and application.[56] In any case, the nineteenth-century biblical debate on the death penalty largely postdated the demise of the execution sermon as a literary genre.

The justifications of capital punishment offered by ministers in the scores of execution sermons published in New England between 1674 and 1825 reflect both strong elements of continuity and unmistakable evidence of change. On the one hand, the basic arguments involving Scripture, natural law, deterrence, and public safety had all been formulated by the early eighteenth century and continued to appear in many sermons over the next hundred years. On the other hand, the relative prominence of the different justifications changed over time, as did the terms in which they were typically formulated. Increasingly the theological language of divine command and communal obligation was replaced by an essentially secular rhetoric of public safety and common good. In addition, some of the later sermons began to question the underlying assumptions of the scriptural defense and suggested a new legal-procedural justification. By the time scriptural arguments returned to vogue during the mid-nineteenth century, the execution sermon genre had itself already expired as a published form.

New England's orthodox ministers emerge from this survey not as isolated Jeremiahs inveighing against the evils of an increasingly alien world but as shrewd, resourceful partisans of entrenched public authority. As a group, they were less firmly committed to a particular line of defense than to the effective vindication of penal severity through the most compelling arguments available at any given time. To that end, they periodically refitted their rhetoric both to changing styles of public discourse and to the shifting contours of penal practice. Indeed, the limits of ministerial flexibility roughly corresponded with the frontiers of public policy. At no point did New England lawmakers of that period actually abolish capital punishment, and, despite a couple of isolated clerical criticisms of *public* hangings (eventually eliminated by Massachusetts and other states during the 1830s), not a single published execution sermon ever condemned the death penalty as such.[57] Like the criminals whose cases they addressed, New England's orthodox ministers were, in the end, constrained only by a line firmly attached to the gallows.

Although the extent of ideological innovation may be somewhat exaggerated by the method of the last two chapters, focused as they are on those ministers who presented new terminology and ideas, the changes were substantial and extended beyond the particular sermons examined here. It is difficult to know whether the new arguments directly mirrored the evolving attitudes of the ministers themselves or were consciously fitted by their authors to changing popular views. Both factors were almost certainly involved, and in either case the sermons suggest a substantial degree of ideological flexibility. It is significant, in that regard, that the major revisions in language and doctrine explored in this chapter invariably corresponded with actual shifts in penal practice or broader social changes. In explaining basic religious concepts like sin and salvation, most ministers simply reiterated traditional beliefs with remarkably little change over the decades. But in discussing more topical issues like crime and punishment, they showed a greater willingness to embrace new ideas, even those that bypassed or challenged existing theological formulations. Even as they faithfully cultivated traditional piety, the authors of New England execution sermons tacitly diverted much of their discourse into a wider secular sphere.

III

Criminals and Innocents:

The Literature of Social Insurgency

6

A Fellowship of Thieves:
Exposing a Criminal Underworld in Eighteenth-Century New England

Even as ministers integrated new ideas into an old genre, printers and criminals turned to new literary forms. The last speeches and longer criminal autobiographies that flourished between 1730 and 1800 had evolved, in part, out of the conversion narratives and pious confessions appended to execution sermons. But in contrast to those earlier forms, many of the newer criminal accounts were increasingly secular in tone and content. In the aftermath of the Revolution, a few of the most popular narratives conveyed messages explicitly hostile to both religious and secular authority, expressing ideological insurgencies that were transforming the cultural landscape of the early republic.[1] The intellectual ferment that reshaped ministerial ideas even as it generated antiauthoritarian narratives was paralleled by a breakdown of social control. As a series of crime waves swept the region during the eighteenth century, particularly after 1760, a new class of offenders started to appear on the gallows of New England.

Many of the criminals executed in the region during the seventeenth century had been social insiders, sinful but integral members of local communities. Most of those hanged during the first thirty years of the eighteenth century had been social outsiders, sailors and pirates from all over the world who typically had few if any ties to the provincial communities in which they were judged and condemned. By contrast, quite a few of the offenders executed during the last seventy years of the eighteenth century were neither insiders, nor outsiders, but undersiders, participants in a flourishing quasi-criminal subculture.[2] Many were chronic property criminals who were finally executed for burglary or robbery. The stories of those social insurgents are told in a surprisingly rich body of broadsides and pamphlets. The lives depicted in those narratives will be the primary subject of this chapter. But before turning to that popular literature, it may be useful to provide a brief overview of the problem of property crime in eighteenth-century New England. Although the focus of the following discussion is on Massachusetts, similar patterns of crime obtained throughout the broader region.

The Problem of Property Crime

The problem of serious property crime had already emerged in Massachusetts during the first decades of European settlement.[3] An early colonial act of 1642 against burglary, robbery, and theft referred to the "many persons of late years" who were "apt to be injurious to the goods and lives of others." In 1651 the records of the General Court of the colony complained that "many crimes" were being committed in Boston "both by night & by day." During the following year, the legislature referred specifically to "theft" as "a sinne of late much growing uppon us" and enacted new legal penalties to combat it.[4] Like alcoholism and prostitution, property crime was just one among a variety of social vices that beset Boston as it developed into a thriving seaport over the course of the seventeenth century.[5]

Not surprisingly, the problem persisted into the provincial period. During the spring and summer of 1712, for example, Boston merchants, shopkeepers, and craftsmen suffered through an extended series of larcenies and burglaries.[6] When a gang of young thieves was arrested and convicted of the crimes, Cotton Mather delivered two sermons bemoaning the problem of theft in Massachusetts. The first of those discourses drew a "Vast Assembly," and both were quickly published, suggesting that the clergyman's alarm may have been shared by the general public.[7] Three years later, in January 1715, Boston's selectmen acknowledged "the great perplexity" felt by townspeople in the face of frequent attempted robberies and offered a monetary reward for the apprehension and conviction of the criminals responsible.[8] That same year, the General Court imposed the death penalty for burglary of dwelling-houses at night.[9] Over the following decades, legislators repeatedly acknowledged the inadequacy of existing laws against property crime, enacting harsher penalties to combat the receiving of stolen goods (1723), theft (1736), robbery (1761), and burglary (1770).[10] Although a more ambitious legislative effort to restructure the province's criminal code was apparently sidetracked in 1765 by the onset of the Stamp Act crisis, such an overhaul was finally enacted by the new state legislature in 1785.[11]

But not even stricter penalties solved the problem. On the contrary, local newspaper coverage suggests that there was an upsurge of property crime in Boston during the decade following the French and Indian War, particularly in the winter months, when demand for labor tended to be relatively low.[12] During that same period, Thomas Hutchinson, the lieutenant governor and chief justice of the Superior Court of Judicature, repeatedly bewailed the epidemic of thefts, burglaries, and robberies.[13] Although the Revolutionary War may have caused a temporary decline in the incidence of property offenses, the problem certainly reemerged with the arrival of peace; there seems to have been a postwar crime wave beginning in the early to mid-1780s.[14] The increased incidence of serious property crime was not only suggested by a renewed stream of newspaper reports but was also reflected in the caseload of the Supreme Judicial Court. There were a dozen indictments for burglary before the state's highest tribunal during the single year of 1784, compared to a total of only four during the preceding four years combined.[15] No fewer than five property criminals, three burglars and two robbers, were executed in the state during that year alone.[16] Not even the legislative revisions of 1785 succeeded in stemming the tide of property crime; rather, such offenses persisted in relatively large numbers into the 1790s and occasionally assumed particularly dangerous forms.[17]

During the winter and early spring of 1797, Boston was one of a number of towns across the country that were struck by a series of house fires, some involving arson and attempted burglary. In one case a conflagration that might have destroyed a large part of the town was only narrowly averted. The residents of Boston quickly mobilized to combat the alarming problem. The crisis was also addressed rhetorically in a sermon delivered by John Lathrop, a local clergyman, in March of that year and published shortly thereafter as *God Our Protector and Refuge in Danger and Trouble*. Although Lathrop affirmed that God was indeed every Christian's ultimate refuge from danger and trouble, the minister also suggested a few more practical remedies. Among other things, he urged energetic governmental action, suggested that the existing system of "police" needed improvement, and called for the erection of large houses of "punishment or industry," modeled on a similar institution recently established in Bavaria, within which "*vagrants*, strolling *mendicants*, and people of suspicious, and of bad character" might be confined.[18] His discussion at once recalled traditional Anglo-American fears of the "strolling poor," reiterated more than a century of local concern over recurrent property crime, and reflected a new era of international penal reform.[19]

Any survey of modern scholarly interpretations of property crime in eighteenth-century Massachusetts ought to begin with the work of Carl Bridenbaugh, whose two classic studies of early American cities, including Boston, concluded that the problem of property crime—along with other forms of urban disorder—increased substantially over the course of the seventeenth and eighteenth centuries.[20] That perception of a rising tide of colonial crime was implicitly challenged by the findings of a ground-breaking quantitative study of criminal prosecutions in provincial Massachusetts produced by David H. Flaherty in 1981. Flaherty calculated rates of prosecution before the Superior Court of Judicature between 1693 and 1769 for various categories of offense. He found relatively low, even declining, rates of criminality throughout the period and concluded that "overall the system of social control did function effectively for the prevention and prosecution of serious crime."[21]

However, a number of even more recent studies of crime in eighteenth-century Massachusetts by Adam Hirsch, Linda Kealey, N. E. H. Hull, and Louis Masur, including two that have carried quantitative calculations based on court records into the last thirty years of the century, have suggested that

Massachusetts faced two crime waves after 1760, one beginning in the early to mid-1760s and probably continuing until the outbreak of the Revolutionary War in the mid-1770s, the other beginning in the early to mid-1780s with the return of peace and apparently continuing into the 1790s.[22] Those twin surges of peacetime property crime apparently coincided with the increasing stratification of wealth in late colonial and revolutionary Boston, the concurrent growth of urban poverty, and the gradual emergence of a sizeable contingent of impoverished transients wandering across the Massachusetts countryside.[23] The proliferation of the "strolling poor" seems to have been a particularly significant, if perhaps only temporary, development. While serious property crime probably remained a predominantly urban phenomenon, there is at least fragmentary evidence that crime increased even more rapidly in rural Massachusetts than in Boston during the second half of the eighteenth century.[24] Although the burgeoning incidence of property crime in rural areas may have been ameliorated by changes in settlement and poor-relief laws during the 1790s, the problem of persistent urban crime seems to have been less easily solved.[25] Indeed, the pattern of surging property crime in Boston during the decades between 1760 and 1800 may represent a transitional phase between the sporadic, or epidemic, outbreaks of the seventeenth and early eighteenth centuries and the endemic problem that had emerged in American cities by the first half of the nineteenth century.[26]

Although David Flaherty's optimistic conclusion concerning the effectiveness of social control in provincial Massachusetts *may* be warranted for the years between 1693 and 1760, such an assessment certainly cannot be sustained for the last four decades of the century. After 1760, and particularly after the end of the French and Indian War, frequent newspaper reports of property offenses suggest that a critical threshold had been crossed both in the actual incidence of such crime and in the public's awareness of it as a serious social problem. The alarms of Thomas Hutchinson and John Lathrop, delivered with apparent urgency from bench and pulpit, simply reinforce that impression. In short, if late provincial and early national Massachusetts was not quite yet a den of thieves, it increasingly was a society chronically beset by those who, to use some venerable legislative language, were "apt to be injurious to the goods and lives of others."[27]

The Popular Literature

Who were the thieves of eighteenth-century Massachusetts? Where did they come from, why did they turn to crime, and how did they pursue their illicit vocation? Contemporary readers interested in those questions could turn to a series of popular eighteenth-century publications closely associated with the gallows. Criminal executions in late provincial and early national New England often evoked last-speech broadsides.[28] Those works did not contain statements delivered by criminals at the gallows but rather short autobiographies prepared in prison during the days before a hanging. During the second half of the century, a few longer criminal memoirs were also published as pamphlets or books. There are good reasons to trust those narratives as social-historical sources. Several studies have affirmed the factual accuracy of similar genres in early modern England.[29] In addition, much of the information on specific crimes, trials, and punishments described in New England narratives is confirmed by surviving court records.[30] Although ministers, printers, and others certainly played active roles in extracting "last speeches" through interrogations in jail and undoubtedly often drafted the statements for illiterate criminals, there is little reason to doubt that condemned men and women actually provided the biographical information that they contain.[31]

The criminals themselves offered various rationales for producing last speeches. A few said that they did so in order to "give Glory to GOD."[32] Many others sought to warn or deter others from their sins and crimes, or even to lead former companions to "sincere Repentance."[33] Such motives suggested the pious and didactic origins of the criminal confession genre. However, a few of the late eighteenth-century criminals also expressed a desire to inform and entertain their readers. In 1787 John Sheehan explained that he sought "to satisfy the curious Publick." Similarly, in 1789 Rachel Wall assumed that "the ever-curious Public" would "be anxious to know every particular circumstance of the Life and Character of a person in my unhappy situation." Later in her account, she described a particularly engaging "adventure" in hopes of "gratifying the curiosity of some particular friends."[34] In fact, much of the success of the genre can probably be explained by simple popular curiosity concerning the lives and exploits of capital criminals. While ostensibly designed to warn against wickedness, last speeches also served contemporary readers, as they will now serve us, as exposés of a developing criminal subculture.

Although domestic property criminals were rarely hanged in Massachusetts before 1730 or after 1800, they constituted a sizeable minority of all offenders executed during the intervening decades.[35] They were correspondingly well represented in the last speeches and longer documentary biographies that flourished during that same period. Eighteen contemporary broadsides and four longer narratives described the lives and careers of a total of twenty-five thieves, burglars, and robbers active in provincial and early national Massachusetts (and often elsewhere in New England), most of whom were executed for their property crimes.[36] (See table.)[37] It should be stressed that those twenty-five offenders were not strictly representative of all contemporary thieves. Rather, they were among the most serious property offenders of that time and place, exceptional both in their capital convictions and in the extraordinary publicity that their cases received in the form of published narratives.

The Sample of Thieves
(listed by order of death)

Name	Birthplace	Vital Dates
Matthew Cushing	Limerick, Ireland	1712–1734
Hugh Henderson	Armagh, Ireland	ca. 1707/9–1737
William Welch	Burchestown, Ireland	ca. 1730/1–1754
John Shearman	Rochester, Massachusetts (?)	ca. 1721/3–1764 (?)
Joseph Lightly	Newcastle, England	ca. 1736/9–1765
Isaac Frasier	North Kingston, Rhode Island	1740–1768
Arthur, a Negro	Taunton, Massachusetts	1747–1768
William Linsey	Palmer, Massachusetts	ca. 1745/6–1770
Levi Ames	Groton, Massachusetts	ca. 1751/2–1773
Daniel Wilson	Bellingham, Massachusetts	1749–1774
William Huggins	Fishkill, New York	1759–1783
John Mansfield	Province of Maine	ca. 1760/1–1783
Dirick Grout	Schenectady, New York	ca. 1747/8–1784
Francis Coven	Marseilles, France	ca. 1761/2–1784
Richard Barrick	Ireland	1763–1784
John Sullivan	Limerick, Ireland	1766–1784
Johnson Green	Bridgewater, Massachusetts	1757–1786
John Sheehan	near Cork, Ireland	ca. 1763/4–1787
Rachel Wall	Carlisle, Pennsylvania	1760–1789
John Bailey	New York, New York	1771–1790
Thomas Mount	Middletown, New Jersey	1764–1791
John Stewart	Ireland	ca. 1777/8–1797
Stephen Smith	Sussex County, Virginia	ca. 1764/70–1797
Samuel Smith	Middletown, Connecticut	1745–1799
Henry Tufts	Newmarket, New Hampshire	1748–1831

The basic demographic characteristics of the thieves described in the popular crime literature are hardly surprising. The offenders generally conformed in gender and age distribution to the patterns found by other investigators of early modern property crime.[38] Only one of the criminals was a woman, and all but six of the twenty-five thieves were executed while in their twenties: Two were in their late teens, one in his thirties, and two in their forties; only Henry Tufts, a wily thief and trickster, managed to cheat the hangman and live to the ripe old age of eighty-two. Although it is possible that those gender and age distributions resulted partly from biases in the apprehension, prosecution, and punishment of such criminals, the sharply skewed figures, along with the similar patterns found in early modern Europe, certainly suggest that most serious property crimes in eighteenth-century New England were committed by young adult males. The last speeches and other narratives provide a wealth of information about the lives of those young felons.

Early Lives: The Turn to Crime

The criminal autobiographies typically opened with formulaic lines identifying the criminal's name, age or birthdate, birthplace, and parentage. "I LEVI AMES," a typical statement began, "aged twenty-one years, was born in *Groton*, in *New-England*, of a credible family, my father's name was *Jacob Ames*, who died when I was but two years old."[39] Such passages suggest a great deal concerning the social origins of the criminals. All three of the property criminals executed before 1760 had been born in Ireland. In contrast, six of the seven thieves in the literary sample executed between 1764 and 1774 seem to have been from New England, all but one of those from Massachusetts itself. The only true outsider had been born in England. Those condemned between 1783 and 1799 represented more of a mix. Four were natives of New England, including two from Massachusetts and one each from Connecticut and New Hampshire. Another five had been born abroad, four in Ireland and one in France. The remaining six thieves executed between 1783 and 1799 were from various non-New England colonies or states, including three from New York and one each from Pennsylvania, New Jersey, and Virginia.[40]

The fact that the three earliest malefactors came from Ireland may suggest the disproportionate role of immigrants in Massachusetts property crime during the first six decades of the eighteenth century, or it may simply reflect a reluctance on the part of local authorities to execute native-born criminals for property offenses. That condemned men in the middle period had nearly all been born in New England, mostly in Massachusetts, may indicate the maturation of an indigenous criminal element in the region, or it may merely signal a greater willingness to crack down on home-grown offenders. The mixed pattern of origins in the final period may indicate the gradual integration of Massachusetts into a wider criminal underworld that apparently flourished up and down the Atlantic seaboard during the second half of the eighteenth century, or it may simply reflect a more general shuffling of population—especially poor, unattached males—stimulated by the Revolutionary upheaval.[41]

In regard to the ethnic origins of the thieves described in the published literature, it should be noted that four were African Americans and seven were Irishmen.[42] Since both of those groups were subject to widespread popular prejudice, it is difficult to know the degree to which their disproportionate presence in the literary sample reflected either economic discrimination (leading to property offenses) or judicial bias (leading to capital convictions and executions).[43] A cultural preoccupation with deviants from "outsider" social groups could also, in theory, have led to literary treatments of blacks and Irish out of proportion to their actual presence at the gallows. In any case, both groups seem to have been popularly stigmatized for their perceived association with serious crime.[44] As early as 1706, a Boston editorialist claimed that blacks were "much addicted to Stealing."[45] More than a century later, in 1817, a minister from Connecticut publicized the "shocking fact" that at least one-third of the criminals sentenced to prison in his state over the previous twenty-six years had been black.[46] The Irish did not enjoy a much better reputation. Richard Barrick, a condemned robber, was almost certainly drawing on popular Anglo-American stereotypes when he satirically claimed that "the *Hibernian* coat of arms" depicted an Irishman dangling from the end of a rope.[47]

Of course, few mothers and fathers, whatever their ethnic origins, expect their children to die on the gallows. The last speeches of several of the condemned thieves suggest that traumatic childhoods may help explain that unfortunate outcome in their cases. For example, William Welch, born in Ireland in 1730 or 1731, testified that his "cruel" stepmother not only "prevented" his "Education" but also helped launch his juvenile career as a petty thief by taking him to markets and fairs to pick pockets and by serving as a receiver of his stolen goods. Richard Barrick, born in Ireland in 1763, explained that he was raised in a foundling hospital and was apprenticed at the age of ten to a silk-weaver. When his master "starved and froze" the boy "almost to death," Barrick "left him, and roved through the streets, and frequently stole small things from shop-windows." He later joined a gang of thieves with whom he picked pockets until he was caught, convicted, and forced to join the navy as an alternative to imprisonment.[48]

Two of the American-born criminals also testified to the formative influence of cruel or dishonest elders. Isaac Frasier was born to parents "in low circumstances" at Kingston, Rhode Island, in 1740 and had the further misfortune of being apprenticed at the age of eight to a shoemaker, with whom he lived for eight years "in the most abject condition." Young Frasier's "allowance of food" was "so small" that he "was often induced by hunger" to steal for his subsistence. Much like Welch's stepmother, Frasier's mistress also encouraged his pilfering of "sundry . . . trifling articles." The case of Stephen Smith, born into slavery in Sussex County, Virginia, during the 1760s, was somewhat similar to those of Welch and Frasier. Despite his father's piety, Smith's mother "encouraged" him "to *Steal*," leading him to commit "many small Thefts" in his youth.[49]

Aside from the cases just mentioned, most of the other convicts offered far more favorable portraits of their parents or guardians, indicating that they turned to crime despite the best efforts of their elders. For example, Levi Ames, born in Groton, Massachusetts, during the early 1750s, reported that he belonged to "a credible family" and was "the first of the family who was ever disgraced." John Mansfield, born in the province of Maine in 1760 or 1761, claimed that his parents had been "reputable" and that his siblings were "well esteemed by those who know them"; he recalled: "My parents have been exceeding kind to me; they took all possible care of my education while I continued with them; I always had their good wishes, and, when opportunity offered, their best advice." And Francis Coven, born in Marseilles, France, during the early 1760s, declared that "he came of reputable Parents" and that "his Father was a Merchant, who brought him up in the Ways of Virtue and gave him a good Education."[50]

A dozen of the other thieves in the literary sample, including two from Massachusetts, six from other colonies or states, and four from abroad, also referred favorably to the characters of their parents or guardians.[51] Although there is certainly a formulaic tone to the literature's composite catalogue of "credible" or "reputable" parents, probably a function of standardized leading questions posed by the jailhouse interviewers who often drafted the last speeches, there is little reason to doubt its underlying accuracy. After all, reports of wicked, even criminal, elders contained in the last speeches of Welch, Barrick, Frasier, and Stephen Smith suggest that far less favorable formulas were available to prison biographers. If the testimony of the majority is to be believed, most of the condemned thieves were not born into a criminal subculture. It should follow that their turns to crime often involved a process of breaking away from the values and authority of pious and respectable elders.

In a few cases the break occurred quite early in life. Matthew Cushing recalled that he was "rebellious and head-strong" from his "Childhood" and that his parents were unable to "rule" him. Arthur, a slave from Taunton, Massachusetts, claimed that his life of "notorious Crimes" began when he ran away from a harsh mistress at the age of fourteen and joined a community of dissolute Indians. Rachel Wall reported that she left her parents "without their consent" at a "very young" age, soon marrying a man who introduced her to "bad company" and a life of crime. Thomas Mount confessed that he "played truant," robbed orchards on Sundays, provided a wicked example for many "boys" of his acquaintance, despised his parents, and considered everything they said to be beneath his regard. Finally, John Stewart's first step into crime was an act of filial betrayal; at the age of fifteen, he defrauded his parents of some property and divided the spoils among his "wicked Companions."[52] Note that in most of those instances the break with the authority of elders was accompanied by involvement with an alternative fellowship of vice, whether Arthur's "Indians," Wall's "bad company," Mount's "boys," or Stewart's "wicked Companions."

Even when the turn to crime occurred later in life, it was sometimes depicted as a consequence of social influence rather than of purely personal depravity. Daniel Wilson, for example, blamed the "advice and persuasion" of a disreputable associate for his own turn to horse-stealing, which followed a diligent and successful career as a house-carpenter. Similarly, after describing how a young man in New York City had led him to a boardinghouse occupied by "bad Women," John Stewart explained how the same individual tempted him to turn to property crime. "One Evening this young Man took me out and told me that I could get more Money in a Night by Thieving, than I could by Work, to which I agreed," he recounted. "On that Night I went into a Shop and stole about the worth of two Dollars."[53] Although one should be cautious in crediting what may be self-serving attempts by criminals to spread the blame for their misdeeds, or efforts by pious redactors to illustrate the dangers of bad company, there is little reason to doubt that accounts of disreputable companionship and criminal tutelage had some basis in fact. If so, those cases suggest that, in turning to theft, the offenders had succumbed less to economic necessity than to personal temptation and the influence of peers.[54]

In several instances, the break with respectable parents and the entry into a world of vice and crime were accomplished through military service. British-born Joseph Lightly joined the king's forces during the Seven Years' War; he recalled: "As soon as my Mother knew of my being inlisted, she told me she hoped she should hear of my being hanged, for my Cruelty of going to leave her against her Will." Despite his mother's parting malediction, Lightly joined his regiment at Dublin; they later marched to Cork, from where they embarked for overseas service. "After my Arrival at *Philadelphia*, in *North-America*, I soon began to forget God," Lightly testified, "and being in the Army, where all Manner of Vice and Wickedness prevail'd, I fell into Cursing and Swearing, taking great Delight therein; as also in contriving all Sorts of Mischief."[55]

A generation later, at the commencement of the American Revolution, Dirick Grout enlisted in the American army although it was against his "Father's Will" and despite his parent's "repeated good Council." When Johnson Green enlisted with the colonial forces near the outset of the same conflict, it was also "contrary" to the "advice" of his mother. A year or two after that, William Huggins enlisted in the army for a five-month term. "During my short stay in the army, I became acquainted with many vices I had not ran into before," Huggins recalled in jail. "I contracted a love for gaming, playing for money and cheating those I played with; took to drinking, and as I grew older those sins became more familiar to me, and harder to part with."[56]

The turn to serious crime typically occurred after the period of military service.[57] Joseph Lightly's last speech featured a classic account of the furloughed soldier turning to a rambling life of transiency and criminality. "After I had intirely left the Army, I went up and down through the Country, in Order to get acquainted with the Roads, for my Intention was to Rob, or do any other Sort of Mischief I could lay my Hands to, for Support," Lightly explained. "In my Progress through the County I stole two Shirts and two Pair of Trowsers." His antisocial stroll through New England was interrupted by his arrest in Hartford in February 1765 on suspicion of having murdered a female companion in Ware, Massachusetts. Although he had admittedly intended to defraud the woman, he denied having killed her; nonetheless, he was convicted and executed for the homicide later that year.[58]

Dirick Grout's turn to crime, nearly twenty years later, took place in an urban setting. After repeatedly enlisting in the American army during the Revolutionary War, Grout left the military in 1780, having committed no crimes during his period of service. Although he initially returned to his home in New York State, Grout eventually made his way to the vicinity of Boston, where he struggled to find work and lodging, with only occasional success. Even as he searched for legitimate employment, the impoverished veteran began to commit a series of property crimes. "The first Theft I committed was at a House at the North-End, where I stole some Fowls and a Jacket," Grout testified, "for which I was detected, tried, convicted and received fifteen Stripes." That initial crime may have been committed in October 1783; afterward, he was induced to steal ten more fowls by a poor companion and was again caught, convicted, and whipped. Later, in March and April 1784, he began committing a series of burglaries, some in conjunction with two other accomplices. In August 1784 Grout was indicted for several of those burglaries and convicted of one of them, for which he was hanged in October of that year.[59]

The linked cases of William Huggins and John Mansfield, described in their jointly published *Last Words*, represent variations on the same theme of social and economic displacement in the wake of war. After Huggins had served for several months in the army and acquired such vices as gaming and drinking, he returned to farming, the occupation to which he had been bred, in his hometown of Fishkill, New York. Finding that civilian work did not agree with him, he reenlisted for another term of six months. After being discharged from that second stint of military service, he once more returned to his parents, probably resuming agricultural employment. But he again became restless at home and moved to Stockbridge, Massachusetts, where he went into the "farming business," squandering his money as quickly as he earned it. At that time he met and became "very intimate" with one John Mansfield.[60]

Huggins's new friend was a young mariner from Maine who had been stripped of all his money and property, down to the buckles on his shoes, when his vessel was seized by a British man-of-war in September 1781. Mansfield was then held on a prison ship in Halifax harbor until May 1782, when he managed to escape. After much hardship and danger, he finally made his way to Beverly, Massachusetts. From there, unwilling to return to his friends in an impoverished state, Mansfield decided to "go into the country, and endeavour to mend . . . [his] fortune," probably through agricultural labor. "I sat out with a design to go to work," Mansfield later explained, "but after trying this method for a small time, I found that I could not get as much for my labour as those who were used to such work; and consequently could not clothe myself as I then wished."[61]

Mansfield eventually "stroled into the country as far as *Stockbridge*," where he befriended William Huggins. "We found each others circumstances to be somewhat similar; and after some consultation, we agreed to go to *Salem* together, and look out for a vessel and take a voyage to sea," Mansfield recalled. "In order to fit ourselves out with clothing and other necessaries, and to furnish us with money to purchase some things to carry with us to trade with, as a venture, we came to the fatal determination . . . to rob and steal from others what we thought would be sufficient for our purpose." The two

Execution broadside on the case of Huggins and Mansfield, combining last speeches and dying verses, published in 1783 by Isaiah Thomas of Worcester, Massachusetts, the most prominent printer of the early republic. *Courtesy, American Antiquarian Society.*

men were soon apprehended and convicted for a burglary in the town of Harvard, Massachusetts, in October 1782 and were executed the following June at Worcester.[62]

The experiences of Lightly, Grout, Huggins, and Mansfield suggest what may be a far broader pattern in the criminal careers of Massachusetts thieves. Another hint of that pattern may lie in the particular years in which the property criminals in the literary sample were put to death. Twenty-three of the twenty-four executed malefactors were hanged during the years 1732–38, 1764–74, or 1783–99. Put another way, only one of the offenders was hanged during the wartime years of 1739–48 (War of Jenkins's Ear; King George's War), 1754–63 (French and Indian War), or 1775–82 (American Revolution). The sole apparent exception was William Welch, executed in April 1754; however, the crime for which he was hanged was actually committed during the peacetime year of 1753.[63]

The pattern is not unique to New England. Contemporary observers and recent historians alike have noted that British property crime rates from the sixteenth through nineteenth centuries seemed to decline with the outbreak of war and to rise with the arrival of peace. That cycle has generally been ascribed to the numerical impact of military enlistments (or conscription) and subsequent demobilization on the pool of young men most likely to engage in criminal activities. Wars tended to remove many potential offenders from civilian society into the armed forces, while the onset of peace resulted in a returning flood of demobilized, often brutalized, commonly jobless, and potentially criminal soldiers and sailors who could not easily be reintegrated into a peacetime economy. It also seems probable that many young men, particularly those at the economic margin, who had not themselves engaged in military service, or been directly displaced by the war, would have been adversely affected by the sudden expansion of the labor pool caused by returning veterans.[64]

Although only a few of the twenty-five thieves in the published accounts depicted wartime displacement or related hardships as causes of criminality, and although it should be emphasized again that those offenders are not offered as a strictly representative sample of all property criminals in Massachusetts, the striking absence among them of malefactors executed during wartime years certainly suggests that the British pattern may have been replicated to some degree in eighteenth-century New England. If so, social displacement and economic hardship must indeed have played a contributory role in turning at least some of the men under study here to criminal pursuits.[65]

Wicked relatives, cruel masters, unruly childhoods, bad companions, military corruption, wartime displacement, and economic hardship; those were the causes cited by condemned thieves for their turns to crime. Many also invoked the old assumption that lesser sins led on to greater offenses, bemoaning such misdeeds as cursing, drinking, Sabbath-breaking, and disobedience to parents.[66] Several similarly described a "progress of vice" within the realm of property crime, implying that early petty thefts of items like pins, eggs, and apples led to more serious misconduct.[67] But in contrast to several generations of orthodox ministers, it is striking how rarely the criminals invoked traditional religious explanations like natural depravity and divine abandonment. There were a few exceptions. Matthew Cushing warned his readers that if they were disobedient to their parents God would "leave them" to fall into many other sins. Nearly forty years later, Levi Ames similarly attributed his downfall to God's "anger" over his filial disobedience and claimed to have been corrupted "by the temptations of the devil."[68] But most of the thieves of eighteenth-century New England, like a growing number of ministers of the same period, already lived in a world of secular explanations.

The Pattern of Crime

After providing basic information concerning birth, parentage, and early lives, most last speeches went on to provide detailed catalogues of criminal careers. A few of the criminals may have been full-time professionals, subsisting entirely on their illicit gains over extended periods of time while performing no honest labor.[69] Most, however, although habitual offenders, also sometimes engaged in noncriminal occupations. The thieves in the literary sample apparently included a shipwright, a housewright, and a bricklayer, along with numerous servants, mariners, and laborers.[70] Such men either committed thefts during periods of lawful employment as a supplement to honest wages or went on temporary sprees of criminality during intervals between legitimate labor. Significantly, most did not describe their capital property offenses as isolated aberrations in their conduct; only two of the condemned thieves portrayed themselves as complete novices in crime.[71]

Whether they were full-time, part-time, or sporadic offenders, the thieves of eighteenth-century Massachusetts stole remarkably similar types of goods in most cases, usually items from one or more of the following categories: money, food, fabrics, finished clothing and accessories, miscellaneous household goods, silverware, and occasionally horses or other livestock. Such goods predominated in larcenies, burglaries, and even robberies, regardless of the size of the haul. The largest thefts, generally burglaries from the shops or warehouses of merchants (although occasionally from the homes of wealthy individuals), could yield loot worth from twenty to two hundred pounds or more. Those crimes sometimes involved a significant amount of advance planning, including prior information on the presence of valuables at a certain location and careful reconnoitering of the scene of the prospective crime.[72] Such high-yield thefts occurred throughout the eighteenth century.[73]

The details of a single provincial case suggest the range and quantity of goods that might be taken in a large commercial heist. In September 1768 William Linsey broke into the shop of Thomas Legatt of Leominster, Massachusetts, and made off with property valued at sixty-six pounds, eight shillings, and ten pence. The specific items stolen were enumerated in the records of the Superior Court of Judicature: a wide variety of fabrics, variously described as linen, chints, taffeta, tammy, calamanco, holland, lawn, serge, buckram, broadcloth, and woolen cloth; such clothing and accessories as handkerchiefs, hats, gloves, hose, and buttons; such food items as cakes, biscuits, raisins, chocolate, nutmeg, and cinnamon; and such miscellaneous household goods as pins, fishing lines, razors, pen knives, ink pots, two spelling books, two primers, two psalm books, one Bible, and more.[74]

While burglaries and thefts thus occasionally involved valuable quantities of goods, most of the property crimes committed by the twenty-five thieves described in the popular literature seem to have yielded much more modest returns. Many thefts from private homes and yards netted goods worth less than twenty pounds, often much less. For example, about two years after looting a shop of goods worth more than sixty-six pounds, William Linsey burglarized a house in Lunenburg, Massachusetts, with much less lucrative results. On the night of September 8, 1770, Linsey broke into the dwelling of Joseph Bellows and stole one beaver hat, one pair of leather breeches, one striped linen shirt, one cotton and linen shirt, one pair of men's shoes, one pair of metal shoe buckles, one pair of garters, one pair of leather spatterdashes, one pair of knee buckles, thirty pounds of pork, ten pounds of beef, and one pair of yarn stockings, to a total listed value of only three pounds, six shillings, and six pence.[75]

Most of the fabrics, clothes, and other household items stolen in large and moderate-sized burglaries and thefts were undoubtedly intended for eventual sale.[76] Yet in many cases, especially those involving relatively small thefts, it is difficult to distinguish items taken for the immediate personal use of the thieves themselves from those intended to be sold. One quantitative study has suggested that thefts for subsistence, committed by unskilled workers just struggling to survive, may have represented an increasing proportion of Massachusetts property crimes during the post-Revolutionary period.[77] In any case, the phenomenon was most apparent in the sprees of opportunistic, often petty theft committed by transient offenders, a pattern frequently depicted in the published narratives. For example, the last speech of "Arthur, a Negro Man," published in 1768, described a string of minor thefts committed by himself, Isaac Frasier, and another companion after their joint escape from the Worcester Jail:

> We then set off for *Boston*. At *Shrewsbury*, we stole a Goose from Mr. *Samuel Jennison*, and from the Widow *Kingsley*, in the same Place, we stole a Kettle, in which we boiled the Goose, in *Westborough* Woods. At *Marlborough*, we broke into a Distill-House, from whence we stole some Cyder Brandy. In the same Town we broke into a Shoe-maker's Shop, and took each of us a pair of Shoes. We likewise broke into Mr. *Ciperon Howe's* House, in the same Place, from whence we stole some Bread, Meat and Rum. At *Sudbury*, we stole each of us a Shirt, and one pair of Stockings.[78]

And so forth. Most of those property crimes seem to have been opportunistic thefts designed to meet the immediate needs of the fleeing felons for food, drink, and clothing.

Henry Tufts also engaged in a long series of petty thefts for subsistence, both in the vicinity of his residence in New Hampshire and on long rambles through other parts of the country. When he was in need of shoes, Tufts sought out a shoemaker's shop and stole a pair or two; when he was hungry, he broke into a milk-house and took "a profusion of butter, cheese, bread and cold meat." Johnson Green's *Life and Confession* (1786) described a similar string of break-ins, along with thefts through open windows or out of wash-tubs, most often involving food, clothing, and money. During the single year of 1784, Green committed at least a dozen such crimes in southern Massachu-setts and Rhode Island, making off with shirts, gowns, stockings, and sheets, along with quantities of pork, beef, and mutton. By his own account, Green disposed of such goods in various ways: "Some of the things I have stolen I have used myself—some of them I have sold—some have been taken from me—some I have hid where I could not find them again—and others I have given to lewd women, who induced me to steal for their maintenance."[79]

Although it may sometimes be possible to distinguish between relatively large-scale larcenies for profit and smaller petty thefts for subsistence, the significance of that distinction ought not to be exaggerated. Several of the criminals described in the published accounts committed both types of of-fenses; it seems probable that particular targets, yields, and dispositions were often a function of opportunity and chance rather than careful forethought or planning. Similarly, the criminals in the literary sample do not seem to have drawn a sharp line between simple larceny and burglary; most committed both types of offense. Choosing between the two modes apparently was often more a matter of circumstance than of settled policy. In contrast, a fairly sharp distinction may be drawn between the thieves/burglars and a third category of property criminals: robbers.

Very few of the property crimes under study here were robberies, that is, thefts from individuals, generally on public thoroughfares, involving the threat or use of violent force. Among the twenty-five criminals described in the literary sample, only Richard Barrick, John Sullivan, and Rachel Wall were executed for robbery. Barrick and Sullivan were condemned in October 1784 for assaulting Cyrus Baldwin on the highway at Winter Hill, in Charles-town, the previous July, robbing him of a watch, a silk handkerchief, a pen-knife, and some silver currency. According to a newspaper report on the incident, Baldwin was severely beaten with a club that cut "his Scalp in several Places." Wall, a habitual offender, was capitally convicted of assaulting Marga-ret Bender on the public highway and robbing her of a bonnet worth seven shillings. Other cases of robbery reported in contemporary newspapers fre-quently involved the brandishing of weapons (such as guns or knives), the actual infliction of physical violence (such as stabbings or beatings), and the theft of money, clothes, and small personal items like watches.[80] While Barrick, Sullivan, and Wall had all been guilty of other larcenies and burglar-ies in the past, very few of the other property criminals treated in the popular literature ever seem to have committed robberies.[81] Robbers, then, were a relatively distinct group of property criminals, often singled out for particularly severe punishment (regardless of yield) on the basis of their resort to physical intimidation and violence.

Although last speeches as a group did not tend to glorify the criminal careers that they documented, a few of the convicts did try to glamorize their more daring or unusual exploits. For example, Arthur playfully described disguising himself as an Indian squaw, outbrawling a cuckolded husband, and quaffing cherry rum stolen from the saddlebags of one of his would-be captors. Similarly, Rachel Wall entertained readers with her account of an attempted jailbreak employing tools hidden in a loaf of bread. However, such picaresque anecdotes, also prominent in Henry Tufts's longer memoirs, were rarely present in most last speeches and were more than counterbalanced by prosaic accounts of criminal poverty, futility, regret. As Johnson Green concluded: "I have lived a hard life, by being obliged to keep in the woods; have suffered much by hunger, nakedness, cold, and the fears of being detected and brought to justice."[82]

The Limits of Social Control

Some last speeches suggest that the judicial system of eighteenth-century Massachusetts operated quite efficiently in detecting and punishing property criminals. For example, the statements of Joseph Lightly, Dirick Grout, William Huggins, and John Mansfield seem to illustrate a system of justice that could rapidly and effectively locate, prosecute, punish, and finally excise criminals from the community. Somewhat similarly, John Sheehan, an Irish immigrant who had served in the American army during the Revolution, and John Bailey, a black mariner from New York City, portrayed themselves as criminal novices who were quickly isolated and disposed of by the court system.[83] Such accounts are certainly consistent with David H. Flaherty's finding that "the system of social control" in provincial Massachusetts "did function effectively for the prevention and prosecution of serious crime."[84]

However, many of the other cases described in the popular literature suggest a far less optimistic assessment of the efficiency of the criminal justice system in provincial and early national Massachusetts. In such cases, property criminals were able to commit numerous larcenies and burglaries over extended periods of time despite the best efforts of judicial authorities. Hugh Henderson, an Irish immigrant, spent a total of nine years in New England; by his own account he "took to *Stealing*" after he had been there only a year and continued the practice thereafter, except for "two or three Years intermission." William Welch, another native of Ireland, seems to have frequently engaged in criminal activities over a period of at least three or four years. "My Crimes are heinous and numberless," he confessed in his *Last Speech*. "Thus I lived in a continued Course of Stealing, picking Pockets, Drinking and Whoring till I have brought myself to the Gallows."[85]

Native-born criminals sometimes proved just as persistent. The criminal career of Isaac Frasier, originally from North Kingston, Rhode Island, spanned a period of about eight years and was particularly active over the last three. The *Brief Account* of his life specifically recorded nearly fifty acts of theft, many involving breaking and entering—and the list was by no means complete. "I acknowledge myself to have been guilty of almost an innumerable number of other thefts," Frasier explained, "but have forgot the order of time in which they were committed." For example, his own account did not specify a single one of the ten thefts described by Arthur, his black cohort, as having been committed with Frasier following their joint escape from the Worcester jail in December 1766.[86] The last speech of William Linsey, born in Palmer, Massachusetts, listed more than twenty acts of fraud or theft committed during a criminal career that spanned five or six years. "Having so often escaped with impunity, for my wretched crimes," he recalled, "I was under no awe or restraint, neither fearing God nor regarding man, resolutely bent upon working wickedness." Johnson Green, a native of Bridgewater, Massachusetts, committed thefts over a period of more than five years but was especially active during the years 1783 through 1786. His last speech listed more than sixty thefts or attempted thefts, many involving break-ins, over the course of his criminal career.[87]

The *Confession* of Thomas Mount, published in pamphlet form, specified no fewer than ninety-five acts of theft attempted by the New Jersey native, beginning during the late 1770s and only ending with his final arrest and execution in 1791. The criminal career of Henry Tufts, born in Newmarket, New Hampshire, in 1748, was even longer than Mount's. He began stealing in the early 1760s and did not stop until receiving a sentence of death for burglary—never carried out—in 1794. Tufts confessed that any "endeavour to particularize the numerous tricks and villainies which first and last I have practised would be a vain and useless task . . . a mere catalogue of which must swell a volume." In fact, Tufts's various offenses do "swell a volume"; the *Narrative* of his life and crimes runs to more than 350 pages. Even allowing for occasional picaresque exaggeration, or sheer invention, it constitutes a formidable record of larceny. Finally, Samuel Smith, a native of Middletown, Connecticut, committed his first thefts before the onset of the American Revolution and continued stealing until his last arrest and hanging in December 1799.[88]

The criminal careers just described varied in a number of significant respects. Frasier, Green, and Mount committed enormous numbers of thefts and burglaries. Linsey alternated between such straightforward larcenies and more crafty commercial frauds and forgeries. In addition to simple thefts, shop-breaking, and horse-stealing, Henry Tufts periodically rambled across the countryside practicing medicine, preaching, telling fortunes, playing cards, and even, one winter, exhibiting "a set of pictures, called *shows*, which were viewed by looking through magnifying glasses." Samuel Smith not only committed larcenies and burglaries but also received stolen silver plate and sometimes counterfeited currency. What all of those different careers shared were a habitual tendency to commit property crimes and an apparent ability to evade or endure penal sanctions over periods ranging from at least three to as many as thirty or more years. The long strings of unadjudicated and unpunished offenses described in several of the narratives also suggest the limited value of court records as measures of the incidence of property crime during the eighteenth century.[89]

Remarkably, those felons managed to achieve such extended criminal careers during a period when, in Massachusetts, some types of burglary were punishable by death on the first offense and simple larceny (to the value of three pounds) was a capital crime after only three convictions. Various factors explain their success. First, the careers of several in the literary sample were undoubtedly lengthened by their frequent—at times, almost perpetual—mobility. Isaac Frasier, Johnson Green, Thomas Mount, and Henry Tufts were preeminently men on the move. Frasier's wanderings carried him throughout southern New England to perpetrate crimes or receive punishments in Boston, Worcester, New Haven, Middletown, Providence, and numerous other locations as well. Johnson Green committed crimes in about twenty different communities, mostly in southeastern Massachusetts and Rhode Island, including Attleboro, Barre, Bridgewater, East Bridgewater, Easton, Halifax, Holden, Johnston, Medford, Natick, Norton, Pawtuxet, Providence, Rutland, Seekonk, Sherborn, Shrewsbury, Stoughton, and Walpole. During intervals between his thefts, he was often "obliged to keep in the woods" to avoid detection.[90]

Thomas Mount's long string of nearly one hundred larcenies stretched up and down the eastern seaboard, all the way from Portsmouth, New Hampshire, in the north to Alexandria, Virginia, in the south. Although many of Henry Tufts's thefts occurred in the vicinity of his longtime home in Lee, New Hampshire, he committed numerous other property offenses while on rambles that took him through Maine, Vermont, Massachusetts, Connecticut, New York, and New Jersey.[91] The frequent movement of those habitual thieves undoubtedly helped them to escape detection and to evade capture even when detected, allowed them to establish themselves repeatedly in new locations, where their reputations for larceny would not have been known, and may have also enabled them to avoid the more serious punishments that sometimes came with multiple convictions, by spreading their crimes over a number of jurisdictions. Such men constituted one segment of a larger transient class of vagrants, vagabonds, or "strolling poor," repeatedly legislated against in Massachusetts over the course of a century and a half.[92]

A second means by which thieves were able to extend their criminal careers was by arranging private settlements of their crimes when they were apprehended.[93] In 1766 the Chief Justice of the Superior Court of Judicature, Thomas Hutchinson, bemoaned the frequency of the offense known as "Theft-bote," whereby "the Person robbed has taken back the Goods stolen, and received a Satisfaction in Order to a Concealment." In fact, private resolutions were repeatedly mentioned in the crime narratives, particularly in Isaac Frasier's account of his criminal activities during the 1760s. In the early part of that decade, while residing in Newtown, Connecticut, Frasier stole "some trifles from Jonathan Booth, was detected, and settled the affair in private." At the same place, he was also accused of taking some money from "one Amos Northrup" but was able to "secrete" the accusation by paying Northrup off. About the same time, he "stole a shirt" from someone in New Milford but "settled the affair without punishment." In 1764 or so, he made off with about twenty pounds worth of goods from a store in Woodstock "but settled the affair with the owner." In July 1765 Frasier broke open and robbed the shop of Trueman Hinman in Woodbury, Connecticut, taking seventy or eighty pounds worth of goods; after being detected, he "settled the affair with the owner without punishment." The notorious thief later stole a hat in Providence and "was taken for it" but again "settled the affair without trial." Finally, in 1768, while already under sentence of death in Connecticut, the fugitive stole some cash and valuables from Beeman's tavern in Shrewsbury, Massachusetts, and after being apprehended on the road between Hatfield and Northampton managed, once again, to settle the "affair . . . without punishment." [94]

Private settlements were occasionally mentioned in the narratives of other thieves as well. In 1768 Arthur recalled a case at Sandwich in which he "stole a Shirt, was detected, and settled the Affair, by paying twenty Shillings." In 1770 William Linsey recounted two instances in which employers arranged "settlements" to shield him from legal action. In 1773 Levi Ames mentioned that he had given the victim of one of his thefts twenty dollars in order to "make up the matter." In 1774 Daniel Wilson described two private arrangements to settle horse thefts, at least one involving monetary compensation. Henry Tufts's lengthy *Narrative* of 1807 told of five or six instances in which he was able to arrange private settlements of his crimes.[95] It is probably significant that all of the examples just cited involve criminals who had been born and raised in New England; private settlements were probably more easily arranged by natives of the region than by foreign immigrants or other strangers.[96]

Another important factor in extending the criminal careers of thieves was the notorious inadequacy of jails in eighteenth-century Massachusetts and surrounding jurisdictions.[97] Escapes from jail were periodically reported in contemporary newspapers.[98] Frequent references to escapes—and attempted escapes—also made their way into court records.[99] Other evidence suggests that the problem of jail security was quite serious. One modern scholar has estimated that 16 percent of all convicts who served time in the prison facility on Castle Island in Boston Harbor between 1785 and 1798 managed to escape.[100] The last speeches and other narratives of condemned thieves in eighteenth-century Massachusetts also suggest that the problem was pervasive. Isaac Frasier's *Brief Account* reported numerous escapes from a variety of jails. Between the years 1760 and 1768 he broke out of facilities in or near Newport, Rhode Island; Goshen, New York; Litchfield, Connecticut; Fairfield, Connecticut (twice); Worcester, Massachusetts (twice); Cambridge, Massachusetts; and finally, while under sentence of death for burglary, New Haven, Connecticut. Frasier also reported several unsuccessful attempts at escape from New England jails; during one such effort, he managed to burn down the jail and court house in Fairfield.[101]

Thomas Mount more than matched the impressive record of Isaac Frasier. He fled twice from military custody in the state of New York, escaped from the prison garrison on Castle-Island in Boston Harbor by swimming three miles on a foggy day, and broke out of jails in Philadelphia, Pennsylvania (twice); Alexandria, Virginia; Newcastle, Delaware; Fairfield, Connecticut; Windham, Connecticut; York, Massachusetts (now Maine); and Portsmouth, New Hampshire. Henry Tufts was hardly less elusive. In addition to breaking out of military custody at West Point, Tufts also escaped from jails in Exeter, New Hampshire (four times!); Newburyport, Massachusetts; Dover, New Hampshire; and Salem, Massachusetts. He also once attempted to escape from the jail at Falmouth (later Portland), Maine, and tried repeatedly to break out of the jail in Ipswich, Massachusetts, but without success.[102]

Several other thieves, including Arthur, Daniel Wilson, Francis Coven, Johnson Green, and Samuel Smith, also reported on one or more successful jailbreaks in their last speeches. In August 1794, shortly before his incarceration on Castle Island following a conviction for breaking and entering and larceny, a writ of habeas corpus had been issued to transfer Samuel Smith from custody in Middlesex County to the jail in Boston. On the writ Attorney General James Sullivan scrawled a brief note that may serve as an apt summary of a century of frustration for legal authorities in Massachusetts and many surrounding jurisdictions. "The Sheriff of Middlesex will have Smith in Boston on Thursday if possible," Sullivan tersely noted; "bets run high that he will escape." Sure enough, although Smith was successfully transported from Concord to Boston, the authorities proved unable to hold him for the duration of his lengthy prison term; during the winter of 1796–97, Smith successfully absconded from Castle Island by crossing a frozen Boston Harbor over the ice.[103]

In addition to criminal mobility, private settlements, and inadequate jails, a final set of factors prolonging criminal careers in provincial and early national Massachusetts related to the nature of contemporary penal sanctions. The common noncapital penalties for property offenses during most of the period were public whipping, public shaming (in the pillory or on the gallows), physical mutilation (branding or ear-cropping), fines and court costs, and (in lieu of monetary payments) servitude. Unfortunately, there was little to stop a thief who had just been whipped, shamed, mutilated, or fined from returning forthwith to a life of crime. For example, after Thomas Mount once received one hundred lashes for a theft and twenty-five more for "giving the court saucy answers," his attitude was anything but contrite. "No sooner was this account settled," he recalled, "but I proceeded in my old way, and stole three large silver spoons." Mount's response was apparently a common one.

"Our thieves after whipping, and a short imprisonment, are set at liberty," a contemporary commentator from a neighboring state explained; "the punishment they have received has destroyed the fear of shame, and produced a desire of revenge, which serves to stimulate their vicious inclination; they improve the next opportunity to repeat the crime, and by practice make themselves masters of the trade."[104]

While servitude, a sanction regularly imposed on convicted thieves in lieu of fines and court costs, theoretically imposed an extreme sort of social control over condemned criminals, the practice was flawed in several respects. When a victim (who was entitled to the convict's labor) was reluctant to employ the felon himself, it sometimes proved impossible to find anyone else willing to purchase the convicted thief as a servant. In his memoirs Henry Tufts recalled one such instance in which he and an accomplice had to be released because, as he playfully put it, "no man in his senses would purchase . . . a brace of condemned malefactors." His case was by no means unique. In 1784 an exasperated correspondent of the *Massachusetts Centinel* complained that it was as difficult to find purchasers for convicted felons as it was "for a thief to become an honest man."[105] Even when someone could be found to take condemned men into servitude, it seems unlikely that such masters would have been any more effective than local jailers in controlling recalcitrant offenders.[106]

As for the penalty of incarceration, imposed with increasing regularity on property criminals during the last fifteen years of the eighteenth century (following the penal reorganization of 1785), it was, as already suggested, greatly limited in its effectiveness by the extreme insecurity of eighteenth-century jails and prisons, even such new facilities as that on Castle Island.[107] In the final analysis, only the gallows could put a certain end to the career of a thief in eighteenth-century Massachusetts. "No, no, that is impossible," the notorious Mount would reply when admonished to reform. "Tommy Mount must be hung for a thief."[108]

A Fellowship of Thieves

In the lengthy *Narrative* of his life, Henry Tufts repeatedly portrayed himself as a figure acting in opposition to the interests and sentiments of the broader community. Early in the work he explained that he was unable to gain employment from hostile neighbors in the vicinity of Lee, New Hampshire, and even described how a mob of locals tried to dismantle his house. "As the vortex of my rapacity enlarged its circumference, in like ratio did the number of my enemies increase," Tufts commented shortly thereafter; "they now reprobated my unjust practices with greater indignation, and wished nothing more sincerely, than an exemplary punishment." Such sentiments only increased with time; as he later noted: "Many were officially anxious that I should be caught and punished, regarding me as a pest to society, and my nefarious misdeeds as altogether insufferable." Indeed, by "robbing friends and foes indiscriminately," Tufts and his associates established themselves as "the scourges of the community."[109]

Yet Tufts and the other thieves of eighteenth-century Massachusetts were not all isolated deviants, each skulking alone in an entirely hostile sea of law-abiding respectability. Rather, at least some of the thieves were part of an alternative fellowship that existed uneasily within the broader society. Fragmentary evidence indicates that property criminals of seventeenth-century Massachusetts may have occasionally acted in small groups, and newspaper reports of the eighteenth century suggest an awareness that thieves continued to operate in gangs.[110] The last speeches and other published narratives of property criminals also indicate that thieves frequently acted with one or more accomplices. A few such cases have already been described. Following their joint flight from the Worcester jail, Arthur committed a series of thefts in company with Isaac Frasier and another young escapee; William Huggins and John Mansfield were intimate friends who together committed a capital burglary; Dirick Grout committed a number of property crimes in conjunction with two dishonest associates; Richard Barrick and John Sullivan were joined by a third accomplice in perpetrating the highway robbery for which two of them were hanged.[111]

The pattern is even more dramatically illustrated by the career of Henry Tufts, a rogue who habitually sought out like-minded companions to join him in the commission of property crimes. Tufts periodically introduced those disreputable associates to the readers of his lengthy *Narrative*. First there was James Dennis, an Irishman, of whom Tufts claimed: "In the formation of our minds there was something congenial, I believe, which, like loadstone and steel, attracted each other." It was at Dennis's urging and in his company that Tufts burglarized a store in Saco, Maine. Other partners followed. "About this period I met with one James Smith, a Dutchman, whose disposition, I perceived, was analogous to my own," Tufts recounted. "As kindred souls naturally agree, we became intimately associated." Smith and Tufts soon embarked on a partnership in thievery in which "hens, turkies, sheep, and the like" became the frequent "victims" of their "rapacious industry." Sometime later he took up with "a droll, unlucky chap" named John Sanborn, a man of his "own kidney," with whom he also willingly "associated" and engaged in many thefts. It is certainly significant, in terms of the general reliability of the Tufts *Narrative* as a social-historical source, that many traces of the criminal activities of his companions—including one or two of Dennis's offenses specifically mentioned by Tufts—litter the records and files of the Massachusetts Superior (later Supreme) Court.[112]

If the *Narrative* of Henry Tufts is useful in suggesting the sometimes intimate quality of criminal partnerships, the *Confession* of Thomas Mount is helpful in suggesting the sheer quantity of such associations over the course of an extended criminal career. A high proportion of the nearly one hundred property crimes catalogued in Thomas Mount's brief autobiography were committed with the assistance of one or more companions. In all, Mount referred by name to no fewer than twenty-eight accomplices with whom, in small groups of between two and four, he committed numerous thefts and burglaries up and down the Atlantic seaboard. Those accomplices included Jack Millar (or Miller), with whom he was convicted before the Massachusetts Supreme Judicial Court of breaking and entering and larceny in August 1785, and Archibald Taylor of Boston, subsequently convicted and hanged for robbery in 1788.[113]

There is some evidence that, by the second half of the eighteenth century, criminal associations were moving beyond isolated local partnerships to encompass larger areas of operation and networks of cooperation. The pattern has already been well documented for colonial counterfeiters.[114] Although there probably was not the same degree of criminal organization among other types of property offenders, some such development does seem to have taken place.[115] Newspaper reports occasionally suggested the widening scope of activities, and the emerging pattern was strikingly confirmed by the accounts of Henry Tufts and Thomas Mount. Not only did Tufts himself ramble throughout virtually all of the northeastern United States, committing numerous property offenses along the way, he also cooperated with a "connected string" of "confidential friends," an apparent network of criminal associates or accomplices, "reaching from Newyork, to the District of Maine; and from thence through Vermont to [the] Canada line."[116]

Similarly, the Reverend William Smith, editor of Thomas Mount's *Confession* of 1791, claimed that Mount was part of an extensive "gang of plunderers," held together by rules, regulations, and a common criminal dialect, that had "infested the United States ever since the late war." According to Smith, the American network of thieves modeled themselves on an earlier British criminal organization known as the Flash Company. The minister concluded that the group had

> spread themselves all over the continent, from Nova-Scotia to the remotest parts of Georgia—that the principal seaport towns are their places of general rendezvous—and that the number of the society at present, are from about 70 to 80 males and females. They have receivers in the principal towns of each State, who not only receive the stolen goods, but point out shops and houses for them to break into and plunder.[117]

Significantly, Henry Tufts claimed to have become acquainted with a number of the "flash fraternity" while in prison on Castle Island during the 1790s.[118] Although Smith (or his informants) may well have exaggerated the size, reach, and cohesiveness of the American Flash Company, at least some widely flung networks of property criminals likely did operate in post-Revolutionary America.

In addition to their immediate associates, the thieves of eighteenth-century Massachusetts participated in a wider quasi-criminal subculture made up of prostitutes, tavern-keepers, receivers of stolen property, and other secondary accomplices. In 1734 Matthew Cushing confessed that he was "much addicted to lewd Women" and claimed to have found "many" in Boston to suit him. Three years later, Hugh Henderson not only confessed to "*Gaming*" and "*Whoring*" but also suggested that Worcester tavern-keepers cheated on weights and measures, tolerated "Disorders" in their houses, and allowed patrons to drink to excess. In 1754 William Welch's *Last Speech* depicted a similarly disreputable urban milieu. The condemned man referred to a safe-house where he had been secreted as a runaway servant and suggested that Boston contained many such havens for "Rogues and Run-aways." Welch complained as well of one particularly "abominable" brothel-keeper who received stolen goods, and he emphasized the role of prostitutes in corrupting him and encouraging him to steal. "I frequented idle Houses, and found many in *Boston*, where were idle Women to decoy the Simple, and gratify the lustful," he explained. "And thus I continued in Stealing and picking Pockets, and spending all on Whores."[119]

Thieves of the late eighteenth century also described a social environment populated by prostitutes, receivers, and other disreputable associates. Johnson Green confessed that he had given many of the proceeds of his crimes to "lewd women, who induced [him] . . . to steal for their maintenance." Henry Tufts described secondary accomplices who provided information about prospective targets and assisted him in the aftermath of his crimes. Thomas Mount provided by far the most lurid picture of underworld camaraderie, recalling how "a company of thieves, with their whores" would often meet after a burglary—"full of plunder"—and engage in "scenes of cursing, singing, dancing, swearing, roaring, lewdness, drunkenness, and every possible sort of brutish behaviour." Mount particularly complained of the receivers, or "fences," as they were called in the flash language. According to him, they not only regularly underpaid and even cheated the thieves but also combined with prostitutes to further exploit them. "These receivers being in league with our whores," Mount explained, "make them very extravagant in their demands upon us, who, after treating them with the best of our spoils, if we do not promise quickly to get them more, threaten to inform against us."[120]

Although a number of offenders may have been isolated deviants, many of the property criminals of eighteenth-century Massachusetts were participants in a loosely knit fellowship of thieves, principals in a quasi-criminal subculture that at once served and exploited them. While some seem to have been driven to crime by bad upbringings, social displacement, and economic hardship, others apparently succumbed to peer pressure and personal temptation. Their deviance thus stemmed both from purely personal goals and frustrations and from such broader social problems as the growth of urban poverty in Boston and the expansion of transiency throughout eighteenth-century New England. Their illicit careers also reflected patterns of property crime prevalent throughout early modern Europe and North America.[121]

Most of the thieves described in the popular literature were not true professionals but marginal, often rootless young men who alternated erratically between honest labor and criminal activity, rarely achieving much success in either sphere. Yet given the weaknesses of existing social controls, they were sometimes able to go on for years, either evading the penal system entirely or simply enduring its clumsy and ineffective noncapital sanctions. Some such thieves may eventually have turned away from larceny to lives of honest labor; for others, as for all but one of those discussed here, the only lasting turn from crime came at the end of a rope. "In one word, a thief or highway-man is a pitiable animal," Thomas Mount concluded grimly; "he risks his life every adventure he engages in, and all the recompence he gets for his pains, is the treachery of his whores and comrades, and last of all an ignominious death."[122]

But the last speeches rarely ended so bitterly. Rather, they typically concluded with traditional expressions of warning and penitence, spiritual hope and social reconciliation. Condemned criminals cautioned children and parents, thanked ministers and jailers, and invoked the mercies of God for the sake of Jesus Christ. Even those few who claimed to be innocent tended to sound conciliatory, acknowledging their general wickedness and forgiving the witnesses who had testified against them.[123] Given such closing passages, it is tempting to see the dying felons as penitent sinners, little different from the subjects of earlier conversion narratives.[124] Yet the densely empirical accounts that dominate most of the narratives suggest a rather different reading. By drawing such attention to extended criminal careers, last speeches presented dying thieves less as penitent sinners than as "suppressed insurgents." They were not so much emblems of divine grace as symbols of a harried society's determination to protect lives and property. But, ironically, the same lengthy catalogues of wrongdoing that implicitly justified the executions may have tended to undermine public confidence in the capacity of social authorities to control crime and disorder. By allowing habitual offenders to document their misspent lives, such accounts exposed the emergence of a criminal subculture whose very existence implicitly mocked traditional communal ideals.

7

Injured Innocents:
Ideological Insurgency in Crime Literature of the Early Republic

Must Thieves who take men's goods away
Be put to death? While fierce blood hounds,
Who do their fellow creatures slay,
Are sav'd from death? This cruel sounds. . . .
But, ah! Alas it seems to me,
That Murder now is passed by
While Priests and Rulers all agree
That this poor Criminal must die.

Although they described a criminal subculture that increasingly threatened the lives and property of law-abiding citizens, relatively few of the literary responses to crime in late eighteenth-century New England directly challenged the ideological assumptions of ministers and magistrates. There were, however, several exceptions, all dealing with alleged miscarriages of justice. One of the first was a poem entitled *Theft and Murder!* evoked by the execution of Levi Ames for burglary in 1773.[1] The anonymous author, quoted above, contrasted the judicial death of Ames with the lenient treatment accorded to the British soldiers involved in the Boston Massacre just a few years earlier. The fact that "Priests" and "Rulers" were together linked to the execution suggested a critique of both religious and secular establishments.

While there is no evidence the defiant poem had any great popular impact, a number of subsequent works that posed explicit challenges to authority were among the most widely read and frequently reprinted crime publications of the early republic. Although one of the antiauthoritarian narratives was an imported piece of fiction, the others dealt with actual American cases. And while only one was originally published in New England, all were reprinted and sold in that region. Despite their shared critical perspective, the works drew on very different sources of inspiration.[2] In fact, they reflected at least three distinct ideological insurgencies that were transforming early national society: a sentimental insurgency most often expressed in contemporary fiction; an evangelical insurgency that spawned several unorthodox denominations; and a philosophical insurgency based on Enlightenment ideology. In the aftermath of a political revolution with profound social implications, a number of extremely popular crime narratives broke away from the literature's earlier service of entrenched authority to challenge or subvert established assumptions concerning social hierarchy, public justice, and orthodox religion.

Ambrose Gwinett: A Victim of Circumstance

One of the first of the popular antiauthoritarian narratives to appear in New England was *The Life and Adventures of Ambrose Gwinett*, a fictional account first published in London. The anonymous work was almost certainly written by Isaac Bickerstaffe, an Irish playwright who delighted English audiences of the late 1760s with a string of popular comedies and comic operas.[3] His fanciful crime narrative first appeared in 1768 in an obscure literary magazine. The story was promptly reprinted in English and French periodicals and was repeatedly reissued as a pamphlet. The second separate edition appeared in London in 1770, a fourth edition a year or so later, a sixth in about 1780, and a number of others during the following decades. So durable was the narrative that it was even included in a series of toybooks published in Glasgow as late as 1850.[4]

The pamphlet's success in Great Britain was matched by its popular reception in the northeastern United States, where it had appeared in more than a dozen editions by 1836. The first reprint appeared in Boston, Massachusetts, in 1782, followed by printings in Philadelphia, Pennsylvania (1784, two editions, one in German); Norwich, Connecticut (1784); Hudson, New York (1786); New London, Connecticut (1795); Fairhaven, Vermont (1799?); Boston, Massachusetts (1800); Cooperstown, New York (1805); Brattleborough, Vermont (1807); Otsego, New York (1812); Providence, Rhode Island (1815); and New York City (1836). An unidentified American printer also issued an edition for "Travelling Booksellers" in 1798, probably in New England or upstate New York.[5]

Although Bickerstaffe's narrative was almost certainly pure fiction, it was presented to early national readers as a factual biography. Ambrose Gwinett (the story went) had been born to reputable parents in the city of Canterbury, where, at the age of sixteen, he was apprenticed to a local attorney. Nearly five years later, in the autumn of 1709, Gwinett set out to visit his sister and her husband in another town. After a day of strenuous walking, the young man sought lodging in a crowded public house. There he was forced to share a room already occupied by a middle-aged man who sat in his nightgown counting some money. That night Gwinett was troubled by hemorrhoids and sought relief in a downstairs privy; by the time he returned to the room, his bedfellow had vanished. He continued on his way early the next morning and soon arrived at the home of his relatives, where he was confronted by three men who accused him of having robbed and murdered his roommate at the public house. After an elaborate circumstantial case had been made against him, Gwinett was imprisoned, tried, convicted, and condemned to be hanged and

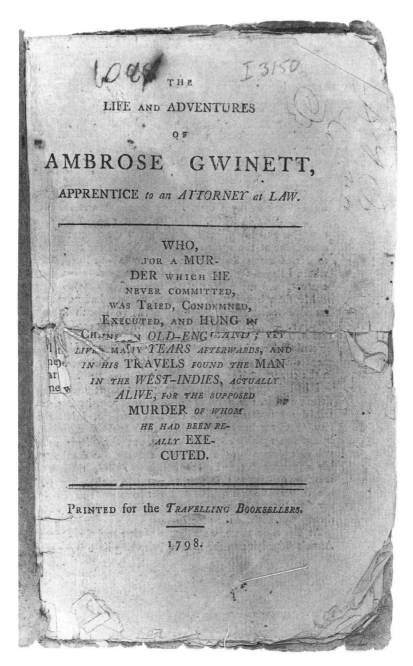

THE

LIFE AND ADVENTURES

OF

AMBROSE GWINETT,

APPRENTICE *to an* ATTORNEY *at* LAW.

WHO,
FOR A MUR-
DER WHICH HE
NEVER COMMITTED,
WAS TRIED, CONDEMNED,
EXECUTED, AND HUNG IN
CHAINS IN *OLD-ENGLAND*; YET
LIVED MANY *YEARS AFTERWARDS,* AND
IN HIS TRAVELS *FOUND THE* MAN
IN THE *WEST-INDIES, ACTUALLY*
ALIVE, FOR THE SUPPOSED
MURDER OF *WHOM*
HE HAD BEEN RE-
ALLY EXE-
CUTED.

PRINTED for the *TRAVELLING BOOKSELLERS.*

1798.

Worn and tattered chapbook edition of *Ambrose Gwinett,* probably published somewhere in the northeastern United States.

145

gibbeted, all despite his persistent claims of innocence. On execution day he miraculously survived his punishment and, with the help of his brother, fled the country on board a privateer.[6]

The remainder of the narrative recounted Gwinett's harrowing adventures abroad. The privateer on which he sailed was captured off the coast of Florida by a Spanish squadron; he was confined for three years at a prison in Cuba, after which he served as a deputy to the governor there; while in Havana, he was astonished to meet the man for whose alleged murder he had been hanged and gibbeted; he arranged to return to England with his supposed victim but mistakenly boarded a pirate vessel and was forced to join the crew; after spending nearly four years with the pirates, he was thrown overboard and left to die; he was eventually rescued by a Spanish vessel and taken to Cadiz for trial, where he was sentenced to the galleys for life; after serving on board a Spanish prison ship for several years, he lost one of his legs and was taken prisoner when the vessel engaged three Algerian rovers in a battle; after a long period of servitude in Algiers, he was eventually released; finally, in 1730, the unfortunate man returned to England, where he was forced to support himself by begging.[7]

The narrative of Ambrose Gwinett combined the engaging motifs of crime, combat, and captivity, all familiar themes in Anglo-American popular literature of the late eighteenth century. However, in a number of editions published in the northeastern United States, the narrative was transformed into something more than a trivial adventure story. In the versions published at Philadelphia and Norwich in 1784, the printers added a note to their title pages that deftly transformed the work into a polemic against an established legal practice. The squib appended to each subtitle described the story as "DEMONSTRATIVELY proving, that Condemnations upon circumstantial Evidence are injurious to INNOCENCE, incompatible with JUSTICE, and therefore ought always to be discountenanced, especially in Cases of LIFE and DEATH."[8] The same note was subsequently included in editions appearing at Hudson (1786), New London (1795), Boston (1800), and Providence (1815).[9] The version produced in Boston even featured a brief prefatory note recommending the work for "the perusal of both Judges and Juries in the United States."[10] Such glosses suggested that Bickerstaffe's fanciful adventure story had serious implications for the administration of justice in the early republic.

Direct evidence indicates that the narrative was actually viewed in that light by at least one American lawyer. In the spring of 1806, Francis Blake, a young veteran of the Worcester bar, was engaged in defending two Irish immigrants accused—on the basis of purely circumstantial evidence—of having robbed and murdered a young man traveling along a turnpike in Wilbraham, a small town in western Massachusetts. Although afflicted with a bad cold, a weak case, and a complete lack of prior experience in capital trials, Blake offered some unusually cogent closing arguments for the defense.[11] After reviewing the evidence at hand and citing a number of standard legal precedents showing the inadequacy of circumstantial evidence in capital cases, Blake referred to a far less conventional authority. The attorney insisted that the unusual source would provide a "striking illustration" of his argument, despite the fact that it was taken from "a two-penny pamphlet instead of a folio, . . . from the pack of the pedlar, and not from the library of the lawyer." Although admittedly unsure as to whether its contents were "true or fabulous," he explained that the little book in question had become familiar to him early in life and had "produced an impression" that could "not be easily effaced." The unlikely story that Blake then recounted had been carefully abstracted from *The Life and Adventures of Ambrose Gwinett*.[12]

Elizabeth Wilson: A Sentimental Insurgent

About four years after the first American appearance of Isaac Bickerstaffe's fanciful narrative, another crime pamphlet received similarly wide distribution. Unlike the story of Ambrose Gwinett, this new account, *A Faithful Narrative of Elizabeth Wilson*, was based on an actual American case. It was evoked by the execution in January 1786 of an unmarried woman from Chester County, Pennsylvania, for the murder of her own infant twins, the last of five illegitimate offspring.[13] Surviving copies were published that year in Carlisle, Pennsylvania; Philadelphia, Pennsylvania; Hudson, New York; and New Haven, Connecticut. Contemporary newspaper advertisements suggest that copies of the work were sold (if not printed) at Hartford and Middletown, Connecticut. A broadside poem on the case was issued in Boston, probably followed by a repackaged version of the prose narrative. Another edition may have also appeared around the same time in New York City.[14] In order to understand why the case aroused such widespread interest, one need only look at the pamphlet itself.

The centerpiece of the narrative was an autobiographical confession delivered by Wilson to two Baptist ministers on the evening of December 6, 1785, the night before her scheduled execution. Its description of her sexual misconduct suggested two distinct modes of discourse, one pious, the other sentimental. She began with a traditional religious explanation of her sexual fall: "From sixteen to twenty-one years of age, I had a religious concern but through the subtilty of Satan and corruption of nature was led away to the soul-destroying sin of fornication, which I believe to be my predominant evil."[15] Invocations of Satan, sin, evil, and natural corruption denoted the confession of a pious penitent. Yet when Wilson went on to describe her sexual relationship with Joseph Deshong, the father of the murdered twins, she did so in terms suggestive of contemporary sentimental fiction: "In the beginning of the year 1784, he insinuated himself into my company, under pretence of courtship, declaring himself a single man, and by repeated promises of marriage deceived and persuaded me to consent to his unlawful embraces."[16] Promises, pretense, insinuation, deception, and persuasion was the typical language of a literary seduction. Wilson's narrative deftly straddled the divide between spiritual and sentimental biography.

Having laid claim to the dual status of pious penitent and sentimental victim, Wilson proceeded to shift the burden of guilt from herself to her faithless lover. As she told it, Joseph Deshong had promised to "bear all the expenses" resulting from her pregnancy. However, as the time for delivery drew near, it became apparent that he had no intention of honoring that commitment. When she sought out Deshong after the twins were born and threatened to sue him for support, he once more feigned sympathy and promised help. But after he had lured her into some woods outside of Chester with the babies, he again reneged. "I have no money for you," he roughly told her, "nor your bastards neither." When she refused his demand that she kill the babies herself, he promptly put a pistol to her breast and trampled the "dear infants" to death before her eyes. "My sins are more in number than the hairs of my head," Wilson acknowledged, "but my Righteous Judge doth know my innocence in respect of that cruel murder."[17]

The condemned murderess's penitent demeanor and persistent claims of innocence apparently carried some weight with the state authorities, who granted Wilson a reprieve of nearly a month. During her last weeks on earth she continued to play the role of pious penitent as if her life depended on it. When ministers visited her, she appeared "deeply affected"; when other prisoners suggested that her religious professions might not be sincere, she became "greatly distressed." On the morning of her execution, the convict's demeanor was "serious, solemn, and devout." Meanwhile, her brother had gone off to Philadelphia in pursuit of another reprieve. He managed to obtain a stay of execution but supposedly arrived at the gallows in Chester just twenty-three minutes too late. His sister had already been hanged. "But here we must drop a tear!" the narrator declared. "What heart so hard, as not to melt at human woe!" Although she had been guilty of concealing the murder of her twin infants, the sympathetic editor concluded, Wilson had probably been "innocent . . . of the crime for which she suffered."[18]

Like a number of the most popular sentimental novels of the early republic, the narrative of Elizabeth Wilson implicitly challenged society's sexual double standard even as it publicized an alleged miscarriage of justice.[19] Given its articulation of increasingly popular cultural themes, it should not be surprising that the narrative was revived, in even more blatantly sentimental form, more than thirty-five years after the death of Elizabeth Wilson. In 1822 a small pamphlet loosely based on her case was issued by John Wilkey, an obscure Boston publisher. The scene of the tragedy had been moved to Dauphin County, Pennsylvania; the name of the condemned woman had been changed to Harriot Wilson; the date of her execution had been altered to 1802; and the narrative had been retitled *The Victim of Seduction!*[20]

Although the new version of her life did not deny that Wilson had killed her infants, it implicitly absolved her of blame, completely shifting the burden of guilt onto her illicit lover. According to the author, sensitive readers would feel nothing but "abhorrence for the seducer, and pity for the unfortunate victim of his arts."[21] The new text even included an explicit diatribe against the sexual double standard.[22] At the same time, Wilkey issued a second pamphlet on the case, consisting largely of pious meditations ostensibly written by the unfortunate woman's brother.[23] The two works were eventually combined and reissued in New York (1838), Philadelphia (1839), and Saint John, New Brunswick (1840).[24] The convergence of her troubled life with the powerful cultural impulses expressed in contemporary fiction had assured that the story of Elizabeth Wilson would long survive her untimely death.

Whiting Sweeting: An Evangelical Insurgent

Five years to the day after the execution of Elizabeth Wilson, a young man was fatally stabbed while assisting in the arrest of an accused thief in Stephentown, New York, just north of Albany and west of the Massachusetts border.[25] His assailant, Whiting Sweeting, another local young man, was convicted of murder during the summer of 1791 and was hanged on August 26 of that year. The case evoked what was probably the most frequently reprinted crime pamphlet in the northeastern United States during the late eighteenth century. The first authorized edition of *The Narrative of Whiting Sweeting* was issued in mid-September 1791 by Silvester Tiffany, a small-town newspaper publisher in Lansingburgh, New York, not far from Stephentown.[26] Even before the appearance of Tiffany's edition, the work was already being pirated by a rival publisher in Albany.[27] The pamphlet was subsequently reprinted in Hartford, Connecticut (1792?); Providence, Rhode Island (1792–94, two editions); Philadelphia, Pennsylvania (1792); Concord, New Hampshire (1793); Exeter, New Hampshire (1793–94, three editions); Dover, New Hampshire (1796); and Windham, Connecticut (1797).[28] Two or three other early editions (without imprints) were probably published in Albany, New York, and copies of the work were advertised in Wilmington, Delaware, in 1792, and in Salem, Massachusetts, in 1795.[29]

The narrative of Whiting Sweeting was a literary pastiche, written almost entirely in the first-person voice, ostensibly by the prisoner himself. It interspersed accounts of the alleged crime and capital trial with various pieces of religious prose and poetry and concluded with a description of Sweeting's behavior in jail by an "intimate acquaintance," William Carter.[30] The pamphlet's exculpatory accounts described the circumstances surrounding Sweeting's alleged crime and capital conviction. It all began when he was falsely accused of stealing an iron kettle. One wintry evening in early January 1791, a group of at least six men, led by a constable, went to Sweeting's house with a warrant for his arrest. The men had brought some rum with them and stopped to drink along the way. Although Sweeting had been warned that a mob was coming for him and tried to escape through the deep snow into the woods, he was quickly spotted by his pursuers, who surrounded him on a large rock

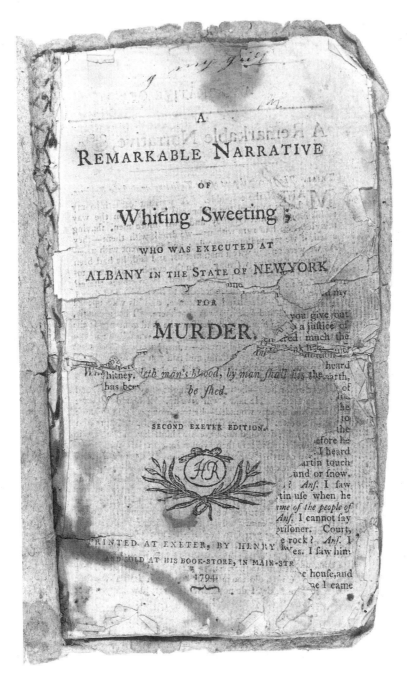

A

REMARKABLE NARRATIVE

OF

Whiting Sweeting;

WHO WAS EXECUTED AT

ALBANY IN THE STATE OF NEW-YORK

FOR

MURDER.

Whoso sheddeth man's blood, by man shall his be shed.

SECOND EXETER EDITION.

PRINTED AT EXETER, BY HENRY RANLET,
AND SOLD AT HIS BOOK-STORE, IN MAIN-STR.

1794.

The second Exeter, New Hampshire, edition of Whiting Sweeting's antiauthoritarian narrative, the most frequently reprinted crime pamphlet of the late eighteenth century. This copy was read to tatters but carefully mended by an early owner.

150

behind his house. Armed with a knife and club, Sweeting threatened to kill the first man who touched him. But when he leaped from the rock and tried to run away, he was tackled by a young man named Darius Quimby. By the time the two men were pulled apart, Quimby had been mortally wounded. One witness at the trial claimed to have seen "the arm of the prisoner move backward and forward as if striking the deceased."[31]

It was unclear from the trial testimony whether Sweeting had any way of knowing that the mob of men who chased him were trying to make a lawful arrest. By his own account, the group "yelled and hallowed beyond description," acting "more like drunken savages than like christians." Although the prosecutor's charge of murder certainly seemed questionable under those circumstances, the defendant's "eminent and learned" counsel played strangely passive roles. After assuring Sweeting that "they would manage the business" for him, the lawyers decided not to offer closing arguments. When the prisoner himself was called on to address the jury in their place, he was surprised and agitated and failed to raise a number of points in his favor. Still, he did manage to insist that he had known of no warrant, feared for his own safety, and had not intentionally hurt anyone. He also claimed that the "prejudiced" witnesses against him were not telling the whole truth. Despite those assertions, the judge's charge virtually directed the jury to convict Sweeting of murder; when they found the prisoner guilty, the magistrate sentenced him to death. Dishonest witnesses, negligent lawyers, a rattled defendant, and a hostile judge all contributed to the alleged miscarriage of justice depicted in the popular pamphlet.[32]

Yet the narrative of Whiting Sweeting was intended not only to expose worldly injustice but also to correct theological error. In the last section of the work, William Carter described Sweeting's spiritual transformation in jail in terms suggestive of many earlier criminal conversion narratives. Although he seemed "exceedingly ignorant" in religious matters when first arrested, Sweeting proved to be an "earnest seeker" of salvation, constantly praying, meditating, reading, and studying Scripture in jail. After only a few weeks behind bars, Sweeting experienced an "extraordinary change," a spiritual and intellectual conversion that left him "calm, composed, pleasant, affable." Soon Sweeting was able to hold his own in sophisticated religious discussions with visiting ministers. "He made surprising progress in the knowledge of scripture," Carter recalled, "and seemed as if he was able to unfold any mysterious passage in the plainest manner."[33] After his condemnation, the jailhouse theologian took pen in hand and filled his narrative with some very provocative religious ideas. In sharp contrast to the orthodox theological assumptions expressed and exemplified by most earlier criminal converts, the writings of Whiting Sweeting constituted a sweeping assault upon traditional religious beliefs, a point-by-point refutation of some of the fundamental tenets of Calvinism.

The first basic point of orthodox dogma, as expressed in the Canons of Dort (1619) and in countless other Calvinist writings, was "unconditional election." Calvinists believed that even before the creation of the world God had chosen a select group of men and women for salvation (or election) and had consigned the rest of humanity to damnation (or reprobation), all without regard to any foreseen merit on the part of the individuals involved.[34] Although Sweeting acknowledged that God indeed knew in advance who would be damned and who would be saved, he insisted on distinguishing between "knowledge," on the one hand, and "power, or agency," on the other. For Sweeting, election was simply a description of God's foresight of who would believe in Christ and hence be saved, and who would not believe and hence be damned. Thus election was not unconditional and predetermined by God but conditional and contingent on human faith.[35]

The second basic tenet of Calvinism was "limited atonement," according to which Christ died not for all humanity but only for the predetermined elect, to whom (and to whom alone) he conferred the holy Spirit or saving grace.[36] As suggested by his critique of unconditional election, Sweeting rejected the notion that "Christ only died for a certain number, elected from eternity." Rather, he believed that Christ's sacrifice had been for the benefit of all mankind, each of whom received "a portion of his blessed Spirit," a measure "freely given without exception." According to Sweeting's scheme, the only restriction on grace was temporal. Every human being experienced a period of uncertain duration during which the indwelling holy Spirit strived with him for his soul; if a person did not respond to the divine efforts during that "day of grace," God would withdraw his Spirit, leaving the person damned for all eternity.[37]

The third basic tenet of Calvinism was "total depravity." According to the orthodox view, all men and women were morally corrupted by Adam's original fall. Yet Calvinist theologians tended to qualify that inherited inclination toward wickedness. The Canons of Dort, for example, described a residual "light of nature" (or natural conscience) that allowed people to know "the difference between good and evil" and to show "some regard for virtue and for good outward behavior."[38] Other early Calvinist thinkers, such as the great English Puritan divine William Perkins, posited the existence of a non-redemptive common grace, distinct from special or saving grace, given by God to all men and women to inhibit them from acting out their most wicked inclinations.[39] However, Whiting Sweeting explicitly denied the existence of "natural conscience" and rejected the distinction between common and saving grace. In Sweeting's view, *all* natural impulses were wicked and *all* divine grace offered salvation. The one and only counterbalance to man's wicked impulses was not natural but spiritual, not merely inhibitive but potentially redemptive: a "special saving grace . . . given all, without exception." In short, Sweeting rejected the Calvinist rationalizations of natural conscience and common grace in favor of an absolute dualism opposing natural depravity and saving grace.[40]

The fourth fundamental doctrine of Calvinism was "irresistible grace." Orthodox theologians believed that the gift of salvation bestowed by God on the elect was not a conditional offer but an irresistible imposition that men and women had no power to refuse or reject.[41] In contrast, Sweeting believed that the essence of spiritual grace was its voluntary nature. "The Spirit and the Bride say come; Behold I stand at the door and knock," he explained metaphorically. "It belongs to us to open the door, and receive the King of Glory in; if we will not open, he will not force; if we bar, he will never break." Not only were men and women theoretically capable of resisting the Holy Spirit, but many in fact did so: "They who are called reprobate, are not made so by an eternal decree . . . but having resisted till their day of grace is past, become such by their own stubbornness and wilfulness." Against the Calvinist assumption that saving grace was irresistible, Sweeting posited the view that God's gift of the Holy Spirit was essentially voluntary and conditional, the object of free human choice.[42]

The fifth and last basic point of Calvinism was "final perseverance of the saints," that is, the assumption that, although those who received God's saving grace might sin, they would never permanently fall from grace or lose their position among the elect.[43] Not surprisingly, given his conditional and voluntaristic conception of grace, Sweeting rejected that view, at least on a theoretical level. He certainly hoped that nobody would ever fall from grace and did not seem to consider it likely; yet he reluctantly concluded that "there can be no impossibility in the supposition, that a soul truly converted may fall back and be condemned." Even after receiving grace, Christians enjoyed no absolute assurance of salvation; they could not depend on past religious experience, however valid, but had always to monitor their current spiritual state. A person's free choice of salvation was not an isolated decision but an ongoing process subject to reversal.[44]

Whiting Sweeting thus rejected many of the fundamental tenets of Calvinist theology. Again and again throughout his narrative, he affirmed the voluntary and conditional nature of God's universal offer of salvation. "I conclude mankind are *free agents*," he wrote, "and have restored to them, by the Redeemer, full power and ability to save or damn themselves; to chuse and obtain life or death, heaven or hell; that they are left to their own free choice."[45] Even the verses accompanying the narrative echoed Sweeting's message of spiritual hope and human volition:

> The Spirit and the Bride, say, come,
> The invitation's strong;
> Oh, fill my heart with fire of love,
> And tarry not too long.[46]
>
> Oh! don't despair of finding rest
> If to the Lord you'd come,
> For there is plenteous pardoning grace,
> And in his house there's room.[47]

It is difficult to determine the source of Whiting Sweeting's unorthodox religious views. By his own account, he had been a scoffer at religion and a believer in universal salvation at the time of his arrest. There is no way to know for certain what spiritual influences might have acted on him in jail. The orthodox ministers who visited him there were certainly not depicted as the sources of his theology but as the foils against whom he defined his own unorthodox views. Rather, the narrative suggested that his new beliefs were the product of his own spiritual illumination and scriptural study. According to William Carter, his intimate acquaintance, Sweeting insisted that he "had not received [his insights] from man, by tradition and education, but from God, by the influence of his holy Spirit."[48] Yet it is hard to believe that a previously ignorant and profane young man could have formulated such a sweeping and sophisticated attack on Calvinism in so short a time, unless he had somehow gained access to a preexisting critique. Although his views actually coincided at many points with doctrinal positions formulated two centuries earlier by the Dutch theologian Arminius and his followers, it seems unlikely that Sweeting would have stumbled across such arcane heretical writings in rural New York.[49] Surely the roots of his theology lay closer to home.

In fact, Stephentown, New York, and the adjacent village of Berlin seem to have been local centers of evangelical activity, small parts of a much larger religious ferment that was transforming the spiritual landscape of New England and upstate New York during the last decades of the eighteenth century.[50] As the older, established religions failed to keep pace with the quickening tempo of geographic expansion and frontier settlement in the aftermath of the Revolution, newer evangelical sects and denominations rushed to fill the gap. Several Baptist churches were established in the neighborhood of Stephentown during the 1780s and 1790s.[51] While some of those congregations adhered to orthodox Calvinist theology, others did not. One of the earliest of those churches was organized in September 1783 as the "Free or Open Communion Baptist Church of Stephentown."[52] Although the founders of that congregation had reportedly migrated from Rhode Island, they embraced theological views nearly identical to those of the Freewill Baptists then spreading throughout northern New England.[53] Significantly, the views expressed in the *Narrative of Whiting Sweeting* coincided in most respects with those of the Freewill Baptists. Both embraced conditional election, universal atonement, resistible grace, and the possibility of backsliding; both recognized that every individual experienced a decisive "day of grace" that might never be renewed; most important, both emphasized that free human choice was the decisive variable in the drama of salvation.[54]

While the precise means of transmission remain unknown, Whiting Sweeting, or whoever was responsible for the theological positions expressed in his narrative, had somehow gained access to many of the free-will doctrines then circulating throughout rural New England, quite possibly through the Open Communion Baptist church in Stephentown. Like the founders of that congregation, Sweeting's own family had migrated to upstate New York from southern New England; maybe some of his relatives belonged to the church.[55] Or perhaps he was proselytized in jail by unrelated members of that congregation. But whatever the derivation of its ideas, Sweeting's narrative was one of the first and most popular literary expressions of anti-Calvinist evangelism issued in the early republic.[56] The compilation thus not only challenged secular authority but also embodied an insurgent religious culture that was shattering the spiritual hegemony of orthodox Calvinism in late eighteenth-century New England.[57] That surviving copies of the *Narrative* are worn nearly to tatters and yet carefully mended by early owners suggests that the subversive message of Sweeting's dense and sophisticated tract was intensively pondered and earnestly embraced by many early national readers.[58]

Stephen Burroughs:
A Philosophical Insurgent

The last edition of Sweeting's pious narrative appeared in Windham, Connecticut, in 1797; that same year, proposals were issued for printing a very different sort of criminal autobiography in Newfield, Connecticut.[59] As it turned out, the first volume of the *Memoirs of Stephen Burroughs* was published the following year, not in Newfield, Connecticut, but in Hanover, New Hampshire, the childhood hometown of its controversial protagonist. In appearance it was a much more impressive volume than Sweeting's ephemeral pamphlet, nearly three hundred pages in length and bound in full leather. A second volume of the *Memoirs*, another two hundred pages long, was published in Boston six years later by Caleb Bingham, an old college friend of the author.[60] The first collected edition of the *Memoirs* appeared in Albany, New York, in 1811, compressed into several hundred pages of tightly packed type.[61] But by then cheaper and more accessible abridged versions of the first volume were already being issued under the title of *Sketch of the Life of the Notorious Stephen Burroughs*. Compact editions of that pocket-sized abridgement of about one hundred pages were published in Hudson, New York (1809); Albany, New York (1810); Otsego, New York (1810); New York City (1811); Greenfield, Massachusetts (1812); Philadelphia, Pennsylvania (1812); Albany, New York (1813); Brookfield, Massachusetts (1814); Wilmington, Delaware (1814); and Hartford, Connecticut (1818).[62] Although no versions of the autobiography, either complete or abridged, seem to have been published during the 1820s, the longer *Memoirs* were revived during the middle decades of the nineteenth century. Substantial editions of a few hundred pages each, typically bound in cloth and including at least portions of the original second volume, appeared in Boston (1832, 1835, 1840), New York City (ca. 1840s, 1851, 1852), Philadelphia (1853), and Amherst, Massachusetts (1858). The complete *Memoirs* were again revived during the twentieth century, with editions appearing in 1924 in both New York and London, featuring an affectionate preface by the poet laureate of New England, Robert Frost. Another edition was issued in 1988, with Frost's preface and a new foreword by Philip Gura.[63]

Today the autobiography of Stephen Burroughs is remembered primarily as an early American example of the picaresque form, its roguish protagonist recalled as a prototype for later generations of literary confidence men.[64] There is much in the *Memoirs* to recommend that view, as suggested by the following summary of its hero's life, drawn primarily from the autobiography but confirmed where possible from outside sources. Stephen Burroughs was born in about 1765, probably in South Killingly, Connecticut, the son of a Presbyterian minister.[65] At about the age of seven, he moved with his family to Hanover, New Hampshire, where his many mischievous pranks earned him a reputation as "the worst boy in town."[66] Following an abortive enlistment in the Continental army at the age of fourteen, young Stephen continued his chronic tricks and petty thefts under the tuition of Joseph Huntington, a respected minister and teacher in Coventry, Connecticut, and throughout his brief attendance at Dartmouth College, back in Hanover, from which he was expelled during his sophomore year in 1782.[67]

After his expulsion from college, Burroughs deftly assumed the mantle of physician and, in January 1783, went to sea as a ship's doctor on a packet to France. After an exciting voyage in which the American vessel fought off the attack of an English privateer, Burroughs toured for a time in France, returned on the same packet, and was briefly imprisoned at Newburyport for allegedly stealing some wine and silk from the ship's cabin. He then returned in a despondent mood to his father's home in Hanover, where he remained unemployed for about a year. In late 1784 and early 1785, Burroughs taught school at Haverhill and Orford, two towns on the Connecticut River north of Hanover. But his employment at Haverhill was abruptly terminated after an intrusive tutor from Dartmouth warned the inhabitants against him. His long-term prospects in New Hampshire were further undermined by his courtship of a married woman and his prosecution for stealing a beehive.[68]

In the spring of 1785, Burroughs borrowed some sermons from his father, assumed his mother's family name of Davis to prevent "disagreeable reports" from preceding him, and set off down the Connecticut River in search of employment as a preacher. Following a successful inaugural performance at Ludlow, Burroughs was hired by a Presbyterian congregation in the town of Pelham, Massachusetts. After preaching there through much of the summer (and providing readers with a hilarious parody of an orthodox sermon), the impostor was forced to flee after being identified by a passing clergyman. In the meantime, Burroughs had himself been hoodwinked in a fraudulent alchemical scheme for transmuting copper into silver and recruited by a friend to assist in a counterfeiting operation. On August 23, 1785, Burroughs was arrested in the town of Springfield, Massachusetts, for attempting to pass two counterfeit coins.[69]

When Burroughs was tried in early October of that year, he was convicted, sentenced to three years' imprisonment, and jailed in Northampton. There he was whipped, chained, and deprived of adequate food, heat, and clothing. Those harsh punishments were partly in retaliation for his own attempts to escape, once by setting fire to the jail. In early 1786 Burroughs was transferred with other convicts to the prison garrison on Castle Island in Boston Harbor. At that new facility, Burroughs again proved to be anything but a model prisoner. He quickly engineered his own escape, along with seven other prisoners, by digging a hole through the chimney with a nail. Once recaptured, he did his best to sabotage the forced labor required of convicts on the island and even organized an unsuccessful insurrection. In late September 1788, Burroughs was released, after more than three years of incarceration.[70]

Upon regaining his freedom, Burroughs initially went to work on his uncle's farm in Charlton, Massachusetts, a flourishing agricultural community in the western part of Worcester County. Soon he began teaching school in that same town. In September 1789 he married Sally Davis, his uncle's daughter. It seemed as though he might finally be settling down. But in October of the following year, he was arrested and accused of attempting to rape two young former students and an older woman. At his trial in April, the embattled schoolteacher was convicted on one count of attempted rape and acquitted on another; on the advice of his lawyers, he pleaded guilty to two other lesser counts of "open gross Lewdness and lascivious behavior." He was sentenced to be whipped, pilloried, imprisoned, and placed on the gallows with a rope around his neck. However, before the entire punishment could be inflicted, Burroughs escaped from the jail in Worcester, reportedly with the assistance of sympathetic locals.[71]

After fleeing Massachusetts, Burroughs went to Long Island, New York, where he again assumed a false identity, going under the name of Stephen Edenson and claiming to have been born in London. He was initially employed as a schoolmaster on Shelter Island, at which time he wrote a series of philosophical essays for the *Long Island Herald* that embroiled him in local controversy. He then gained a more lucrative teaching position in Bridgehampton, Long Island, and managed to retain that position even after his true identity became known. However, he later became involved in a bitter struggle with the local minister, Aaron Woolworth, and several other prominent citizens for control of a newly established village library.[72] In the spring of 1793, the anti-Burroughs faction issued a proclamation demanding that he leave town and later unsuccessfully tried to expel him under the state poor law. His enemies then, by his own account, engineered a charge of attempted rape against him. When Burroughs was convicted only on the lesser charge of assault, he viewed it as a moral victory. But his opponents continued to harass him, and he was finally forced to leave Long Island after being successfully sued for debt.[73]

In April 1794 Burroughs left his pregnant wife and two little children and began to travel southward, intending to join an old school friend whom he believed to be practicing law in Georgia. Along the way he was forced to beg for money from various acquaintances and strangers. In late spring or early summer, he arrived in Washington, Georgia, only to discover that his friend had left the state. He nonetheless managed to gain employment as rector of a local academy, where he stayed for about six or eight months. After engaging in various land speculations and trading ventures, he returned to New England near the end of 1795. There he was reunited with his family and spent the next few years in Hanover, managing his father's farm. After falling out with his father in about April 1799, Burroughs moved to the town of Stanstead in Lower Canada, where he managed a farm and some mills belonging to his wealthy father-in-law for at least two or three years. So ended the original two volumes of the *Memoirs of Stephen Burroughs.*[74]

Drawing on several accounts appended to subsequent editions of the autobiography and on other materials, it is possible to offer a brief sketch of the remaining years of his life. During the first decade of the nineteenth century, Burroughs led a ring of counterfeiters in Canada that reproduced the bills of various banks in the United States. In the spring of 1811, he was reportedly in prison, awaiting trial on some unspecified charge.[75] However, by the following year he was said to be teaching school in the town of Three Rivers in Lower Canada.[76] At some point he reportedly repented and, having converted to Catholicism, remained a respectable schoolmaster until his death in 1840. According to a visitor who saw him at about the age of seventy, Burroughs was a brilliant conversationalist, "never serious, certainly not sad, and not often grave or solemn, but more commonly playful and always cheerful."[77]

Throughout his autobiography Burroughs depicted himself as a figure at war with social authority. As a child, he attacked the dignity of his elders by ridiculing them with pranks; as a youth, he continued to mock his social superiors at school and at college. As a fraudulent preacher, he subverted the authority of the ministry; as a counterfeiter, he undercut the authority of government and property; as a defendant, he questioned the authority of the court; as a prisoner, he defied the authority of his keepers; and as a newcomer to Bridgehampton, he challenged the authority of a community's established social elite. He characterized his relationship with the government of Massachusetts as one of "open war." His enemies on Long Island later accused him of trying to "overthrow all the *good old establishments.*"[78]

Significantly, Burroughs did not portray his chronic social insubordination as mere roguery or willful wickedness but repeatedly insisted that his actions were grounded in principle or justified by circumstance. Again and again throughout his autobiography, he stressed that his intentions were honorable, even benevolent. In impersonating a minister, he was simply trying to earn a livelihood; in passing counterfeit money, he was merely doing a favor for a friend. "I think my motive for this undertaking is founded on the principles of uprightness," he told himself shortly before his arrest in Springfield. "I think the sentiment of friendship is the uppermost object in this undertaking." Similarly, after helping a fellow prisoner to escape, he congratulated himself for having been "guided by the principles of philanthropy." Following his controversy with the established leaders of Bridgehampton, he reassured himself that he had pursued "the course of rectitude." Burroughs did not claim to be infallible, simply well-meaning. "That I had done wrong in many instances, through imprudence, the impetuosity of feelings, and a misconception of things, I was perfectly sensible," he acknowledged, "but that it had uniformly and ever been my desire to render good, rather than evil, and to avoid injuring every person, so far as my judgment would serve, was a truth my whole soul responded to with pleasure."[79]

Burroughs not only insisted on justifying his intentions both to himself and to his readers but also challenged the capacity of others to judge them accurately. He insisted that moral conduct could only be evaluated circumstantially but, at the same time, claimed that it was virtually impossible for anyone else to understand all the circumstances governing his behavior. In a world characterized by deception, delusion, and prejudice, it was not surprising that his intentions were frequently misread.[80] "I know the world will blame me, but I wish to justify my conduct to myself let the world think what it may," he insisted. "Indeed, I know they are not capable of judging upon the matter, with any propriety, because they ever will and ever must remain ignorant of the particular causes which brought these events into existence."[81]

In addition to defending his own intentions, Burroughs also regularly challenged the motives of his persecutors and the fairness of the legal proceedings undertaken against him. By his own account, each of his major convictions was a gross miscarriage of justice. In regard to his prosecution for counterfeiting, he contended that a hostile story appearing in the Springfield newspaper prior to his trial had been "calculated to fix an invincible prejudice" against him in the minds of prospective jurors. Because the sole witness at that trial stood to receive a reward from the government if he was convicted, thereby giving him an interest in the outcome, Burroughs argued that his testimony should have been excluded. He further claimed that the prosecutor, by bringing up old and unproven aspersions against his character in his opening remarks to the jury, had acted "contrary to every principle of law and justice." Finally, he condemned the judges for failing to prevent such "flagrant violations of all rules of order," expressing astonishment at seeing "all justice and virtue fled from the bench."[82]

In regard to his prosecution on three counts of attempted rape in Worcester County, Burroughs not only offered his own exculpatory version of events in his *Memoirs* but also inserted another sympathetic trial account, ostensibly written by an elderly lawyer. According to Burroughs, the charges had been trumped up by a prominent local citizen who was both jealous of the young schoolteacher and eager to curry favor with government officials. Burroughs's wife claimed, in a letter also included in his *Memoirs*, that the "evidence brought forward in support of these charges were of a kind too ridiculous to mention." He himself pointed out how preposterous it was for him to be charged with "open lewdness" for acts that all witnesses agreed had been performed in private. He implied as well that two of the three judges had been unfairly hostile to his cause in their addresses to the jury. His own and his wife's version of events was amplified and confirmed by the elderly attorney's supplementary account, which suggested that the alleged victims had dissembled on the stand in order to salvage their tarnished reputations. The old lawyer concluded that Burroughs may have been a seducer but was certainly no rapist.[83]

Burroughs depicted his subsequent trial for attempted rape on Long Island as a similar travesty of justice. He claimed that the charges had been fabricated by the established social elite of Bridgehampton, led by a minister and a judge, acting in collusion with a local woman of bad character. After his arrest the malicious minister traveled to Massachusetts in order to dredge up old accusations against him and then planted a report about them in the Springfield and Long Island newspapers in order to prejudice public opinion. Before his trial Burroughs contacted a local attorney, who promised to represent him. But when the proceedings opened he was shocked to find that lawyer assisting the county prosecutor, leaving him to defend himself as best he could. When a key defense witness proved unable to appear in court and Burroughs requested a continuance until the following term, he was granted only a single day's delay.[84]

"You have no witness in your cause, and no chance to get any," one of his enemies brutally warned him. "You have no person to assist you in managing your trial, and two powerful lawyers against you; besides all this, the court is against you." That assessment was generally confirmed by the proceedings themselves. When Burroughs tried to cross-examine the key witness against him, one of the judges helped the woman to formulate her answers; when Burroughs tried to address the jury, he was "continually interrupted" by the prosecutors. Yet despite all of the unfair tactics employed against him, the jurors refused to find Burroughs guilty of attempted rape, convicting him only on the lesser charge of assault.[85]

As well as complaining about his treatment in court, Burroughs also assailed the penal sanctions applied against him, particularly those that followed his conviction for counterfeiting. He claimed that the extraordinary punishments administered by the sheriff during his imprisonment in Northampton—the whippings, chainings, and deprivations of food, heat, and clothing—were cruel, barbarous, and inconsistent with the most basic of civil rights. "The fundamental principles upon which our liberties and privileges are founded, are the trial by jury, that no unnatural and cruel punishment shall be inflicted, and that a person shall never be punished, but by due course of law," he explained. "In the punishments inflicted on me, none of these preliminaries have been attended to, but I have been subjected to the arbitrary will of a petty tyrant." Burroughs also cited revolutionary rhetoric on the preciousness of liberty in arguing against the sanction of imprisonment and further denied the effectiveness of incarceration as an instrument of moral reform, describing Castle Island as a "perfect school of vice."[86]

Although Burroughs's critique of imprisonment may have run against the dominant trend of public policy in the early republic, his advocacy of individual rights against the coercive powers of the state, particularly in regard to criminal prosecutions, was quite consistent with the drift of post-Revolutionary reformist thought. Legal historian William E. Nelson has described a grow-ing sensitivity to the plight of criminal defendants among lawyers of early national Massachusetts, a concern that evoked various "libertarian" reforms designed to provide greater procedural protections for the accused. By dra-matizing the vulnerability of defendants and convicts to abuses by public officials, the popular autobiography of Stephen Burroughs surely contrib-uted to that new awareness. As the old lawyer who commented on the trial of Burroughs for attempted rape noted, it was all too easy for the popular clamor aroused by "men in eminent stations" to drown out "the small voice of the individual."[87]

The challenge to authority posed by Burroughs went far beyond his solici-tude for the rights of defendants and prisoners. His autobiography actually implied a sweeping rejection of traditional dogmas and hierarchies in favor of an egalitarian social order based on natural reason and fraternal benevolence. He articulated a theory of education based on gentle guidance rather than harsh coercion and an ideal of familial relations based on equality rather than tyranny.[88] Those views reflected a broad "revolution against patriarchal au-thority" that was transforming generational attitudes during the second half of the eighteenth century.[89] The model relationships embraced by Burroughs were not those of superior to inferior, master to servant, or ruler to subject but equal to equal, brother to brother, and friend to friend.[90] Given the common origin of the species, he insisted that all people stood on "the footing of brethren of the same family, entitled to equal privileges and immunities."[91] It was an outlook well suited to the new "horizontal" peer society that was emerging in the early republic in place of the traditional "vertical" social order of the colonial period.[92]

In expressing his distaste for established social values and hierarchies, Stephen Burroughs posed as an enlightened philosopher bestowing cosmopoli-tan wisdom on a narrow provincial audience.[93] That role was particularly evident in his dealings with the "uninformed" people of Long Island.[94] There he assumed pedagogic functions not only as a schoolteacher but also as a contributor to the local newspaper and as the chief organizer of a local library. Shortly after his arrival in New York, Burroughs wrote a series of essays for the *Long Island Herald*, a newly established paper that would support the Jeffersonian Republicans.[95] His articles attacked prejudice and intolerance in the language of a *philosophe*, calling for "the establishment of the principle of universal benevolence, on the ruins of superstition."[96] In the subsequent con-troversy over a new village library, Burroughs opposed those who insisted on filling the shelves with theological writings and instead sought to acquire works by such pillars of the Enlightenment as Hume and Voltaire.[97]

Burroughs appealed not only to the enlightened benevolence of his read-ers but also to their aroused emotions. As a child, he had been an eager reader of novels and romances. And as an adult, he celebrated "those exqui-site joys, which flow from a heart of sensibility." Especially in the second volume of his *Memoirs*, Burroughs presented himself as a sentimental victim, forced to witness the suffering of his family and then cruelly separated from his beloved wife and little children by the machinations of his enemies. At times, by his own account, he was driven to the point of despair: "Horror stalked around my dwelling. Wild dismay was my pillow companion. The most excruciating agony perpetually harrowed my almost exhausted spirits." When obliged to abandon his family on Long Island in 1794, Burroughs claimed to suffer the "heart-cutting pangs" of a "person of feeling." The following year, upon hearing news of his absent family, Burroughs experienced a "confused chaos of pleasure, intermixed with the keenest pain." Like any good sentimentalist, Burroughs often "fell sacrifice to too great a degree of sensibility."[98]

Of course, for all his pretensions, Stephen Burroughs was both a rogue and a fraud, a man who once described himself as "full of all deceit, hypocrisy, and duplicity."[99] Yet that was not how he chose to present himself in his *Memoirs*. Between the covers of his own book, at least, he was less a fraud than a philosopher, less a rogue than an injured innocent, a figure with serious ideas about society and with serious grievances against those who dominated it.[100] As an author very much in control of his text, Burroughs (or his designated defenders) always got the last word, wreaking literary vengeance for past sanctions and humiliations. Other cultural rebels were free to savor his revenge; it was said, for example, that one of the favorite boyhood books of Joseph Smith, founder of Mormonism, was the *Memoirs of Stephen Burroughs*.[101] As for the various figures of authority assailed and lampooned in his work—the hypocritical judges, lawyers, sheriffs, deacons, and ministers— they could, like Burroughs at the whipping post, do little more than squirm and take their punishment.

Although they did so in a variety of ways, several of the most popular criminal narratives of the early national period depicted their subjects as victims of injustice. The story of Ambrose Gwinett illustrated the dangers of circumstantial evidence; the account of Elizabeth Wilson exposed the unfairness of contemporary sexual standards; the narrative of Whiting Sweeting assailed both legal injustice and theological error; the memoirs of Stephen Burroughs attacked the cruelty and hypocrisy of public officials. Those varied exposés of social injustice drew upon a number of powerful ideological insurgencies that were challenging traditional values during the last decades of the eighteenth century. Wilson embodied literary sentimentalism; Sweeting articulated anti-Calvinist evangelism; and Burroughs, after impersonating and parodying an orthodox minister, boldly trumpeted the values of both Enlightenment benevolence and literary sentimentalism.[102] All four of the narratives also reflected an emerging libertarian concern over the treatment of criminal defendants, potential victims of the massive coercive powers of the state.

While only Burroughs actually hailed from New England, all four narratives were quickly incorporated into the literature of that region, repeatedly printed and marketed there. Even the geographical locus of the popular accounts gradually edged their way into the neighborhood: Gwinett began in England; Wilson sinned and repented in Pennsylvania; Sweeting lived in upstate New York, just west of the Massachusetts border; and Burroughs emerged from the Connecticut Valley heartland of New England itself. As ministers and magistrates undoubtedly looked on in dismay, the region's literature of crime and punishment, once committed to the service of entrenched elites and established ideologies, came to express the antiauthoritarian convictions of a revolutionary age. Judging by their persuasive force and extraordinary popularity, as well as by the intensity with which they were read and the painstaking care with which they were preserved, it seems likely that those polemical works did not merely reflect ideological changes but actively reshaped public attitudes and values.[103]

IV

Trials and Tribulations:
The Literature of Legal Romanticism

8

The Story of Jason Fairbanks:
Trial Reports and the Rise
of Sentimental Fiction

During the first half of the nineteenth century, cultural entrepreneurs transformed New England's literature of crime and punishment, replacing the established genres of execution sermons and last speeches with trial reports, romantic biographies, crime novels, and expanded newspaper coverage. While ministers rechanneled their fascination with crime and punishment into a vast polemical literature of penal reform, an assortment of lawyers, newspaper editors and reporters, stenographers, and hack writers became more active in the popular marketplace, creating crime genres suited to both their own expertise and the preferences of a pluralistic culture increasingly committed to legal and romantic values.[1] The case of Jason Fairbanks, examined in this chapter, documents the rapid transition after 1800 from old forms to new. The case of Albert J. Tirrell, treated in the next, illustrates the new literature as it had evolved by midcentury. Like many other highly publicized criminal cases of the period, both affairs revolved around issues of gender, courtship, illicit sex, and sexual violence, all central preoccupations of contemporary fiction.[2] In dealing with such issues, those cases established the threatening figure of the "sexual predator" as a dominant image in the popular literature of crime and punishment. While it cannot be claimed that the Fairbanks and Tirrell publications are strictly "typical" or "representative" of that vast and varied literature, they certainly do embody a number of its most powerful and pervasive themes.

Seduction and its baleful consequences were the preeminent themes of late eighteenth-century fiction. The dramatic motif of female virtue under assault, popularized by Samuel Richardson in *Pamela* (1740) and *Clarissa* (1748), was eagerly reenacted by countless imitators over the following decades.[3] Treatments of the subject were not only sentimental but also often sensational. One modern critic has observed that "rape, jealous frenzy and murder" pervaded British novels of the period 1770 to 1800.[4] Early American fiction showed a similar preoccupation with illicit sex and untimely death. No fewer than nine of the eleven tales contained in the first volume of a New England literary journal issued in 1789 were "accounts of seductions and the resultant misery."[5]

That same year, the first American novel, William Hill Brown's *The Power of Sympathy*, appeared as an exposé of "the dangerous consequences of seduction." Brown described several tragic deaths resulting from affairs of the heart in the novel's main plot and two subsidiary tales.[6] Two of the most popular American novels of the late eighteenth century, Susanna Rowson's *Charlotte Temple* (1791) and Hannah Foster's *The Coquette* (1797), also explored the fatal consequences of illicit sexual relations.[7]

Although American literary seductions were certainly influenced by Richardsonian models, they also drew on materials much closer to home. Indeed, several of the most successful early novels were actually "docudramas" based on cases of local interest. A seamless blending of the factual and the fanciful, so prominent in nineteenth-century crime coverage, was a constitutive characteristic of American fiction at the very moment of its birth. Thus one of the subsidiary tales in *The Power of Sympathy* was based on the real-life scandal of Frances Theodora Apthorp, a young socialite from Boston who committed suicide in 1788 after having an affair with her brother-in-law and giving birth to an illegitimate child. The tragedy caused a local furor and was the subject of much newspaper comment.[8] Similarly, the seduction and death of Susanna Rowson's fictional heroine in *Charlotte Temple* were supposedly modeled on the experiences of one Charlotte Stanley, an unfortunate woman whose grave might be seen at Trinity churchyard in New York City.[9] Likewise, Hannah Foster's *Coquette* was based on the life of her husband's cousin, Elizabeth Whitman of Hartford, Connecticut. The story of Whitman's illegitimate pregnancy and subsequent death was widely circulated in New England newspapers of the late 1780s.[10] In a cultural setting in which fiction was still very much subject to attack as a species of falsehood, authors regularly defended novels by asserting their actual (or ostensible) rootedness in real life.[11]

While the contemporary claim that "every town and village affords some example of a ruined female" may have been an exaggeration, it seems clear that premarital sexual intercourse was much more than a purely literary phenomenon in late eighteenth-century America.[12] And the direction of influence may not all have been one way. Although art undoubtedly followed life, contemporary spokesmen also insisted that life followed art. Moralists of the day regularly blamed sentimental fiction for corrupting the virtue of susceptible readers. "Everyone knows what an effect the general style of Novels has on untutored minds," one critic claimed in 1791; "they are written with an intent to captivate the feelings, and do in fact lead many on to the path of vice." Similarly, another observer insisted in 1797 that novels "not only pollute the imaginations of young women, but likewise give them false ideas of life, which too often make them act improperly." Ironically, such criticisms frequently appeared in contemporary novels and in magazines specializing in shorter works of sentimental fiction.[13]

In fact, modern demographers have detected a gradual rise in premarital pregnancies in America, including New England, beginning as early as the late seventeenth century. The trend reached a peak during the second half of the eighteenth century when, in some New England communities, more than 30 percent of first births took place less than nine months after marriage.[14] The increase evidently reflected a decline in traditional parental and communal controls on sexual activity among the young, one small part of a much broader shift from community-oriented values and behavior toward greater individual assertion and autonomy in a variety of social spheres.[15] Of course, the peak in premarital pregnancies at the end of the century also coincided with the emergence of a new literary ideal of autonomous romantic courtship; contemporary sentimental fiction both celebrated romantic love and condemned parental efforts to dictate the marital choices of children.[16] Although it is difficult to gauge the impact of that literature on the actual conduct of young men and women, it seems clear that romantic love played an increasingly prominent role in the culture of early national New England, both as a literary ideal and as a social expectation.[17]

Whatever its cause, the eighteenth-century rise in premarital pregnancy did not mark a permanent trend in American demography. Although traditional external controls were not restored, rates of premarital pregnancy gradually subsided after 1800, as young men and women apparently internalized a new ethic of sexual self-control. That new ethic was part of a much broader project of self-discipline and repression, one designed to counteract the potential for social chaos implicit in the emergence of liberal individualism as a dominant cultural ethos in early nineteenth-century America.[18] Ironically, then, the most complete triumph of the literary ideal of romantic love coincided in time with the reassertion of sexual restraint among America's youth.[19] By 1850 rates of prenuptial conception had returned to levels nearly as low as those of 150 years earlier.[20] The start of the nineteenth century thus roughly coincided with a transition from an unstable pattern of widespread premarital sexual activity in defiance of traditional norms to a stable system of autonomous courtship based on internalized restraint. Yet even the most noble self-discipline was sometimes sorely tested when adverse economic circumstances, or other obstacles, prevented the legitimate consummation of romantic love in marriage.[21] During the spring of 1801, some such crisis seems to have been reached in the troubled courtship of Jason Fairbanks and Eliza Fales.[22]

By the beginning of the nineteenth century, the town of Dedham had drifted far from its beginnings as a harmonious farming community of Puritan peasants established several miles south of Boston during the Great Migration of the 1630s. To be sure, a vast majority of the inhabitants still tilled the soil; workshops and factories were just barely beginning to alter the economic landscape of eastern Massachusetts. But time had gradually attenuated the spiritual fervor and collectivist orientation of the Dedhamites, while population growth and resulting land scarcity led to a widening of economic divisions. Political developments in the early republic had also polarized the town, with a majority of Jeffersonian yeomen at war with local Federalists under the formidable leadership of Fisher Ames. Not even religion provided a reliable basis for unity; various Protestant denominations had gained a foothold in the town, and even Congregationalists sometimes fought bitterly among themselves. As if the once placid community did not have enough sources of contention, Dedham would soon be further divided by a local tragedy.[23]

One afternoon in May 1801, Herman Mann, the publisher of the *Columbian Minerva*, a weekly newspaper issued in Dedham, was called to the scene of a violent death. He would describe the affair at length in the next issue of his paper, under the heading "MELANCHOLY CATASTROPHE!" According to Mann's account, Jason Fairbanks and Elizabeth Fales, two young Dedham residents of respectable families, had been engaged in a courtship long frustrated by certain unspecified "obstacles." On the afternoon of Monday, May 18, 1801, the couple met by agreement at a thicket of birches not far from the Fales residence in order, as Fairbanks ambiguously put it, to reach a "final determination." Sometime later, at about three o'clock, Fairbanks appeared at the Fales house, covered with blood and holding a knife, and announced that Eliza had killed herself and that he had tried to do the same. When the girl's relatives rushed to the grove of birches, they found Eliza lying on the ground with her throat cut and her body lacerated by multiple stab wounds; the young woman died after "a few struggles and gasps." Jason was not much better off, with a cut throat and various other knife wounds. The following morning, Mann reported that Fairbanks was "still alive, but in a most deplorable situation."[24]

In covering the untimely death of Eliza Fales, Mann did not simply provide an objective statement of the facts in the case. Rather, he laced his account with language suggestive of the sentimental fiction that had begun to flood New England over the preceding decades. The publisher described the murder scene as "tragic," "melancholy," and "heart rending," referred to his own report on the matter as a "sympathetic effusion," and suggested that the event would evoke the "sympathizing grief of every one susceptible of the passions of humanity." He concluded by inviting readers to join in sentimental lamentation: "Ye who have experienced, or learned from your natural sympathy—come, and with me, drop a tear."[25] Mann was clearly attuned to the contemporary cult of sensibility and assumed that at least some in his audience were as well.

A verse broadside issued shortly afterward, perhaps also by Mann, adopted a similar tone. Although the anonymous author of *A Mournful Tragedy* called on readers to shed a "friendly tear" for the "afflicted parents," the closing lines of the piece hinted that parental opposition to the courtship might have been responsible for Eliza's death:

> Now parents all where'er you be,
> Who hear this sad catastrophe;
> Now let you this one caution take,
> Where love is fix'd—don't matches break.[26]

The poet thus implicitly endorsed the ideal of autonomous romantic courtship that was becoming increasingly powerful in American culture of the early republic.

Meanwhile, Jason Fairbanks was too badly wounded to be moved in the immediate aftermath of Eliza's death. In what must have been an uncomfortable arrangement, he was taken into the Fales home and treated by a number of doctors. Already in fragile health with a crippled right arm and an undiagnosed case of tuberculosis, Jason had wounds in his throat, chest, abdomen, right side, right arm, and thigh. During the following days, a wound in the abdomen began to mortify, bringing on symptoms of lockjaw; at least one of the doctors in attendance doubted that he would recover. Elizabeth Fales was buried on May 20, following an enormous procession attended by nearly two thousand mourners, a number that approximated the total population of the town. The next day, with a coroner's jury having already named Fairbanks as a probable "accessory" to Eliza's death, Jason was removed from the Fales residence and carried to jail in a litter. While implicitly blaming Eliza's parents for her demise, the author of *A Mournful Tragedy* had indicated uncertainty as to whether her death was murder or suicide. That the coroner's jury named Fairbanks only as an "accessory" to Eliza's "murder" suggests that the poet was not the only one with doubts as to what had really happened in the thicket of birches.[27]

But when Fairbanks came to trial before the state Supreme Judicial Court the following August, he was charged with murder. So many spectators of both sexes flocked to the trial at Dedham that the judges were forced to move the proceedings from the usual courthouse chamber into a nearby meetinghouse.[28] James Sullivan, the Republican attorney general of Massachusetts, handled the prosecution; Harrison Gray Otis and John Lowell, Jr., two prominent Federalist lawyers, stood for the defense.[29] It should be noted that Otis and Lowell were key members of a younger generation of Federalist politicians who abandoned the open elitism of their conservative elders and shrewdly imitated the democratic political rhetoric and tactics of their rival Jeffersonian Republicans.[30] As we shall see, they proved equally willing to exploit the insurgent cultural forms of literary sentimentalism. Their client was arraigned on Wednesday, August 5; the trial itself took place on August 6 and 7. About forty witnesses appeared, most for the prosecution; the testimony concluded at eleven on the morning of the second day.[31]

The witnesses provided the jury with a detailed picture of the background and immediate circumstances of the tragedy. The two principals were Jason Fairbanks, a sickly young man of about twenty-one years of age, and Elizabeth (also referred to as Betsey or Eliza) Fales, a healthy girl of about eighteen. The pair had been courting, at least sporadically, over a period of several years, despite Jason's poor health and the opposition of Betsey's family and friends. At times Fairbanks apparently became frustrated by the situation; witnesses testified that he had made threatening remarks concerning both Betsey and her mother. Still, the couple often met together at the Fairbanks residence, at friends' houses, and outdoors, occasionally spending the night together alone. Although members of the Fales family denied it under oath, other witnesses, particularly young friends, testified that their attachment seemed strong and mutual.[32]

On Sunday, May 17, the day before the tragedy, Jason's niece playfully forged a marriage certificate for Fairbanks and Fales. That same day Jason told a friend, Reuben Farrington, that he "planned to meet Betsey, in order to have the matter settled," explaining that he "either intended to violate her chastity, or carry her to Wrentham, to be married, for he had waited long enough." Farrington saw Fairbanks twice the next morning; Jason seemed "cheerful, and merry as usual" but claimed to be too weak to help him with some gardening. At one-thirty that afternoon, Fairbanks told Farrington that he would let him know in about an hour what he had decided to do about his courtship.[33] In the meantime, Betsey Fales had spent Monday morning helping with household chores. Both her mother and sister claimed that she had appeared "cheerful and merry as usual." After drinking some milk for lunch, she went between twelve and one o'clock to a neighbor's house to retrieve a novel, *Julia Mandeville*. She stayed there for a bit more than an hour, amusing herself by reading the book, a melodramatic piece of British fiction that climaxed with the sudden and tragic deaths of two young lovers who had been engaged to be married. After laying the novel aside, Betsey played for a few minutes with a little child and left. At about three o'clock, two of her friends repeatedly heard Betsey Fales's voice coming from some nearby woods; at first one thought she was laughing, but then both thought they heard cries of distress. Fifteen minutes later they learned that Betsey was dead.[34]

All of the circumstances surrounding the discovery of Betsey Fales in the birch grove confirmed that Jason Fairbanks had been with her at the time she received her mortal wounds. Fairbanks himself directed her relatives to the spot where she lay. In his hand was the bloody jackknife with which both of them had apparently been wounded; he had borrowed it earlier in the day in order to mend a pen. Witnesses found Jason's overcoat and pocketbook near Betsey's body, along with fragments of the marriage certificate that Jason's niece had given him the previous day. Although Jason's claim that Betsey had committed suicide was excluded from trial testimony, it seemed clear that she had either taken her own life or been murdered by Fairbanks.[35]

Lawyers on both sides sought to resolve the issue in their favor by marshaling evidence concerning Betsey's wounds and Jason's physical condition. Betsey, it appeared, had one deep wound on her neck, four on her breasts, six on her left arm, and two on her left side, as well as cuts on one or both of her thumbs, two scratches on her right arm, and a small wound on her back, a little below the shoulder blade. Witnesses disagreed on a number of relevant points, including the precise angle and seriousness of the cut on her back. Could Fales have inflicted such wounds herself? That possibility, however unlikely, was never definitively ruled out by expert testimony. After all, Fairbanks had without doubt inflicted nearly as many wounds on his own body.

Indeed, the prosecution's chief medical witness acknowledged that even the cut on Betsey's back might have been self-inflicted.[36] On the other hand, could the weak and sickly Fairbanks, with a crippled and shrunken right arm, stiff at the elbow, have inflicted such wounds in the face of resistance by a healthy young woman of middling stature? Sympathetic witnesses for the defense testified to Jason's extreme weakness, noting that he was unable to work, needed the assistance of his mother in getting dressed, and had been easily bested in a recent scuffle with a younger niece. However, prosecution witnesses recalled incidents in which Jason had tussled effectively with other young men. In short, much of the testimony concerning Betsey's wounds and Fairbanks's physical strength was either contradictory or inconclusive.[37]

After all the testimony had been given, the lawyers delivered their closing arguments. The two defense counsel talked for a total of six hours; according to a contemporary newspaper account, their speeches constituted "a torrent of eloquence, with all that ingenuity, sagacity and learning, which the genius and wisdom of man could invent." Although the prosecutor's final address was only a third as long, it was, according to the same report, "a masterly and pathetic plea."[38] In addition to presenting self-serving recapitulations of ambiguous testimony, the closing arguments of both defense and prosecution also offered imaginative reconstructions of the fatal scene, based on divergent assessments of character and motive. The scenario offered by Harrison Gray Otis centered on his portrait of Betsey Fales as a passionate young woman whose head was "filled with melancholy romances and legendary tales." She was, in short, very much like those misguided and impressionable female readers described by contemporary critics of sentimental fiction. Otis further suggested that Betsey had been driven to despair by her love for Jason, a sickly young man whose suit was opposed by her parents and whose health was too fragile to allow him to support her himself. Finally, amid the birches, realizing the hopelessness of their courtship, Betsey had frantically seized Jason's knife and taken her own life.[39] Significantly, Otis sought to bolster the credibility of his version of events by invoking the authority of literature:

> This is his simple tale—Is it impossible? Is it improbable? Has disappointed love never produced despair? Has despair never induced Suicide? Has the softer sex been peculiarly exempt from these feelings and these results? No—Every annal, and every novel writer will establish the assertion, that no passion has so often terminated fatally as love, and no circumstances have so frequently given it a *fatal direction* as injudicious restraint.[40]

Otis then tried to clinch his case by sketching a melodramatic vignette that might easily have been extracted from a contemporary romance; the key prop in his little drama was the forged marriage certificate, itself a "fiction," whose fragments had been found at the scene of the crime:

> When their conversation turned upon their future prospects, and the small hopes which they entertained of a happy union, Jason produced this certificate, and after relating the history of its origin, with a desperate and melan-

Portrait of Harrison Gray Otis, defense attorney for Jason Fairbanks. Painted by Gilbert Stuart in 1809. *Courtesy, Society for the Preservation of New England Antiquities, Boston. Photograph by David Bohl.*

choly look, correspondent to their feelings, he observed, "I fear we shall never be nearer to the gratification of our fond expectations; I fear that this little *fiction* is the highest consummation of our bliss, which we shall ever realize;" and tearing in pieces the scroll on which their names were united, "thus, said he, our tenderest hopes are scattered to the winds." Perhaps this little *incident*, more than all others, contributed to rouse that phrenzy and despair, which induced her rashly to terminate, by *her own* hand, her *own* existence.[41]

While Otis invoked the epistemological authority of novels and even adopted their narrative strategies, his reconstruction tended to confirm the contemporary critique of fiction as corrupting immature minds and stimulating unhealthy passions. Like many authors of early sentimental tales and novels, Otis shrewdly hedged his bets by implicitly condemning fictive modes even as he employed them.

James Sullivan's competing reconstruction of events centered on his characterization of Jason Fairbanks as a sickly young man corrupted by idleness, parental overindulgence, depraved companions, and unhealthy lusts, a classic example of the "progress of vice." Such themes were certainly familiar to readers of execution sermons; in fact, Sullivan at one point launched into a little jeremiad on the "great defects of education" in the early republic, particularly criticizing "false fondness and misapplied tenderness towards children."[42] Yet Sullivan's description of Fairbanks as an idle, pampered, and lustful young man coincided not only with traditional sermon themes but also with characterizations occasionally found in contemporary fiction.[43] Indeed, Sullivan was no more averse to invoking the authority of literature than his opponent. Thus, in rejecting the idea that Fales might have slashed herself to death, he explained: "Even in the most romantic pictures and visionary tales, we find the fair sex, when sick of life, generally avoiding the ghastly wound of the knife and dagger, and seeking an avenue through the water, or by poison, or strangling."[44]

In place of Otis's melodramatic reconstruction, the prosecutor appealed directly to the imaginations of the jurors with his own recreation of the fatal scene, one just as compelling and almost as creative as his opponent's, and one that also hinged on that tantalizing "fiction," the spurious marriage certificate:

> I now again call your imaginations to an image from whence the eye turns with horror, and of which language refuses a description.
>
> When he [Fairbanks] had produced the false certificate, and she had with a virtuous indignation torn the imposition in pieces, he became enraged:—Perhaps the knife was first exhibited to obtain by terror, what he feared he could not obtain by force. She turned on her face, the stab on her back altered her position. . . . When her arms defended her throat the wounds were given in her bosom to remove the obstruction, and her arms and hands mangled to gain access to the neck. Thus far led on, he found no retreat; but gave the ghastly wound, which more immediately produced her death.—But I quit the horrid and distressing scene.[45]

According to Sullivan, the basic problem with his opponent's argument was not that it conformed to the contemporary literary imagination but that it exceeded even its spacious bounds. "The most extravagant fictions are recurred to, in order to bring the unnatural conjecture within the lines of possibility," he declared. "But these [fictions] run away and refuse to recognize this scene, as one of their family."[46]

If the jury had any doubts as to which imaginative reconstruction of the crime to believe, they were probably resolved by the closing charge of the judges. In recapitulating the evidence, the jurists "called their attention to . . . the improbability of her giving the wounds in her breast, side and arms, even if she had intended to destroy her own life; and to the impossibility of her making that in her back, if it was in place and form as described by the witnesses." One of the judges even claimed that if Jason had simply encouraged or abetted Betsey's suicide he was still as culpable under the indictment as if he had killed her "with his own hand."[47] At about ten-thirty in the evening on August 7, the twelve men retired to deliberate. They returned the next morning at eight with a verdict of guilty. In receiving his sentence of death, Fairbanks appeared to be "the only one, amidst a crouded assembly, who remained insensible and unmoved," a fact noted with wonder in the newspaper accounts. "No trial in our courts of justice, has excited so much sympathy and horror," the *Boston Gazette* concluded on August 10, "and nothing perhaps in history *or fiction*, exceeded the remarkable facts which gave it rise."[48]

In contrast to most criminal proceedings of the eighteenth century, the trial of Jason Fairbanks received fairly extensive coverage in the local press. A particularly detailed account of the trial, prepared by a "Gentleman on the Spot," appeared in the August 10 issue of the *Independent Chronicle* and was reprinted by at least two other Boston newspapers.[49] In addition, the "correct and concise" account, occupying nearly two complete columns in the densely packed newspaper typography of the day, was quickly reprinted, both in Boston and in Salem, as an eight-page pamphlet.[50] Those reprints are certainly among the earliest American examples of newspaper trial reports reissued as pamphlets, a practice subsequently popularized during the middle decades of the century.[51] The Salem edition was emphatically entitled *A Deed of Horror! Trial of Jason Fairbanks . . . for the Murder of . . . His Sweetheart!!!* In giving the pamphlet at least a veneer of melodramatic romance, that title tended to integrate the report into a sentimental discourse already initiated by Herman Mann's *Columbian Minerva*, the anonymous poet's *Mournful Tragedy*, and the lawyers' courtroom arguments.

At eight o'clock on Thursday morning, September 10, following an abortive escape that quickly became entangled in the aroused political passions of the day, Jason Fairbanks was taken from a jail in Boston and placed in an open coach, accompanied by the Reverend Peter Thacher of Boston and two peace officers.[52] The condemned man stopped briefly at the jail in Dedham and then walked to the scaffold on the town common in his shroud, in the midst of a late summer thunderstorm, guarded along the way by two companies of cavalry and a detachment of Dedham's own volunteer infantry. In addition to the official procession, thousands of curious spectators jammed the roads leading to the gallows. On the morning of the execution, a lady of Roxbury counted no fewer than 711 carriages along the route to Dedham. An estimated ten thousand spectators (about five times the total population of the town), including many women and children, packed the common in order to witness the execution. Shortly before three in the afternoon, after a solemn prayer by the Reverend Thacher, Fairbanks dropped his handkerchief as a signal of readiness and was launched into eternity.[53] Throughout the ceremony Jason exhibited his usual impassive demeanor, a fact carefully noted in subsequent newspaper reports. In the *Columbian Minerva*, for example, Mann speculated at length on the significance of Fairbanks's stoic manner, managing to insert a plug for one of his forthcoming publications in the process. Did the prisoner's steadfast bearing suggest the callous insensibility of a brute or the magnanimous fortitude of a martyr, hero, or sage? The public themselves could judge once they had read Jason's own "last communication to the world," a statement to be issued, of course, by Herman Mann.[54]

Even before the execution, local printers were preparing a new round of publications on the controversial case. On Tuesday, September 8, Russell and Cutler of Boston inserted a notice in the *Columbian Minerva* announcing that *The Trial of Jason Fairbanks* was then in press and would be appearing within a few days. The publishers explained that their report had been delayed by difficulties in procuring "accurate and authentic copies" of relevant trial documents but promised that the forthcoming work would provide "a full, correct, and authentic detail of the Proceedings." Just two days later, as Fairbanks was being hanged in Dedham, an advertisement in the *Independent Chronicle* announced that Russell and Cutler's report had indeed been published and was then on sale in Boston. Within less than a week, a second edition of the trial account was being sold by Russell and Cutler in Boston, Herman Mann in Dedham, and other booksellers in Boston, Salem, Newburyport, and Portland. A third edition was published at the beginning of October, and a fourth had been issued before the end of the year.[55]

Russell and Cutler's *Report of the Trial of Jason Fairbanks* was an eighty-seven-page report of the proceedings, consisting of verbatim transcripts of trial testimony; third-person synopses of lawyers' arguments; detailed summaries of charge, verdict, and sentence; and supplementary accounts of the prisoner's escape, recapture, and execution.[56] Although the bulk of the report was secular and objective in tone, it was carefully framed by statements depicting the trial account in moral and religious terms. In a florid preface, Russell and Cutler offered their report as a warning to both parents and children, citing with approval the attorney general's strictures on "the danger of idle habits, overweening fondness in parents, and the importance to youth of a virtuous education." Similarly, in some moralistic passages appended to the work, they reminded readers "of the frailty of virtue, of the treachery and perverseness of the human heart, and of the immense importance and inestimable value of the power of religion."[57] The pious verities embedded in generations of New England execution sermons showed remarkable cultural resilience, reemerging not only in the arguments of lawyers but in the pompous reflections of report editors as well.

But Russell and Cutler's *Trial* was marketed to readers not simply as a quasi-official record of a legal proceeding, or as a carrier of traditional religious and moral values, but also as an account of intrinsic fascination and horror, one that was at once undoubtedly "real" and yet as emotionally engaging as imaginative literature. To that end, newspaper advertisements (using language borrowed from the defense counsel's closing argument) described the case as "without exaggeration, without the aid of fancy, one of the most awful catastrophes ever exhibited in real life, in any age or country, or sketched by the most excentric imagination of the most melancholy poet."[58]

Even in denying any dependence on such fictional attributes as "fancy" and "excentric imagination," the publishers invoked precisely those qualities to arouse public interest in their report.

Local printers also issued several more ephemeral responses to the case at about the time of the hanging. Two verse broadsides seem to have been issued on the day of the execution itself, probably sold to the crowds gathered at the gallows on Dedham common. Although they retained some of the moral warnings and pious affirmations typically embedded in eighteenth-century gallows poetry, the verses also invoked themes of romantic love, seduction, and betrayal, all staples of contemporary fiction.[59] A prose broadside that appeared in at least three variant editions during the days immediately following the execution illustrated the transitional quality of literary responses to the Fairbanks case even more dramatically. All surviving versions of the work, entitled *Biography of Mr. Jason Fairbanks and Miss Eliza Fales*, were issued in Boston, almost certainly by Nathaniel Coverly, Jr., a prolific publisher of popular broadsides and pamphlets.[60] Coverly was the son of an itinerant printer who in 1789 had launched one of the earliest literary magazines in New England, a journal devoted to sentimental fiction.[61] The son would now parody what the father had once purveyed.

The earliest version of the *Biography* was quite similar in format to a standard last-speech broadside. Like those earlier works, it was printed on one side of a folio sheet. Topped by woodcuts of two coffins and a gallows, its text descended in narrow columns of small type set off by funereal black borders. In fact, the first edition of the *Biography* was explicitly offered as a substitute for a conventional last speech. A preliminary note explained that although "the PUBLIC" had "been anxiously waiting to be informed of the Life, Character, and last DYING WORDS of JASON FAIRBANKS," they had been disappointed by the murderer's reserve. In lieu of a terse first-person narrative of the type commonly produced during the last decades of the eighteenth century, the biographer, ostensibly a local gentleman (but quite possibly Coverly himself), offered flowery third-person sketches of both criminal and victim, replete with stereotypes familiar to readers of contemporary sentimental fiction.[62]

Although its genteel author was identified as a former schoolmate, the *Biography* depicted Fairbanks in extremely unflattering terms. Much as in Sullivan's courtroom sketch, Jason was described as a proud, passionate, indolent, and insincere young man who refused to work for a living. Eliza Fales, in turn, was the quintessential sentimental heroine, complete with graceful ringlets of auburn hair, well-turned shoulders, alabaster bosom, tapered waist, virgin blush, and heart of softest sensibility. She was, of course, helplessly susceptible to the winning manners and dissembling assurances of her seducer, soon catching his "tender passion" and returning it with "reciprocal ardor." The anonymous author even compared her unrestrained love to that of Werther, an early tragic hero of European romantic fiction.[63]

Nathaniel Coverly, Jr.'s satirical broadside on the Fairbanks case. This is probably the second or third edition. *Courtesy, Boston Anthenaeum.*

In addition to its colorful biographical sketches, the broadside also included journalistic accounts of Jason's escape, recapture, and execution, along with an accurate factual summary of the evidence in the case, including a recitation of Eliza's activities on the day of the crime and close descriptions of the wounds suffered by both Fales and Fairbanks. The latter material was taken verbatim from the detailed trial account that had first appeared in the *Independent Chronicle* and then been reprinted in various forms.[64] Near the end of his pastiche, the author repeated the defense counsel's familiar description of the Dedham tragedy as "without the aid of fancy, one of the most awful catastrophes, ever exhibited in real life . . . or sketched by the most excentric imagination, of the most melancholly poet." He then incongruously concluded with a description of Eliza's ascent to "the blissful abodes of Paradise," where she would live in ecstasy with "myriads of the heavenly choir, who on golden harps are continually chanting Canto's of Thanksgiving and Praise to the Deity."[65]

Two subsequent editions of the broadside biography further accentuated the sentimental and satirical components of the work. All reference to the *Biography* as a substitute for the traditional last speech was omitted, as was the journalistic account of Jason's escape and recapture. In their place the revised versions featured new invocations of feminine sensibility, playful literary allusions, and fresh infusions of ludicrously florid prose. The biographer inserted an ornate description of a romantic evening excursion by Fales and Fairbanks, an extended excerpt on Adam and Eve from Milton's *Paradise Lost*, and an imaginative account of Jason's torments in hell, matching his description of Eliza's ascent to heaven.[66] Someone, again probably Coverly, even sentimentalized the broadside's iconography, replacing the crude woodcut of Eliza's coffin at the top of the page with a monographed urn beneath a weeping willow. Both revised versions also included a satirical diatribe against women who attended public hangings, and one (probably the later) featured a pair of humorous addresses to the ladies of Concord, Massachusetts, the site of another execution less than two years earlier. One of those addresses included a buoyantly patriotic vignette of America's departed military heroes, led by Washington, feasting on ambrosia in heavenly bliss. Some vestige of order was maintained by a series of chapter headings with such engaging titles as "The Lovers' Ramble, by Moon Light," "The Shade of the Murdered Eliza Ascended to Paradise," and "The Ghost of Fairbanks in Pandamonium." In terms of their demarcated episodic structure, the broadsides were virtual novels in embryo.[67] Having produced engaging montages of the accurate and the imaginary, the anonymous biographer expressed his hope that readers would be able to "discriminate between a little innocent fiction, and more plain and sober matter of fact."[68]

There are several internal clues as to the intended audience for Coverly's broadside. Although a note attached to the first edition implied that it was addressed to "the Public at large," the two subsequent versions seemed to denote a more selective audience. Both included a narrative aside to "a young Sentimentalist of eighteen." One also featured a pair of addresses to a group of genteel "Ladies of Concord."[69] Perhaps those hints of a young, genteel, female audience were simply part of the parody; coarse young men may have been even more likely to enjoy the irreverent broadside than polite young ladies.[70] Still, it does seem significant that the author implied a readership quite similar to those denoted by many contemporary works of sentimental fiction.[71] Clearly, no one could fully appreciate the playful satire without being familiar with the cult of sensibility. That the readers of eastern Massachusetts were already so attuned is suggested by the avid reception of Coverly's broadside. A note attached to both revised editions claimed that the printer's office had been "throng'd with purchasers for three days: and altho' the Press has been groaning night and day since [the execution] . . . yet we have not been able to supply the urgent demand."[72]

The primary function of Coverly's broadside undoubtedly was to provide its publisher with a profit. Yet even literary hacks can sometimes carry an ideological load. So it was with the broadside biographer, who conveyed two very different critiques of social misconduct from the vantage point of an emerging culture of gentility. The sentimental account of Fairbanks and Fales depicted Jason as an insincere seducer who concealed his dishonorable intentions behind a genteel facade. The broadside arraigned his "dissembling vices," "scyphocant's art and dissimulation," and "assumed and winning manners." In selfishly pursuing a liberal education beyond his father's means, Jason was judged guilty of "meanly aping the manners of a gentleman." Whether gentility was defined in terms of moral character or material resources, Jason Fairbanks was a fraud, an insight that the author intended to make "publicly known."[73] Like many other sentimental tales of the period, the *Biography* exposed male pretense and duplicity to the critical gaze of female readers.[74]

If Jason Fairbanks personified ungentlemanly concealment, public executions embodied an equally offensive pattern of vulgar exposure. According to the author's satirical account of the execution of burglar Samuel Smith at Concord in 1799, the gallows attracted a "heterogeneous, motely *assemblage*" of male and female, maid and married, old and young, black and white. They gathered to witness a man *"suspended by the aid of Hemp from the Gallows, dancing a Spanish Fandango in the air—and* screwing *up the muscles of his phiz, into the most ghastly distortions."* The women in the crowd completed the ritual by fainting away, exposing their private parts to the gaze of male spectators. Although it may have been perceived by deluded participants as a "Scene of Sentiment," the promiscuous intermingling of age, race, and gender; the dying man's grotesque loss of bodily control; and the attending women's theatrical immodesty all suggested a far less sympathetic construction. "Oh! Sentiment, how are thou polluted!" the author exclaimed. In fact, his satire of gallows ritual playfully anticipated a revolution in attitudes that would culminate in the abolition of public executions by an antebellum public increasingly committed to genteel norms of social segregation, female domesticity, and personal self-control.[75]

In pandering to both the public's passing fascination with the Dedham tragedy and much broader movements in cultural preoccupation and taste, the revised editions of Coverly's broadside subverted generic categories even more blatantly than the original. In format the *Biography* resembled a last speech; but in style and content it alternated motifs of sentimental fiction, romantic biography, literary parody, social satire, and journalistic reportage.

The broadside flirted with a number of genres but never really embraced any one. In effect the *Biography*, particularly in its later redactions, was an "episte-mological text," that is, one in which generic vacillation and structural confusion paralleled perceptual uncertainty within the plot itself.[76] It was not at all clear that purchasers would be any more successful in deciphering the broad-side biographer's hybrid text than Eliza in reading Jason's duplicitous char-acter or the ladies of Concord in interpreting a public execution. Given the epistemological havoc that they wrought, it was appropriate that the two revised versions of the *Biography* were issued as imprints of the "Pandamo-nium Press."[77] As late as December 1799, the execution of Samuel Smith had evoked an entirely conventional last-speech broadside; less than two years later, Nathaniel Coverly helped to bury the genre in an avalanche of sentimen-tal and satirical motifs, vindicating the earlier literary judgments of Susanna Rowson and Royall Tyler.[78] By blasting through the formulaic constraints of an established form, the *Biography* raucously heralded the arrival of a new cultural regime.

But the old order was not so easily shouted down; the Fairbanks case also produced a residual measure of moral and religious commentary. On the Sunday following Jason's execution, Thaddeus Mason Harris, a prominent minister from Dorchester, preached an unscheduled discourse in the first parish of Dedham. Having been invited on short notice, Harris was unable to prepare a new talk for the occasion but instead borrowed from his files a sermon originally delivered several years earlier. The discourse was addressed especially to young people, warning them against various "bad principles and habits" as they planned their future lives. Among other things, Harris offered the standard contemporary critique of novels and related fiction. "Peruse not idle and romantic books," the clergyman warned. "They give wrong ideas of human life, inflame the passions, delude the imagination, and corrupt the heart." Although Harris did not directly mention the Fairbanks case in his sermon, he closed with oblique references to the local ill feeling and contro-versy aroused by the case, pleading that "harmony and quiet once more prevail through this perplexed and distressed vicinity!"[79]

On that same Sunday, September 13, 1801, Thomas Thacher delivered a sermon to his congregation in the third parish of Dedham. In addition to offering the usual pious and moral advice, Thacher's sermon, unlike Harris's, treated the Fairbanks tragedy at some length, describing his own visits with the alleged murderer in prison both before and after his condemnation. The minister clearly sympathized with Fairbanks, denying reports of his impiety and lack of sensibility (a key criterion of sentimental judgment), but remained noncommittal on the issue of his guilt. "The facts relating to that are pub-lished to the world," the minister explained; "every one must judge according to his conscience, and the degree of probability and evidence which are of-fered to his mind."[80] Even more striking was Thacher's description of Jason's conduct at his execution, a characterization suggestive of Herman Mann's subsequent speculation in the *Columbian Minerva*. "Had the same measure of fortitude been possessed by a truly virtuous man," the outspoken minister insisted, "it might have made him a martyr for religion; a patriot bleeding on the scaffold for vindicating the rights of his country; or a hero crowned with glory expiring on the bed of honor." Finally, Thacher offered a lurid description of the disorderly behavior of the crowd in Dedham on hanging day and issued a forceful condemnation of public executions, suggesting that their "Gothic savageness" tended to "harden the heart" of spectators. On that point, at least, the minister and the broadside biographer would presumably have agreed.[81]

Both sermons evoked by the Fairbanks case eventually made their way into print. On the evening of September 13, within hours after the two clergymen had spoken, Herman Mann wrote Harris requesting a copy of his discourse for publication.[82] A notice in the *Columbian Minerva* of September 29 announced that the sermon was in press, and an advertisement the following week informed the public of its issue. "Those parents who would train up their children in the way they should go," Mann's plug read, "will not fail to purchase this excellent Discourse."[83] Although Harris did not explicitly mention Fairbanks once in his sermon, the murderer's name on the title page appeared in larger type than the author's; Mann was clearly counting on the public's sustained interest in the Fairbanks case to help sell the pamphlet. Nearly two months later, on December 1, Mann announced in the *Minerva* that a subscription had been opened at his office for the publication of Thacher's sermon, stressing that the work contained minute "particulars" concerning the "conversation, character, and conduct" of the late Fairbanks. The same newspaper announced the actual appearance of Thacher's work in a notice dated January 16, 1802; more than four months after his execution, the case of Jason Fairbanks was still being addressed in print.[84]

In terms of their pious affirmations and moral advice, the discourses of Harris and Thacher were very much a part of New England's long tradition of gallows sermons. Yet in a number of respects they signaled a weakening of that tradition. First, neither one of the lectures was a true execution sermon, that is, a discourse addressed both to a condemned prisoner and to the wider community during the days or hours immediately preceding an execution. Rather, each sermon had been delivered on the Sunday *following* the hanging of Fairbanks, obviously precluding any address to the condemned man; in contrast to traditional gallows sermons, the discourses of Harris and Thacher were quite literally afterthoughts. The essential detachment of Harris's sermon from the Fairbanks case was reinforced by the fact that the piece had been prepared several years earlier for delivery in a completely different social context. Only the sentimental pleas for communal harmony and conciliation appended to the prepared talk addressed the Dedham tragedy, and even then only obliquely. As for Thacher's discourse, much of its appeal seemed to lie in its sympathetic account of Jason's character and its condemnation of public executions rather than in its orthodox religious messages. In contrast to the traditional status of New England ministers as authoritative communal spokesmen, Harris and Thacher seem to have adopted the emerging nineteenth-century clerical roles of sentimental conciliator (Harris) and moral gadfly (Thacher).[85] It was fitting that by the end of January 1802 Herman Mann was offering Thacher's discourse as a complimentary bonus to purchasers of a secular compilation on the Fairbanks case; such sermons had indeed become little more than gratuitous vestiges of a disintegrating literary regime.[86]

Even as Mann collected subscriptions for Thacher's discourse, the enterprising publisher prepared to issue a work that would more forcefully vindicate the character of Jason Fairbanks. On December 8, Mann announced that *The Solemn Declaration of the Late Unfortunate Jason Fairbanks* was already in press; the work was actually published by about December 17.[87] It consisted of three parts: a first-person statement by Jason himself; a longer third-person account of the convict's "Life and Character," ostensibly written by Jason's older brother with some outside assistance; and corrected extracts of trial testimony. The tone of the *Declaration* was suggested by its iconography. Above its half-title was a funereal vase initialed J. F. and entwined by vines; in seeking to evoke sympathy for its departed subject, the pamphlet matched Coverly's hostile broadside urn for urn.[88] A second edition of the work appeared almost immediately, and a third appeared sometime the following year, suggesting that the public was quite interested in—and perhaps receptive to—the Fairbanks side of the story.[89]

According to his own statement, Jason had been acquainted with Betsey Fales from "a very early age" and had eventually become her "favored lover." Although her family initially treated him with "respect and affection," the relationship turned sour when two minor incidents aroused the hostility of Betsey's sister and mother, forcing the young lovers to separate. When a chance meeting led to a renewal of the courtship a year later, the couple arranged a series of rendezvous in the grove of birches, in one of her father's outbuildings, and at the homes of neighbors. As Jason's health deteriorated, Betsey began visiting him at his father's house, commonly staying until one in the morning and once even remaining the entire night. During at least one of those trysts the couple had sexual intercourse. Finally, in May 1801, with Jason's health much improved, the couple arranged a meeting in the thicket of birches in order to discuss their situation.[90]

Here Jason provided yet another account of the fatal meeting in the grove, one similar to the version offered by Harrison Gray Otis at the trial but differing from it in a few crucial details. According to Jason, the couple was engaged in a "long conversation upon the subject of marriage" when he recalled the fictitious marriage certificate prepared for him by his niece the previous day. He showed Betsey the spurious document, commented (in terms quite similar to those presented by his lawyer) that it was as close to marriage as they would ever get, and tore the certificate to pieces. While

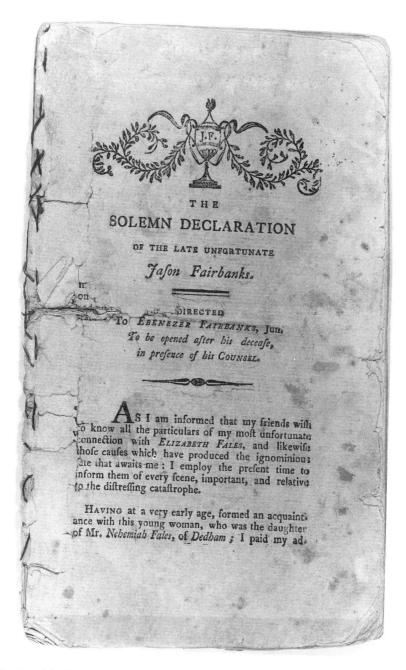

THE

SOLEMN DECLARATION

OF THE LATE UNFORTUNATE

Jason Fairbanks.

DIRECTED

To *EBENEZER FAIRBANKS,* Jun.
*To be opened after his decease,
in presence of his* COUNSEL.

AS I am informed that my friends wish
to know all the particulars of my most unfortunate
connection with *ELIZABETH FALES,* and likewise
those causes which have produced the ignominious
fate that awaits me : I employ the present time to
inform them of every scene, important, and relative
to the distressing catastrophe.

HAVING at a very early age, formed an acquaintance with this young woman, who was the daughter
of Mr. *Nehemiah Fales,* of *Dedham* ; I paid my ad-

Caption title of Jason Fairbanks's *Solemn Declaration*, topped by a funereal urn.

assuring Fales of his willingness to wed her instantly, he acknowledged that she would even then have to continue living at her father's house, since he had "no means, nor any place of . . . [his] own to carry her to." Betsey thereupon began to "weep bitterly," saying that such an arrangement would be impossible since her mother would immediately "turn her out" of the house. She also questioned Jason's sincerity, noting that her sisters and another acquaintance, a Mrs. Whiting, had told her that Fairbanks did not really love her. Jason's statement then reached a crucial juncture, recounting an exchange that had not been included in his lawyer's version of events:

> And now with all sorrow, and blame to myself, do I pursue the remainder of this melancholly history; for I replied angrily and roughly, that if she were capable, and willing to believe all that her sisters and Mrs. *Whiting* said upon the subject, she might go to the devil with them, since she so well knew that I had already *possessed her person, and received the pledge of her most tender attachment!*
>
> She then, with great quickness, demanded of me—"*if I had ever told any one of our connection?*" I rashly, but sincerely, answered, that I had indeed entrusted our secret to my intimate friends, *Reuben Farrington* and *Isaac Whiting.*—Upon which she violently exclaimed, "*Oh! you are a monster!*— and looking on me, as I sat whittling a small piece of wood with a pen-knife, she cried out "*give me that knife, I will put an end to my existence, you false-hearted man!—for I had rather die than live!*"
>
> At the same time, stretching out her hand, she took the knife, and began, as if in a state of distraction, to stab her breast and body—screaming out, and walking violently from me . . . ; while I, struck with astonishment, remained without power, and in a cold state of insensibility; but was too— too soon awakened from this dreadful stupefaction, by her coming, and either falling or sitting down by me.—Her throat was cut—which seeing, I immediately seized that cruel knife which had robbed me of all my fond heart held dear! and while it yet remained wet with her blood, stabbed myself in many and repeated places; only leaving off when I had finished cutting my own throat, and when I believed all was over with me![91]

If Jason's melodramatic account was to be believed, the immediate cause of Betsey's death was not her virtuous refusal to submit to Jason's sexual advances (as argued by the attorney general), or her romantic despair over their inability to marry (as postulated by the defense), but rather her rage over Jason's indiscretion in revealing the consummation of their love to his male friends. Yet it should be noted that, in each of those scenarios, tragedy resulted from the conflict between personal impulse or desire and the resurgent cultural norm requiring marriage as a precondition for sexual intercourse and romantic fulfillment. Sullivan alleged that Fairbanks's failure to adopt the self-restraints exercised by Betsey Fales led directly to his attempt to rape her. Otis implied that both Fairbanks and Fales had embraced the new ethic of sexual self-control, leading to their romantic despair and attempted suicides. Jason's own account suggested that neither of the pair had successfully internalized the new inhibitions; yet Betsey felt so humiliated by that failure that she killed herself in a rage when she learned that her weakness had been exposed to Fairbanks's friends. Whichever version one accepts, the tragedy would seem to be illustrative of tensions accompanying a major transition in courtship patterns at the beginning of the nineteenth century.[92]

The biography of Jason Fairbanks appended to his own declaration was an earnest attempt to vindicate the condemned murderer's character and salvage the reputation of his family. It was explicitly offered as a refutation of various "false and defaming publications" that had been "printed and exposed for sale in every corner of the country," particularly the hostile *Biography of Mr. Jason Fairbanks and Miss Eliza Fales*.[93] In contrast to the broadside biographer's unflattering portrait of Jason Fairbanks as a dissolute idler and unscrupulous seducer, the new narrative depicted Jason as a gifted, industrious, and sensitive young man whose bright prospects in life were first stymied by physical infirmity and then blasted by unforeseen tragedy. According to the sympathetic account, Jason was raised with intense affection and indulgence. "Never was a child so caressed, so beloved, or who appeared to have so many claims upon the attachment of his surrounding family," the author recalled; "for as he grew in stature, his prepossessing form, his intelligent mind, and his affectionate temper, made him the hope, the delight, the boast of his connections." Unfortunately, his early promise was repeatedly frustrated by chronic poor health. Not only was his naturally weak physical constitution undermined at the age of twelve by a bout with smallpox that left his right arm withered and immobile, but he also suffered from coughs, headaches, fever, and "bleeding at the lungs."[94]

To counteract the view of Jason as a malingering loafer, the account detailed his valiant efforts to apply himself in the face of physical adversity. Even with his crippled arm and other malignant symptoms, young Fairbanks often expressed a desire to work on the family farm and repeatedly attempted to do so, despite its impact on his health. His older brother was finally forced to forbid Jason's agricultural employment, explaining that his "labor would not indemnify the costs of his recovery." Similarly, after enrolling in a local academy, Jason's "brilliant prospects" were ruined by his "excruciating nervous headaches." Even after he had returned home in distress, family members were forced to hide Jason's books in order to guard him against his own debilitating intellectual pursuits. After he had recovered somewhat, Jason obtained work as a clerk for the Register of Deeds. Although its impact on his health was predictably disastrous, Jason persevered until "*compelled* to retire." Finally, when Jason insisted on reentering the academy, his awful symptoms returned, resulting in a "total and complete bodily incapacity for exertion of every kind" that continued to the day of his attempted suicide.[95]

In addition to defending him against charges of idleness, the sympathetic author offered a detailed account of Jason's relationship with Elizabeth Fales, describing their courtship in sentimental terms. The two had been drawn together when Jason was only sixteen by a shared interest in music; "it was the mutual harmony of sweet sounds, that first awakened their young hearts to affection." Indeed, their harmony was more than simply musical. Since a "most melting sensibility was the reigning principle of both their minds," they actually enjoyed a "reciprocal and delightful unison of disposition." Yet their relationship was also described as a joining of contrasts, one in which Fales rather than Fairbanks played the more dominant and assertive role: "She was healthy, active, animated, and of opinions the most decided, energetic and undeviating—he, weakly, sedentary, conciliating and pacific."[96] While such a formulation may have grated against contemporary gender stereotypes, it neatly meshed with Jason's version of events in the fatal grove.

As in the closing arguments of Harrison Gray Otis, the author also stressed the role of romantic fiction in shaping and stimulating the affections of Betsey Fales. In contrast to Jason's varied reading in "politics, novels, history and philosophy," Betsey's literary pursuits were much more limited. "Like his, her delight was studiously to devote her few leisure hours to reading; but the books of her choice were usually confined to works of fiction and moral amusement, in which the passion of love was generally transcendant," the author explained. "Hence her sensible heart became more tenderly attached, while her fond imagination was continually tracing through each romantic description, some resemblance of the fancied perfections of her own lover."[97] In light of the circumstances of her death, that account—confirmed in part by trial testimony concerning Betsey's reading of *Julia Mandeville* on May 18—suggested the contemporary critique of sentimental fiction as tending to "inflame the passions, delude the imagination, and corrupt the heart."[98]

Although the condemned murderer's older brother claimed that the "Life and Character" had been drafted for him by a local "gentleman of liberal education," there is some reason to believe that it was actually written by a woman. In an April 1802 letter, Thomas Boylston Adams scornfully dismissed the sketch as the product of a "female biographer," particularly disparaging its "gorgeous decorations" and "tinsel splendor."[99] An account of the Fairbanks case published in the late 1860s was less abusive but more specific, attributing the work to Sarah Wentworth Morton, a beautiful Boston socialite and frequent contributor to local literary magazines whose poetical effusions had at one time earned her considerable renown as "the American Sappho."[100]

While such a late attribution may not be entirely convincing by itself, several other bits of evidence (in addition to the Adams reference) tend to lend it circumstantial support. As the daughter of a wealthy merchant and the wife of a prominent lawyer who eventually became attorney general of Massachusetts, Sarah Wentworth Morton was part of a sparkling social circle that included Jason's counsel, Harrison Gray Otis.[101] It certainly seems plausible that Otis, passionately convinced of his client's innocence, might have brought his melodramatic case to the attention of a sympathetic acquaintance like Sarah Morton. It seems equally plausible that Mrs. Morton, known as a woman prone to befriend and patronize young persons of both sexes, might have taken a personal interest in the fascinating cause célèbre.[102]

One or two other circumstances in Sarah Morton's personal life might also

Unfinished portrait of Mrs. Sarah Wentworth Morton, probable author of a sympathetic biography of Jason Fairbanks. Painted by Gilbert Stuart in about 1802. *Courtesy, Worcester Art Museum, Worcester, Massachusetts.*

have led her to sympathize with Jason Fairbanks. The socialite's only son, a teenager at the time of the tragedy in Dedham, was a promising but sickly youth whose life she later described in terms strikingly similar to those applied to Jason Fairbanks in the biographical sketch. "In his very early childhood he appeared a prodigy of genius," Morton wrote of her son many years after his untimely death. "But his whole existence was that of suffering, owing to the original feebleness of his constitution and the energetic sensibility of his mind."[103] Morton's sympathies might well have been aroused by the similarity of Jason's intellectual aspirations, acute sensibilities, and bodily sufferings to those of her own child.

Another motive for Morton's interest in Jason Fairbanks may have been provided by her earlier involvement, during the late 1780s, in a highly publicized sex scandal that was in some respects analogous to the Dedham tragedy. Her husband, Perez Morton, and her sister, Frances Theodora Apthorp, had been the guilty principals in the infamous case of adulterous incest and suicide recounted in the novel *The Power of Sympathy* (1789). Having been intimately familiar with Frances Apthorp's suicide in the face of her father's patriarchal outrage, the romantic poet may have found it particularly credible that Betsey Fales would have taken her own life in despair over her parents' disapproval of Jason Fairbanks. Since Sarah Morton's personal sympathies at the time of Apthorp's suicide were not with her judgmental father but with her philandering husband and guilty sister, it would not be surprising if she had sympathized with two other illicit lovers in a subsequent romantic tragedy.[104]

Finally, the case for Sarah Morton's authorship of the short biography of Jason Fairbanks is strengthened by the fact that at least two other mid-nineteenth century literary sources linked the condemned murderer to a woman matching her description. In an essay published in 1856, Lucius M. Sargent described sympathetic ladies of "respectable standing" who visited Jason Fairbanks in his cell and recalled in particular one unnamed woman of "some literary celebrity" who smuggled a knife to the condemned prisoner. Similarly, in his biography of James Sullivan published in 1859, Thomas C. Amory referred to a tradition which held that Jason's abortive escape had been engineered with the help of "a lady of beauty and much literary reputation, the wife of one already eminent at the bar, and who subsequently rose to its highest office." There can be little doubt that Amory's detailed reference was to Sarah Morton, the beautiful literary wife of an attorney general, while Sargent's sketchy description, although somewhat less definitive, also neatly fit "the American Sappho."[105]

Whether or not Mrs. Morton actually wrote the Fairbanks biography, the mere fact that the attribution was plausible suggests the shifting literary tone and cultural context of criminal narratives at the beginning of the nineteenth century. Those new influences were apparent in many other literary responses to the Fairbanks tragedy and were particularly prominent in successive editions of Nathaniel Coverly's flamboyant *Biography of Mr. Jason Fairbanks and Miss Eliza Fales*. Although the hostile *Biography* and the sympathetic "Life and Character" may have differed sharply in their portrayal of the condemned murderer, they actually shared a common body of language and sentiment. Another literary response to the Dedham tragedy apparently issued at the time—unfortunately no copies seem to have survived—took the matter one step further, directly into the realm of fiction. That work, entitled *Life of Jason Fairbanks, a Novel Founded on Fact*, was evidently one of the earliest American novels based on an actual murder case.[106] During subsequent decades many other criminal biographies, particularly those involving cases of sexual intrigue, would have at least as much in common with contemporary romantic fiction as with the pious spiritual biographies and skeletal last speeches of earlier cultural regimes.[107]

If the case of Jason Fairbanks suggested the growing cultural influence of sentimental fiction, it also illustrated an emerging trend toward expanded newspaper coverage of crimes and trials. Although journalistic treatments of the case were quite modest in comparison with later antebellum coverage of sensational murders, the florid report of the tragedy in the *Columbian Minerva* and the detailed trial account in the *Independent Chronicle* were both exceptionally elaborate by eighteenth-century standards. It is probably no coincidence that, several weeks after the execution on Dedham common, Fisher Ames, a prominent Federalist of that same town, published a thoughtful essay assailing the extensive coverage being given by local newspapers to such tragedies as murders and suicides. Among other things, Ames suggested that the detailed discussion of unusual disasters tended to frighten the timid, inspire the foolish, and corrupt the "public taste and morals." While acknowledging that such events should be "mentioned" by the press, he insisted that coverage should be "cursory" and objected particularly to the presentation of those "horrid details that make each particular hair stiffen and stand upright in the reader's head." Since he had earlier complained in private correspondence of the local hysteria aroused by the Fairbanks affair, it is likely that Ames wrote with that particular case in mind. As an astute reader of the public press, Ames perceived the sensationalistic trend of newspaper coverage; as a staunch social conservative, he deplored it.[108]

The Fairbanks case not only illustrated the growing influence of sentimental fiction and the gradual expansion of newspaper coverage but also demonstrated the emerging importance of the trial report as a central literary response to the subjects of crime and punishment. Detailed summaries of the Fairbanks trial were provided by local newspapers, and one was reprinted at least twice in pamphlet form; a much longer synopsis of the proceedings was also quickly published. That longer report, issued by Russell and Cutler of Boston, achieved immediate commercial success, appearing in four editions within a matter of months. In addition to their appearance in newspapers and in separate pamphlets, summaries or excerpts of trial testimony were also included in such works as Coverly's *Biography* and Fairbanks's *Solemn Declaration*, establishing a pattern of literary agglomeration that would persist into the antebellum period.[109] Unlike most colonial publications, which treated crime and punishment without much regard to the intervening process of adjudication, trial reports were central to the nineteenth-century literature.

The rise of the novel and allied genres, the development of modern journalism, and the popularization of the trial report were related cultural developments. Each literary form offered realistic portrayals of social events within an essentially secular epistemology. Newspapers, biographies, and novels borrowed materials from criminal proceedings, and trials themselves reflected the influence of a new literary sensibility. The ease with which legal and romantic treatments of crime could blend within the culture of nineteenth-century New England is neatly suggested by Thomas C. Amory's retrospective assessment of the Fairbanks case:

The incidents of the tragedy have been made the subject of romance; and persons, residing near the scene of its occurrence, relate the simple particulars of the story with a pathos which requires no aid from the embellishments of fiction. It is one of the legends of New England; and the fast hold it still retains upon popular sympathy has not been probably the less enduring for the charm with which the eloquence of the eminent counsel, Otis, Lowell and Sullivan, have invested it.[110]

According to James Sullivan's biographer, the process of legal adjudication did not inhibit romanticization of the Fairbanks story but actually enhanced its status as local legend. Far from being the antithesis of sentimental expression, nineteenth-century legal advocacy could be its very essence.

Literary responses to the Dedham tragedy of 1801 suggest that the dawn of the nineteenth century may have marked a key transition in the cultural history of New England; it certainly did in regard to the region's crime literature.[111] In addressing the case of Jason Fairbanks, execution sermons appeared only as attenuated afterthoughts; the dry husk of the last-speech broadside was exploded by an infusion of motifs from sentimental fiction; expanded newspaper treatments of crime suggested the coming flood of journalistic reportage; and early trial reports illustrated the legalistic component of a new cultural regime. By the 1830s and 1840s, the transition was complete: execution sermons and last-speech broadsides had vanished; sensationalistic newspaper accounts, legalistic trial reports, and romantic biographies had become the primary media of crime coverage. An older literature of Protestant piety had been overwhelmed by a new culture of legal romanticism.

Before moving on to the Tirrell affair of the 1840s, it may be helpful to set fictive aspects of the Fairbanks case into historiographic perspective. The classic account of fiction's stunning rise to literary predominance during the last decades of the eighteenth century was formulated in 1797 by the American novelist Royall Tyler. "No sooner was a taste for amusing literature diffused," he claimed, "than all orders of country life with one accord forsook the sober sermons and Practical Pieties of their fathers for the gay stories and splendid impieties of the Traveller and the Novelist." Although not the view of a disinterested observer, Tyler's assessment was still being echoed and endorsed by literary scholars 150 years later.[112]

However, two recent studies of book production and diffusion in rural Massachusetts have challenged the notion that fiction rapidly conquered the New England countryside. In a perceptive survey of the printing and bookselling business of the Merriam family of Brookfield, Jack Larkin notes the relative scarcity of fiction in the output and sales of that firm. "Fiction could be found on the country bookstore's shelves, but up to the early 1830s it seems to have played no transforming role in the cultural lives of ordinary rural people," Larkin generalizes. "Fiction moved slowly, in minuscule numbers, against the predominantly orthodox cultural grain of central Massachusetts, where Puritan-bred suspicions of novels remained powerful."[113] That view has been reinforced by the skillful reconstruction of two early social libraries in Concord by Robert A. Gross, who finds that fewer than 7 percent of the volumes in a collection assembled between 1795 and 1820 were works of fiction. After explicitly challenging one of Tyler's extravagant claims, Gross notes that "only a handful of novels, and all of those highly moral, made it onto the shelves."[114]

Although Larkin and Gross make a strong case against the Tyler thesis, many of the circumstances surrounding the Dedham tragedy of 1801 tend to support the idea that a revolution in literary culture had already been accomplished in eastern Massachusetts by the beginning of the nineteenth century. Trial testimony indicated that Betsey Fales had shared at least one melodramatic novel with her neighbors during the spring of 1801.[115] Supporters of Jason Fairbanks argued that romantic fiction played a crucial role in shaping Betsey's love for Jason and in precipitating her violent demise.[116] Herman Mann's initial newspaper report of the tragedy was interspersed with evocative phrases drawn from sentimental discourse, which suggests that he expected local readers to be attuned to the language of literary sensibility.[117] Other published treatments of the case were also infused with motifs typical of contemporary tales and romances.[118] Lawyers on both sides of the case not only adopted narrative strategies suggestive of fiction in their reconstructions of events but also invoked the epistemological authority of imaginative literature in their arguments.[119] In short, fictive themes pervaded cultural responses to two of the most serious events that could ever confront a community: a murder (or suicide) and a capital trial. The readers of Dedham and vicinity had not simply found a new literary diversion; sentimental fiction offered them a new language, a new sensibility, and a new way of perceiving the world around them.

There are several ways to reconcile the striking cultural pattern exposed by the Fairbanks case with the findings of Larkin and Gross. First, sentimental motifs could be widely diffused through the culture by vehicles other than fiction. As suggested by the Fairbanks case, even readers who scrupulously avoided novels might still be exposed to the new discourse in newspapers, trial reports, and other publications.[120] Second, there may have been a significant time lag in the diffusion of the "fiction revolution" across the state of Massachusetts. Sentimental novels may have reached Dedham, a community within the cultural orbit of Boston, long before they arrived in substantial numbers at inland Brookfield. Third, the relatively genteel social libraries of Concord were probably not representative of popular reading habits throughout eastern Massachusetts. As Jesse H. Shera has demonstrated, the commercial circulating libraries that flourished in the region during the late eighteenth and early nineteenth centuries actually specialized in novels and other works of fiction.[121] Fourth, Larkin and Gross provide evidence suggesting that some young people in both Brookfield and Concord ignored literary proscriptions and embraced novel reading despite the disapproval of their elders.

According to Larkin, purchases by apprentices in the Merriam printing office accounted for more than half of the firm's total sales of fiction.[122] It is only reasonable to assume that the literary tastes of those young men were shared (along with the actual novels) by at least some of their local friends. Similarly, Gross reports that one Mary Wilder Van Schalkwyck, a well-connected young widow in her early twenties, read fiction with enthusiasm in Concord during the 1790s and early 1800s. Van Schalkwyck not only owned novels herself but also lent them to and borrowed them from her friends and regaled her companions with vivid renditions of fictional plots.[123] In short, the reading habits of young working men in Brookfield and young women of leisure in Concord, along with the reported literary interests of the social circle of Fairbanks and Fales in Dedham, all suggest that locally flourishing "youth cultures" in early national Massachusetts were committed to the consumption of novels, whether their elders approved or not.[124]

But there was more to the fiction revolution than that. Herman Mann highlighted sentimental motifs in his newspaper account (presumably directed at adult readers) and lawyers on both sides of the Fairbanks case incorporated fictional themes into their arguments (certainly directed at adult judges and jurors), suggesting that young people were not the only ones being seduced by the new literary forms. Editors and lawyers not only used sentimental language themselves but seemed to assume that their mature neighbors were attuned to fictive discourse as well. As they struggled to retain power and influence in an increasingly egalitarian public culture, young Federalists like Harrison Gray Otis were at least as willing to employ fashionable literary motifs as they were to embrace innovative political tactics.[125] Literary sentimentalism was not merely a resource for the socially powerless but was becoming an effective tool of established elites.[126] In fact, some of those elites may have themselves been seduced by the new ethos. Chief Justice Dana of the Massachusetts Supreme Court reportedly sobbed while imposing the death penalty on Jason Fairbanks.[127] And John Lowell, Jr., Otis's high-strung co-counsel, was supposedly so distraught by the outcome of the Fairbanks case that he suffered a nervous breakdown and never again resumed the practice of law. Surely those were signs of true sensibility![128]

Whether manipulative cynics or sincere proselytes, the authors of sentimentalized crime coverage and commentary were active agents of cultural change, carrying new values to those outside the still limited circle of committed fiction readers. The presence of sentimental themes in courtroom proceedings was particularly significant. As Lawrence M. Friedman has observed, "arguments presented in trials are often important clues to what stories count as good, or true, or compelling stories, within a particular culture."[129] Indeed, the arguments of Otis and Sullivan suggest that sentimentalism had successfully infiltrated the "spontaneous philosophy" of early nineteenth-century popular culture.[130] While old-fashioned moralists, who feared and despised novels, may have taken grim satisfaction in the tragic ending to the Fairbanks story, they could only have been alarmed by the many fictive versions of the tale that were told and retold by the cultural arbiters of Dedham. Their trepidation was entirely justified: By integrating the motifs of imaginative literature into the authoritative discourses of law and journalism, published responses to the deaths of Eliza Fales and Jason Fairbanks legitimized, even as they critiqued, the birth of a sentimental culture.

9

The Prostitute and the Somnambulist:
Rufus Choate and the Triumph
of Romantic Advocacy

If the Fairbanks case exposed a transitional stage in literary responses to crime and punishment in New England, an equally sensational melodrama played out in Boston more than forty years later illustrated the new cultural regime in full and lurid flower. The discovery of the charred corpse of a young woman, Maria A. Bickford, at a disreputable boarding house in late October 1845 led to successive trials of a wealthy young rake, Albert J. Tirrell, for murder and arson. From its beginning the affair aroused great popular interest and excitement in Boston. The city's numerous daily newspapers and other local periodicals provided extensive coverage of the case over a period of many months; a number of biographical accounts of both victim and suspect appeared in the newspapers or were issued as pamphlets; a novel based on the case was quickly published; and, when the case finally reached the courts, detailed trial summaries were reported in the daily press, in weekly periodicals, and in separate pamphlets.[1]

Journalistic coverage of the Bickford affair was much more extensive and sustained than it would have been had the tragedy occurred a mere twenty years earlier. That heightened attention reflected the emergence during the 1830s of the penny press, cheap urban daily newspapers that catered to an enormous audience drawn largely from the middle and working classes. The rise of the penny press and related print ephemera, based in large part on the great marketability of crime accounts and trial reports as literary commodities, was one aspect of the much broader development of a mass consumer culture in antebellum New England. The new consumerism accompanied a complex process of agricultural change and economic diversification that caused thousands of young men and women to leave rural areas in pursuit of economic opportunities in growing factory towns and commercial centers. Between 1820 and 1845, the population of Boston rose from under forty-four thousand to nearly one hundred thousand, while many other smaller towns in southern New England crossed the urban threshold both demographically and culturally. Within just a few decades, the heart of a largely rural and agricultural region had become predominantly urban and industrial.[2]

One particularly troubling aspect of the emerging consumer culture of industrializing New England was the commercialization of urban prostitution. Although Boston had long been notorious for its whores, Barbara Hobson has pointed out that legislation enacted in Massachusetts during the mid-nineteenth century reflected "an awareness of prostitution as an increasingly commercialized trade with more middlemen and merchandisers."[3] At least one antebellum commentator also applied the language of modern commerce to fallen women by characterizing youthful prostitutes as a "marketable commodity."[4] Yet that image may convey too passive an impression of the prostitutes, who themselves increasingly acted like aggressive entrepreneurs. According to one outraged moral reformer, base women thrust their calling cards into the hands of young men in Boston stores, while debauched candy vendors boldly solicited passing clergymen on the streets.[5] Overall, the peddlers of sex in cities like Boston provided antebellum consumers with an ever expanding array of products and services, ranging from the vicarious titillation offered by prurient crime coverage in penny dailies, trial reports, and other cheap pamphlets to the more direct, and somewhat more costly, gratification promised by disreputable women in brothels, dancehalls, and houses of assignation.[6] In life Maria Bickford had been a minor participant in a major growth industry; in death she would play a more prominent role.

So much antebellum crime coverage revolved around courtroom cases that a number of prominent criminal lawyers became media celebrities. One of the most famous was Rufus Choate, a personal friend, political protégé, and legal rival of Daniel Webster.[7] Because Choate was to play a key part in the trials of Albert Tirrell, it may be useful to provide a brief sketch of his life and career up to the mid-1840s. The son of bookish parents of old Yankee stock, Rufus Choate had been born in Essex County, Massachusetts, in 1799. After a childhood of precocious reading on the family farm and a brief stint at a local academy, he entered Dartmouth College in 1815. There Choate distinguished himself by his academic brilliance, joining a circle of talented young scholars greatly influenced by such apostles of European romanticism as Scott, Byron, Wordsworth, Coleridge, and Madame de Staël.[8] Although for a time he leaned toward an academic career, Choate had decided by 1819 to become a lawyer. More than one biographer has ascribed Choate's change of vocational plans to the impression made on him by Daniel Webster's memorable arguments in *The Trustees of Dartmouth College v. Woodward* (1817–19), the famous litigation involving their shared alma mater.[9]

Yet it seems extremely unlikely that Choate actually heard Webster's arguments in the Dartmouth College case, and, when he came to eulogize his idol in 1853, Choate chose not to invoke memories of that renowned constitutional contest. Instead, he recalled the great advocate's "exuberant" display of "power" in the criminal trial of one Joseph Jackman for robbery. It was a performance observed with evident fascination by Choate while at home from Dartmouth in poor health during the spring of 1818.[10] To judge by his earlier defense of two brothers accused of the same crime, Webster almost certainly impugned the integrity of Jackman's alleged victim and postulated that the complainant, a wealthy and reputable merchant from Bangor, Maine, had actually staged an elaborate sham robbery, possibly in order to avoid paying some debts.[11] Thus young Choate saw Webster defeat a criminal charge by assassinating the character of the supposed victim—who was also a key prosecution witness—and by offering an imaginative reconstruction of events surrounding the crime that was consistent with his client's innocence. It may be no coincidence that those were two techniques of which Choate himself would eventually become an effective and controversial master.[12]

Whether or not Webster's performance in the Jackman case was his immediate inspiration, Rufus Choate did pursue a legal career after leaving Dartmouth. After a few months at Harvard Law School in 1820, Choate served an apprenticeship in the office of U.S. Attorney General William Wirt in Washington. Having gained some additional training back in Massachusetts, Choate was admitted to the bar of Essex County in 1823. He began his practice in the village of South Danvers, Massachusetts, moving to the successively larger venues of nearby Salem in 1828 and Boston in 1834. During his early years at the bar, Choate was perceived as a strikingly beautiful young man, tall and slender, awkward in manner and careless in dress, with a profusion of jet black hair and a strangely exotic look about him. His appearance was at once that of a Byronic hero and an uncouth provincial; he was, as one bemused contemporary noted, "an Apollo with a *slouch*."[13]

It was as a criminal lawyer that Choate first gained public and professional notice; he became widely known for defending such petty miscreants as an accused turkey thief and a group of alleged dancehall rioters. Choate's striking appearance, excited eloquence, and flamboyant courtroom manner lent those causes a crowd-pleasing drama hardly justified by their otherwise trivial character. His striking methods not only drew spectators—and raised eyebrows—but also won cases. Legend had it that Choate never lost a criminal trial while in practice in Essex County.[14] As with his mentor, Daniel Webster, the young advocate's courtroom triumphs helped launch a successful political career. Choate served in both houses of the Massachusetts legislature during the late 1820s, in the U.S. House of Representatives during the early 1830s, and in the U.S. Senate during the early 1840s. Yet Choate remained immersed in legal matters even while holding political office and was primarily identified, both by himself and by the public, as a courtroom lawyer.[15]

Contemporary observers and modern scholars alike have struggled to convey the magical intensity of Rufus Choate's courtroom performances, with their fantastic blend of broad learning, keen logic, vivid imagination, captivating eloquence, savage insinuations, ludicrous exaggerations, and vehement gestures, complete with trembling hands, blazing eyes, wild hair, and disheveled clothing.[16] But behind all the extravagance of demeanor and erudition lay a fairly simple and consistent courtroom method. Choate almost invariably sought to portray the character of his client in as favorable a light as possible, blacken the reputations of opposing parties and witnesses, and offer hypothetical reconstructions of disputed events that were consistent with his client's innocence.[17] In portraying good and evil characters and in sketching plausible human motives and actions, Choate engaged in an imaginative and expressive enterprise closely analogous to that of a novelist or other creative writer, a point understood by perceptive contemporaries.

The anonymous author of a biographical sketch of Choate that appeared in the *American Review* in early 1847 claimed that the advocate argued his case as though writing a "romantic poem," portrayed his client as the "hero of the narrative," and treated his jury like the "reader of a romance." The same writer also implied that Choate's powerful identification with his clients was like that of a great author with his fictional characters. "Ideas, suppositions, possibilities, drawn into his own imagination, are vitalized into realities," the writer explained, "and he sees them as living things—sees them as Dante saw Farinata rise from his glowing tomb—as Shakspeare saw Cordelia bending over Lear."[18] According to E. P. Whipple, another contemporary biographer, Choate was so successful in turning "the dryest law-case" into "a thrilling tragedy or tragi-comedy" that even his clients—who of all people should have known better—were often moved to tears by the lawyer's plausible stories, weeping irrepressibly at the "eloquent recapitulation of what they had suffered and done." Thus did Choate transform dubious, even criminal, characters into "poetic personages, worthy of the pen of Scott or Dickens." Although many miscreants were undoubtedly liberated over the years by Choate's expansive eloquence, Whipple concluded that the great lawyer's remarkable "power of lifting, of idealizing his clients, of making them the heroes or heroines of a domestic or sensational novel, was never more brilliantly illustrated than in the celebrated Tirrell trial."[19]

By the time of his return to Boston from the Senate in 1845, Choate was at the height of his legal powers, professional reputation, and public celebrity. He was an acknowledged leader of the Boston bar, involved in numerous civil and criminal cases.[20] His courtroom performances were the subject of frequent coverage and favorable comment in the Boston press.[21] Yet Choate's legal preeminence was maintained in the face of stiff competition; antebellum Boston enjoyed a wealth of legal talent. "In no city in the Union, we think, can such a brilliant galaxy of eminent counsellors be found, as in this city," a reporter for the *Boston Daily Times* proudly claimed in 1846, "and however distinguished one may become at the bar here, there are always others prepared to dispute his claims to greater eminence."[22]

Indeed, despite his impressive record and reputation, Choate was by no means invincible, not even in front of a jury. Opponents could defeat him not by matching or exceeding him in flowery oratory and enchanting eloquence—after all, nobody could out-Choate Choate—but by *dis*enchanting the jurors with plain talk and common sense.[23] During the early autumn of 1845, shortly before the sensational Tirrell affair splashed across the pages of Boston's newspapers, Choate defended three merchants accused of forty-five counts of commercial fraud in the case of *Commonwealth v. Eastman, Fonday & Com-*

pany. Opposing him in the litigation was a man nearly twenty years his senior, the veteran public attorney for Suffolk County, Samuel D. Parker. Much like Choate, Parker had reportedly achieved his early reputation at the bar as a criminal defense lawyer, a protector of rogues and prostitutes. In fact, published records of the Boston Municipal Court confirm that between 1823 and 1832 Parker defended an assortment of accused thieves, gamblers, rioters, counterfeiters, and wanton and lascivious women. But the Boston native and son of a prominent local clergyman finally switched sides during the early 1830s; as county attorney over the next two decades, Parker routinely prosecuted unsavory characters of the type he had once ably defended.[24]

Despite their shared background as criminal defense lawyers, the courtroom styles of Choate and Parker contrasted sharply. While Choate was verbose, imaginative, and flowery, Parker tended to be concise, logical, and systematic, prone to organizing his oral arguments around tight sets of numbered propositions. "He was direct, close and pointed," one reporter wrote of Parker's courtroom manner in the case of *Eastman, Fonday & Company.* "Possessing none of the graces of rhetoric, he yet bore down, in plain language to be sure, but with iron-linked arguments."[25] The sharply divergent personal styles of Choate and Parker, along with their natural rivalry as prominent Boston lawyers, may have contributed to a testy misunderstanding that developed between them during the course of the trial.[26] In any case, Parker endured Choate's clever courtroom sparring and eventually got the better of his younger opponent; after deliberations of nearly five hours, the jury came in with a verdict of guilty on all but three of the forty-five counts.[27] Within a matter of months, the two legal combatants would have a highly publicized rematch in the murder trial of Albert J. Tirrell.

The legal troubles of Albert Tirrell were first reported by the Boston press in a mildly satirical squib appearing on Monday, September 29, 1845, in the *Daily Evening Transcript.* The brief story, entitled "A Love Affair," contained the report of one Colonel Hatch, a correspondent to the Boston newspapers, concerning the arrest in New Bedford the previous Saturday of an unnamed "young blood" accused of "some indelicacies with a young woman." According to Hatch's report, the young man had been armed with a six-barreled pistol and a dirk and had only been apprehended after "a hard chase of about a mile." The report concluded by noting that the suspect was to be brought to Boston that Monday to stand trial. The trivial scoop was promptly picked up by two of Boston's most widely circulated penny newspapers, the *Daily Times* and *Daily Mail,* whose editors were always on the lookout for engaging filler to pad their spacious sheets.[28]

The following day the *Boston Post*'s regular Municipal Court column offered a more detailed account of the arrest in New Bedford, identifying the captured man as "Albert J. Tirrell, gentleman, of Weymouth." According to the *Post,* Tirrell had been indicted the previous May for an adultery allegedly committed in Suffolk County. He had eluded arrest at the time and had remained at large until his dramatic flight and apprehension by the New Bedford officers. His unnamed paramour, reportedly present with him at a house in New Bedford, had successfully fled in another direction. Following his arrest and transfer to Boston, Tirrell was formally arraigned on the adultery charge and committed to jail pending trial at the next term of the Municipal Court.[29]

As it turned out, Tirrell did not have to spend much time in jail, posting bail on October 2. About a week later, a number of his friends and relatives, including his young wife, wrote letters to Samuel D. Parker, the county prosecutor, requesting a stay of proceedings on the adultery indictment in the hope that Tirrell might be reformed. Parker presented those letters to the judges of the Municipal Court, who agreed to suspend prosecution for six months, with Tirrell paying court costs and posting bond as a guarantee of his good behavior. On October 21 Tirrell came to court, paid costs, and posted bond. Then, in defiance of the terms of his recognizance, he went off to meet his paramour, joining her the following day at a disreputable lodging house on Cedar Lane, near the western end of Beacon Hill.[30]

Less than a week later, at nine o'clock on the morning of Monday, October 27, the second edition of the *Daily Mail* reported the initial details of a gruesome case of murder and attempted arson. It seemed that a woman named Bickford had been killed several hours earlier at a house on Cedar Lane; the victim's throat had been "cut nearly from ear to ear," and her bed had been set on fire. Later that same day, at two o'clock in the afternoon, the *Mail* produced an "extra" edition providing more sensational details on the fast-breaking case. The disreputable dwelling where the mutilated body was discovered had long been occupied by one Joel Lawrence and his wife, who had used it in recent years as a "house of assignation." The victim was identified as Maria A. Bickford, a young married woman from Maine, separated from her husband for some time. According to the *Mail*, she had been a woman of "slight, graceful figure, and very beautiful."[31]

At about five o'clock that morning, Mr. and Mrs. Lawrence and another young woman living in the house had heard a shriek upstairs, followed by a heavy thud; immediately afterward, someone had stumbled down the stairs and rushed out the door of the building. Bickford's body was discovered in an upstairs room shortly thereafter. The dead woman's jugular vein and windpipe had been completely severed, her hair had been partly consumed by fire, and her face had been "charred and blackened" by flames. A number of fires had been set in the room where the body was discovered, the walls of the room were splattered with blood, a nearby washbowl contained a quantity of bloody water, and a bloodstained razor was found at the foot of her bed. Some articles of men's clothing were found in the room, along with a letter initialed A. J. T. to M. A. B. According to the *Mail* reporter, the murder had almost certainly been committed by Albert J. Tirrell.[32]

Additional details provided by the Boston press over the following several days only strengthened that inference; a number of particularly damaging

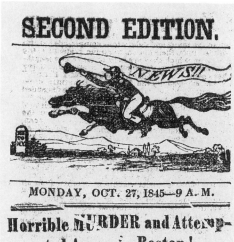

SECOND EDITION.

MONDAY, OCT. 27, 1845—9 A. M.

Horrible MURDER and Attempted Arson in Boston!

A woman was murdered this morning about 4 o'clock, at a house in Cedar Lane, near Cambridge Bridge, recently occupied as a house of prostitution by the notorious Julia King. Of the present character of the house we are not informed.

The murdered person was a Mrs. Bickford; and her husband is now absent in the state of Maine. *Her throat was cut nearly from ear to ear,* and the bed set on fire in order to conceal this act of atrocity.

We are requested not to give further particulars until the holding of the Coroner's Inquest, which we trust will develop the mysteries of this horrid affair, and be the means of bringing the murderer to justice.

One of the first journalistic reports of the death of Maria Bickford, which appeared in the *Boston Daily Mail* **within hours of the crime.** *Courtesy, Massachusetts Historical Society.*

facts emerged at the official inquest, held the day after Bickford's death. The proceedings were closely covered by local newspapers, a few of which provided nearly verbatim transcripts. Nine witnesses testified before the coroner's jury, including Joel Lawrence, his wife, his teenage son, and Priscilla Blood, a young woman living with the family. According to those members of the Lawrence household, Maria Bickford had come to stay with them nine or ten days before and had frequently been visited there by Tirrell, who stayed overnight on at least one or two occasions. On the afternoon before the murder, Priscilla Blood heard the couple exchange angry words; shortly afterward, Bickford explained to Blood that she liked to quarrel with Tirrell because "they had such a good time making up."[33]

Tirrell left the house early that evening but was back in his paramour's bedroom within a couple of hours; at about nine o'clock, as the Lawrence family was preparing to retire for the night, Bickford came to Priscilla Blood's room and asked her for some water for Albert. That was the last anyone saw or heard of the couple until early the next morning, when the Lawrence household was roused by a commotion upstairs, followed by billows of smoke and fire. At about five-thirty that morning, a young man matching Tirrell's description came to a nearby stable and requested a horse to carry him to Weymouth, Tirrell's hometown, explaining that "he had got into a little difficulty and wanted to go to his wife's father." During the course of the inquest, a number of witnesses identified a vest and a cane subsequently found at the scene of the crime as belonging to Tirrell. On the basis of that web of purely circumstantial evidence, the coroner's jury concluded that Bickford had been murdered by her paramour, Albert J. Tirrell.[34]

As the newspapers printed a succession of false rumors concerning Tirrell's whereabouts over the following weeks, they also began examining the life and character of his alleged victim.[35] While all seemed to agree that Maria Bickford had been young, beautiful, and fallen, competing accounts offered very different versions of her life and suggested widely varying degrees of sympathy. One early and largely inaccurate account in the *Daily Mail* of October 31 claimed that Maria was an "unsophisticated girl" who had been lured into adultery shortly after her marriage by a depraved companion. Although her conduct and character had deteriorated thereafter, she had managed to pause before the brink of "utter degradation and ruin" and was about to be reclaimed by an old lover—who planned to elope with her to western New York—at the time of her death. Bickford had allegedly told an acquaintance that "she was tired of the way she had been living, and was resolved that her future life should atone for her past follies."[36]

The narrative continued with a poignant description of various articles found in the dead woman's room, including several rings and trinkets worn by her on the day before her death, a collection of perfumes and cosmetics neatly arranged on the mantelpiece, a bundle of letters containing an endearing epistle from her mother, a number of gilt-framed prints, and a daguerreotype of Bickford herself in which she appeared "uncommonly lovely and innocent." That inventory of genteel feminine possessions was clearly designed to arouse sympathy for the fallen woman. The reporter finally speculated on Maria's thoughts during the hours before her sudden death. "Who knows the joys, the promised hope, that revealed itself for future life?" he asked rhetorically. "She was the victim of jealousy and revenge, and he who committed the bloody act, cannot go unpunished."[37]

An anonymous poem that appeared on November 10 in the *Boston Post* offered a similarly sympathetic view of Maria Bickford as a "sentimental victim." It began by describing the fallen woman asleep in bed, dreaming of her long lost days of childhood innocence, as a sexual predator prepared to cut her throat with "cold, cold hands and ruthless steel." While acknowledging Maria's faults, the poet attributed far greater depravity to her killer—and

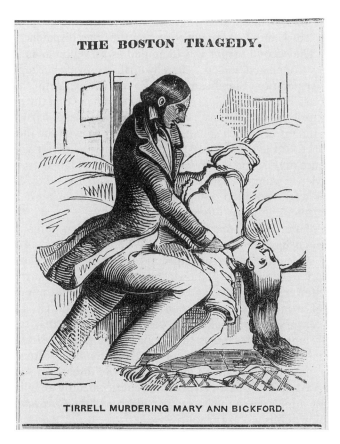

THE BOSTON TRAGEDY.

TIRRELL MURDERING MARY ANN BICKFORD.

Graphic representation of the alleged murder of Bickford by Tirrell from the
National Police Gazette, **a nationally distributed periodical devoted to crime cover-**
age, published in New York City. *Courtesy, American Antiquarian Society.*

to mankind in general—suggesting that even the worst of women was purer
than the best of men. Outrage at the murder of a prostitute had inspired a
powerful critique of male corruption and violence. Like the sympathetic *Mail*
reporter, the poet concluded with an indignant call for vengeance:

> O may they find who did this deed.
> And may the jury try him;
> And may the judge his sentence read,
> And may the sheriff hang him![38]

But not all newspaper treatments were sympathetic toward Bickford; on the
contrary, some portrayed the slain woman less as a sentimental victim than as a
sexual predator in her own right. For example, one early report, first appearing
in the fledgling *Boston Daily Whig* on November 1, suggested that Bickford had

been responsible for the deaths of at least two men. One had allegedly been stabbed with a dirk and then cruelly poisoned, the other dispatched by unspecified means. The second victim was identified as a "yellow man" with whom Bickford had "connected herself," thereby further sullying her reputation with a hint of miscegenation. Significantly, the *Whig* story explicitly challenged the sympathetic account that had just appeared in the *Daily Mail* the previous day. "Maria Bickford was notoriously a woman of the vilest passions, without any of those redeeming traits which sometimes characterize even the most depraved and abandoned of the sex," the *Whig* reporter insisted. "Her whole life furnishes evidence of this, and the endeavors made by the Mail to get up sympathy for the murdered woman is anything but commendable." Excerpts from the hostile story were reprinted, sometimes with accompanying denials by her estranged husband, in many other newspapers.[39]

Charges of murderous treachery on the part of a fallen woman, far-fetched though they may have been in the Bickford case, had a great deal of resonance in the moralistic culture of early Victorian America. While most social observers of the period would have acknowledged the exceptional purity of virtuous women, far fewer would have agreed with the anonymous poet's claim that the worst of women was purer than the best of men. On the contrary, nineteenth-century moral spokesmen commonly argued that fallen women were actually more depraved than their male counterparts. Fearing the aggressive potential of female sexuality, nervous commentators often transmuted the vision of a sentimental victim into the far more threatening counterimage of a sexual predator.[40] Such an alchemy was performed by an editorial on the Bickford case appearing in the November 13 issue of the *Christian Reflector*, a Baptist weekly published in Boston:

> However amiable, and lovely, and true, a woman may have been in innocence, she is, in the degradation of lost virtue, like a fallen angel. She may retain her smiles, and charm still with her winning ways, but she is as *devilish* as she is sensual. No crime is too horrid for her to commit, if her passions be aroused or her interest involved. She is two-fold more the child of hell, than even the fiend who effected her ruin.[41]

Given such widely shared assumptions, it is not surprising that Maria Bickford could be portrayed as a villainess even in connection with her presumed murderer. Thus a story appearing in the *Daily Mail* of December 6, 1845, based on an interview with a relative of Tirrell (probably a cousin from New Bedford), suggested far more sympathy for the suspected killer than for his alleged victim. According to the report, Tirrell had been an "unfortunate young man" who was naturally "generous, warm-hearted and affectionate to his friends." Indeed, he would probably have become a "useful and respected member of society" had it not been for the "terrible . . . influence of a depraved and fascinating woman."[42]

The *Mail*'s informant supported his claims with anecdotal evidence. The person had accompanied Bickford and Tirrell on a trip to New York, Philadelphia, and Baltimore the previous year and reported that Bickford had repeatedly forced "her unfortunate and infatuated paramour" to endure "the most reckless extravagance and dissipation." He went on to claim that Bickford's "selfish extravagance and riotous living" had eventually "despoiled her victim of every dollar of his patrimony" and suggested that Tirrell, financially depleted and fanatically jealous, may have finally murdered Bickford in order to prevent her from becoming the mistress of another man. The story also provided a number of details on Bickford's alleged murder of a "colored man" who had been her lover in New Bedford, again raising the specter of miscegenation. "That Mrs. Bickford was a depraved and hardened woman, her course for the last few years bears ample testimony," the *Mail* report concluded. "It is the opinion universally of those who have known her of late years, that there are few unfortunate females of her class who possessed fewer redeeming qualities."[43]

Mediating between the polar images of Maria Bickford as sentimental victim and sexual predator was the more complex view embedded in a biographical sketch provided to the Boston press by her estranged husband, James Bickford. His story initially appeared on December 1 in the *Boston Post* and was often reprinted in other local newspapers and periodicals, becoming the most widely circulated account of Maria Bickford during the months preceding Tirrell's trial. It was probably fairly accurate; at least a few key details can be verified from local records. According to Mr. Bickford's sketch, his wife had been born in Bath, Maine, under the name of Mary Ann Dunn. Her parents had soon moved to Bangor, where Maria went to work as a domestic servant at the age of fifteen. A year or two later, in 1839, she married Mr. Bickford, with whom she lived "happily" for the next three years. The couple had only one child, who died young.[44]

At about the time of her child's death, several of her female friends convinced young Mrs. Bickford to join them on a trip to Boston. "While in the city, she appeared delighted with everything she saw—completely captivated," Mr. Bickford recalled, "and on her return home [she] expressed a desire to reside permanently in Boston." Thereafter she became "dissatisfied with her humble condition," particularly with her husband's inability to satisfy her passion for "dressing extravagantly." She became less affectionate toward her husband and even flirted with an attractive young man who frequented their boardinghouse. In her disgruntled state of mind, Maria was an easy target for the young seducer, whose "prepossessing appearance and winning address" soon put her "completely in his power." In October 1842 Mrs. Bickford and her new paramour eloped to Newburyport, where she was deserted by him less than three months later. "Ere she became acquainted with this man she was one of the most virtuous of her sex," Mr. Bickford insisted, "but his insinuating plausibility quickly drew her into the whirlpool of vice."[45]

After being abandoned by her lover, Maria moved to Boston and from there wrote her husband, complaining that she was "sick and destitute, and wished to see him very much." But when Mr. Bickford came to the city and finally found her in a "house of ill-fame," she declared that she would never return to Bangor. Having by then become "completely depraved," she resided at various brothels in Boston before moving to New Bedford in July 1844. There Maria first met Albert J. Tirrell, soon becoming his "acknowledged mistress." After cohabiting for several months in New Bedford, traveling together throughout the northeastern United States, and residing at a number of Boston hotels, the illicit couple rented an elegantly furnished house of their own in Boston during the spring of 1845, complete with "two or three female boarders." Because the police were already in pursuit of Tirrell on the charge of adultery, the dwelling was occupied under the fictitious name of Maria Welch.[46]

When Albert disbanded the household in June 1845 after an apparent quarrel with his lover, Maria began traveling frequently, sometimes with Albert and sometimes in an effort to escape him. During that period she was frequently in touch with her husband, who occasionally handled her baggage and begged her to come home. Even while resisting that advice, Maria informed him that "Tirrell abused her, that she was afraid of him, and was determined to get clear from him." After receiving one last letter from Maria in October 1845 describing Tirrell's arrest for adultery in New Bedford and her own erratic travels from that city to New Hampshire, Niagara Falls, Montreal, Vermont, New York, and finally back to Boston, James Bickford heard nothing more from his wife.[47]

After reporting Mr. Bickford's account, the *Post* reiterated his claim that Maria had been "anxious to escape" from her paramour and suggested that her murder had probably resulted from Tirrell's infatuated jealousy. The newspaper concluded by appending Mr. Bickford's refutations of two earlier newspaper stories on his estranged wife, one sympathetically fabricating her planned elopement to western New York and the other maliciously implicating her in the deaths of two men.[48] Aside from those specific denials, Bickford's plausible account of his wife's life actually mediated between the polar depictions of Maria Bickford as sentimental victim and sexual predator, suggesting that Maria had been a willful and frustrated young woman, at once vulnerable *and* seductive. After finding herself trapped in an unsatisfying marriage to a man of limited means, she had rebelled against social conventions, turned to prostitution, and plunged into a dangerous sexual relationship from which she eventually sought to extricate herself but which finally destroyed her.

Although Tirrell was not the subject of as much biographical reportage as Maria Bickford, treatments of his life and character tended to cover an analogous spectrum of judgment. The extreme views have already been discussed. The poem printed in the *Post* portrayed Tirrell as a heartless seducer and sexual predator; the sympathetic *Mail* report of December 6 depicted him as a fundamentally decent—but hopelessly infatuated—young man. Other accounts put aside the stereotypes long enough to provide some concrete biographical details. The suspected murderer was the son of a prominent shoe manufacturer from Weymouth. The elder Tirrell had accumulated a fortune of about twenty-five thousand dollars, much of it in real estate, and had served for twelve years as a representative in the state legislature. When his father died in the spring of 1844, Albert's share of the inheritance was worth about eight thousand dollars. He was twenty-one years of age at the time and already a married father. After becoming infatuated with Maria Bickford in New Bedford during the summer of that same year, he squandered his fortune on her at a rapid rate until his arrest for adultery in September 1845.[49] Whether they evoked sympathy or revulsion, Albert's wealthy background and respectable lineage only seemed to increase the public's fascination with the bloody aftermath of his compulsive binge.

The sensational affair that culminated in the murder and arson on Cedar Lane was not only addressed by a succession of contradictory journalistic accounts but was also treated in a number of essentially fictional works published in pamphlet form. For the most part, those works simply elaborated on the competing characterizations of Bickford and Tirrell already familiar to newspaper readers. The first of the pamphlets, entitled *The Life and Death of Mrs. Maria Bickford*, was initially issued and advertised in the Boston press on December 9, 1845.[50] Although the title page announced that it had been written by a clergyman from Maine, the work was actually copyrighted and probably compiled by one Silas Estabrook, an obscure printer and journalist who had recently moved from New York City to Boston.[51] According to a questionable characterization contained in the pamphlet itself, Estabrook was an "obscure and shrivelled compositor" much given to "plans and projects for astonishing the world."[52] Although it may be too much to claim that Estabrook accomplished that grandiose aim in publishing his biography of Maria Bickford, he did succeed in producing a remarkably popular piece of literary ephemera, priced to sell in the mass market at a mere $12\frac{1}{2}$ cents per copy.[53] At least four editions of the work appeared over the following months, and Estabrook himself apparently claimed in February 1846 that it had been perused by no fewer than "one hundred thousand persons."[54]

As an engaging hodgepodge of melodrama, satire, and social exposé, Silas Estabrook's biography of Maria Bickford lurches from one literary cliché to another, alternately characterizing its subject as romantic heroine, sentimental victim, and sexual predator. The printer begins by portraying Bickford as a romantic and mysterious young woman—the subject of ominous prophesies and alarming dreams, much given to philosophical speculations, contemplative trances, and solitary communions with nature. Having thus endowed Maria with the standard accoutrements of a romantic heroine, Estabrook goes on to portray his subject as a sentimental victim, the pathetic dupe of a lustful seducer. The villain in Estabrook's little melodrama is Theodore Maxwell, a suitably despicable medical student from the state of Georgia who was pursuing his education in Brunswick, Maine. Young Maxwell's southern pedigree allows Estabrook to assume, in passing, the mantle of social critic, decrying

the atrocity of the domestic slave trade and assailing the "swaggering empti-
ness" of "Southern chivalry."[55]

Even while venting his antisouthern spleen, Estabrook proceeds with his
story. Having won Maria's heart and enjoyed her body, Theodore Maxwell
treats his young lover with "repulsive brutality." As a sentimental victim,
Maria initially responds to the southerner's "iron scoffs" with "tears, tenderness, and supplications." But after Maxwell mockingly proposes that Maria
consign herself for sale as a white slave in Georgia, the young victim is transfigured by a new lust for vengeance; for the moment, at least, Estabrook's
heroine has become a sexual predator. "Bravely will I play my part," Maria
tells herself. "I will smile when I curse. I will win to destroy."[56]

But Maria's threatening resolve quickly fades, and she resumes the familiar role of sentimental victim. When she travels to Boston by steamer and is
unable to afford the fare, she is brutally seduced—even raped—by "a portly,
well dressed man" who offers to pay her passage. Estabrook here assures his
readers in one of many informative footnotes that the practice of entrapping
young women into prostitution on board Eastern steamboats is common,
ruining no fewer than "five thousand poor girls . . . every year." After arriving in Boston the following morning, Maria is quickly accosted by a cab driver.
When she tells him that she is seeking housing and employment, the treacherous cabby smiles and deposits her in a brothel. Here Maria once again submits
to male lust, settling into a "seraglio of vice" patronized by aristocrats, bank-
ers, sailors, artisans, swindlers, Harvard students, deacons, and even ministers. On that cue, Estabrook inserts a footnote listing a short catalog of well-
known clergymen notorious for their sexual transgressions.[57]

After being arrested in a police raid and deposited in the local jail, Maria
is, according to Estabrook, rescued by "celebrated philanthropist" John Augustus, a well-known figure in antebellum Boston who was involved in reforming local prostitutes.[58] With the help of her new benefactor, Maria secures
employment in a tailoring establishment on Washington Street and finds lodging in a wooden garret. Estabrook describes her sitting by the fire in her
humble dwelling four months later, an appropriately maudlin penitent: "Her
face was worn but not melancholy, and her bosom heaved a sigh and her voice
trembled, while she sung the song of 'Home, sweet home.'" Alas, Maria's
salvation proves to be only passing; she falls ill, loses her job, and is forced to
succumb to the amorous embraces of yet another treacherous, upper-class
patron—in this case, a lustful physician.[59]

It is only after several months in the arms of the lascivious doctor that
Maria returns to Maine, where she quickly meets and marries Mr. Bickford,
an "honest and worthy" bootmaker. However, the match proves to be an
unhappy one for Maria, leading toward a future of "poverty, contention, and
disappointment."[60] She thereupon decides to abandon her marriage and move
to Boston, undergoing in the process yet another dramatic change of character, a metamorphosis from bored housewife to sexual predator, described
with blood-curdling exuberance by Silas Estabrook:

When she had concluded to remove to Boston, there to reside permanently, a new tide rushed in upon her destiny. SHE WAS LOST. The fountain of tears was dry. Despair laid its iron fingers upon the strings of her heart. And now began that career of madness and crime which rendered her name a signal of terror to the licentious, who thronged the dens of prostitution. She laughed and was happy in her revengeful determination.—Revenge! at whose shrine of blood she did reverence! . . .

For a period of over four years, she led the van in the battle of Extermination to Man, the plunderer of her life's joys, her innocence—Man, the rock of her ruin! She saw but to conquer. The devotees of pomatum swarmed about her, lavishing sickening adulations upon her charms. She inwardly mocked at their hollowness, and Murder whetted its beak upon their lies. Twice were her hands imbrued in the blood of her paramours; and, had her existence been prolonged a few more days, it is highly probable that [another man] . . . would have fallen a victim to her avenging steel.[61]

On that horrific note, Estabrook concludes his biographical sketch of Maria Bickford, resuming his pamphlet with a somewhat shorter account of Albert J. Tirrell. The portrait is not an attractive one: "His flushed cheeks, his beak-like, pimpled nose, his gallynipper lips, rendered his demeanor the beau ideal of a sucker-sharp. His tongue could rattle off more lies and oaths in a minute than that of any other sucker in Boston, excepting one." The printer concludes his ephemeral best-seller with a reprinted newspaper account of Tirrell's arrest in New Orleans (inserted into the second and subsequent editions) and a reprint of James Bickford's account of his wife in the *Boston Post*. In addition to filling out the thirty-two-page pamphlet, those last appended materials undoubtedly served to strengthen the somewhat tenuous link between Estabrook's fanciful narrative and the factual case still being reported in the local press.[62]

Although Estabrook does not portray his heroine as a consistently passive and penitent victim, his overall portrait of Maria Bickford—with its blending of sentimental, romantic, and even gothic motifs—presents a powerfully sympathetic image of the fallen women. Young Maria is pictured as the repeated victim of male treachery and lust who turns to vengeance only as a last and justifiable resort. Lurid accounts of the wrongs suffered by Estabrook's heroine are interspersed with footnotes documenting and deploring a number of related social vices of the day, to the point that it almost becomes unclear whether the work is literary melodrama masquerading as social criticism, or social criticism posing as literary melodrama.

That the author intends to present a sympathetic portrait of his subject and that he wants, at the same time, to be seen as exposing contemporary social vices is suggested by an early advertisement for the work that appeared in the *Boston Daily Bee*. "It [the pamphlet] gives a brief history of this unfortunate woman, from her birth to her awful death, and dwells with much earnestness upon her misfortunes and wrongs," the newspaper notice explains. "She is represented as a gifted and accomplished female, and the author lashes Tirrel,

and other abandoned rakes most unmercifully, and exposes, with great bold-
ness, the licentious and murderous practices of the day."[63] That promotional
blurb, presumably delivered tongue-in-cheek, provides a suitable epitaph for
the printer's playful and engaging work.

Silas Estabrook was apparently so pleased with the public's reception of
his fanciful biography of Maria Bickford that he produced two similar pamphlets on the same case. The first of those works, *Eccentricities & Anecdotes
of Albert John Tirrell*, was briefly but prominently advertised in Boston newspapers at the end of January 1846. The pamphlet is divided into eleven cantos
and an appendix and is, if anything, even more preposterous than Estabrook's
first effort. It opens with a brief but florid disquisition on the nature of
murder, and the next three cantos consist of a rambling letter allegedly written
by Tirrell to his mother from a prison in New Orleans. In it he describes his
abortive flight from justice, in which he frantically tries to escape from the
horrifying ghost of Maria Bickford, complete with gaping throat, that follows
him wherever he goes. "*Yet I did not kill her; she was her own murderer!*" he
desperately concludes. "Why do they all say *I* did it?"[64]

Although the opening section of the work sets a gothic tone and suggests a
measure of sympathy for Tirrell's plight, Estabrook reverses himself in the
following seven cantos. These constitute an episodic comic narrative of
Tirrell's life from childhood, ostensibly compiled by a widow from Weymouth, documenting his many repulsive traits and eccentricities: his violent
harassment of school masters; his remarkable ability to train animals, illustrated by his success in teaching three cats to play the dulcimer and six turkeys
to dance a jig; his invention of a mechanical fly-swatter; his abandonment of
his wife on their wedding day; his career of depravity in New Bedford; his
escapades with Maria Bickford in New York; his remarkable proficiency at
billiards; his novel method of pulling teeth with a pistol; and so forth. At the
close of the unflattering memoir, Estabrook assures his readers that he does
not intend to prejudge Tirrell's guilt and offers a brief attack on the death
penalty. The pamphlet concludes with a detailed synopsis of the coroner's
inquest on Bickford's death, undoubtedly taken from a contemporary newspaper, thereby linking the comic narrative to the real case that it seeks to
exploit.[65]

Like his first pamphlet on the Bickford case, Estabrook's *Eccentricities
and Anecdotes* also contains some class-conscious social criticism, particularly in his description of New England's greatest whaling center. "Society in New Bedford is organized upon a different basis from that of any
other city of the United States," he notes. "The wealth of the place is
entirely under the . . . control of a small number of aristocratic families,
who have grown . . . fat from sperm oil and whale-bone." He goes on to
explain how the community's worthy seamen are systematically swindled out
of their rightful earnings by the aristocratic vultures. He also describes the
plight of the city's numerous prostitutes, who are at once tools and victims of
the exploitative class system. While following their corrupt trade, those des-

perate women frequently die by murder or suicide; Estabrook cites a sexton's report from New Bedford of "thirty-four secret burials within the space of five months, from the houses of ill-fame." Had Maria Bickford's death occurred in New Bedford, Estabrook implies, the public might never have heard of it. "These are the true characteristics of the American Sodom," he concludes. "Whoever goeth there may read on every wall: *Aristocracy—Murder—Prostitution—Hypocrisy, and Hell.*"[66]

Silas Estabrook's third pamphlet on the Bickford affair, *The Early Love Letters, and Later Literary Remains of Maria Bickford*, had ostensibly been compiled by the same minister responsible for her earlier biography.[67] Its publication was advertised in the *Daily Times* at the beginning of March 1846, just a few weeks before Tirrell's trial for murder.[68] The work features a series of fabricated love letters written by Maria to her fictional seducer—the southern medical student, Theodore Maxwell—and an equally spurious "private journal" allegedly kept by her during her last years in Boston. It also contains several other epistles attributed to Maria, including two genuine notes from her to James Bickford, previously reproduced in the latter's account of his wife's life in the *Boston Post*.[69] Like the journalistic reports appended to Estabrook's two earlier pamphlets, those genuine letters undoubtedly served to strengthen the perceived link between an essentially fictional compilation and the factual case on which it was very loosely based.

As in Estabrook's earlier biography, Maria is portrayed in her letters and literary remains both as a sentimental victim and as a sexual predator. "She was a victim to her own free impulses and affections," the editor explains of her early fall. "She entrusted her virtue and good name to the guidance of betraying man while yet the rose of youth was on her cheek."[70] Once fallen, she naturally seeks revenge against all mankind. "Since there is no humanity or decency in the male race, it shall be my part to plunder and ruin all whom I am able to decoy," Maria declares in her journal. "I have been *their* victim, they shall now be *mine*."[71] Yet despite her vengeful attitude, the fallen woman is given an essentially sympathetic portrayal. Indeed, her letters and journal reveal Maria to be a woman of exquisite sensibility and lively literary judgment. At various points she pertly comments on the writings of Goldsmith, Mackenzie, Scott, Bulwer-Lytton, Cooper, Dickens, and Sigourney.[72] She also discusses erudite sermons, attends fashionable theaters, and sentimentally communes with the dead at Mount Auburn Cemetery.[73] Estabrook's compilation tends to establish that, despite the denials of her "heartless calumniators," Maria Bickford did in fact possess "an intellect of no ordinary character, and a generous, confiding heart."[74] Such natural virtues stand in sharp contrast to the hypocrisy of Maria's social betters. "Seduction and unbridled indulgence in Maine are regarded as a matter of course by nearly all lawyers, doctors, ministers, and other professional men," she notes in her journal; "though they expiate, as with iron lungs, upon the enormity of these evils, themselves are the first and most greedy participators in them."[75] Here again the author spices his literary concoction with a dash of social criticism.

What are we to make of Silas Estabrook's three pamphlets on the case of Maria Bickford? First, it should be clear that they elaborated on the two polar views of the fallen woman as sentimental victim and sexual predator, images firmly embedded in the general culture and already evident in journalistic accounts of the Bickford affair. Second, the pamphlets illustrated the degree to which nineteenth-century literary treatments of real-life crime could be suffused by the motifs of sentimental and romantic fiction. In such extreme cases, crime literature actually became a form—or a parody—of such fiction. Third, despite their playful quality, the works embodied a powerful artisanal critique of the commercial and professional classes. They thus perpetuated, albeit in secular form, the traditional role of crime publications as vehicles for social exposé and criticism, even as they contributed to a very substantial antebellum literature of "subversive reform."[76]

Meanwhile, just about seven weeks after the death of Maria Bickford and only a few days after the appearance of Estabrook's first pamphlet, one of Boston's most popular newspapers was reviewing a novel inspired by the Bickford affair. On December 13, 1845, the editor of the *Boston Daily Mail* reported his receipt from the local publishing house of H. L. Williams of a work entitled *Julia Bicknell: or, Love and Murder! Founded on a Recent Terrible Domestic Tragedy.* "We suppose it will be considered a work of fiction by those who are not familiar with the cold blooded murder recently committed in our city," the writer explained, "but to our citizens generally it may and probably will appear like a picture of truth, with an occasional tint borrowed from imagination to give it a proper coloring." The reviewer proceeded to report favorably on the novel and suggested that it would gratify the "curiosity" of those eager to learn more about the real-life "mystery." He concluded by predicting that the work would find an exceptionally "ready sale" because the subject matter could not fail "to interest a very large portion of the community."[77] That the paperback novel was priced at only twenty-five cents could only have enhanced its prospects for a wide readership.[78]

Although he was not identified by the newspaper reviewer, the author of *Julia Bicknell* was a prolific novelist named Osgood Bradbury. Like Maria Bickford herself, Bradbury had been born and raised in Maine. After working as a clerk in a country store and attending an academy, Bradbury taught school, practiced law in several towns, and served two years in the Maine state legislature before moving to Boston in 1840. Bradbury was listed in contemporary city directories as a "counsellor," and his achievements at the bar were highly touted in advertisements for his fiction. One plugged him as an "eminent lawyer" with a "long and successful practice"; another noted that he served "at the same bar as Choate, Webster, and other eminent counsellors." An enthusiastic copywriter even claimed that Bradbury had brought "conviction and consequent punishment upon many of the more guilty criminals."[79]

In reality Bradbury seems to have devoted the bulk of his energies during the mid-1840s to literary pursuits, both newspaper reporting and fiction writing. Between about 1844 and 1849, Bradbury produced no fewer than thirty-one short novels, many of them published by Henry L. Williams, an enterprising purveyor of cheap, sensational fiction with offices in Boston and New York. Williams's pamphlets, which circulated by the rails as far west as Michigan, were close forerunners of the famous "dime novels" of the second half of the nineteenth century. Williams (and two of his brothers) produced not only countless paperbound novels but also a string of cheap literary magazines. Those journals, with patriotic titles like *Uncle Sam* and *The Yankee*, were pioneer "story papers" of the kind that would soon be drawing enormous numbers of readers of the middle and working classes, dwarfing even the circulation figures of the urban penny dailies. Many of Bradbury's short novels were published both as pamphlets and as serials in the story papers. He was apparently paid by the piece; one of his early novels was reportedly purchased by a Boston publisher for fifty dollars. Bradbury continued to produce a stream of cheap novels into the 1850s and 1860s. A couple even appeared after his return to Maine and his assumption of the associate editorship of the *Portland Advertiser* in 1862. At various times a lawyer, novelist, and journalist, Bradbury participated in all three of the rising professions most directly responsible for the transformation of New England crime literature during the antebellum period.[80]

As an author of cheap, romantic fiction, Osgood Bradbury fit very much in the mold of J. H. Ingraham, his better known and even more prolific contemporary.[81] "A new American Novelist has arisen. His name is Professor Ingraham," Longfellow wrote a friend in 1838. "He is a tremendous ass!! really *tremendous*! I think he may say he has written the worst novels ever written by anybody. But they sell." A contemporary periodical similarly dismissed Ingraham as a "romance writer merely—trash, trash, trash!" Such critics might just as easily have been speaking of Osgood Bradbury. In fact, Ingraham and Bradbury were the two chief workhorses in the Williams literary stable throughout the 1840s, dominating both their periodical and pamphlet production. Hacks like Bradbury and Ingraham, while still nominally artisanal in their crafting of individualized products, operated very much in the spirit of an emerging industrial order; their output was characterized by mass production, cheap prices, and interchangeable plots.[82]

Although Bradbury wrote a number of adventure stories about Indians, he also specialized in lurid exposés of urban vice, stressing the evils of libertinism, intemperance, and gambling. Such works were undoubtedly inspired, at least in part, by the writings of the popular French novelist Eugene Sue. Just two years after the first appearance of Sue's classic *The Mysteries of Paris* (1842), Bradbury came out with his own modest *The Mysteries of Boston* (1844) and *Mysteries of Lowell* (1844).[83] In general Bradbury approached his fictional work with labored energy, meager artistry, and a penchant for resolving his melodramatic plots with violent deaths.[84] The sordid tragedy of Maria Bickford and Albert Tirrell provided suitable fodder for his literary cannon. An advertisement in one of the Williams papers breathlessly promised that the story could not fail to "appal the stoutest hearts and 'send its readers weeping to their beds.' "[85]

There can be no doubt that *Julia Bicknell*, written within weeks after the murder in Cedar Lane, was loosely based on the Bickford affair. The main characters in the novel are Frederick Searsmont, a young married rake who expects to inherit a fortune from his dying father, Catherine Searsmont, his mawkishly devoted but troubled wife, and Julia Bicknell, his thoroughly depraved mistress. The character of Frederick Searsmont is clearly based on Albert Tirrell, while that of Julia Bicknell is even more obviously modeled, down to the similarity in names, on Maria Bickford. In addition, the character of Julia's estranged husband, an obsequious shoemaker who appears briefly in Bradbury's novel, unmistakably resembles Maria's legal spouse, James Bickford.[86]

Much of the action of *Julia Bicknell* takes place in "a country village" outside Boston, where Catherine Searsmont regularly waits for her husband to return from his suspiciously frequent and ill-explained jaunts to the city. When not moping alone at home or banging away at her piano, Catherine stays busy confiding her well-founded doubts concerning Frederick's moral character to a sympathetic local widow. When even his parents finally recognize Frederick's licentiousness, they decide to disinherit their wayward son. Meanwhile, of course, young Searsmont is spending much of his time in Boston, drinking, gambling, breaking his marriage vows, and plotting even worse forms of mischief with his dissolute mistress, Julia Bicknell.[87]

If Estabrook's Maria Bickford is an essentially sympathetic victim, Bradbury's Julia Bicknell is a thoroughly corrupt sexual predator without redeeming qualities. Although originally an "innocent and virtuous girl" from rural Maine, Bicknell has since abandoned her husband, moved to Boston, and plunged into a life of dissipation. She is, according to Bradbury, a prime illustration of the principle that "females, when they make a false step, not only become more abandoned and reckless than the opposite sex, and plunge deeper into crime, but also go the downward road with greater speed." In her first appearance in the novel, she is closeted with her paramour in a Boston brothel, coolly plotting the murder of her shoemaker husband, who has threatened to prosecute them for adultery. But when Julia discovers that Frederick has been disinherited by his father, she backs out of their murder plan and begins to turn her affections toward a wealthy young alcoholic named Charles Medford, who is both richer and handsomer than the suddenly dispensable Searsmont.[88]

When Frederick realizes that Bicknell is abandoning him, his heart is filled with thoughts of revenge; one Sabbath afternoon, he reaches a final determination to kill her. That evening he goes to her chamber in the brothel and as she sleeps, at half-past three in the morning, cuts her throat with a razor: It is a blood-chilling account of one sexual predator preying on another. After washing his hands in her room and hiring a wagon to carry him from the city, he arrives home to discover that his father has died that very night! Not satisfied with those two dramatic deaths, Bradbury completes his short novel with a lurid description of the demise of Charles Medford, the young drunkard, on the floor of an oyster saloon during a fit of delirium tremens. "May we all learn profitable lessons from these sad developments in human life, and be taught to avoid the crying sins of the age in which we live," Bradbury unctuously concludes. "Libertinism, gambling, and intemperance, are the great moral evils which so easily beset our race, and directly or indirectly lead to the commission of all the crimes found in the catalogue of human offences."[89]

Somewhat like Silas Estabrook's three pamphlets, Osgood Bradbury's novel about the Bickford case lingers ambiguously on the threshold between fact and fiction. Unlike Estabrook, however, Bradbury acknowledges his work's liminal status by packaging it as a novel-based-on-fact and by providing fictional names for the leading characters. Bradbury's work also differs sharply from Estabrook's in its portrayal of the figure representing Maria Bickford. While Estabrook offers an essentially sympathetic and somewhat complex portrayal of Bickford as a sentimental victim turned seductress, Bradbury's picture of Bicknell is relentlessly hostile and one-dimensional. All of the reader's sympathies in Bradbury's novel are directed toward Tirrell's devoted wife and pious parents—characters largely ignored in Estabrook's accounts—leaving Julia Bicknell as a stock villainess. Like Estabrook, Bradbury also laces his work with social criticism. But in contrast to the printer's sharp assaults on the respectable classes, Bradbury's diatribes are safely conservative and conventional, restricted to the usual bromides against gambling, licentiousness, and strong drink. Bradbury's work may have been racy, but it was not radical.[90]

It should be noted that the explosion of cheap fiction, represented in New England by the works of Estabrook, Bradbury, and Ingraham, was actually an international phenomenon. By the 1840s romantic novels designed for a mass reading public, issued in both cheap periodicals and paperbound pamphlets, spewed from presses in England and France as well as the United States. In fact, the output of English and American publishers was boosted by frequent plagiarisms both from each other and from the wildly successful French serials of Sue and others. In that spirit of rampant "borrowing" in the pursuit of profit, Bradbury's novel on the Bickford case was published within a year or two of its first Boston appearance by Edward Lloyd of London, a key figure in the development of England's cheap working-class fiction industry during the 1830s and 1840s. The work appeared anonymously in serial form under the title *The Unhappy Bride; or, the Grave of the Forsaken.* As an early "penny dreadful," each number (or installment) of the serial could be purchased separately for a single penny. Even mass culture did not get much cheaper than that.[91]

During the five months following the discovery of Maria Bickford's mutilated corpse in a burning house on Cedar Lane, the Boston press depicted the murdered woman in a variety of ways. Competing views were conveyed both by newspaper accounts and by longer fictional pamphlets. At one extreme

Maria was portrayed as a sentimental victim, at the other as a sexual predator. Those stereotypes reflected an ambivalence concerning female character deeply rooted in antebellum culture. Mediating between those polar views was the more complex and realistic portrayal offered by her estranged husband, James Bickford. Although Albert Tirrell, the chief suspect in the case, did not receive quite as much journalistic and literary attention as his alleged victim, he too was the subject of widely varying portrayals. In one newspaper report based on an interview with a sympathetic relative, he was depicted as a fundamentally decent young man entrapped by his passion for a depraved seductress. But in other accounts he was described as a heartless seducer and sexual predator in his own right. Over a period of months, those competing images of Bickford and Tirrell were aggressively marketed at bookstores and periodical depots and by dozens of ragged urchins selling newspapers and pamphlets on the streets. "Hear's the lyfe of Albert J. Turrel and the crewill murder of Maryer a Bikford!" the newsboys reportedly hollered. "Here's the Lyfe of the misfortynait Maryer a Bickford!"[92] It remained to be seen what effect the competing images of victim and suspect might have on the actual trial of Tirrell.

Early on the morning of October 27, Albert Tirrell had fled from the burning house on Cedar Lane and gone to a nearby stable to hire a horse and wagon. He drove to the house of some relatives in Weymouth who concealed him from pursuing officers for the next day or so and provided him with money to escape from Massachusetts. The following day he headed west with his brother-in-law and then continued north on his own, probably through the state of Vermont, into Canada. On November 8 he wrote his family from Montreal, announcing that he was to sail that day for Liverpool. But the vessel was forced to turn back by bad weather, and later that month he boarded a ship in New York City bound for New Orleans. After receiving a tip that the fugitive was headed their way, authorities in Louisiana arrested Tirrell on board a vessel in the Gulf on December 5.[93]

Meanwhile, Bostonians were outraged by the seemingly successful flight of a suspected murderer. Although Samuel Parker, the prosecuting attorney for Suffolk County, had quickly engaged a number of officers to pursue the suspect, other branches of the local government responded more slowly. The mayor, near death from illness, apparently did nothing, and the city council waited several days before offering a reward of one thousand dollars for the apprehension of Tirrell. The *Daily Times* noted widespread public complaints over the sluggish official response and blasted the city government as "essentially and thoroughly imbecile."[94] During November and early December, Boston newspapers occasionally reported rumored sightings or arrests of Tirrell; some of those stories seemed to presuppose the guilt—and even the eventual execution—of the absconded suspect.[95]

On December 20 news of Tirrell's arrest in New Orleans reached Massachusetts and was widely reported in the Boston press. On December 24 the

Daily Times indicated that the governor had dispatched two officers to Louisiana to retrieve the suspect. Less than a week later, it reported that the witnesses against Tirrell had been called by the Supreme Judicial Court to arrange for their appearance at a future trial. In mid-January Boston papers reprinted a letter from Tirrell to the *New Orleans Picayune* in which he asserted his innocence, complained of his unfair treatment in the press, and denied earlier reports that he had attempted suicide. On February 5 the *Times* announced that Tirrell had safely arrived in Boston and been placed in the Leverett Street jail. The following day hundreds of Bostonians flocked to the Police Court—mistakenly believing that Tirrell was to be examined there—in hopes of catching a glimpse of the suspected murderer, who had already become something of a celebrity.[96]

On February 7 the *Daily Times* cited unconfirmed reports that Daniel Webster and Rufus Choate had been engaged as defense counsel by Tirrell's friends. Only half of the rumor turned out to be true; several days later Choate returned home from Washington to assume direction of Tirrell's defense in association with two junior counsel, Annis and Amos B. Merrill.[97] One of those two brothers had known the suspect in Weymouth several years earlier, when Tirrell was still a schoolboy.[98] On February 16, when Tirrell was arraigned for murder before the Supreme Judicial Court, the press reported favorably on the prisoner's courtroom manner. "Tirrell is a young man . . . of a manly and prepossessing appearance," the *Daily Times* observed. "His demeanor in Court was perfectly cool and placid, without the appearance of being at all bold or otherwise objectionable." As they would on future occasions, newspapers also took note of the suspect's fashionable clothing; at his arraignment he wore a "sporting" mulberry dress coat, black pants, and a satin vest. He pleaded not guilty to the murder charge, and his trial was set for March 24.[99]

Early that March morning the court house and every avenue leading to it were "thronged by an eager multitude" waiting to catch a glimpse of the prisoner. When Tirrell was brought into the courtroom at nine o'clock, he faced a "gaping crowd of spectators—besides a full *corps* of Reporters and Lawyers, who were all eyes and ears." According to one sardonic press account, the "anxious countenances" of the assembled multitude seemed to suggest that "some great event was about to take place, or some new era burst upon the world."[100] On the bench were three associate justices of the Supreme Judicial Court; the prosecution was to be conducted by Samuel D. Parker, while the defense was to be handled by Rufus Choate and the brothers Merrill. After the jury had been selected and the indictment read, the trial itself got under way with the opening statement of the prosecuting attorney. Advance copies of Parker's prepared text were probably supplied to the Boston press, since the transcripts in the various newspaper reports are virtually identical.[101]

After defining the crime of murder and explaining the nature of circumstantial evidence, Parker devoted the bulk of his opening statement to a forceful recapitulation of the same web of circumstances implicating Tirrell in Bickford's death that had already been developed at the coroner's inquest and in many press reports. Although he once referred to the defendant as an "unhappy young man," his account was predictably hostile toward Tirrell. He implied that the prisoner's legal marriage had been forced by a premarital pregnancy, described his subsequent adultery as "bold and unfeeling," suggested that he had been "severe and cruel" towards his victim, and claimed that he had even "threatened her life." Somewhat surprisingly, Parker's characterization of Maria Bickford was equally unsympathetic. He described her as "an unblushing harlot and an undisguised adulteress," a condemnation hardly mitigated by Parker's obligatory reminder that "murder loses not its guilt in the baseness of its victim." Even more surprising, he concluded his opening not with a denunciation of the accused murderer but with a quotation from Proverbs concerning the destruction of "the young man void of understanding" by "the harlot." "He goeth after her straightway, as an ox goeth to the slaughter," the biblical passage read. "For she hath cast down many wounded; Yea, many strong men hath been slain by her." It hardly seemed clear from Parker's opening argument who was the greater victim in the case—and who ought to be on trial: "young man" Tirrell or "harlot" Bickford.[102]

Parker called various witnesses for the prosecution: the coroner; a physician consulted at the inquest; several members of the Lawrence household, including Priscilla Blood and her paramour, William Patterson; a number of neighbors, including Theodore Bowker, a local fireman who had helped extinguish the flames in Bickford's room; two men from the stable to which Tirrell had apparently fled; a married couple who had been visited by Tirrell on the morning of the murder; the victim's husband; Tirrell's brother-in-law; and so forth. Their testimony, completed by noon of the second day of the trial, provided a fairly detailed picture of the events surrounding Bickford's violent death. The result was a strong circumstantial case against Tirrell. It seemed clear that Tirrell had been adulterously connected with Bickford, that he had been staying with her regularly during the days immediately preceding her death, that he had been with her at the Lawrence house on the evening of October 26, and that he had fled from the burning building during the early morning of October 27.[103]

However, prosecution witnesses also brought out a number of facts that would prove quite helpful to the defense. First, Joseph Moriarty, the coroner's physician, conceded that Maria Bickford's neck wound might have been self-inflicted and even acknowledged that suicide was "the natural death of the prostitute." Second, Theodore Bowker, the local fireman, testified that Joel Lawrence initially tried to prevent him from going upstairs to put out the blaze in and around Maria Bickford's room; Choate would later draw damaging inferences from Lawrence's reluctance to allow Bowker to enter his burning building. Third, several members of the Lawrence household described a strangely stifled scream or groan coming from the yard immediately after

Tirrell had fled the building; the nature and significance of that sound became a key component in the prisoner's defense. Fourth, Mary and Samuel Head, a married couple, testified that Tirrell had come to their house early on the morning of the crime in order to pick up some clothes, apparently just before or after going to the stable. The Heads testified that Tirrell made a "strange noise" and "appeared to be in a strange state, as asleep or crazy." When Mr. Head took hold of him and shook him, Tirrell "sort of moved or waked out of a kind of stupor" and asked Mr. Head: "Sam, how came I here?" Tirrell's mental state at that time would also be a key element in his defense. Fifth, Nathaniel W. Bayley, Tirrell's brother-in-law, testified that when Albert arrived in Weymouth he claimed to be fleeing from the old adultery indictment. When Bayley informed him of the murder charge, Albert seemed genuinely surprised and, until dissuaded by his relative, apparently intended to return to Boston to face the accusation. Bayley's account thus suggested an explanation for Tirrell's flight that was consistent with his innocence of the murder charge.[104]

Following the completion of the prosecution case, Annis Merrill delivered his opening argument for the defense. As with Parker's address, advance copies of Merrill's speech seem to have been provided to the Boston press.[105] The junior counsel began by deploring the flood of unfavorable publicity that had already prejudiced the case of his client. "The press has given to the world the most shocking and exaggerated accounts of the death of the deceased," he complained. "Pamphlets and histories of his [Tirrell's] pretended follies and crimes, have been poured over the country . . . exciting public indignation against him . . . till the public mind has been poisoned, and most people have begun to regard his guilt as fully established." In the face of that hostile popular sentiment, Merrill pleaded with the jurors to judge Tirrell's case with benevolence, kindness, charity, and, most of all, a presumption of innocence.[106] Merrill went on to discuss the unreliability of circumstantial evidence, particularly when derived from "polluted sources." In doing so he broached a major defense aim: to destroy the credibility of the Lawrences and their disreputable lodgers. Merrill promised to demonstrate "by their own confessions, by the records of courts of justice, and by the testimony of multitudes of witnesses" that their lives were thoroughly immersed in "falsehood, pollution and crime." In order to illustrate his more general point, Merrill also cited a number of cases in which persons convicted and executed on the basis of circumstantial evidence were later proved to have been innocent.[107]

Merrill went on to offer several hypothetical reconstructions of Bickford's death that were consistent with his client's innocence of the murder charge. First, he suggested that Bickford might have cut her own throat, pointing out that suicide was "almost the natural death of persons of her character." Second, he suggested that "some other person" might have crept into Bickford's room and killed her, either out of "revenge or jealousy, or for her money." Third, he stressed that even if Bickford had died at Tirrell's hands, it did not necessarily follow that he was guilty of a capital charge. "If it was done in a quarrel—it was not murder, but manslaughter," Merrill pointed out. "If it was done in a fit of derangement or accidentally, it would not be pretended that he was guilty of Murder."[108]

Merrill also addressed two key issues of motive. On the one hand, he pointed out that Tirrell's flight was no proof of his guilt of murder, since he already had ample reason to flee from the old adultery indictment; he had, after all, violated his recognizance by returning to Bickford. On the other hand, Merrill pointed out that the prosecution had established no plausible motive for Tirrell's alleged murder of his illicit lover. "He had become perfectly enamored, infatuated, and spell-bound by the fascinations of that depraved and lascivious woman," the junior counsel cogently argued. "Is it reasonable, that a man, captivated and enamored as the defendant was with this woman, and without a motive, would have premeditated one of the most atrocious crimes against the individual, to whom of all others he was most devoted, though *criminally* attached?" Merrill thus stressed Tirrell's lack of motive while reminding the jurors of Bickford's repugnant moral character.[109]

After Merrill had spoken for about an hour and a half, the court adjourned for a dinner break; following the recess the junior counsel resumed his opening argument, introducing what was to become a central—and certainly the most unusual and controversial—aspect of the defense. It was, Merrill acknowledged, a somewhat "peculiar" and "novel" line of argument. Yet it was one that held "the key" to all of the "mysterious and suspicious circumstances" in the case, reconciling them "with each other and with the innocence of the defendant." His claim was that Tirrell was a lifelong and habitual somnambulist, or sleepwalker, who often committed acts of violence while in a somnambulistic state. According to Merrill, who cited numerous medical authorities, somnambulism was an established disease, a species of insanity or mental derangement. If Tirrell did actually kill Bickford—and Merrill did not concede that he had—he must have done so while sleepwalking and hence was not legally responsible for his act.[110]

Merrill closed his long opening statement with two last lines of argument. First he announced that the defense intended to vindicate the general reputation of Albert Tirrell. "Since the Attorney for the government has gone somewhat out of his way to assail the character of the defendant," Merrill explained, "it is due to him and his very respectable connexions to say, that his character was good, up to the time of his acquaintance with the deceased, and this we are prepared to prove by unimpeachable testimony." Then he challenged the notion that the death penalty served any useful social purpose. While acknowledging that jurors should not tamper with existing laws, he implied that—given the enormity and doubtful utility of the extreme sanction—they could legitimately demand a very high level of proof before reaching a guilty verdict in a capital case. Merrill thus sought to link his client's cause to a very active and powerful antebellum movement against the death penalty.[111]

In the midst of Merrill's opening address, a sensation was created in the crowded courtroom by the entrance of "a rosy cheeked young looking woman leading a beautiful little girl about four years old, accompanied by an elderly gentleman." The woman was the wife that Albert had abandoned in his obsessive pursuit of Maria Bickford. The little girl was their first child. The elderly man was Albert's father-in-law, a Weymouth farmer. One reporter noted that the daughter stood bareheaded on her mother's lap, glancing with bright eyes over the audience in the courtroom and particularly beaming at her father.[112] Albert had married his distant cousin, Orient Tirrell, in February 1843. As implied by the prosecuting attorney, the wedding took place under scandalous circumstances, little more than a month before Orient delivered their first child.[113] One suspects from the relatively long delay between pregnancy and marriage that Albert may have been a reluctant groom, finally pressured into the union by irate relatives. But whatever his true feelings toward the young wife and child, they served as useful courtroom props, arousing sympathy for Tirrell just as his lawyers were launching their case.

During his opening argument, Merrill had promised to call "multitudes of witnesses" to destroy the credibility of the Lawrences and their boarders. To that end, the first defense witness was a constable whom he asked about the reputation of Joel Lawrence's house. However, the prosecutor objected to the question, and the lawyers debated the issue at some length. Choate claimed that Lawrence and his wife were "unworthy of belief" and belonged in the House of Correction; he insisted that the couple's depraved character should be given "due weight" in Tirrell's trial. But the court ruled the constable's evidence inadmissible, thereby depriving the defense of one key weapon in its strategic arsenal.

Stymied in their efforts to attack the Lawrences, the defense team went on to call a succession of Albert's relatives, friends, and acquaintances, beginning with his widowed mother, Nabby Tirrell. Those witnesses testified on a number of points. First, they provided much evidence concerning Albert's habitual somnambulism. According to his mother and older brother, Albert had been "in the habit" of sleepwalking since early childhood; indeed, the spells had increased in severity and frequency as Albert grew older. On many occasions in his youth, Albert had forcibly grabbed hold of his brother during the night while sleeping; sometimes he had also pulled down curtains and broken windows in his room. One old neighbor confirmed seeing Albert sleepwalking on three occasions, and another testified to replacing panes of glass in Tirrell's bedroom. As recently as late September 1845, a cousin claimed, Albert had pulled him out of bed in his sleep and brandished a knife. Another acquaintance was prepared to testify that Maria Bickford had complained of Tirrell's striking her while he was asleep, but that hearsay was ruled inadmissible. To complete the cycle of evidence, the chief cook on board the vessel that carried Tirrell to New Orleans reported that the defendant had alarmed a number of the other passengers by sleepwalking. All those witnesses affirmed that Tirrell's bouts of somnambulism had been accompanied by a loud, strange, gasping noise or groan.[114]

A number of friends and relatives also gave evidence concerning Maria Bickford and her relationship with the defendant: Bickford had been good-looking, well-dressed, and skilled in playing the accordion and piano; however, she had also been willful, manipulative, and quarrelsome—a woman who drank to excess, never worked, carried razors and dirks, treated her lover scornfully, and regularly threw tantrums when frustrated. Witnesses testified to fits of temper in which she stamped on her bonnet, tossed grapes around the room, threw a washbowl at Albert, and hurled a decanter of brandy into the fireplace. After one quarrel with Albert, she threatened to run a knife through him; on two other occasions, she endangered her own life by swallowing laudanum. Conversely, Tirrell generally treated Bickford with affectionate indulgence, trying to steer her away from liquor, pleading with her to avoid disreputable dancehalls, and showering her with expensive dresses and other gifts, once even buying "all the spangles in a store" so that nobody would be able to match her glitter. Maria's response to Albert's largess was far from gracious. After once telling Tirrell's cousin that she wanted a new silk dress, Maria allegedly turned to her doting paramour and told him that if she ever failed to get what she wanted while she was with him she would cut her own throat. In short, according to the witnesses for the defense, Albert Tirrell was a hopelessly infatuated paramour and Maria Bickford anything but an innocent victim.[115]

Defense lawyers called a series of minor supplemental witnesses to add finishing touches to their sympathetic portrait of the prisoner and unflattering counterimage of his alleged victim. A series of acquaintances from Weymouth testified to Tirrell's peaceable reputation and good character; one former neighbor described Albert as "a whole-souled, good-hearted young fellow." On the other hand, a black landlord from one of Boston's notorious vice districts testified that Maria Bickford had boarded with him for a week in 1844. Another witness recalled seeing her in the company of a Creole named Frank Carr; when the witness was asked whether Bickford had ever quarreled with the man or struck him, the question was ruled inadmissible. Still, Tirrell's lawyers had undoubtedly achieved their main goal of further sullying the dead woman's reputation by raising the twin specters of prostitution and miscegenation.[116]

The last important witnesses to be called for the defense were the medical experts, including four physicians, among them the eminent Walter Channing, longtime professor and dean of the Harvard Medical School, and Samuel Woodward, superintendent of the State Lunatic Asylum at Worcester. The doctors testified to a number of crucial points. First, they insisted that Maria Bickford's throat wound might have been self-inflicted. Second, they suggested that even after receiving the wound she might have been able to leap from her blood-soaked bed onto the floor where she was found. Third, they discussed the general phenomenon of somnambulism, implicitly vouching for its legitimacy as a medical condition. Fourth, they affirmed that the previous testimony indicated that Tirrell had been a sleepwalker; in particular, they suggested that the strange gasping noise made by him was a symptom of that condition. Finally, they claimed that a person in a somnambulistic state might very well rise in the night, dress himself, commit a murder, set fire to a house, and run out into the street. In short, the doctors offered strong support for two key components of the defense case: that Maria Bickford might have committed suicide, and that if Tirrell did kill her he probably did so in a somnambulistic trance.[117]

After all of the many defense witnesses had been heard, the stage was set for Choate's closing argument. On the morning of the trial's fourth day, the combination of pleasant weather and intense anticipation drew an immense crowd to the courthouse and its vicinity; the "elbowing and pushing" for a place in the courtroom was even greater than on the previous days. People of various social classes, including law students, ministers, medical men, and "the masses," flocked to hear the great advocate.[118] By all accounts Choate was more than equal to the task. One playful report in the *Boston Daily Mail* was particularly evocative, using detailed physical description, along with scientific analogies and religious allusions, to convey the almost electric excitement aroused and manipulated by the quintessential master of romantic advocacy, the "great galvanic battery of human oratory":

> The orator arose and commenced his argument. His manner is peculiarly animated and thrilling. When he rose, his dark hair . . . was standing in knotty curls over his finely formed head, his black eyes sparkled with great brilliancy, his underlip tremulously protruded, and his hands quivered, all showing . . . that this great battery was highly charged with Heaven's own fire. He commenced—every ear was open and every heart beating with half suppressed emotions; the masses stood cheek to breast and shoulder to shoulder, excited, anxious, listening most intensely, and all forming a chain for the electric fluid to pass and do its work on the soul. His first words were slow and solemn. All were hushed into deep silence. After addressing a few remarks to the jury, he turned to the weeping, trembling prisoner— pointed his tremulous finger at him—rose upon the ends of his toes— turned to the venerable judges—spoke a moment most eloquently to them—wiped his perspiring brow—thrust his fingers through the curls of his hair, and then, looking over the crowded audience, addressed the jury again, often shaking off the electric sparks from the very ends of his tremulous fingers, over judges, jurors, lawyers, and spectators, as the Roman Catholic Priest scatters the holy water upon his devout and worshipping audience.[119]

To judge by the *Mail*'s account, Choate's commanding manner generated both intense intellectual energy and quasi-religious power; in addressing dramatic issues of crime and punishment, the romantic advocate had evidently supplanted the orthodox minister as both cultural icon and social authority.

Choate began by assuring the jurors that he did not intend to expend much of his energy—or take up much of their time—in arguing Tirrell's case. In fact, he started talking at a few minutes past nine in the morning, continued uninterrupted till the dinner break five hours later, and resumed for an hour

Portrait of Rufus Choate, engraved at about the time of the Tirrell trials. From the *American Review,* **January 1847.** *Courtesy, American Antiquarian Society.*

and a half during the afternoon; in all, his address lasted about six and a half hours.[120] But in contrast to the opening speeches, advance copies of Choate's closing argument were not provided to the press; as a result the synopses reported in contemporary newspapers varied a great deal in language and detail.[121] The discrepancies probably stemmed in part from Choate's legendary velocity of speech; one stenographer is said to have exclaimed of his oratory in frustration: "Who can report chain lightning?"[122] Even if every word had been accurately taken down, no transcript could possibly have captured the magic of Choate's manner and inflection.[123] Still, the imperfect newspaper synopses provide a generally accurate impression of the lawyer's argument, particularly when viewed collectively. As Choate himself supposedly responded when asked whether a particular report of his pleading in another case was accurate: "Not verbally, not verbally, but the general nonsense of the thing they have got."[124]

At the outset of his address, Choate tried to rouse sympathy for Tirrell's plight, reminding the jury in hackneyed phrases of his extreme youth, comely features, widowed mother, and loving wife and children. Tirrell had not wandered so far from virtue, Choate suggested, that he might not eventually be reclaimed. Later Choate returned to the issue of Tirrell's character, claiming that he had been "agreeably surprised" by his own impressions of the prisoner. He referred with approval to a witness's description of Albert as a "whole-souled fellow" and claimed that the prisoner exhibited a "free, frank, and manly nature." Choate's only concessions were that Tirrell may have been "irregular in his habits" and "too fond of handsome women."[125] As in many of his other pleas, Choate painted as favorable a portrait of his client as the circumstances would allow. Near the outset Choate also tried to link incipient sympathies for Tirrell—and uncertainties regarding his guilt—with more general doubts concerning the death penalty; to that end he read excerpts from a contemporary article in the *North American Review* opposing capital punishment, particularly passages relating to the dangers of circumstantial evidence.[126]

After attempting to rouse jurors' sympathies for the prisoner and against the death penalty, Choate went on to stress the weakness of the prosecution's case, particularly the absence of positive testimony establishing Tirrell's guilt. According to a report in the *Boston Daily Bee*, Choate hammered away at that point by offering a series of rhetorical questions in parallel form, each punctuated by a resounding negative:

> How far does the testimony lead you? Did any human being see the prisoner strike the blow? No. Did any human being see him in that house after 9 o'clock the previous evening? No. Did any human being see him run from the house? No. Did any human being see him with a drop of blood upon his hands? No. Can any one say that she did not take her own life? No. Can any one say that on that night he was not laboring under a disease to which he was subject from his youth? No. Has he ever made a confession of the deed? To friend or thief taker, not one word.[127]

The *Daily Times* offered a somewhat different version of the last lines: "Has he ever made any confession of guilt? *No, never, never*; neither to relative or friend; never to any officer, or thief-stealer—never, *never, never*."[128] Although the reports in the *Bee* and the *Times* may have differed in verbal detail, each effectively conveyed the same substantive argument and highlighted Choate's masterful use of repetition as a dramatic rhetorical device.

In addition to stressing the absence of conclusive testimony, Choate ridiculed the prosecutor's reconstruction of events, suggesting that Parker had failed to establish a plausible motive for the crime. Again and again Choate reiterated that Tirrell's affection for the deceased had been deep, consistent, and abiding, despite her unattractive traits. Therefore, the proposition that he would have suddenly murdered her was all but beyond the realm of human possibility. "The defendant, who for 12 or 15 months had been idolatrously attached to Maria Bickford,—so fondly attached that he left wife, children, mother, workshop, and the grave of his father—went to sleep in the arms of this woman, the same fond, foolish love existing, woke up in the night, and cut her throat," Choate postulated sarcastically. "How improbable."[129]

The heart of Choate's argument lay in a series of hypothetical reconstructions of what *might* have happened during the early morning of October 27. First, like his associate Merrill, he stressed the possibility that Bickford might have committed suicide, demonstrating in the process his genius for imaginative—and persuasive—speculation. "Gentlemen, you cannot say that this abandoned woman, waking when Albert slept, ruminating on the probability of Albert's return to his family, sadly reflecting on the past and the future, her husband forever alienated from her, did not take her own life," he suggested. "How very natural, that she died thus, the natural death of her class." In that regard Choate approvingly cited Dr. Moriarty's remark that suicide was "the natural death of the prostitute." He also reminded the jury of Bickford's two attempts to swallow laudanum and her peevish threat to cut her own throat. She had been, after all, a "spoiled child" and a "ruined woman" given to "recklessness and violence." Choate concluded with typical extravagance that the odds in favor of Bickford having committed suicide—as against her having been murdered—were a thousand to one; no, ten thousand to one![130]

But if Bickford had committed suicide, how had the fire been set? Beyond the possibility that Bickford had started the conflagration before killing herself, or that Lawrence had set his own building ablaze, Choate offered an even more intricate reconstruction of events that also explained a number of other seemingly damaging pieces of evidence, such as the presence of Bickford's mutilated body on the floor and the placement of burning clothes in the hallway. Perhaps, Choate ingeniously suggested, Tirrell had been awakened by the gushing blood of his suicidal lover, frantically snatched her from the soiled bed, grabbed a lamp from the mantelpiece, rushed to the closet to find some material to staunch the wound, accidentally set fire to the dresses in the closet with his light, entangled his feet in some burning clothes, inadvertently dragged them out into the hall, and then stumbled down the stairs to safety. "Is there any thing improbable in this?" Choate demanded. "Not at all."[131]

In addition to suggesting that Bickford might have killed herself, Choate cast aspersions on a variety of other persons, both known and unknown. He referred scornfully to the "reckless and depraved characters" of those relied upon as witnesses for the prosecution. Joel Lawrence and his wife were "shameless keepers of a house of ill-fame"; Priscilla Blood was a "notorious prostitute." Citing the local fireman's testimony concerning Lawrence's initial refusal to allow him to enter the burning building, Choate postulated that the inmates of the house wanted time to alter evidence in Bickford's room and that Lawrence wanted the flames to destroy his own dwelling. Like Merrill, he also raised the possibility that someone else might have entered the house and murdered the woman. "Many of her acquaintances and many of Lawrence's acquaintances knew of her having jewelry and valuable clothes," he pointed out. "I do not suppose the external guards to that house were any stronger than the internal virtue."[132]

Shortly before the adjournment at two o'clock, Choate finally broached the issue of somnambulism. He continued to elaborate on that novel defense after the recess, during much of the last hour and a half of his address. He cited the evidence of defense witnesses establishing that Tirrell had been a sleepwalker since childhood; he referred to the opinions of the doctors confirming Tirrell's somnambulism; he noted the testimony of key prosecution witnesses concerning the "strange extraordinary noise" heard on the morning of the crime; and he particularly stressed Mr. and Mrs. Head's descriptions of Tirrell's bizarre behavior later that same morning. According to Choate, no fewer than twelve witnesses had testified to the facts relating to Tirrell's somnambulism, and not one had been impeached or contradicted. How natural that Tirrell would sleep, dream, and under the control of that dream commit the crime! "Somnambulism explain[s] . . . the killing without a motive," Choate insisted. "Premeditated murder does not." The great lawyer's closing peroration, resonant with the imagery of classical republicanism, was characteristically florid but to the point. "In old Rome . . . it was always the practice to bestow a civic wreath on him who saved a citizen's life; a wreath to which all the laurels of Caesar were but weeds," he told the jury. "Do your duty today, and you may earn that wreath."[133]

"Mr Choate's argument for the defence was agreed by all to be a masterpiece of pleading," the editor of the *Evening Transcript* raved the following day. "Ingenious in its arguments . . . eloquent in all its bearings . . . startling in its *possibilities*, profound in its thoughtfulness, pathetic in its appeals, and remarkable in its logic."[134] In fact, it was little more than a melodramatic recapitulation of the points already raised by Annis Merrill in his opening argument. As indicated in the *Daily Times* report, Choate's closing address consisted of three principal assertions: "1st, That the evidence did not contradict the idea of suicide; 2nd, That not the slightest degree of evidence had been shown that a third party had not done the deed; and 3d, If the deed was committed by the prisoner, it must have been done while in the somnambulistic state."[135]

Each one of Choate's propositions implied a hypothetical reconstruction of events on the morning of Bickford's death that was consistent with his client's legal innocence. Much like the author of a historical novel (a genre of which he was an avid booster), Choate took advantage of gaps and ambiguities in the factual evidence to build imaginative yet plausible scenarios.[136] At the same time, he manipulated the emotions of his audience in order to create sympathy for certain characters and distaste for others. As a novelist sought to move readers, so Choate sought to move jurors. In defending the life of Albert J. Tirrell, Rufus Choate combined the rational arguments and rhetorical devices of a legal advocate with the imaginative constructions and evocative characterizations of a literary artist.

After Choate had concluded his "splendid" address at half-past four in the afternoon, the court took a short recess.[137] When the proceedings resumed, Samuel Parker rose to offer the closing argument for the prosecution, one that would last less than half as long as that of his opponent. As in the case of *Eastman, Fonday & Company*, Parker did not try to match his younger rival in spellbinding oratory but sought to disenthrall the jurors with systematic reasoning and common sense. He began by offering a series of numbered propositions, tersely summarized by one reporter as follows:

Portrait of Samuel D. Parker before the bench that appeared shortly after Tirrell's murder trial. From the [Boston] *City Crier and Country Advertiser*, April 1846. *Courtesy, American Antiquarian Society.*

1st. A murder by some human hand.
2d. Not self-murder or suicide.
3d. By no resident in the house.
4th. It was done by Albert J. Tirrell.
5th. Being done by him it was not authorised by law, not justifiable, not excusable.
6th. It was a felonious homicide.
7th. It was not manslaughter.
8th. It was murder.[138]

Parker then proceeded to apply relevant testimony from the trial to each of his propositions. In the process he gamely sought to turn Choate's emphasis on Tirrell's obsessive love to the government's advantage. He first pointed out that Maria's tight hold on Albert's affections, affirmed by the defense, tended to undercut Choate's suggestion that she might have committed suicide out of fear of losing him.[139] Similarly and somewhat paradoxically, Parker also argued that Tirrell's obsessive love for Bickford actually provided him with a plausible motive for killing her. "He idolized this woman—his money was all gone, and in moments of contrition he wanted to go home," the public prosecutor explained. "How could he disenthrall himself but by dashing this idol to pieces. Here is a motive."[140]

Yet as cogent as Parker's counterpoints may have been, they probably undercut his case by confirming Choate's imaginative reconstruction of the relationship between Bickford and Tirrell, with Maria depicted as a manipulative seductress and Albert as an infatuated slave to her charms. Even as he made a strong case against suicide and for murder, he undoubtedly strengthened the male jurors' prejudices against Bickford and their sympathies for Tirrell. "Would it be extraordinary that a woman of her disposition and character should provoke to such a degree as to urge the doing of a desperate deed[?]" Parker demanded. "If suicide is the common death of the prostitute, then murder is of frequent occurrence in the house of ill-fame."[141] Such arguments, logical though they may have been, could hardly have aroused much sympathy for the victim; without such sympathy, and in the absence of positive evidence, it seemed unlikely that a jury would be willing to condemn a man to death. Still, Parker forged on, methodically building his case point by point. "The jury should weigh the matter fairly, and give the prisoner the benefit of every doubt," he concluded wistfully. "The law casts a shield over all, the virtuous and the wicked."[142]

On the morning of Saturday, March 28, 1846, the fifth day of the trial, Judge Dewey of the Supreme Judicial Court delivered his charge to the jury. He spoke for about an hour and a half, reviewing the central issues in the case. According to Dewey, the main question facing the jury was whether Bickford had died by suicide or murder. In that regard, he reminded the jury of the medical testimony holding that she might have killed herself, as well as the other evidence concerning her depraved character, carrying of dirks and razors, taking of laudanum, and threatening to cut her own throat. The judge also endorsed defense claims concerning Tirrell's love for the deceased, pointed out that the prisoner's flight from the scene was not necessarily an indication of guilt, and even expressed support for the novel plea of sleepwalking. "Somnambulism is insanity, to be treated as such," he bluntly asserted. "If proved, this is a proper ground of defence." Although Dewey's charge was not entirely one-sided—and certainly did not direct an acquittal—his framing of the issues must have been encouraging to defense lawyers.[143]

When Dewey concluded his charge at a quarter to eleven in the morning, the jury immediately retired to deliberate. The panel consisted of twelve men, including two housewrights, a mason, a mastmaker, a furniture dealer, a druggist, and a clerk.[144] After about two hours of discussion, the group returned to the courtroom in agreement. Before the outcome was announced, the sheriff warned the crowd in the courtroom not to respond to the decision with any noise or disorder. But when the verdict of not guilty was declared by the foreman, Tirrell broke into tears and the spectators in the courtroom burst into applause. As news of the decision flew down the stairs and out into the street, it was greeted by "a roof-shaking hurra" from the more than one thousand people gathered at the scene.[145] After the crowd in the courtroom had been hushed, Parker demanded to know whether the verdict had been based on the defense of somnambulism; the foreman declared that the issue had not even been considered by the jury. As in so much of the pretrial commentary, it may finally have come down to a question of female character—or male misogyny. "Oh! we didn't care a sixpence for that stuff about som-nam-bulism," one of the jurors is said to have explained defensively to jeering companions, "but then, you know, we couldn't believe the testimony of them abandoned women. Now, could we?"[146]

Even before the proceedings began, it had become clear that Tirrell's sensational trial would provide a boon for Boston's newspaper publishers, particularly for the proprietors of its largest penny dailies, the *Times* and the *Mail*. On March 21, a few days before the trial opened, the *Times* announced that it would provide "the fullest and most satisfactory" reports on the case and warned its agents and carriers to notify the paper early of expected increases in orders. On March 25, the day after the proceedings began, the morning *Times* announced that it would issue extras at twelve o'clock and at five in the afternoon every day, with updated courtroom coverage, for as long as the contest continued.[147] The daily trial reports consisted of nearly verbatim synopses, even transcripts, of speeches and testimony, filling as many as eight or more columns of tiny print in a single issue. Several of Boston's other newspapers, particularly the rival *Mail*, scrambled to match, or at least approximate, that comprehensive coverage.[148] Trial reports were also reprinted in at least two of the weekly periodicals issued by newspaper publishers.[149]

Boston's publishers marketed their coverage of the Tirrell trial in the form of pamphlets as well. Even before the trial was over, both the *Times* and the *Mail* announced that they would issue composite reports once the verdict was reached. The *Times* boasted in a notice on March 26 that their report would "unquestionably be the fullest and most complete of any that will be published." Not to be outdone, a boldface advertisement in the *Mail* the following day announced that their "very superior and correct Report" would be issued in an "Illustrated Octavo Edition of 20,000 COPIES!!"[150] Those first compilations hit the streets on Monday, March 30, just two days after the verdict, marketed by newspaper agents and by various book and periodical dealers.[151] By April 16, a fourth edition of the *Mail* report was being advertised in the newspaper; the *Times* version also appeared in at least two printings.[152] A third trial pamphlet, evidently a composite of reports in the *Mail* and the *Daily Bee*, was issued by Boston publisher H. B. Skinner under the title-heading "Warning to Young Men."[153] Other Tirrell trial pamphlets may also have been issued at the time.[154] Most of the reports seem to have been priced at a mere $6\frac{1}{4}$ cents per copy, suggesting that the publishers were aiming to attract a mass audience nearly as large as that for the penny dailies themselves; judging by the number and reported size of editions, they may have succeeded.[155]

The Tirrell trial pamphlets probably appealed to their popular audience on a number of levels. First, of course, the comprehensive reports were a logical extension of the journalistic function served by the partial reports printed daily in the newspapers, simply informing the public of a newsworthy event of great local interest. Further, by preserving the factual record in a more permanent form than the daily newspaper, the pamphlets may have made a transition from journalism to history. An advertisement in the *Mail* thus cited the "value" of the Tirrell trial report "as a *history* of an unparalleled crime."[156] Yet the trial pamphlets had an appeal—and a significance—that went beyond their role as journalism or history. One additional function was as a form of cautionary literature; as suggested by the heading of Skinner's edition, the trial of Albert Tirrell could serve as a powerful "Warning to Young Men." As vehicles of admonition, trial reports of the antebellum period were part of a long tradition of New England crime publications dating back to the Puritan execution sermons of the late seventeenth century. Another more modern function of the Tirrell trial reports was as a repository of legal precedents; according to the advertisement in the *Mail*, the report was of "importance to the members of the legal profession by reason of the authorities cited, and the rules of evidence established by the Court."[157] As already discussed, the popularization of trial reports reflected an earlier transformation in the criminal trial system and coincided in time with the development of professional case reporting.[158]

Yet the primary function of the Tirrell trial reports was probably to entertain. As we have already seen, Rufus Choate's defense of Albert Tirrell was not only novel but novel-like, and the appeal of the trial reports was probably quite similar to that of contemporary romantic fiction. That this is indeed the

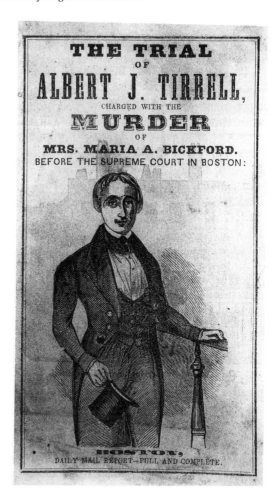

Title page of the *Boston Daily Mail's* pamphlet report of Tirrell's murder trial, with dignified portrait of the nattily attired defendant. *Courtesy, American Antiquarian Society.*

primary literary context within which the reports ought to be seen is suggested by the publisher's advertisement appended to one of them. The back wrapper of the *Times* report was not devoted to journalist notices, religious works, or legal publications but to a short catalog of novels issued by the prolific local publisher of sensational fiction, Henry L. Williams. The list featured not only numerous volumes by Osgood Bradbury, including *Julia Bicknell*, but also a number of works by J. H. Ingraham, among them novels based on two other recent cases of murder and sexual intrigue: those of Helen Jewett and Mary Rogers.[159] The latter case, of course, also provided the basis for Edgar Allan Poe's classic detective story "The Mystery of Marie Rogêt" (1842).[160] Trial reports on the case of Albert Tirrell were thus small parts of a much broader romantic literary complex—permeated by sex, crime, and violence—that was even then giving birth to modern detective fiction.[161]

Maria A. Bickford.

**Sentimental depiction of Maria Bickford, appended to the *Boston Daily Mail's*
pamphlet report of Tirrell's murder trial. The sympathetic tone of this portrait
contrasts jarringly with the relentlessly hostile image of Bickford conveyed by the
judicial proceedings themselves.** *Courtesy, American Antiquarian Society.*

Although extensive crime reportage and trial coverage in newspapers and
pamphlets may have reinforced the dominance of legal elites in antebellum
society, it probably also democratized antebellum culture by providing popular oversight over police practices and judicial proceedings. Crime stories and
trial reports amplified the legal profession's authoritative discourse on crime
and punishment but did so in ways that conservative jurists occasionally found
threatening and disruptive. The *Boston Daily Times*, for example, noted that
Chief Justice Shaw had "expressed a most prejudiced and unjust feeling to the
newspaper press for their notices and reports of criminal cases as interfering
with the trial of causes." The *Times* editor playfully replied that, since newspapers provided more accurate accounts than those contained in the judge's own
notes, Shaw should have been grateful to the press for their services. He also
cited a New York paper's defense of crime reportage as a valuable antidote to
the "exaggerations and distortions" of oral rumor and gossip. More fundamental, the *Times* editor implied that such coverage was an indispensable compo-

nent of "true liberty" and "freedom of the press."[162] Journalistic reportage of crimes and trials at once privileged the authority of print culture, confirmed the hegemony of legal forms and institutions, and enshrined the antebellum public's right to know.

Beginning on the Monday following the verdict—and for weeks afterward— the trial of Albert Tirrell was the subject of intense editorial scrutiny both in Boston and throughout the country. Responses ranged from forthright endorse- ments of the acquittal to outright condemnations. When the respectable *Eve- ning Transcript*, edited by Cornelia W. Walter, launched an editorial campaign against the verdict, the boisterous *Daily Times* countered with its own sustained defense of the outcome, assailing the *Transcript*'s crusade as "NEWSPAPER TWATTLE AND OLD WOMANISM."[163] Although sexual issues were not at all prominent in the substance of the posttrial debate, that choice of epithets— along with Walter's status as the only female newspaper editor in the city— suggests that at least some of the men and women of Boston may have been responding to the case along gender lines.[164] Several of Boston's other newspa- pers seem to have adopted a conciliatory middle course, expressing some dis- comfort with aspects of the trial—especially the outcome—without actually condemning the local tribunal.[165] Although newspapers throughout the coun- try also adopted various views on the case, most seem to have ridiculed the defense of somnambulism and deplored the verdict.[166] While editors fussed and fulminated in print, other Americans responded to the verdict in a variety of ways, with somnambulism suddenly emerging as the defense of choice for petty criminals from Boston to Baltimore.[167]

Meanwhile, as the public furor swirled around him, Albert J. Tirrell re- mained in a Boston jail, awaiting trial on the pending charges of adultery and arson. On Monday, May 18, Tirrell was arraigned in Boston Municipal Court on the morals charges, pleading nolo contendere to two counts against him and not guilty to three others. Sentencing was delayed until the next court term, and Samuel Parker agreed not to prosecute Tirrell on the three addi- tional counts. In failing to contest the two counts of adultery and lascivious habitation, Tirrell made himself liable to a term of six years in the state prison. About a month after his arraignment on the adultery charges, on June 16, Tirrell was brought before the Supreme Judicial Court on the capital charge of arson. However, the proceedings were delayed until a subsequent term be- cause of the illness of a key defense witness.[168]

Although the judicial proceedings had been delayed, the case of Maria Bickford and Albert Tirrell continued to be addressed in print. On April 12, 1846, just a couple of weeks after the conclusion of Tirrell's first trial, James Bickford handed his late wife's correspondence over to a friend who would arrange its publication. He also provided the friend with biographical informa- tion about Mrs. Bickford, explaining that he wanted the material made public in order to refute other fictitious accounts, probably the pamphlets of Silas Estabrook. Beginning on June 9, just a week before Tirrell's trial for arson was scheduled to begin, James Bickford's new biography, *The Authentic Life of Mrs. Mary Ann Bickford*, was widely advertised in Boston newspapers and hawked at periodical depots throughout the city.[169] The publishers may have timed publication so soon before the expected trial in order to influence public opinion or simply to maximize sales.

Newspaper advertisements for the new work packaged it as an exposé of urban vice and corruption. "The Truth Must be Told!" the notices declared in boldface print. "LET THE GUILTY SQUIRM!" The advertisers promised to "reveal to the world a mass of ASTOUNDING FACTS, implicating some well known individuals, conspicuous in the fashionable circles of Boston"; they also vowed to "show conclusively that some of aristocratic and wealthy origin acted a prominent part in the scenes which led to her [Bickford's] final ruin and premature death." Such exposures of the "fashionable," "wealthy," and "aristocratic" would probably have appealed to the working- and middle-class readerships of the penny dailies in which the *Authentic Life* was heavily advertised. Yet its appeal may have been even broader than that; as the notices confidently declared: "All classes may be instructed and benefitted by a perusal of this singular pamphlet." The advertisers also took pains to distinguish their publication from earlier spurious pamphlets—almost certainly those by Silas Estabrook—on the Bickford case. "About the authenticity and genuineness of this work there is no mistake," they insisted. "It is not like the catch-penny affairs issued from the press a few months ago, purporting to give the Biography and Letters of Mrs Bickford, which were fictitious and worthless, and were got up merely to humbug the community and make money by the sale of the most contemptible trash."[170]

The new work consisted of a series of letters written by Maria Bickford and a number of correspondents, particularly her husband and her last lover. The letters were linked in the lengthy pamphlet by interspersed biographical narrative presumably based on material provided by James Bickford. Following an initial discussion of Maria's early life, the correspondence commenced chronologically with a letter by her dated December 6, 1842, not long after she had abandoned her husband, and concluded with a note written by a friend on October 27, 1845, informing James Bickford of his wife's violent death. Appended to that main body of letters was some additional "miscellaneous correspondence" between Mrs. Bickford and a number of other prostitutes and paramours. There is little reason to doubt the authenticity of the correspondence or the general accuracy of the accompanying narrative. In fact, a few of the key details of Bickford's earlier life are confirmed by local records in Maine, and several of the letters from Tirrell had actually been admitted as evidence for the prosecution at his murder trial and identified in court as having been in the possession of James Bickford.[171]

The picture of Maria Bickford conveyed by the new pamphlet was essentially an elaboration of the image already embedded in the account earlier provided to the newspapers by her husband. She emerges from the new work as an impulsive, manipulative, and self-centered young woman driven less by

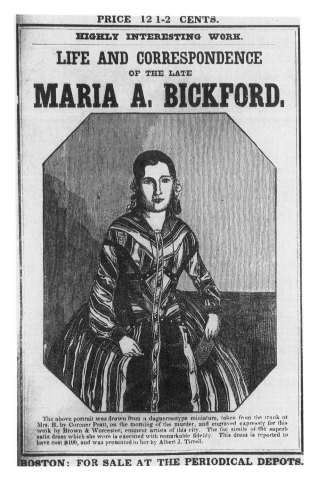

PRICE 12 1-2 CENTS.

HIGHLY INTERESTING WORK.

LIFE AND CORRESPONDENCE
OF THE LATE

MARIA A. BICKFORD,

The above portrait was drawn from a daguerreotype miniature, taken from the trunk of Mrs. B. by Coroner Pratt, on the morning of the murder, and engraved expressly for this work by Brown & Worcester, eminent artists of this city. The fac simile of the superb satin dress which she wore is executed with remarkable fidelity. This dress is reported to have cost $100, and was presented to her by Albert J. Tirrell.

BOSTON: FOR SALE AT THE PERIODICAL DEPOTS.

Front cover of *The Authentic Life of Mrs. Mary Ann Bickford* (1846), with a striking portrait of its subject and a caption focusing the reader's attention on her "superb" dress. *Courtesy, American Antiquarian Society.*

romantic fantasies or sexual passion than by her lust for the products of an emerging consumer culture. Here, for example, is the biographer's description of Maria's first visit to Boston, where she was captivated by the material wealth and display of the metropolis:

> While in the city, she appeared highly delighted with everything she saw. The gorgeous jewelry and splendid goods of every description displayed for sale in the windows of the various stores on Washington street, she would often refer to, and as often express a strong desire to remain here [in Boston] permanently. On returning home, *Boston* was the all-absorbing

theme of her conversation—fine houses; fine carriages; ladies with fine dresses; gentlemen looking prim; commotion, bustle, variety—all had fairly turned her head! Henceforth she became an altered woman, and seemed dissatisfied with her humble and retired condition in life. She was always passionately fond of dress; but the husband's limited means would not permit her to make the gay appearance she so much desired to do, and this was a great source of vexation to her.[172]

After running away from her husband and taking up with a succession of lovers, Maria continued to be obsessed by material commodities. In a letter to a female friend back in Maine, she described her relationship with a young Bostonian named Frank in terms of the material opulence that he provided and even embodied:

> Oh, I ride with the handsomest fellow that Boston affords; and we have three of the most magnificent robes that you ever saw; you don't have none of them down east, and he has got me a most splendid foot muff, and, oh, such a splendid sleigh! and he drives two of the most splendid horses you ever saw. . . . His coat is light velvet; there is not another in the city, and it attracts attention, I can tell you; he is immensely rich. . . . He is the richest man's son there is in Boston. . . . I shall bring my fellow with me when I come [to Maine].[173]

Note Maria's ecstatic emphasis on such consumer luxuries as the robes, the muff, the sleigh, and the velvet coat. Even her description of Frank himself suggests that he is a human commodity to be displayed, admired, and bragged about.

Maria's later description of her urban lodgings in a letter to the same friend reveals a similar infatuation with the material artifacts of a middle-class consumer culture:

> I am keeping house, and am very pleasantly situated; I have four rooms, and they are all to myself; it is a tenement by itself, and no one is with me; I have a very pretty parlor, a parlor chamber and bed room, and a dear little kitchen. I have just got my house furnished; I have got a beautiful carpet and very handsome cane seat chairs and a rocking chair; a very large glass, and a very pretty card table, and covering for it. In my chamber I have a very pretty bedstead, two beautiful matrasses and spread, half a dozen cane seat chairs and a large chair, washstand and toilet table. My kitchen is furnished accordingly. The other day I had the present of a beautiful piece of sheeting. I have got two beds and every thing handy.[174]

Once again, note Maria's enthralled invocation of consumer commodities: the "beautiful carpet," "very handsome cane chairs," "very pretty card table," "very pretty bedstead," "two beautiful matrassess," "beautiful piece of sheeting," and so forth.

If Maria Bickford was indeed a victim of seduction, her *Authentic Life* suggests that she had been seduced less by the lustful men in her life than by the material commodities that their sexual patronage allowed her to enjoy.

Although the resulting portrait is not entirely attractive, it is more plausible than the sentimental victim and sexual predator of other accounts. Perhaps it is even, as advertised, authentic. But accurate or not, Bickford's *Authentic Life* proved to be of great interest to Boston readers; the first issue was quickly exhausted by a "tremendous" rush of purchasers, and a new edition was at the periodical depots within a week.[175]

As it turned out, Tirrell's trial for arson was delayed until early the following year. A couple of weeks before it began, at the end of December 1846, a traveling wax museum opened for business on Washington Street, just a few doors away from the Old South Church. Its statues and tableaus were reportedly exhibited to the clatter of drum, fiddle, and banjo—musical instruments associated during the antebellum period with dancing-saloons frequented by prostitutes.[176] Two of its featured attractions were wax figures of Albert J. Tirrell and Maria A. Bickford. Maria's husband was reportedly hired to superintend the exhibition, where he stood by the figure of his late wife and commented on its likeness to the original.[177] Advertisements for the exhibit in the *Times* and the *Mail* also focused particularly on the statue of the dead woman. "Mrs Bickford's figure will be dressed in the identical dress that was given her by Tirrell and which cost so much money," the press notices read; "also the jewelry and other ornaments worn by her in Boston; all of which have been obtained of Mr James Bickford . . . at a great cost."[178]

In order to acquire the consumer commodities that she so coveted, Maria Bickford had—by resorting to prostitution—turned herself into a commodity for the purchase and enjoyment of male consumers. In the end, as a sexual commodity, she was literally consumed by flames and by Albert Tirrell's fatal passion. Her posthumous appearance on Washington Street as a wax dummy in an elegant dress and expensive jewelry—gaped at by hordes of Boston consumers and their country cousins—was the ironic culmination of a process that Maria herself had set in motion more than four years earlier when, as a raw teenager from provincial Maine, she had gazed longingly into the windows of the fashionable shops on Washington Street, infatuated by the "gorgeous jewelry and splendid goods" placed there on display.[179] The story of Maria Bickford, like the flood of cheap trial reports, romantic biographies, and sensational newspaper accounts of her case, embodied the triumph of an American consumer culture that has endured from that day to this.[180]

On Monday, January 11, 1847, with the wax dummies still on display in Washington Street, another set of actors gathered at a Boston courthouse to play familiar roles: Samuel D. Parker stood for the prosecution; Rufus Choate and Annis Merrill appeared for the defense; three judges of the Supreme Judicial Court presided on the bench; and Albert J. Tirrell sat once again in the dock, on trial for his life. All that had changed was the charge, which was now arson rather than murder. Initially it was unclear how much coverage Tirrell's second capital trial would receive in the Boston press. "As most of the evidence published before will apply to this case," the *Daily Times* noted on January 11, "it will not become necessary to detail it again." But just two days later, the *Times* editors reversed themselves, explaining that they would provide a "full Report" of the proceedings in deference to the public's sustained interest in the case. The rival *Mail* naturally followed suit; as the editor of the *Daily Chronotype* put it on January 13: "The Boston Mail is almost wholly occupied with the new trial of St. Albert J. Tirrell for arson, whose former trial for murder gained the Mail so much patronage that he may be said to be its patron saint."[181] While the largest penny dailies thus provided detailed reports of the trial, coverage by other local newspapers varied widely, with some, like the *Chronotype*, all but ignoring it.[182] Beyond the uneven daily coverage, at least one composite report of the trial was published in pamphlet form.[183]

As suggested by the comment in the *Times* at its opening, Tirrell's second capital trial was largely a replay of the first. Yet one or two important new witnesses, along with a flood of additional minor witnesses, were called by each side. Appearing for the first time for the prosecution was Caroline L. Warren, a dressmaker of dubious character, who was staying in a basement room in the Lawrence house at the time of Bickford's death. Although she had not appeared at the first trial, she now claimed to have seen Tirrell leaving the building early on the morning of October 27. While Warren's testimony helped establish that Tirrell had stayed with Bickford through the night and had fled from the scene of the crime the following morning, her mere presence on the stand may have helped the defense even more than the prosecution by further damaging the already shaky credibility of the Lawrences, who had failed to mention her presence in the building during the first trial.[184] Another significant new witness for the prosecution was Samuel Stetson, an uncle of Tirrell who had seen the fugitive on the morning of the crime. According to Stetson, Tirrell had told him that he had fled from a burning house that morning between four and five o'clock; even more important, Stetson testified that Tirrell was bleeding from a deep cut on the forefinger of his left hand. Since the defendant was left-handed, he would presumably have used that hand in slashing his lover's throat with the razor and might easily have cut himself in the process.[185]

One important new witness for the defense, Jeremiah Palmer, had lived next door to the Lawrences in October 1845. Palmer seriously diminished the already vanishing credibility of his former neighbors by testifying that he heard a person enter their house at around ten o'clock on the evening of October 26, even though Lawrence and his wife had sworn that they had locked their door at nine o'clock and no one had been admitted thereafter. He also claimed that he had heard someone leave the Lawrence's building by the front door at about four o'clock on the following morning. Since all other witnesses agreed that Tirrell had fled by the back door, Palmer's testimony raised the possibility that some unknown person might have arrived at the Lawrences late in the evening, murdered Bickford, set fire to the building, and then fled before daybreak.[186]

Both sides called a veritable flood of additional minor witnesses. The prosecution called numerous observers from Weymouth to refute defense claims concerning Tirrell's habitual somnambulism and produced many others to disparage the character of Eben Tirrell, a key defense witness. For their part, defense lawyers obtained new testimony defending their own witness's reputation and verifying the prisoner's somnambulism. In fact, both sides seem to have scraped the bottom of the evidentiary barrel. For example, Jonathan Bigelow, a minister from Rochester, Massachusetts, testified for the defense that "while in a state of somnambulism, he had composed a sermon and read it aloud, read hymns and made prayers, and performed entire church service[s]; this he had done as often as thirty or forty times, and should perhaps have repeated it oftener, if his wife had not awoke him." Such witnesses helped drag out the proceedings for nearly a week.[187]

Choate's closing speech, delivered on the seventh day of the trial, largely recapitulated his argument in the earlier case; if anything, it was even more melodramatic. Once again he conveyed sympathetic images of his client, disparaged the characters of opposing witnesses, and offered hypothetical reconstructions of disputed events. His characterization of Bickford and his description of Tirrell's feelings for her were particularly powerful and evocative. The deceased was a low prostitute, Choate insisted, "a woman of dirks and knives, like a Spanish girl, coarse, strong and masculine," who had repeatedly attempted suicide; and yet the prisoner had "loved her with the love of forty thousand brothers." To Choate, it all seemed so obvious! "How much more likely that she should have taken her own life," he explained, "than that he should have deliberately murdered her."[188]

After resurrecting the old suicide defense—which was not strictly relevant, since the current charge was arson, not murder—Choate went on to savage the credibility of the new witness for the prosecution, Caroline L. Warren. He contended that her testimony should be completely disregarded by the jury. "A more base and more lying wretch never existed," he insisted; "a more coarse and reckless prostitute never lived." How did he know? Surely it was proved by her "flippant and saucy expression, by her brazen countenance and every shade of her prostitute manner."[189] Choate was hardly more gentle in his treatment of the Lawrences, conceding only that they probably had not murdered Bickford themselves.[190] In addition to exhibiting his undiminished talent for character assassination, the romantic advocate demonstrated his masterful ability to sketch an imaginative scene:

> We will thus state the case: Albert J. Tirrell, if he was there [in Bickford's room], was awakened from the insanity of sleep by the warm blood of the desperate suicide; half-waking he sees the object of his licentious affection or love gasping by his side—he springs from the bed—takes the body gently in his arms and lays it upon the floor—stoops over her and presses upon her lips the last kiss of love and affection; and then crazed, half-sleeping and half-waking, seizes his clothes, rushes out [into] . . . the yard and cries fire.[191]

The lawyer's scene was dramatic, compelling, and essentially irrelevant to the charge of arson; as for the last kiss, it was a touch of pure genius, worthy of the pen of Osgood Bradbury. After entering "heart and soul into the case" and haranguing the jurors for five and a half or six hours, Choate finally subsided, leaving the floor to his older opponent.[192]

When Samuel Parker rose to offer his own closing speech, he could hardly contain his frustration. He pleaded with the jurors to "take a calm and common sense view of the cause" and begged them to be "guided and governed by the plain truth, divested of all metaphor or rhetorical flourish." He also "trusted that they would estimate the arguments by their weight, and not by the vehemence with which they were urged." In trying to disenthrall the jurors, his scorn for Choate's theatrical tactics was obvious. "And may I not beg you to consider carefully what I say," he asked the jurors, "although I resort to no violence of gesture or tone, and do not advance up to you, and scream in your faces what I consider important parts of the case?"[193] After ridiculing Choate's courtroom manner, Parker proceeded to build his usual methodical argument on a series of numbered questions:

1st. Was the house mentioned in the indictment, on fire on the 27th of October, 1845?
2d. Was it Joel Lawrence's house, and was his family in it at the time?
3d. Was the fire accidental or designed?
4th. Did the prisoner maliciously and wilfully set it on fire?
5th. Was it in the night time or day time?
6th. If the prisoner did it, was he then and there an accountable and moral agent?[194]

It was all quite logical and all completely futile. The following day, after a balanced three-hour charge by Chief Justice Shaw, the jurors deliberated for another few hours and returned with a verdict of not guilty. As after the first trial, upon hearing the decision the usually cool prisoner reportedly burst into tears.[195]

Just two days after his acquittal on the capital charge of arson, Albert Tirrell was brought into Boston's Municipal Court for sentencing on the charges of adultery and lascivious cohabitation to which he had earlier pleaded nolo contendere. At the hearing Amos B. Merrill, Tirrell's lawyer, asked for a postponement of sentencing and a reduction in bail to allow his client an opportunity to visit friends and put his business affairs in order. In making that request, he adopted tactics similar to those used in the capital trials: "The eloquent counsel was going on to paint the arts and witchery by which his unfortunate client had been seduced into adulterous connexion with Mrs. Bickford." But the judge abruptly interrupted Merrill's argument, refused the motion for a postponement, and announced that sentencing would take place at two o'clock that afternoon.[196]

When the hearing reconvened, Merrill tried to retract Tirrell's earlier plea and obtain a full trial on the adultery charges, but the magistrate again rejected his motion. Merrill then attempted to have the sentence reduced to a fine. Although the judge rejected that idea as well, he did suggest that the two counts be merged into one, so as to effectively halve the prison sentence. The county attorney, Samuel D. Parker, who had vigorously opposed the earlier attempts at mitigation, agreed to the judge's suggestion. And so Tirrell was sentenced to three years at hard labor in the state prison. Although apparently disappointed by the outcome, he received his sentence calmly. As he was taken out to the carriage, he was followed by a "general rush of the spectators" eager for a last look at the guilty man.[197] Near the end of the following month, the *Daily Times* completed its coverage of the affair with a brief and anticlimactic squib: "It is said that Tirrell is put to work in the copper plate engraving in prison—a very good and pleasant business."[198] That same day, the traveling wax museum on Washington Street finally closed its doors.[199]

Despite two appeals for pardons to the governor, Albert Tirrell was forced to serve out the full three years of his sentence for adultery. His release, at the end of January 1850, sparked a renewed flurry of notices in the Boston press.[200] Albert promptly returned by train to his hometown of Weymouth, where he took up what must initially have been an uncomfortable residence with his wife Orient and two young daughters in his father-in-law's house. Despite past infidelity, Tirrell wasted little time in reasserting his conjugal rights; Orient became pregnant within a few weeks of his return. In November 1850 she gave birth to their third daughter. Perhaps in a symbolic attempt to patch up their frayed marriage, the little girl was named after both parents: Orient Albertine Tirrell.[201]

Aside from a stint in the Union army during the Civil War, Albert seems to have stayed in Weymouth for the rest of his life, as did his wife and three daughters. One somehow doubts that they were a happy family; they certainly were not a prosperous one. In the census of 1850, taken shortly after his release from prison, Albert was listed as a "shoe manufacturer." Shoemaking was the dominant industry in Weymouth, introduced to the town early in the nineteenth century by a member of the large Tirrell family. Albert's own father had also prospered in that line of business, as would his older brother. Yet unlike his father, brother, and many other Weymouth Tirrells, Albert did not manage to secure great wealth through shoes or even maintain a foothold in that thriving and rapidly expanding industry. His employment listings in the state and federal censuses suggest a record of gradual decline. In 1850 Tirrell was described as a "shoe manufacturer," in 1855 as a "speculator," in 1865 as a "trader," in 1870 as a "huckster," and finally in 1880, just a few months before his death of a brain hemorrhage, as "unemployed."[202]

As it turned out, Albert was much less efficient in accumulating money than he had been in squandering it. According to the federal censuses of 1860 and 1870, Tirrell owned no real estate and only one hundred dollars in personal wealth. It was the same amount of money that he had once lavished on a single gaudy dress for Maria Bickford, the sort of estate one might have expected of a factory worker just starting out in life, not of the middle-aged son of a wealthy manufacturer. At times economic distress may have even forced the family apart. In 1860 Albert's three daughters, aged nine, fifteen, and seventeen, were all living in the home of a neighbor, while two boys of similar ages and an elderly woman were living with Albert and Orient. That was a curious arrangement, possibly designed to generate family income by putting the daughters out as household servants and taking in paying boarders. But perhaps it also reflected some underlying tension or discomfort within the family circle. In any case, none of Tirrell's daughters were sufficiently impressed by the delights of matrimony ever to try it for themselves. Or maybe nobody was willing to marry the daughter of an impecunious huckster and presumed murderer.[203]

For whatever reason, the three daughters of Albert Tirrell remained single and largely dependent, living out their years in Weymouth, shuttling occasionally between the homes of parents, neighbors, and relatives. The eldest, Catherine Augusta, was the last to die. The *Weymouth Gazette* reported her passing in August 1917 with a brief notice: "Miss Kate Tirrell died at the Town Home on Monday. She was 74 years old a daughter of the late Albert J. Tirrell. She was born and always lived in this town."[204] There is no way of knowing whether, during her last years of obscure poverty, Miss Tirrell had any recollection of her experience in a crowded Boston courtroom more than seventy years earlier. Did she remember how "a beautiful little girl," just three years old, had caused such a stir simply by walking into the chamber, clasping her mother's hand? Did she recall standing bareheaded on her mamma's lap, flitting her gaze over the assembled multitude, and beaming at her handsome father in the dock? And did she retain any memory whatsoever of the uncouth and flamboyant man who had saved her father's life? Any hope of answering those questions died with Albert's eldest daughter.

Rufus Choate never fully lived down his role in the acquittal of Albert Tirrell. During the following years, he was besieged by criminal defendants eager to obtain his services. In order to escape such distasteful obligations, Choate briefly assumed the office of state attorney general. Yet he was unsuited to the role of prosecutor, reportedly inhibited by his fear of convicting an innocent man.[205] After relinquishing that office in 1854, he continued in private practice until his death five years later. But the notoriety of his criminal practice, and particularly of his role in the Tirrell case, pursued him even to the grave; he was savagely eulogized by Wendell Phillips, among others, as the lawyer "who made it safe to murder."[206]

One of Choate's supporters, Benjamin R. Curtis of the U.S. Supreme Court, replied that critics fundamentally misconceived the American judicial process. "Such persons begin with the false assumption that in the complicated cases which are brought to trial here, one party is altogether right and the other altogether wrong," Curtis explained. "They are ignorant, that in nearly all cases there is truth and justice and law on both sides; and that it is for the tribunal to discover how much of these belongs to each, and to balance them, and ascertain which preponderates."[207] The role of each advocate under such a system was to marshal all of the "justice, truth, and law" on that side of the case, Curtis explained, leaving judges and jurors to mediate between the frankly partial and partisan presentations.[208] Defenders of Choate thus embraced an epistemology at once pluralistic and relativistic, one grounded not in the monologic expression of legal (or religious) authority, but in the intensely competitive and fragmented discourse of an adversarial trial system.

In the eyes of many contemporaries, Choate was at once an oddity and an exemplar; all agreed that he was unique in manner and method, yet younger lawyers often attempted to imitate his style, much to the dismay of older jurists.[209] After all, Choate was very much the product of his age, the embodiment of a mode of elocutionary oratory that achieved its greatest popularity during the first half of the nineteenth century.[210] Much like Osgood Bradbury, his obscure contemporary at the bar, Choate catered to the tastes of a romantic generation. But by the 1850s the romantic style embodied by Choate was already passing, being replaced in the courts by more restrained and technical modes of pleading.[211] "We have heard Rufus Choate argue with vivacity and vehemence," Edward G. Parker observed in 1857, "but the fetters of 'the decisions' manacled his action, and curbed in the leapings of his intellect." Choate's death two years later marked the end of an era. "When he died the sunlight faded from the forum," Parker noted sadly, "and thenceforth the atmosphere of the courts became the cold, prosaic air of daily business details." Richard H. Dana, Jr., put it even more starkly. "The 'golden bowl is broken,'" he eulogized. "The age of miracles has passed."[212]

Literary historian Robert A. Ferguson has described an all but forgotten "configuration of law and letters" that dominated American culture in the early republic. The tradition was shaped by a succession of lawyer-writers who collectively produced an early national literature committed to republican values and neoclassical aesthetics. It was a durable configuration that only broke apart during the mid-nineteenth century, as legal practice became more narrow and technical and literary figures abandoned neoclassicism in favor of the romanticism of the American Renaissance.[213] According to Ferguson, Rufus Choate was one of the last powerful embodiments of—and spokesmen for—that neoclassical tradition.[214]

While his political career and civic oratory certainly support Ferguson's interpretation, a number of Choate's imaginative criminal pleadings suggest that he was also part of a newer and far less distinguished configuration of law and letters, one embodied in his own forensic arguments, in trial reports, and in the cheap fiction of authors like Osgood Bradbury. It was a popular tradition committed not to neoclassical republicanism but to an unstable cultural compound that might best be described as "legal romanticism." For all its volatility, it would prove even more durable than the neoclassical. Although it may have been squeezed out of many courtrooms during the second half of the nineteenth century by more technical modes of pleading, the discourse of legal romanticism has more than held its own in the broader American marketplace. In emphasizing the split between law and literature within the bounds of an elite canon, scholars like Ferguson have neglected a powerful countertendency in antebellum popular culture to amalgamate legal forms and romantic sensibilities.

The early mass-circulation newspapers, with their lurid stories and elaborate trial reports, fully embodied the culture of legal romanticism. In perceptive studies of the nineteenth-century popular press, Dan Schiller and David Ray Papke have argued that antebellum crime coverage was highly politicized and polarized along class lines. In particular, they claim that penny dailies and other cheap journals catered to the ideological preferences of the working and middle classes.[215] There is certainly some evidence of that tendency in literary responses to the Tirrell affair. Silas Estabrook's fictionalized accounts of the case featured class-conscious social criticism.[216] And James Bickford's pamphlet biography was advertised in the penny press as an exposé of upper-class depravity.[217] Since the former was a printer and the latter a shoemaker, one might reasonably—and quite correctly—argue that their popular pamphlets embodied an artisanal critique of elite corruption.

However, the polemical thrust of Estabrook's prose was vitiated by its playful quality, and the class hostility evident in the newspaper advertisement for Bickford's biography was less prominent in the pamphlet itself. Nor was the penny press any more single-minded in its championing of working-class interests. The same daily paper that carried James Bickford's advertisement also defended the jury's verdict in favor of a wealthy rake.[218] And the same newspaper that first depicted Maria Bickford as a genteel victim later portrayed her as a low seductress.[219] Of course, several of the jurors were themselves artisans, and gender prejudices may sometimes have overridden those of class. But one is left with the general impression that editors, reporters, and hack writers responded to the case opportunistically rather than programmatically. They did not so much adhere to a fixed ideological agenda as pick and chose at will from a varied menu of popular, if often contradictory, cultural motifs. Unresolved class tensions and conflicting gender stereotypes were at once expressed and subsumed within a flexible, pluralistic, and highly profitable discourse of legal romanticism.

Published responses to the violent death of Maria A. Bickford and to the subsequent trials of Albert J. Tirrell illustrate at least three major developments in New England crime literature during the first half of the nineteenth century. First, newspaper coverage of sensational crimes and trials expanded dramatically. Second, motifs from sentimental and romantic fiction flooded into the literature. Third, trial reports emerged as popular scripts for the drama of crime and punishment. Those three developments were intricately related. Trial reports and melodramatic accounts were primary media of journalistic coverage; crimes of sex and violence already pervaded contemporary fiction; and criminal trials themselves became stages for the expression of romantic values and perceptions. Like the broader culture that it reflected, antebellum crime literature was at once journalistic, legalistic, and romantic. Those same elements also coalesced into a distinctive pattern of forensic advocacy that catered to popular tastes even as it shaped judicial outcomes. More than anyone else of his generation, Rufus Choate embodied that new courtroom style; his flamboyant arguments challenged reporters, astounded readers, and captivated jurors. As the quintessential romantic advocate, he saved lives, destroyed reputations, and expressed both the sense and the sensibilities of an age.

10

Conclusion

The transformation of New England crime literature between 1674 and 1860 is vividly represented by the four vignettes that opened this book. The case of James Morgan reflected a religious culture preoccupied by the social and spiritual consequences of human alienation from God. The story of the Boston currier both dramatized that alienation and provided a program for spiritual reconciliation under the guidance of local ministers. Morgan's case was valuable to those ministers not because it was exceptional but because it was so very typical. In the final analysis, his crime was no different from any other act of human wickedness; all sins were enormities in the sight of God. His plight was no different from that of any other unsaved person; all labored under a spiritual sentence of death. His solution was no different from that required of any other sinner; all had to turn to Christ for life. The image of James Morgan as penitent sinner embodied a paradigm at the heart of Puritan theology and social theory.

The cases of William Fly and Whiting Sweeting represented a culture in which public order and authority were increasingly under attack. Although international piracy was successfully extirpated during the first few decades of the eighteenth century, subsequent crime waves struck much closer to home, threatening the lives and property of private citizens. At the same time, a succession of larger social movements, notably the Great Awakening, the American Revolution, the New Light Stir, and Shays's Rebellion, assaulted the foundations of religious and secular authority. In that context crime narratives of the eighteenth century offered conflicting messages, some tending to reinforce authority, others to undermine it. By describing the successful repression of social bandits, some criminal last speeches probably bolstered the forces of order by assuring readers that insurgents would be apprehended and destroyed. However, the elaborately documented success of other property offenders in pursuing criminal careers that lasted for years, or even decades, probably undermined public confidence in the penal system. And by portraying condemned criminals as victims of injustice, several of the most popular crime narratives of the late eighteenth century explicitly challenged elite values and institutions. The images of the suppressed insurgent and the injured innocent expressed two powerful—and competing—cultural impulses in an era of social upheaval and revolution.

The case of Maria Bickford illustrated the preoccupation of nineteenth-century literature with illicit sexuality, particularly crimes of violence by men against women. Although that preoccupation may have expressed abeyant impulses released by the breakdown of Puritan controls over the course of the eighteenth century, it also reflected dilemmas peculiar to an emerging culture of consumption. Young men of the early republic were repeatedly enjoined to exercise vigilant self-discipline as competitors in the marketplace. At the same time, the very products of that marketplace offered endless temptations to self-indulgence. The resulting conflict between arousal and restraint was most exquisitely manifested in intimate relations between the sexes, where a pattern of widespread sexual activity out of wedlock was successfully challenged by an ideal of voluntary abstinence. Ironically, that transition to greater sexual control coincided with the triumph of popular literary genres that glorified romantic love and emotional intimacy as essential components of courtship and marriage. The resulting tension between romantic indulgence and sexual restraint created a vast market for literary representations of criminal sexuality that warned against the consequences of impulsive behavior while providing a vicarious taste of forbidden fruit.[1] The image of the sexual predator, who could figure either as man or woman, killer or victim, but whose transgressions invariably led to violent death, was a powerful expression of cultural ambivalence and frustration. It was an image that coexisted uneasily with the optimistic conceptions of human nature widely embraced in nineteenth-century America. By substituting sexual predators for penitent sinners, trial reporters and romantic biographers reversed the old alchemy of Puritan ministers, transforming monuments of grace into pillars of salt.

From the harsh gallows sermons of Samuel Danforth and Increase Mather to the fanciful and romantic potboilers of Silas Estabrook and Osgood Bradbury, New England's literature of crime and punishment evolved not at random but in accordance with broader social and cultural rhythms. The first publications, especially those issued between 1674 and 1700, reflected a cohesive and disciplined Puritan culture in which orthodox ministers were authoritative spokesmen for the community as a whole. Dissidents on the subjects of crime and punishment undoubtedly existed, but their views seldom made it into print.[2] In early execution sermons, clergymen portrayed crime in theological terms, relating it to original sin, natural depravity, the individual's need for salvation through Christ, and the community's obligation to an avenging God. Criminal conversion narratives reinforced those pious messages by illustrating the validity of ministerial doctrines in flesh and blood. Indeed, the elaborately documented success of local ministers in reintegrating condemned men and women into the moral order of the orthodox community was a measure of both the persuasive power and the inclusive intent of the dominant religious ideology.

Undergirding the early literature was an epistemology that was also firmly embedded in Puritan belief. For the ministers who wrote early execution sermons and conversion narratives, the truth was certain, unitary, and rigidly patterned. Clergymen addressed the details of particular crimes and criminals not out of any conviction that each case was unique but from a certainty that every case conformed to fixed patterns of behavior and significance. Both the path to the gallows and the road to heaven were easily charted; the steps of sinful wayfarers invariably conformed to familiar religious models. As examples of early modern spiritual biography, criminal conversion narratives were less oracles of a nascent individualism than exemplars of an enduring devotional communalism. In form, language, message, and underlying intellectual assumptions, New England's earliest crime literature was dominated by Puritan belief, with orthodox ministers enjoying a virtual monopoly on literary expression.

But almost from the beginning, ministers and printers began tinkering with the religious literature of crime, trying to strengthen its message and broaden its appeal. Before the end of the seventeenth century, execution sermons began to appear in volumes containing dying confessions, warnings, prayers, dialogues, and crime accounts. Those supplementary materials provided an entering wedge for literary voices other than those of the ministers. Even the words of pious criminals like Esther Rodgers subtly subverted clerical domination of public discourse. Other added materials reflected an increasingly secular interest in the details of capital cases. When pirates like William Fly openly defied ministers and magistrates, their words and conduct were faithfully presented to local readers. By establishing conventions of documentary reportage and eagerly cultivating a popular readership, ministers like Cotton Mather helped open the door to new literary approaches to crime and punishment.

After 1700 printers experimented with a number of imported English crime genres, turning by the 1730s to execution broadsides as popular literary alternatives to the gallows sermon. Although the earliest last speeches were dominated by pious warnings and confessions, most subsequent examples were largely secular in tone and autobiographical in content. That shift may have resulted in part from a switch in literary mediators; the printers who produced last speeches were presumably less interested than clergymen in affirming religious values and more interested in producing engaging and marketable narratives. The new tone and content of last speeches probably also reflected changes in the types of criminals executed in the region. After 1730 condemned offenders tended to be participants in a quasi-criminal subculture that gradually developed in New England over the course of the eighteenth century. As documentary biographies, many last speeches explored a profane underworld that implicitly mocked traditional values, exposing the old Puritan ideal of the covenanted community united in its struggle against sin as an anachronism. The decline of cultural cohesion went hand in hand with an equally threatening breakdown of social control; both trends were illustrated by the new broadside literature.

Underlying the last speeches was an epistemology very different from that implicit in the earlier religious literature. Although the pious formulas that generally framed the broadside narratives imitated older Puritan models, the naive empiricism of the last speeches—with their linear catalogues of names, dates, places, and actions—suggested the particularism of early modern philosophical realism, bolstered by a long-standing faith, sanctioned by Anglo-American legal practice, in the veracity of statements by dying men and women.[3] Given that intellectual stance, a single reliable narrative could still adequately encompass a person's life, but the truth depicted was dynamic, unpredictable, and highly individuated, unique to the constantly shifting circumstances of that individual. Reality no longer conformed to a few patterns of universal significance but consisted instead of a theoretically endless number of ongoing, intersecting narratives, each conveying the truth about a single life. Unlike the highly patterned, theologically ordered spiritual biographies of the Puritans, many documentary criminal autobiographies of the mid- to late eighteenth century sprawled without fixed meaning across an increasingly varied and disordered social and literary landscape.

Although last speeches may have subtly undermined orthodox social values and intellectual categories, they did not offer explicit ethical alternatives. But several longer narratives published in the aftermath of the American Revolution did just that, embodying powerful ideological insurgencies that shook the social and cultural order of early national New England. The poignant account of Elizabeth Wilson exemplified a sentimental insurgency that was undermining patriarchal values; the polemical narrative of Whiting Sweeting expressed an evangelical insurgency that was shattering the hegemony of Calvinist orthodoxy; and the subversive memoirs of Stephen Burroughs not only ridiculed orthodox religion and reflected sentimental values but also embodied a philosophical insurgency, grounded in the cosmopolitan Enlightenment, that was attacking the entrenched values and prejudices of provincial elites. Those same antiauthoritarian narratives also implicitly challenged the naive empiricism of most last speeches by suggesting that appearances were often deceptive and the truth elusive.

If local clergymen failed to reassert effective ideological control, it was not for lack of trying. New England ministers continued to deliver execution sermons well into the nineteenth century, and printers continued to publish them. However, many of the arguments presented in the new sermons reflected the same breakdown of ideological coherence signaled by the criminal biographies. Explanations of crime based on theological doctrines like original sin and natural depravity were increasingly supplemented by arguments involving faulty pedagogy, romantic contingency, and flawed social policy. Justifications of capital punishment based on scriptural authority were gradually supplemented, or even replaced, by secular arguments based on social need and legal procedure. A new intellectual pluralism had infected even the spokesmen for New England's earlier ideological unity, transforming them into unwitting agents of secularization. It was not that the ministers were abandoning religion itself—they assuredly were not—but that they were gradually narrowing the range of social situations to which they applied spiritual solutions and theological explanations. Without any intention of abandoning the piety of their forbears, many children of the Puritans were intuitively consigning large areas of social experience, including many aspects of crime and punishment, to an ever expanding secular sphere.

The long period of cultural transformation finally climaxed at the beginning of the nineteenth century with the emergence of a new configuration of crime publications. Execution sermons and last speeches gradually disappeared and were replaced by trial reports, romantic biographies and novels, and expanded newspaper coverage. The literature as a whole was at once legalized and romanticized, reflecting two of the dominant cultural currents in antebellum America. The monolithic system of religious expression and authority that had broken down during the eighteenth century was replaced by a pluralistic structure of literary communication and control, organized into complementary professions. Lawyers and judges replaced ministers as the primary spokesmen of public authority. Trial reports may have recaptured crime literature as an instrument of social order, but they did so by appealing to legal rather than religious values. At the same time, novelists and newspaper reporters emerged as key arbiters of public sentiment and taste. While ministers were by no means silenced, they now shared the press with a variety of other cultural spokesmen. If the new configuration of legal romanticism was a form of cultural hegemony, it was an extremely "open" hegemony, one whose very essence encompassed ideological pluralism and social conflict.[4]

The new crime literature suggested an epistemology that was well suited to a legalistic, romantic, and pluralistic culture. The truth was no longer certain, monolithic, and rigidly patterned, conforming to a few fixed spiritual models; nor was it simple, linear, and naively empirical, corresponding to a single reliable narrative. Rather, it was complex, elusive, and fragmented, approximated only by balancing the conflicting testimony of fallible witnesses and the competing arguments of partisan advocates; adversarial trial reports were natural vehicles for the expression of that new approach to reality. An awareness of the contingent quality of human knowledge and experience was reflected not only in trial reports but also in romantic biographies, novels, and newspaper stories that emphasized the subjective, the emotional, the irrational, and the bizarre. Criminal docudramas that seamlessly blended the factual and the fanciful were not so much evidence of generic deterioration as natural extensions of the creative strategies pursued by early sentimental novelists like William Hill Brown, Susanna Rowson, and Hannah Foster. The notion that there was, during the first half of the nineteenth century, a normative genre of purely "fictional" novels, unalloyed by elements of social documentary or reportage, is itself an analytical fiction.[5]

The overall model of change in New England crime literature was one of initial coherence followed by gradual breakdown and insurgency, leading to a new pattern of generic and ideological pluralism. Once formal censorship had ended, Puritan domination of the literature broke down for a number of reasons: a proliferation of local printers, booksellers, and publishers who were decreasingly dependent on the patronage of Puritan ministers and magistrates, and increasingly prone to take initiatives in the pursuit of profit; the ready availability of various generic alternatives to the execution sermon in popular British crime literature; a decline of ideological coherence within the New England ministry that allowed new attitudes toward crime to infiltrate even the execution sermon genre; and the emergence of a number of cultural insurgencies in the aftermath of the Revolution (partly imported and partly indigenous) that won the loyalty of various printers, authors, criminals, and readers. In the end, a cohesive literature of Protestant piety was replaced by a more secular and diverse print culture widely committed to both legal and romantic values. The essential components of that new configuration had all emerged by the first decade of the nineteenth century; the technological innovations of the following years allowed for the elaboration of that cultural transformation but did not fundamentally challenge it. While the artifacts of legal romanticism may have been among the most successful products in America's early industrial revolution, they had been faithfully adapted from an earlier mode of literary production. Trial reports and romantic crime narratives resulted from cultural, not technological, innovations.[6]

Perhaps more than ever before, the subjects of crime and punishment dominate American popular culture. Treatments in books, newspapers, magazines, movies, and television shows range from "straight news" to based-on-fact docudramas to outright fictions. As Lawrence M. Friedman has wryly observed of the dominant medium, modern television "would shrivel up and die without cops, detectives, crimes, judges, prisons, guns, and trials."[7] While technological innovations have allowed for a degree of popular penetration unmatched even by the mass literary culture of the antebellum period, most of the defining characteristics of modern crime coverage can be traced back to the earlier literature. In fact, several key elements had emerged almost from the outset. First, New England printers and booksellers of the late seventeenth century were already well aware of the potential of crime coverage as a profitable literary commodity, an awareness that has never lapsed. From then till now, cultural entrepreneurs have persistently produced crime coverage in a quantity and at a price that made it widely accessible to all but the most impoverished of consumers. Second, printers like Richard Pierce and ministers like Cotton Mather together helped establish a reportorial style, based heavily on interviews, transcripts, and eyewitness accounts, that closely resembles modern documentary practice. The religious motives that animated the originals have long since vanished, but the pattern of documentary reportage largely remains. Third, compilers of criminal conversion narratives cultivated an attention to the subjective experiences of social outcasts and subordinates that still flourishes in other forms today. Although the articulation of that interest has become largely sociological and psychological rather than spiritual, the venues of crime and punishment are still among the only arenas in which the general public becomes at all attentive to the lives of impoverished racial minorities and other social pariahs. Fourth, the authors and printers of early execution pamphlets sought to balance the imperatives of didacticism and sensationalism, generating a creative tension that has continued to shape literary responses to crime ever since. Some modern television writers may be less conscientious than Puritan ministers in fitting morals to their stories, but most still at least go through the motions.

Several other key aspects of modern crime coverage would not emerge until the late eighteenth and early nineteenth centuries. A powerful anti-authoritarian strain, generated by alleged miscarriages of justice, first flourished in the aftermath of the American Revolution—and remains prominent today. A new configuration of legal romanticism, conflating legal forms with romantic sensibilities, coalesced at the dawn of the nineteenth century—and still largely dominates the popular culture of crime.[8] Two key aspects of that configuration were its preoccupation with illicit sexuality and sexual violence—obsessions as consuming now as they were then. Modern responses to crime are thus, in part, the products of cultural breakdown, transformation, and reconsolidation during the revolutionary and early national periods. But perhaps the most fundamental aspect of modern crime coverage was among the earliest to appear, an ambivalence that long predated the upheavals of the late eighteenth and early nineteenth centuries. Like us, the Puritans struggled with conflicting impulses to expel the criminal and to draw him or her back into the fold. The difference today lies in our own inability to reconcile those impulses through faith. We have lost the spiritual gumption to proudly hang a saint, but our cultural landscape is still littered with pillars of salt.

Notes

Abbreviations

Abbreviations for Court Records:

SC, Recs.   Massachusetts Superior Court of Judicature, Records, 1686–
             1780.
SJC, Recs.   Massachusetts Supreme Judicial Court, Records, 1781–1799.
Ct. Files   Files of the Massachusetts Superior and Supreme Courts,
             1686–1799.

All of the above records and files were located for many years in the office of the Clerk of the Supreme Judicial Court for Suffolk County, Suffolk County Court House, Boston, but have now been moved to the State Archives, Boston. The Supreme Judicial Court (SJC) was the post-Revolutionary successor to the provincial Superior Court of Judicature (SC).

Abbreviations for Standard Biographical and Bibliographical References:

American Imprints	Richard H. Shoemaker, comp., *A Checklist of American Imprints for 1820[–1829]*, [10] vols. (New York/Metuchen, N.J.: Scarecrow Press, 1964–71) and successor volumes [year covered used in place of volume number].
BMC	*British Museum General Catalogue of Printed Books*, 263 vols. (London: Trustees of the British Museum, 1959–66).
Bristol	Roger P. Bristol, comp., *Supplement to Charles Evans' American Bibliography* (Charlottesville: University Press of Virginia, 1970).
DAB	Dumas Malone, ed., *Dictionary of American Biography*, 20 vols. (New York: Charles Scribner's Sons, 1928–37).
Dexter	Franklin Bowditch Dexter, *Biographical Sketches of the Graduates of Yale College*, 6 vols. (New York: Henry Holt, 1885–1912).
DNB	Sir Leslie Stephen and Sir Sidney Lee, eds., *The Dictionary of National Biography*, 22 vols. (1885–1901; rpt. London: Oxford University Press, 1937–38).
Evans	Charles Evans, comp., *American Bibliography*, 14 vols. (New York: Peter Smith and Worcester: American Antiquarian Society, 1941–59).
Evans Microprint	Readex Microprint series of Clifford K. Shipton, ed., *Early American Imprints 1639–1800* (Worcester, Ma.: American Antiquarian Society, 1955–68) [refers to notes on microcards].

McDade   Thomas M. McDade, comp., *The Annals of Murder: A Bibliography of Books and Pamphlets on American Murders from Colonial Times to 1900* (Norman: University of Oklahoma Press, 1961).

NUC   *National Union Catalog Pre-1956 Imprints*, 754 vols. (London/Chicago: Mansell, 1968–81).

Ritz   Wilfred J. Ritz, comp., *American Judicial Proceedings First Printed Before 1801* (Westport, Conn.: Greenwood Press, 1984).

Shaw and Shoemaker   Ralph R. Shaw and Richard H. Shoemaker, comps., *American Bibliography: A Preliminary Checklist for 1801[–1819]*, [19] vols. (New York: Scarecrow Press, 1958–63) [year covered used in place of volume number].

Sibley   John Langdon Sibley and Clifford K. Shipton, eds. *Biographical Sketches of Those Who Attended Harvard College* [titles vary], 17 vols. (Cambridge: Charles William Sever/Harvard University Press and Boston: Massachusetts Historical Society, 1873–1975).

Sprague   William B. Sprague, *Annals of the American Pulpit*, 9 vols. (New York: Robert Carter and Brothers, 1857–69).

Wing   Donald Wing, comp., *Short-Title Catalogue of Books Printed in England, Scotland, Ireland, Wales, and British America . . . 1641–1700*, 3 vols. (New York: Columbia University Press, 1945–51).

Preface

1. For citations of those works published before 1801, see *Ritz*; for many of those published between 1680 and 1820, see Allan C. Tappe, "Who Was to Blame? Responsibility for Capital Crimes in America, 1680–1820" (unpublished research paper, Brandeis University, n.d.), pp. 57–64; for those relating to American murder cases through 1860 and beyond, see *McDade*; also see Ronald A. Bosco, "Early American Gallows Literature: An Annotated Checklist," *Resources for American Literary Study* 8 (1978): 81–107. Most of those works are also cited in one or another of the following standard bibliographies of early American imprints: *Evans, Bristol, Shaw and Shoemaker*, and *American Imprints*.

2. The generic identities of most New England crime publications are not problematic. Works within a given genre tend to share strong "family resemblances" in size, structure, subject, style, mood, authorship, and social context or occasion. Genres like execution sermons, last speeches, and trial reports are also denoted in individual works by generic allusions (e.g., references to earlier works within the genre) and by formulaic titles, subtitles, openings, and closings. Those generic signals would have been as obvious to most contemporary readers as they are to modern scholars. Only occasionally do identifications become tricky; for example, the formulaic titles associated with last-speech broadsides were applied to a number of distinct (albeit related) genres over the course of three centuries; on that point, see discussion in text and notes of chapters 1, 6, and 8 below. For a theoretical overview of the concept of genre that

informs my discussion in this note, see Alastair Fowler, *Kinds of Literature: An Introduction to the Theory of Genres and Modes* (Cambridge: Harvard University Press, 1982); on the concept of family resemblance in particular, see pp. 40–44.

Chapter 1. *An Overview*

1. See John Dunton, *Letters Written from New England* (1867; rpt. New York: Burt Franklin, n.d.), pp. 118 and 135; John Rogers, *Death the Certain Wages of Sin* (Boston: B. Green and J. Allen, 1701), p. 153; also see references in note 3 below. Short titles (with capitalizations standardized) and abbreviated imprints are used for primary sources in this and subsequent notes.

2. On the various extraordinary occasions that evoked sermons in early New England, see Harry S. Stout, *The New England Soul: Preaching and Religious Culture in Colonial New England* (New York: Oxford University Press, 1986), passim. For scholarly discussions of New England execution sermons, see Louis P. Masur, "The Culture of Executions and the Conflict over Capital Punishment in America, 1776–1860" (Ph.D. diss., Princeton University, 1985), pp. 8–56; David Levin, *Cotton Mather: The Young Life of the Lord's Remembrancer, 1663–1703* (Cambridge: Harvard University Press, 1978), pp. 119–27; Ronald A. Bosco, "Lectures at the Pillory: The Early American Execution Sermon," *American Quarterly* 30 (Summer 1978): 156–76; Eli Faber, "Puritan Criminals: The Economic, Social, and Intellectual Background to Crime in Seventeenth-Century Massachusetts," *Perspectives in American History* 11 (1977–78): 85–96; Faber, "The Evil That Men Do: Crime and Transgression in Colonial Massachusetts" (Ph.D. diss., Columbia University, 1974), pp. 31–40, 126–73, and 229–56, passim; Walter Lazenby, "Exhortation as Exorcism: Cotton Mather's Sermons to Murderers," *Quarterly Journal of Speech* 57 (Feb. 1971): 50–56; Wayne C. Minnick, "The New England Execution Sermon, 1639–1800," *Speech Monographs* 35 (March 1968): 77–89; Daniel J. Boorstin, *The Americans: The Colonial Experience* (New York: Vintage, 1958), pp. 13–14. I define an execution sermon as a sermon explicitly occasioned by an execution, generally delivered prior to the hanging and generally addressed to both the condemned criminal and the community at large.

3. See Cotton Mather, *Diary*, 2 vols. (New York: Frederick Ungar, [1957]), vol. 1, pp. 122, 165, and 279, quoted at 279; Samuel Sewall, *The Diary*, ed. M. Halsey Thomas, 2 vols. (New York: Farrar, Straus and Giroux, 1973), vol. 1, pp. 99, 310, and 400; and Dunton, *Letters*, p. 135.

4. Such sermons were often revised somewhat for publication; for references to discrepancies, revisions, or enlargements in preparing execution sermons for publication, see Cotton Mather, *Speedy Repentance Urged* (Boston: S. Green, 1690), p. [vi]; Thomas Foxcroft, *Lessons of Caution to Young Sinners* (Boston: S. Kneeland and T. Green, 1733), pp. [i]–ii; Samson Occom, *A Sermon, Preached at the Execution of Moses Paul* (New London: T. Green, [1772]), p. [2]; Ephraim Clark, *Sovereign Grace Displayed* (Boston: J. Boyles, 1773), p. [2]; Thaddeus MacCarty, *The Guilt of Innocent Blood Put Away* (Norwich: J. Trumbull, 1778), p. 19; Peres Fobes, *The Paradise of God* (Providence: B. Wheeler, 1784), p. [4]; Matthew Merriam and Joseph Buckminster, *Sermons Preached to Joshua Abbot* ([Newburyport]: J. Mycall, [1792]), pp. [6] and [49]; Timothy Langdon, *A Sermon* (Danbury: Douglas & Nichols, 1798), p. [4]; Leland Howard, *A Sermon* (Windsor, Vt.: A. & W. Spooner, 1818), p. [2]; Jonathan

Going, *A Discourse* (Worcester: W. Manning, 1825), p. [2]. For one case where a minister claimed to publish a sermon as actually delivered, see Andrew Eliot, *Christ's Promise to the Penitent Thief* (Boston: J. Boyles, 1773), p. [2].

5. Cotton Mather, *Pillars of Salt* (Boston: B. Green and J. Allen for S. Phillips, 1699), p. [2].

6. That claim is based on a page-by-page scan of A. W. Pollard and G. R. Redgrave, comps., *A Short-Title Catalogue of Books Printed in England, Scotland, & Ireland . . . 1475–1640* (London: Bibliographical Society, 1948); *Wing*. I do not know whether execution sermons were published elsewhere in early modern Europe.

7. Synopses of sermons to condemned men were generally included in the *Accounts* regularly compiled by the Ordinary (chaplain) of Newgate in conjunction with criminal executions in London; see P. Linebaugh, "The Ordinary of Newgate and His *Account*," in J. S. Cockburn, ed., *Crime in England 1550–1800* (Princeton: Princeton University Press, 1977), p. 248. Also see the sermons appended to Nicholas Barnard, *The Penitent Death of a Woefull Sinner*, 2d ed. (London: G. M. for W. Bladen, 1642), pp. 79–179; Randolph Yearwood, *The Penitent Murderer* (London: T. Newcomb, 1657), pp. 53–69; and [Richard Alleine], *A Murder Punished and Pardoned* (London: 1668), pp. 49–72; note, however, that at least two of those discourses were actually funeral sermons, all three were delivered *after* the execution of the criminal, and all were appended to volumes containing primarily nonsermonic material.

8. On the general status and character of the Ordinaries of Newgate Prison in England, see Linebaugh, "Ordinary of Newgate," pp. 246–69; for biographical and bibliographical information on one such Ordinary, see H. O. White, ed., *The Works of Thomas Purney* (Oxford: Basil Blackwell, 1933), especially pp. xiv–xxiv and 91–92; on the backgrounds of the American ministers who produced execution sermons, see Minnick, "New England Execution Sermon," p. 78. The much maligned Ordinaries of Newgate should be distinguished from the often more reputable ministers involved in the production of English criminal conversion narratives of the seventeenth century, as described in chapter 2 below.

9. Bartholomew Green, who printed at least ten volumes of execution sermons, has been described as "the most distinguished American printer from 1690 to 1730"; see Benjamin Franklin V, *Boston Printers, Publishers, and Booksellers: 1640–1800* (Boston: G. K. Hall, 1980), pp. 213–19, quoted at 213. For citations of the execution volumes printed by him, see *Evans*, nos. 655, 795, 856, 877, 879, 902, 1020, 1452, 1729, and 2251. On Fleet, Kneeland, and Thomas, see Franklin, *Boston Printers*, pp. 162–70, 323–29, and 464–72.

10. S[amuel] D[anforth], *The Cry of Sodom Enquired Into* (Cambridge, Mass.: M. Johnson, 1674); Going, *Discourse Delivered at Worcester*. Crime-related sermons *were* issued after 1825; see, for example, William Buell Sprague, *Wicked Men Ensnared* (Springfield: Tannatt, 1826); William I. Budington, *Capital Punishment* (Boston: T. R. Marvin, 1843); Lyman Whiting, *Sin Found Out* (Lynn, Mass.: H. J. Butterfield, 1850); however, none of those was delivered in conjunction with a criminal execution. For an execution "address," arguably a sermon of sorts, published *outside* of New England after 1825, see O[restes] A. Brownson, *An Address, Prepared at the Request of Guy C. Clark* (Ithaca: S. S. Chatterton, 1832); I am grateful to William J. Gilmore-Lehne for bringing that pamphlet to my attention.

11. Of the more than sixty volumes of American execution sermons published before 1800, I have been able to locate only two originating outside of New England: Chauncy Graham, *God Will Trouble the Troublers of His People* (New York: H. Gaine,

1759); Holloway Whitfield Hunt, *A Sermon* (Newton, N.J.: 1796). At least one additional execution discourse from outside New England was published as part of a collection of American sermons; see Uzal Ogden, "The Reward of Iniquity," in David Austin, ed., *The American Preacher; or, A Collection of Sermons*, 3 vols. (Elizabethtown, N.J.: S. Kollock, 1791), vol. 3, pp. 185–98.

12. For advertisements of execution sermons, see C. Mather, *Pillars of Salt*, p. 112; John Tulley, *An Almanack for the Year of our Lord, 1699* (Boston: B. Green and J. Allen, 1699), p. [16]; *Boston News-Letter* [cited hereafter as *News-Letter*], Sept. 28, 1713, p. 2; July 11, 1715, p. 2; Dec. 9, 1717, p. 2. Although an attempt to establish a newspaper had been made in 1690, it was immediately suppressed; for more on that episode, see sources cited in note 67 below.

13. For example, in the case of William Fly and his fellow pirates, Benjamin Colman's sermon was delivered on July 10, 1726; the pirates were executed on July 12; and the printed sermon was advertised as being published on July 22; see Benjamin Colman, *It Is a Fearful Thing to Fall into the Hands of the Living God* (Boston: J. Phillips and T. Hancock, 1726); *News-Letter*, July 14, 1726, p. 2; July 21, 1726, p. 2. On the length of time usually taken to bring less newsworthy sermons into print, see Rollo G. Silver, *Publishing in Boston, 1726–1757: The Accounts of Daniel Henchman* (Worcester: American Antiquarian Society, 1956), p. 20.

14. See John Tebbel, *A History of Book Publishing in the United States*, 4 vols. (New York: R. R. Bowker, 1972–81), vol. 1, pp. 27–28; Kenneth Silverman, *The Life and Times of Cotton Mather* (New York: Harper & Row, 1984), p. 281; Michael G. Hall, *The Last American Puritan: The Life of Increase Mather, 1639–1723* (Middletown, Conn.: Wesleyan University Press, 1988), p. 338; Carl Bridenbaugh, *Cities in the Wilderness: The First Century of Urban Life in America, 1625–1742* (1938; rpt. New York: Oxford University Press, 1971), p. 292. It should be noted that the functions of printer, publisher, and bookseller were not entirely distinct during the seventeenth and eighteenth centuries; many individuals combined two or more of those activities; see Tebbel, *History of Book Publishing*, vol. 1, pp. 3–4 and passim.

15. C. Mather, *Diary*, vol. 1, p. 65; *News-Letter*, April 16, 1705, p. 2. Gray must have enjoyed a brisk business; according to the *News-Letter*, he left behind a "considerable Estate."

16. See Worthington Chauncey Ford, *The Boston Book Market, 1679–1700* (1917; rpt. New York: Burt Franklin, 1972), pp. 174, 178, and 182. A somewhat cryptic early inscription on a volume of execution sermons published in 1686 may indicate that it sold for four pence; for a photograph of the inscription, see Hall, *Last American Puritan*, p. 196; Hall takes no note of the inscription or its possible significance.

17. On the daily wages of rural laborers in New England during the first decade of the eighteenth century, see David W. Galenson, "Labor Market Behavior in Colonial America: Servitude, Slavery, and Free Labor," in Galenson, ed., *Markets in History: Economic Studies of the Past* (Cambridge: Cambridge University Press, 1989), p. 89. If one takes the median daily wage rate of 24 pence and assumes a retail price of 3 pence for a stitched execution sermon (which allows a generous markup of 50 percent—assuming 2 pence was the wholesale price), the sermon would cost just one-eighth of a worker's daily wage; this would be almost identical to the cost (as a fraction of daily wages) of a $4.95 mass-market paperback for an unskilled worker today earning about $5.00 an hour. In chapter 9 below, I make a very similar calculation in regard to cheap crime pamphlets of the mid-nineteenth century. Obviously, before precise conclusions could be drawn, account would have to be taken of changes in the relative cost of food,

housing, health care, and so forth. One would also want to note the modern availability of much cheaper newspapers and periodicals, and the greater number of pages provided by modern paperbacks as compared to early sermons. Still, those crude calculations at least suggest the possibility that there has been much less change in the relative pricing of some types of "popular" publications in New England between 1700 and today than heretofore assumed. My immediate point, of course, is not that farm laborers were the primary—or even frequent—purchasers of execution sermons, but rather that the pricing of such works placed them well within the financial reach of most readers of the middling orders and even some of the lower sort.

18. On the practice of giving authors complimentary copies, see Tebbel, *History of Book Publishing* , vol. 1, p. 57; Silver, *Publishing in Boston*, pp. 18–19.

19. See C. Mather, *Diary*, vol. 1, pp. 65, 518 (quoted), 520, 539, 548; vol 2, 14, 26–27, 105, 109. Many of those pages are cited in Silverman, *Life and Times*, pp. 198 and 445.

20. For example, in May 1726 the Reverend Timothy Edwards (father of Jonathan Edwards) of Windsor Farms, Connecticut, lent to "neighbor Rockwell" a copy of Cotton Mather's *Pillars of Salt* (1699), along with a little devotional manual; see John A. Stoughton, *A Corner Stone of Colonial Commerce* (Boston: Little, Brown, 1911), p. 52.

21. See Cotton Mather, *The Vial Poured Out upon the Sea* (Boston: T. Fleet for N. Belknap, 1726), pp. 16–17.

22. See Kenneth A. Lockridge, *Literacy in Colonial New England* (New York: W. W. Norton, 1974), p. 17 and passim. Since those estimates are based on wills signed late in life, since elementary education was generally received during childhood or youth, and since the consistent trajectory of literacy rates was upward, it seems likely that the actual rates at each point in time were substantially higher for boys, adolescent males, and young men, demographic cohorts often targeted by the authors of execution sermons. Also, it should be noted that most experts believe that the level of signatures (upon which the above figures are based) is almost always somewhat below the level of reading ability, suggesting that Lockridge's figure may actually be underestimates of reading skills (see p. 109).

23. See ibid., pp. 13–43, passim. E. Jennifer Monaghan suggests that Lockridge may have underestimated the percentage of colonial women able to read; see Monaghan, "Literacy Instruction and Gender in Colonial New England," in Cathy N. Davidson, ed., *Reading in America: Literature and Social History* (Baltimore: Johns Hopkins University Press, 1989), p. 73.

24. See C. Mather, *Diary*, vol. 1, pp. 122–23; vol. 2, pp. 459–60, 462, and 491. For references to the size of early sermon editions, see Rollo G. Silver, "Financing the Publication of Early New England Sermons," *Studies in Bibliography* 11 (1958): 165, 167–69, 172, and esp. 173. On the marketplace of literary scarcity, see David D. Hall, "Introduction: The Uses of Literacy in New England, 1600–1850," in William L. Joyce et al., eds., *Printing and Society in Early America* (Worcester: American Antiquarian Society, 1983), pp. 1–2, 23, and 26–27; Richard D. Brown, "Afterword: From Cohesion to Competition," in Joyce et al., eds., *Printing and Society*, p. 300.

25. Boston's population in 1717 was estimated at twelve thousand; see Samuel A. Drake, *Old Landmarks and Historic Personages of Boston* (1900; rpt. Detroit: Singing Tree Press, 1970), p. 20. Of course, as already indicated, such sermons were distributed far beyond the bounds of Boston itself.

26. On the double audience of execution sermons, see, for example, C. Mather, *Speedy Repentance*, pp. 1–2; William Shurtleff, *The Faith and Prayer of a Dying Malefactor* (Boston: J. Draper, 1740), p. 2; Sylvanus Conant, *The Blood of Abel* (Boston: Edes and Gill, 1764), p. 5.

27. See C. Mather, *Diary*, vol. 1, p. 122; C. Mather, *The Call of the Gospel Applyed* (Boston: R. Pierce, 1687) [bound and paginated with Increase Mather, *A Sermon Occasioned by the Execution of a Man*, 2d ed.], p. 38; Joshua Moody, *An Exhortation to a Condemned Malefactor* [bound and paginated with I. Mather, *Sermon Occasioned*], p. [84]; C. Mather, *Speedy Repentance*, p. [v]; C. Mather, *The Converted Sinner* (Boston: N. Belknap, 1724), p. 2; Samuel Checkley, *Sinners Minded of a Future Judgment* (Boston: T. Fleet, 1733) [bound with Checkley, *Murder a Great and Crying Sin*], p. 24; Moses Baldwin, *The Ungodly Condemned in Judgment* (Boston: Kneeland and Adams, 1771), p. 15; Eliot, *Christ's Promise*, t.p.; Samuel Stillman, *Two Sermons* (Boston: E. Russell, 1773), t.p.; Joshua Spalding, *The Prayer of a True Penitent for Mercy* (Salem: Dabney and Cushing, 1787), p. 5; James Dana, *The Intent of Capital Punishment* (New Haven: T. and S. Green, 1790), p. 22; Nathan Strong, *A Sermon*, 2d ed. (Hartford: E. Babcock, 1797), p. [3]; Langdon, *Sermon*, p. 16. Of course, it is possible that ministers (or others) sometimes solicited such requests from the criminals.

28. For general discussions of seventeenth-century Puritan sermons, see Stout, *New England Soul*, pp. 13–123; Perry Miller, *The New England Mind: The Seventeenth Century* (1939; rpt. Boston: Beacon Press, 1961), pp. 331–62 and passim.

29. Increase Mather, *The Wicked Man's Portion* (Boston: J. Foster, 1675), p. [iii]; also see C. Mather, *Speedy Repentance*, p. [vi]; Stillman, *Two Sermons*, p. [3]; Spalding, *Prayer of a True Penitent*, p. 5.

30. For a perceptive discussion of the relationship of the doctrine of "divine providence" to popular literature, see David P. Nord, "Teleology and News: The Religious Roots of American Journalism, 1630–1730," *Journal of American History* 77 (June 1990): 9–38.

31. The first two published execution sermons were Danforth, *Cry of Sodom*, and Increase Mather, *Wicked Man's Portion*.

32. For citations of the sermons published between 1686 and 1726, see *Ritz*, pp. 250–55 and cross-references therein.

33. See works by Yearwood and Alleine cited in note 7 above; also see other relevant English works cited in chapter 2 below.

34. See discussion in chapters 2 and 3 below.

35. See *The Last Speeches of the Five Notorious Traytors and Jesuits* ([London: 1679]), passim; one of the condemned men declared: "The words of dying Persons have always been esteem'd of greatest Authority because uttered then, when shortly after they are to be cited before the high Tribunal of the Almighty God" (p. 2); Jonathan Edwards, "Memoirs of Brainerd," in Clarence H. Faust and Thomas H. Johnson, eds., *Jonathan Edwards: Representative Selections* (1935; rpt. New York: Hill and Wang, 1962), pp. 257–58 (I am grateful to Chandos M. Brown for bringing this passage to my attention). For an early attack on the routinely privileged status of criminal confessions, see J[ohn] Q[uick], *Hell Open'd, or, The Infernal Sin of Murther Punished* (London: F. Eglesfield, 1676), p. 79.

36. On confessions as a "principal ingredient" of true repentance, see Q[uick], *Hell Open'd*, p. 33, quoted; I. Mather, *Wicked Man's Portion*, p. 24. On the value of confessions in clarifying issues of guilt and innocence, see, for example, Increase

Mather's urgings that two servants (who had together been convicted of murdering their master) confess, partly (he implies) in order to clarify which one of them had actually committed the crime (p. 24).

37. On the use made of criminal confessions as instruments of warning, see chapter 2 below.

38. However, it should be noted that even those accounts had links to the pious tradition of "remarkable providences."

39. See Cotton Mather, *The Sad Effects of Sin* (Boston: J. Allen for N. Boone, 1713); C. Mather, *Instructions to the Living, from the Condition of the Dead* (Boston: J. Allen for N. Boone); for another volume in which the factual account preceded the sermon, see C. Mather, *The Vial Poured Out upon the Sea* (Boston: T. Fleet for N. Belknap, 1726). Title-page typography was particularly significant during the early modern period when (in England, at least) title pages were sometimes posted in public places as a primitive form of advertising; see H. S. Bennett, *English Books & Readers, 1558 to 1603* (Cambridge, Eng.: Cambridge University Press, 1965), p. 291; Ford, *Boston Book Market*, p. 62.

40. See *News-Letter* [cited hereafter as *News-Letter*, despite variant titles], Dec. 9, 1717, p. 2. For a similar contrast between a title-page and a newspaper advertisement, compare Cotton Mather, *A Sorrowful Spectacle* (Boston: T. Fleet & T. Crump for S. Gerrish, 1715) with the advertisement in the *News-Letter*, July 11, 1715, p. 2.

41. For a broader discussion of the Puritan origins of modern American journalism, see Nord, "Teleology and News."

42. For a comprehensive listing of American execution sermons published before 1801, see *Ritz*, pp. 249–62 and cross-references. For citations of New England execution sermons published between 1801 and 1825, see notes to chapters 4 and 5 below, passim. My figures on the total number of volumes of execution sermons published in New England between 1674 and 1825 are based on a page-by-page scan of *Evans*, *Bristol*, *Shaw and Shoemaker*, and *American Imprints* through 1833. In this and all subsequent cases in which I provide statistics on the numbers of a given genre within a given period, I refer to the total number of distinct titles; reprints and new editions are not counted as separate works. Of course, more than one title could be issued on any given case.

43. See Occom, *Sermon* [*Ritz*, no. 5.04(3)(b)].

44. See Baldwin, *Ungodly Condemned* [*Ritz*, no. 5.02(26)(b)]; Stillman, *Two Sermons* [*Ritz*, no. 5.02(32)(k)].

45. The advertisements ran in the *News-Letter* between October 28 and December 30, 1773; also see *Ritz*, no. 5.02(32)(k).

46. See *News-Letter*, Nov. 4, 1773, p. 3. That was comparable to the prices of chapbooks of the same period and only a few pennies more than almanacs; see Victor Neuburg, "Chapbooks in America: Reconstructing the Popular Reading of Early America," in Davidson, *Reading in America*, pp. 92 and 94; Tebbel, *History of Book Publishing*, vol. 1, p. 154.

47. See, for example, *News-Letter*, Nov. 11, 1773, p. 2.

48. On the broader process of anglicization, see John M. Murrin, "Anglicizing an American Colony" (Ph.D. diss., Yale University, 1966); Jack P. Greene, "Search for Identity: An Interpretation of Selected Patterns of Social Response in Eighteenth-Century America," *Journal of Social History* 3 (Spring 1970): 205–17; Stout, *New England Soul*, pp. 127–47.

49. For a recent scholarly discussion of such works, see Daniel E. Williams, "'Be-

hold a Tragic Scene Strangely Changed into a Theater of Mercy': The Structure and Significance of Criminal Conversion Narratives in Early New England," *American Quarterly* 38 (Winter 1986): 827–47. Although his analysis is otherwise quite perceptive, Williams does not seem to be aware of the English and European origins of the genre.

50. See works by Alleine, Barnard, and Yearwood cited in note 7 above and similar works cited in chapter 2 below.

51. See Cecilia Tichi, "Spiritual Biography and the 'Lords Remembrancers,' " in Sacvan Bercovitch, ed., *The American Puritan Imagination* (London: Cambridge University Press, 1974), pp. 56–73; Owen C. Watkins, *The Puritan Experience: Studies in Spiritual Autobiography* (New York: Schocken, 1972); Paul Delany, *British Autobiography in the Seventeenth Century* (London: Routledge & Kegan Paul and New York: Columbia University Press, 1969), pp. 27–104; G. A. Starr, *Defoe and Spiritual Autobiography* (Princeton: Princeton University Press, 1965), pp. 3–50.

52. See I. Mather, *Sermon Occasioned* [other titles bound in]; Rogers, *Death*, pp. 118–53.

53. Samuel Moodey, *Summary Account of the Life and Death of Joseph Quasson, Indian* (Boston: S. Gerrish, 1726); Samuel and Joseph Moody, *Faithful Narrative of the Wicked Life and Remarkable Conversion of Patience Boston* (Boston: S. Kneeland and T. Green, 1738).

54. For examples of subsequent works depicting the spiritual transformations of condemned criminals, see *The Execution Hymn, Composed on Levi Ames* ([Boston]: E. Russell, [1773]), broadside; Edmund Fortis, *The Last Words and Dying Speech* (Exeter, [N.H.?]: 1795).

55. *An Account of the Behaviour and Last Dying Speeches of the Six Pirates* (Boston: N. Boone, 1704). Because a copy of this rare broadsheet was found in the files of the *News-Letter* at the Massachusetts Historical Society, it has been characterized (I think, on the whole, misleadingly) as an "extra" of that newspaper; see John Franklin Jameson, *Privateering and Piracy in the Colonial Period: Illustrative Documents* (New York: Macmillan, 1923), p. 278 n. 1. On Boone, see Franklin, *Boston Printers*, pp. 46–52; George Emery Littlefield, *Early Boston Booksellers, 1642–1711* (1900; rpt. New York: Burt Franklin, 1969), pp. 192–200.

56. For examples of seventeenth-century Ordinary's *Accounts*, see Samuel Smith, *The True Account of the Behaviour and Confession of the Criminals, Condemned on Thursday the 15th Day of April, 1686* (London: E. Mallet, 1686); Samuel Smith, *A True Account of the Behaviour, Confessions and Last Dying Speeches of the Criminals That Were Executed at Tyburn, on Wednesday the Second of March, 1691/2* (London: L. Curtiss, 1692); *An Account of the Behaviour, Dying Speeches, and Execution of Mr. John Murphey [et al.] . . . on Wednesday the 25th November, 1696* (London: T. Crownfield, 1696); many other examples are listed in *Wing*. For citations of eighteenth-century Ordinary's *Accounts*, see J. N. Adams and G. Averley, *A Bibliography of Eighteenth-Century Legal Literature* (Newcastle upon Tyne, Eng.: Avero Publications, 1982), pp. 354, 371, 375, and 392–95; for a modern scholarly discussion of them, see Linebaugh, "Ordinary of Newgate."

57. Compare Boone's broadsheet with the late seventeenth-century Ordinary's *Accounts* cited in note 56.

58. See [*An Account of the Pirates, with Divers of Their Speeches*] ([Boston?: 1723]), surviving only as an appendix to [Cotton Mather], *Useful Remarks* (New London: T. Green, 1723), pp. 29–45, and in reprint of 1769; see *Ritz*, no. 1.03(1).

59. See, for example, *The Tryal of Spencer Cowper, Esq.* (London: 1699); many other examples are listed in *Wing*; for earlier examples, see Joseph H. Marshburn, *Murder and Witchcraft in England, 1550–1640* (Norman: University of Oklahoma Press, 1971), pp. 55, 70, 148–49, and passim.

60. See Cotton Mather, *The Wonders of the Invisible World* ([1692, postdated] 1693; rpt. London: J. R. Smith, 1862), pp. 120–59. For a thorough bibliographic discussion of that work, see Thomas J. Holmes, *Cotton Mather: A Bibliography of His Works*, 3 vols. (1940; rpt. Newton, Mass.: Crofton, 1974), vol. 3, 1234–66.

61. See *The Arraignment, Tryal and Condemnation, Capt. John Quelch, and Others of His Company* ([Boston, 1704]; rpt. London: B. Bragg, 1705) [cited hereafter as *Tryal of Quelch*]; on the original American edition of the Quelch trial report, see *Ritz*, no. 1.02(3)(c), and Cecil Headlam, ed., *Calendar of State Papers, Colonial Series, America and West Indies, 1704–1705* (1916; rpt. Vaduz: Kraus, 1964) [hereafter cites to this series will be by date only], pp. 216 and 585; *The Trials of Eight Persons Indicted for Piracy* (Boston: B. Green for J. Edwards, 1718); *Tryals of Thirty-Six Persons for Piracy* (Boston: S. Kneeland, 1723); *The Trials of Five Persons for Piracy, Felony and Robbery* (Boston: T. Fleet for S. Gerrish, 1726); *The Tryals of Sixteen Persons for Piracy* (Boston: J. Edwards, 1726).

62. For scholarly discussions of that campaign, see Robert C. Ritchie, *Captain Kidd and the War Against the Pirates* (Cambridge: Harvard University Press, 1986); Marcus Rediker, "'Under the Banner of King Death': The Social World of Anglo-American Pirates, 1716 to 1726," *William and Mary Quarterly*, 3d ser., 38 (April 1981): 203–27.

63. See Danby Pickering, *The Statutes at Large*, 109 vols. (Cambridge, Eng.: J. Bentham for C. Bathurst [imprints vary], vol. 10, p. 323; also see Headlam, *1722–1723*, p. 306.

64. See Headlam, *1704–1705*, pp. 216 and 585. Contemporary records suggest that this report was jointly prepared by Paul Dudley, the queen's advocate and attorney general of Massachusetts, and John Valentine, the register of the Special Court of Admiralty; see *Acts and Resolves, Public and Private, of the Province of the Massachusetts Bay* (Boston: Wright & Potter, 1895), vol. 8, p. 396.

65. See citations in note 61 above. Also see Headlam, *Aug. 1717–Dec. 1718*, pp. 285–86; *1724–1725*, pp. 206–7 (there are no surviving copies of this report, if indeed it was ever printed); *1726–1727*, pp. 137–38. For advertisements of the reports in local newspapers, suggesting sale to the general public, see *News-Letter*, July 3, 1704, p. 2; July 21, 1726, p. 2; *Boston Gazette*, July 25, 1726, p. 2.

66. For a more detailed discussion of American trial reports of the seventeenth and eighteenth centuries, see Daniel A. Cohen, "Pillars of Salt: The Transformation of New England Crime Literature" (Ph.D. diss., Brandeis University, 1988), chapter 8.

67. See Frank Luther Mott, *American Journalism: A History of Newspapers in the United States Through 260 Years: 1690 to 1950*, rev. ed. (New York: Macmillan, 1950), pp. 11–14; Robert W. Jones, *Journalism in the United States* (New York: E. P. Dutton, 1947), pp. 34–43; Willard Grosvenor Bleyer, *Main Currents in the History of American Journalism* (Boston: Houghton Mifflin, 1927), pp. 47–51; Frederic Hudson, *Journalism in the United States, from 1690 to 1872* (New York: Harper & Brothers, 1873), pp. 51–58. In 1690 Benjamin Harris had issued a single newspaper in Boston, but the project was immediately suppressed by the governor and council; see Mott, *American Journalism*, pp. 9–11; Jones, *Journalism in the United States*, pp. 22–33; Bleyer, *Main Currents*, pp. 44–47; Hudson, *Journalism in the United States*, pp. 43–50.

68. See Charles E. Clark, "The Public Prints: The Origins of the Anglo-American Newspaper, 1665–1750" (unpublished manuscript, University of New Hampshire, ca. 1989), chapter 2, p. 22; chapter 5, quoted at p. 1.

69. On the English newspapers that proliferated after the expiration of the Licensing Act in 1695, see Jeremy Black, *The English Press in the Eighteenth Century* (Philadelphia: University of Pennsylvania Press, 1987); James Sutherland, *The Restoration Newspaper and Its Development* (Cambridge, Eng.: Cambridge University Press, 1986); G. A. Cranfield, *The Development of the Provincial Newspaper 1700–1760* (Oxford: Clarendon Press, 1962). On the similarity of the *News-Letter* to such English newspapers, see Clark, "Public Prints," chapter 5, pp. 4–5 and 16–17; Mott, *American Journalism*, p. 11; Bleyer, *Main Currents*, p. 47; Hudson, *Journalism in the United States*, p. 56.

70. On crime coverage in English newspapers during the mid-seventeenth century, see Joseph Frank, *The Beginnings of the English Newspaper* (Cambridge: Harvard University Press, 1961), pp. 202, 212, 223, 226, 239, 241, and 244–46. On crime coverage in the newspapers of the late seventeenth and eighteenth centuries, see Black, *English Press*, pp. 41 and 79–81; Sutherland, *Restoration Newspaper*, pp. 44–90, passim, 98–99, and 103–4; Cranfield, *Development of the Provincial Newspaper*, pp. 65–92, passim.

71. See *News-Letter*, May 29, 1704, pp. 1–2; June 5, 1704, pp. 1–2; June 12, 1704, p. 2; June 19, 1704, p. 2; June 26, 1704, pp. 1–2; July 3, 1704, p. 2; July 31, 1704, p. 2; Aug. 14, 1704, p. 2.

72. On the elite readerships of early American newspapers through the 1820s, see Clark, "Public Prints," chapter 5, pp. 8–13; Michael Schudson, *Discovering the News: A Social History of American Newspapers* (New York: Basic Books, 1978), p. 15; Willard Grosvenor Bleyer, *Main Currents*, pp. 135 and 153.

73. C. Mather, *Diary*, vol. 2, p. 242.

74. J. A. Leo Lemay and P. M. Zall, eds., *Benjamin Franklin's Autobiography* (New York: W. W. Norton, 1986), p. 10. Teach was killed while resisting capture in November 1718, and B. Franklin had left Boston by about September 1723; those two dates establish the temporal parameters within which the Teach ballad must have been composed and printed. Lemay and Zall suggest that it was probably inspired by the appearance of a report of the death of Teach in a Boston paper on March 2, 1719. On James Franklin's hostility toward the Boston establishments and his English training and orientation, see Clark, "Public Prints," chapter 7; Mott, *American Journalism*, pp. 15–21; Clyde Augustus Duniway, *The Development of Freedom of the Press in Massachusetts* (Cambridge: Harvard University Press, 1906), pp. 97–103. Parson Weems claimed to have recalled one stanza of Franklin's ballad on Teach; see James Parton, *Life and Times of Benjamin Franklin*, 2 vols. (1864; rpt. New York: Da Capo Press, 1971), vol. 1, pp. 56–57. For one of the earliest surviving broadside ballads published in New England (also by James Franklin), with a tune given to which the verses could be sung, see *The Rebels' Reward, or, English Courage Displayed* (Boston: J. Franklin, 1724). It is quite possible that other ballads of this type were published by the Boston printer Thomas Fleet during the second and third decades of the eighteenth century; Isaiah Thomas suggests that Fleet printed many "ballads" during the period between about 1712 and 1733; see Thomas, *The History of Printing in America*, 2d ed. (1874; rpt. New York: Weathervane Books, 1970), p. 94, but also see my discussion in note 80 below. For examples of other early modern pirate ballads, see W. Chappell and J. Woodfall Ebsworth, eds., *The Roxburghe Ballads*, 8 vols. (1869–1901; rpt. New

York: AMS Press, 1966), vol. 1, pp. 9–17; *An Old Story Revived* (New York: Broun-Green, 1901); John Franklin Jameson, *Privateering and Piracy in the Colonial Period: Illustrative Documents* (New York: Macmillan, 1923), pp. 253–57.

75. On the crime waves after 1760, see chapter 6 below. On American ballads in general, Worthington Chauncey Ford concludes: "The ballad did not come into popular use until after the War for Independence, and never, indeed, attained the popularity it enjoyed in England"; Ford, *Broadsides, Ballads, Etc. Printed in Massachusetts, 1639–1800* (Boston: Massachusetts Historical Society, 1922), p. ix. Actually, Ford's own bibliography suggests that ballads on military themes became fairly popular after about 1740.

76. See Richard D. Brown, *Knowledge Is Power: The Diffusion of Information in Early America, 1700–1865* (New York: Oxford University Press, 1989), pp. 16–18; G. B. Warden, *Boston, 1689–1776* (Boston: Little, Brown, 1970), pp. 3–126; Duniway, *Development of Freedom of the Press*, pp. 83–103.

77. For citations of New England execution broadsides, see *Ritz*, pp. 187–233, passim, and chapter 6 below. For scholarly discussions of such broadsides, see Daniel E. Williams, "Rogues, Rascals and Scoundrels: The Underworld Literature of Early America," *American Studies* 24 (Fall 1983): 5–19; Lawrence W. Towner, "True Confessions and Dying Warnings in Colonial New England," in *Sibley's Heir: A Volume in Memory of Clifford Kenyon Shipton* (Boston: Colonial Society of Massachusetts, 1982), pp. 523–39. Although none seems to survive from before the 1730s, it is certainly possible that execution broadsides were published in New England during earlier decades.

78. An example of an obscure bookman who produced an execution broadside is Benjamin Gray of Boston; in partnership with Alford Butler, he produced *Poor Julleyoun's Warnings to Children and Servants* in 1733. Gray is characterized by Isaiah Thomas as "not a very considerable bookseller" who worked for many years at bookbinding; see Thomas, *History of Printing in America*, pp. 196–97. An example of a somewhat disreputable printer who specialized in execution broadsides and similar works is Ezekiel Russell, the bulk of whose output has been judgmentally described by modern scholars as "depraved"; see Franklin, *Boston Printers*, pp. 438–42, quoted at 441; for an example of a Russell execution broadside, see John Sheehan, *Life, Last Words and Dying Speech* ([1787]). An example of a prominent Massachusetts printer who issued execution broadsides (in addition to Thomas Fleet, Timothy Green, and Samuel Kneeland, discussed below) is Isaiah Thomas himself, by far the most famous and influential bookman in late eighteenth-century New England; for an example of a Thomas execution broadside, see Johnson Green, *The Life and Confession* (1786).

79. *News-Letter*, Dec. 21, 1769, p. 1. See citations in note 81 below.

80. This claim is based on Thomas, *History of Printing*, p. 94. However, it should be noted that Thomas Fleet's *known* output before 1730 (based on surviving examples and advertisements) does *not* support Thomas's claim that Fleet specialized in ballads and small books for children from the beginning of his career in Boston. In fact, there is little in his known output (consisting largely of religious pamphlets and almanacs) to distinguish him from any of the other printers active in Boston during the second and third decades of the eighteenth century. The earliest known ballads, chapbooks, and similar children's books produced by Fleet did not appear before the 1730s and 1740s, the same decades when (as far as we know) he also began issuing execution broadsides. Those facts raise two possibilities. First, it may be that Thomas's characterization of Fleet's output is accurate and that the absence of surviving examples simply reflects the

extremely ephemeral quality of such works. A second, and in my view equally plausible, explanation is that Fleet produced few (if any) ballads and chapbooks before 1730, and that his production of such works after that date reflected the increasingly secular character of his business (see other indicators of that trend in text below). Thomas (who was not even alive during the decades in question) or his informants may have erroneously extrapolated backwards from Fleet's later output. In either case, Fleet is a key transitional figure in the Boston book trade of the first half of the eighteenth century. The above discussion is based on a systematic scanning of all Fleet imprints listed in the relevant sections of *Evans*; *Bristol*; Ford, *Broadsides, Ballads*; Oscar Wegelin, *Early American Poetry*, 2d ed., 2 vols. (in 1) (1930; rpt. Gloucester, Mass.: Peter Smith, 1965); and d'Alte A. Welch, *A Bibliography of American Children's Books Printed Prior to 1821* (Worcester: American Antiquarian Society and Barre Publishers, 1972).

81. The contrast between Fleet as a "secular" printer and Kneeland and Green as "religious" printers should not be overdrawn; as mentioned in the previous note, Fleet issued many religious pamphlets, including a number by various Mathers, and Kneeland (sometimes in partnership with Green) produced two newspapers and was the official printer for the Massachusetts House of Representatives between 1723 and 1728 and again from 1732 until 1761. On Thomas Fleet, see Franklin, *Boston Printers*, pp. 162–70, and Thomas, *History of Printing*, pp. 93–100 and 246–54; on Timothy Green II and Samuel Kneeland, see Franklin, *Boston Printers*, pp. 245–48 and 323–29, and Thomas, *History of Printing in America*, pp. 101–4 and 118. For examples of early execution broadsides produced by Fleet, see *The Wages of Sin; or, Robbery Justly Rewarded* (1732); *Advice from the Dead to the Living* (1733); Julian [*sic*], *The Last Speech and Dying Advice* (1733); *A Mournful Poem on the Death of John Ormsby and Matthew Cushing* (1734); John Ormsby, *The Last Speech and Dying Words* (1734); *The Dying Lamentation and Advice of Philip Kennison* (1738). For examples produced by Kneeland and Green, see Rebekah Chamblit, *The Declaration, Dying Warning and Advice* (1733); Matthew Cushing, *The Declaration & Confession* (1734); *A Few Lines Upon the Awful Execution of John Ormsby and Matth. Cushing* (1734); Hugh Henderson, *The Confession and Dying Warning* (1737); *A Poem Occasioned by the Untimely Death of Hugh Henderson* (1737).

82. See reference to "Travelling-Traders" in John Bailey, *Life, Last Words and Dying Confession* (Boston: E. Russell, [1790]), broadside; to "the Flying-Traders" in [John] Baptist Collins, Emanuel Furtado, and Augustus Palacha, *Dying Confession* ([Boston: E. Russell, 1794]), broadside; and to "travelling TRADERS, in Town & COUNTRY" in Ebenezer Mason, *The Last Words* (Boston: Printed for the Purchasers, [1802]), broadside.

83. See, for example, Levi Ames, *The Last Words and Dying Speech* (Boston: [1773]), broadside; Ames, *Last Words* (Salem: [1773]), broadside; Robert Young, *The Last Words and Dying Speech* (Worcester: [1779]), broadside; Young, *Last Words* (New London: [1779]), broadside.

84. See *Poor Julleyoun's Warnings*; for an example of a broadside apparently aimed at a wider audience, see John Ormsby, *Last Speech and Dying Words*, which is "Recommended to all People." Also see my discussion below in this chapter (and note 164) of the critiques of last speeches offered by Royall Tyler and Susanna Rowson.

85. While pricing information on early execution broadsides is scarce, all but one of about a dozen such works published between 1745 and 1812 for which information is available were priced between three and six pence or cents each; the exception, a

particularly large illustrated broadside with densely packed prose, cost nine pence and then a shilling in successive editions. See *Boston Evening-Post*, Oct. 28, 1745, p. 2, adv. [6 pence]; *News-Letter*, Oct. 21, 1773, p. 2, adv. [6 coppers]; Valentine Dukett, *The Life, Last Words, and Dying Speech* ([Boston: 1774]) [6 coppers]; *A Poem Occasioned by the Most Shocking and Cruel Murder* ([Boston: E. Russell, 1782?]) [6 coppers]; Samuel Frost, *Confession and Dying Words* (Worcester: I. Thomas, [1793] [6 pence; another advertised at 3 pence]; Collins, Furtado, and Palacha, *Dying Confession* [4 pence]; Jonathan Plummer, Jr., *Dying Confession of Pomp, a Negro Man* (n.p.: J. Plummer, Jr., [1795]) [6 pence]; *Biography of Mr. Jason Fairbanks and Miss Eliza Fales* (Boston: [Nathaniel Coverly, Jr.], 1801) [variant editions priced at 9 pence and a shilling each]; *A Mournful Tragedy* (n.p.: ca. 1801) [variant editions priced at 3 and 4 cents each]; *The Last Words of Samuel Tully* ([Boston]: Timothy Longlive [pseud.?], [1812]) [6 cents]. As a point of comparison, almanacs (of the period 1766–75), the most widely circulated form of "cheap literature" in eighteenth-century Anglo-America, typically retailed for about five cents each; see Tebbel, *History of Book Publishing in the United States*, vol. 1, p. 154. On the shifting—and confusing—relationship between pence and cents in eighteenth- and early nineteenth-century America, see U. S. Bureau of Labor Statistics, *History of Wages in the United States from Colonial Times to 1928* (1934; rpt. Detroit: Gale Research, 1966), pp. 16–26, passim.

86. See citations in *Ritz*, pp. 187–233, passim; the claim that more than twenty-five were published between 1732 and 1799 is based on my own page-by-page scan of *Evans* and *Bristol*. Later examples are listed in *Shaw and Shoemaker*.

87. For citations of such broadside elegies, see Wegelin, *Early American Poetry*, pp. 106–9 and passim; for reproductions of the broadsides themselves, see Georgia B. Bumgardner, ed., *American Broadsides* (Barre, Mass.: Imprint Society, 1971), nos. 35–39; *Some Early Massachusetts Broadsides* (Boston: Massachusetts Historical Society, 1964), nos. 2 and 13; Ola Elizabeth Winslow, ed., *American Broadside Verse* (1930; rpt. New York: AMS Press, 1974), nos. 2–30.

88. For examples of hanging ballads, see Chappell and Ebsworth, *Roxburghe Ballads*, passim; Marshburn, *Murder and Witchcraft*, passim.

89. Execution verses were being sung in England as late as the mid-nineteenth century; see Henry Mayhew, *London Labour and the London Poor*, 4 vols. (1861–62; rpt. New York: Dover, 1968), vol. 1, p. 283.

90. See *Groans from the Dungeon; or, the Sorrowful Lamentation of James Dick* ([Glasgow?: 1792]), broadside; *The Sorrowful Reflections of Millesius Roderic Macuillan* ([Edinburgh?: 1797]), broadside; *A Sorrowful Lamentation, for John M'Millan* ([Glasgow?: 1798]), broadside.

91. See, for example, *Poor Julleyoun's Warnings* (Boston: B. Gray and A. Butler, [1733]), broadside; *Dying Lamentation and Advice of Philip Kennison*; *The Dying Penitent; or, the Affecting Speech of Levi Ames* ([Boston: 1773]), broadside; Robert Young [?], *The Dying Criminal: A Poem* ([Worcester: I. Thomas, 1779]), broadside. On the convention of criminal authorship in English execution verses, see Charles Hindley, *The History of the Catnach Press* (London: C. Hindley, 1887), pp. [xxvi] and 65; Mayhew, *London Labour*, vol. 1, p. 281.

92. See Young, *Dying Criminal*.

93. Elhanan Winchester, *The Execution Hymn* ([Boston]: E. Russell, [1773]), broadside. Winchester later became a prominent Univeralist; see Frederick Lewis Weis, *The Colonial Clergy and the Colonial Churches of New England* (Lancaster,

Mass.: Society of the Descendants of the Colonial Clergy, 1936; rpt. 1961), p. 232; Stephen A. Marini, *Radical Sects of Revolutionary New England* (Cambridge: Harvard University Press, 1982), pp. 69–71.

94. Thomas, *History of Printing*, 154. That "young woman" may have written the second poem that appears on Winchester, *Execution Hymn*.

95. See Isaac B. Choate, "Thomas Shaw of Standish: 'A Down-East Homer,' " in Windsor Daggett, *A Down-East Yankee from the District of Maine* (Portland, Me.: A. J. Huston, 1920), pp. 57–74. Another such character was Jonathan Plummer, Jr., of Newburyport, Massachusetts, who characterized himself as "a travelling preacher, Physician, Poet, and Trader"; for a sampling of his ephemeral output, see Wegelin, *Early American Poetry*, vol. 1, pp. 62–63; vol. 2, pp. 196–97.

96. On the proto-journalistic function of early English broadside ballads, see Leslie Shepard, *The History of Street Literature* (Detroit: Singing Tree Press, 1973), pp. 14–21.

97. For example, compare the prose and verse accounts in Johnson Green, *The Life and Confession* (Worcester: [I. Thomas, 1786]), broadside.

98. See citations in *Ritz*, pp. 187–233, passim. My claim that copies of more than thirty-five prose broadsides survive from between 1733 and 1799 is based on a page-by-page scan of *Evans* and *Bristol*. For examples of prose broadsides that apparently have not survived, see Bristol [*sic*], *The Dying Speech* ([Boston: Fleet, 1763?]), adv. in *Boston Evening-Post*, Dec. 5, 1763, p. 3; Solomon Goodwin, *The Last Words and Dying Speech* (Salem: [1772]), cited in *Ritz*, no. 5.02(28)(a).

99. Ormsby, *Last Speech*; Joseph Lightly, *The Last Words and Dying Speech* ([Boston: 1765]), broadside; Rachel Wall, *Life, Last Words and Dying Confession* ([Boston: 1789]), broadside.

100. See, for example, *The Speech of the Late Lord Russel* (London: J. Darby, 1683); many of those last speeches were collected and published in *The Dying Speeches and Behaviour of the Several State Prisoners* (London: J. Brotherton and W. Meadows, 1720). For scholarly discussions of those confessions, see Lacey Baldwin Smith, "English Treason Trials and Confessions in the Sixteenth Century," *Journal of the History of Ideas* 15 (1954): 471–98; J. A. Sharpe, "'Last Dying Speeches': Religion, Ideology and Public Execution in Seventeenth-Century England," *Past and Present*, no. 107 (May 1985): 157–58 and 165. Such political confessions often took the form of written statements prepared in prison before the execution, sometimes but not always delivered orally at the gallows. They consisted primarily of statements of religious and political conviction, as well as accounts (often self-exculpatory) of the treasonous activities for which the prisoners had been condemned; they rarely included much general autobiographical information.

101. See, for example, Yearwood, *Penitent Murderer*, pp. 15–35; Samuel Smith, *A True Account of the Behavior, Confession, and Last Dying Speeches of the Prisoners That Were Executed at Tyburn on the 23d of October, 1689* (London: L. Curtiss, 1689), p. 2; I. Mather, *Sermon Occasioned*, pp. 22–23 and 35–36. For a scholarly discussion of such confessions in England, see Sharpe, "Last Dying Speeches," 144–67. Like their political counterparts, such confessions often took the form of written statements prepared in prison and only sometimes recorded words actually delivered at the gallows, and they rarely included much biographical information, although some was often provided in other sections of the same publications.

102. Thomas Green and John Madder, *The Last Speeches and Dying Words* (Edinburgh: 1705; rpt. London: S. Bridge, [1705?]), broadside; *The Last Words and Confes-*

sion of Christian Adam (Edinburgh: J. M., 1709), broadside [actually a third-person account]; Peter Dalton, *The Last Speech and Dying Words* (Dublin: 1712), broadside; Henery Watts, Philip Reily, and Edward Fox, *The Last Speech Confession and Dying Words* (Dublin: C. Hicks, 1723), broadside; William Wood, *The Last Speech and Dying Words* (Dublin: J. Harding, 1724), broadside. The confessions of Dalton, Watts, and Reily are all first-person autobiographical statements quite similar to those later issued in New England. Similar statements were being included in the Newgate Ordinary's *Accounts* by the 1730s, if not earlier; see [James Guthrie], *The Ordinary of Newgate His Account of the Behaviour, Confession, and Dying Words of the Malefactors, Who Were Executed . . . the 18th of January* (London: J. Applebee, 1738), pp. 13–16; [James Guthrie], *The Ordinary of Newgate, His Account of the Behaviour, Confession, and Dying Words, of James Hall* (London: J. Applebee, 1741), pp. 7–15.

103. Thomas Foxcroft, *Lessons of Caution to Young Sinners* (Boston: S. Kneeland and T. Green, 1733), pp. [69–72], appends text of Chamblit, *Declaration*; John Campbell, *After Souls by Death are Separated from their Bodies* (Boston: S. Kneeland and T. Green, 1738), pp. 34–36, appends text of Henderson, *Confession*. Another early broadside confession with much religious and moralistic content was Julian, *Last Speech*.

104. On naive empiricism as a characteristic, if controversial, epistemological stance in early modern narrative, see Michael McKeon, *The Origins of the English Novel, 1600–1740* (Baltimore: Johns Hopkins University Press, 1987), pp. 47–52 and passim.

105. For examples of picaresque motifs in last speeches, see Arthur, a Negro Man [*sic*], *The Life and Dying Speech* (Boston: [1768]), broadside; Wall, *Life*. Michael McKeon has posited "a characteristic tension" in early modern criminal biography between "the historicizing truth of the individual life and a countervailing movement of moralizing and repentance"; see McKeon, *Origins of the English Novel*, pp. 96–100, quoted at 100. New England's last speeches reflected over time a gradual shift in emphasis from the latter to the former.

106. On the process by which ministers and condemned criminals collaborated in the preparation of early confessions, see C. Mather, *Sorrowful Spectacle*, p. 83.

107. For evidence of the role of ministers in the production of an early last-speech broadside, see Henderson, *Confession*. For evidence of the role of printers in the production of last speeches, see Julian, *Last Speech*; Foxcroft, *Lessons*, p. [72]. For evidence of the role of prison officials in the production of "last speeches," see Ames, *Last Words*; Dirick Grout and Francis Coven, *The Life, Last Words and Dying Speech* ([Boston: 1784]), broadside; John Sheehan, *Life, Last Words and Dying Speech* (Boston: E. Russell, [1787]), broadside; Wall, *Life*.

108. For reproductions of the signature marks of apparently illiterate criminals, see Henderson, *Confession*; James Buchanan, Ezra Ross, and William Brooks, *The Last Words and Dying Speech* (Boston: Draper and Folsom, [1778]), broadside; Green, *Life*; Edmund Fortis, *The Last Words and Dying Speech* (n.p.: [1794]), broadside.

109. For Kneeland and Green's last speeches, see Chamblit, *Declaration*; Cushing, *Declaration*; Henderson, *Confession*. For Fleet's last speeches, see Julian, *Last Speech*; Ormsby, *Last Speech*. Fleet also published a somewhat longer first-person criminal narrative: Philip Kennison, *Short and Plain, but Faithful Narrative of the Wicked Life* (Boston: T. Fleet, 1738); although no copies of this pamphlet survive, it was advertised as having been "written with his own Hand" while in jail awaiting

execution; see *Boston Evening-Post*, Sept. 11, 1738, p. 2; Sept. 18, 1738, p. 2; *Ritz*, no. 5.02(12). Julian, a young Indian servant, concluded his statement with the following caveat: "These Things I declare freely and voluntarily, and desire Mr. *Fleet* to Print the same for the Benefit of the Living: And I do hereby utterly disown and disclaim all other Speeches, Papers or Declarations that may be printed in my Name, as Witness my Hand this 21st. of *March*, 1733." But again, the contrast between the two firms should not be overdrawn; Fleet's earliest last speech was quite pious and didactic in tone, and the version of Chamblit's last speech appended to a sermon by Thomas Foxcroft identified it as having been given directly to Samuel Kneeland; see Foxcroft, *Lessons*, p. [72].

110. For a discussion similar to that contained in this and the following paragraph, see Towner, "True Confessions," pp. 537–38.

111. For an extended discussion of such criminals, see chapter 6 below.

112. How, for example, might readers have internalized some of the picaresque passages in Arthur, *Life and Dying Speech*?

113. See Ames, *Last Words*, broadside; Ames, *The Life, Last Words, and Dying Speech* ([Boston?: 1773?]), 8 pp.; Buchanan, Ross, and Brooks, *Last Words*, broadside; Ross, Buchanan, and Brooks, *The Lives, Last Words and Dying Speech* ([Worcester: 1778?]), 8 pp.; Fortis, *Last Words*, broadside; Fortis, *Last Words* (Exeter: 1795), 12 pp.

114. See Stephen Burroughs, *Memoirs*, vol. 1 (Hanover, N.H.: B. True, 1798) and vol. 2 (Boston: E. Lincoln for C. Bingham, 1804); Henry Tufts, *A Narrative of the Life, Adventures, Travels and Sufferings of Henry Tufts* (Dover, N.H.: S. Bragg, Jr., 1807).

115. See works discussed in chapter 7 below.

116. See Clark, "Public Prints," chapter 6; Richard D. Brown, *Knowledge Is Power*, p. 111; Ian K. Steele, *The English Atlantic: An Exploration of Communication and Community* (Oxford: Oxford University Press, 1986), pp. 145–67; Brown, "Afterword," p. 303; Richard L. Merritt, *Symbols of American Community 1735–1775* (New Haven: Yale University Press, 1966); Bleyer, *Main Currents*, pp. 88–89.

117. For a perceptive discussion of the complex interdependence of rural printing and commercialization, see William J. Gilmore, *Reading Becomes a Necessity of Life: Material and Cultural Life in Rural New England, 1780–1835* (Knoxville: University of Tennessee Press, 1989). According to William Charvat, the decentralization of printing in New England was more extreme and longer lasting than in other American regions; see Charvat, *Literary Publishing in America, 1790–1850*, pp. 30–36.

118. On the proliferation of small-town printers, see Brown, "Afterword," pp. 305–6; Milton W. Hamilton, *The Country Printer: New York State, 1785–1830* (New York: Columbia University Press, 1936), pp. 49, 86–89, and passim.

119. [Isaac Bickerstaffe], *The Life and Adventures of Ambrose Gwinett* (1768; rpt. Boston: J. White, 1800), p. [2]; for a full discussion of this work and citations of other American printings, see chapter 7 (text and notes) below.

120. See, for example, *Narrative of the Life and Dying Confession of Henry Mills* (Boston: H. Trumbull, 1817); *Narrative of the Pious Death of the Penitent Henry Mills* (Boston: H. Trumbull, 1817); *Particulars of the Late Horrid Murder, of the Accomplished—but Unfortunate Miss Maria Pattan* (Boston: Coverly, [1817?]; rpt. New York: 1817); *A Faithful Account of the Massacre of the Family of Gerald Watson* (Boston: N. Coverly, 1819); see *McDade*, p. vi and nos. 500 and 682. For a discussion of one of the most prolific mid- to late-nineteenth-century publishers of journalistic fictions, see Thomas M. McDade, "Lurid Literature of the Last Century: The Publi-

cations of E. E. Barclay," *Pennsylvania Magazine of History and Biography* 80 (Oct. 1956): 452–64.

121. See chapter 7 below. For the author who challenged the fitness of others to judge his behavior, see Burroughs, *Memoirs*, vol. 1, p. 191. For another provocative treatment of antiauthoritarian crime narratives of the late eighteenth and early nineteenth centuries, see Eric Cummins, "'Anarchia' and the Emerging State," *Radical History Review* 48 (1990): 32–62.

122. For examples of early nineteenth-century execution broadsides that were not autobiographical narratives, see Mason, *Last Words*; *Last Words of Samuel Tully*; Henry Phillips, *Declaration and Dying Speech* ([Boston: 1817]). The last-speech broadside form disintegrated at almost precisely the same time in Scotland (despite a similar persistence of formulaic titles), suggesting that the underlying shift in cultural preferences or sensibilities was transatlantic. For some reason, probably relating to the rise of sentimentalism and romanticism, the short, naively empirical broadside autobiographies of the eighteenth century no longer satisfied. The rise of the penny press and the abolition of public executions in New England will be documented below. It should be noted that at least a few stray crime broadsides did appear in the region after 1840; see, for example, Mary G. Doe [pseud.?], *Soliloquy, of Prof. John W. Webster, After the Disappearance of Dr. Geo. Parkman Up to the Time of His Execution* (Biddeford, Me.: Advertiser Press, ca. 1850), broadside.

123. On nineteenth-century execution broadsides (and other forms of crime literature) in England, see Richard D. Altick, *Victorian Studies in Scarlet* (London: J. M. Dent, 1970); Hindley, *History of the Catnach Press*; and Mayhew, *London Labour*, vol. 1, pp. 213–323, passim. On the best-selling broadsides of the mid-nineteenth century, see Hindley, *History of the Catnach Press*, p. 92; Mayhew, *London Labor*, vol. 1, p. 284. On the relative prices of English newspapers and execution broadsides, see Mayhew, *London Labour*, vol. 1, pp. 222, 230, 285, and 291; Raymond Williams, *The Long Revolution* (New York: Columbia University Press, 1961), pp. 191 and 193. On the development of cheap newspapers and periodicals in England, see Louis James, *Fiction for the Working Man, 1830–1850* (London: Oxford University Press, 1963), pp. 12–44; Richard D. Altick, *The English Common Reader: A Social History of the Mass Reading Public, 1800–1900* (Chicago: University of Chicago Press, 1957), pp. 332–64. It should be noted that there were "penny weeklies" in England during the 1830s and 1840s; however, those that were not suppressed were literary magazines, not newspapers. On the abolition of public executions in England, see David D. Cooper, *The Lesson of the Scaffold* (Athens: Ohio University Press, 1974), p. 174 and passim. On the gradual spread of working-class literacy, see Altick, *English Common Reader*, p. 171 and passim. On the demise of a similar street literature in France after 1860, see James Smith Allen, *Popular French Romanticism: Authors, Readers, and Books in the 19th Century* (Syracuse, N.Y.: Syracuse University Press, 1981), p. 146.

124. At least ten volumes of execution sermons were issued during the 1770s, and eight more were published in each of the next three decades; however, only five appeared during the years 1810 to 1819, and only one or two thereafter. About a dozen last-speech broadsides were published during the 1770s, nearly as many appeared during the 1780s, and eight more were issued during the last decade of the century; however, few if any were issued after 1800. Although many crime broadsides appeared during the first half of the nineteenth century, they rarely if ever adopted the first-person autobiographical last-speech format; and although autobiographical narratives continued to be issued, they generally took the form of longer pamphlets. Those

findings are based largely on a page-by-page scan of *Evans, Bristol, Shaw and Shoemaker*, and *American Imprints* through 1833; for citations of such sermons and broadsides through 1800, see *Ritz*, pp. 187–233 and 249–61, passim, and cross-references.

125. On a somewhat analogous transition from execution broadsides and ballads to trial reports and journalistic crime coverage in England after 1860, see Mike Hepworth and Bryan S. Turner, *Confession: Studies in Deviance and Religion* (London: Routledge & Kegan Paul, 1982), pp. 113–14.

126. My generalizations and statistics on the incidence of published trial reports are largely based on a page-by-page scan of *Evans, Bristol, Shaw and Shoemaker*, and *American Imprints* through 1833; for citations of such reports through 1800, see *Ritz*, pp. [3]–45. The trial report genre became popular in New York and Pennsylvania between 1787 and 1800, that is, somewhat earlier than in New England; see Cohen, "Pillars of Salt," pp. 342–78.

127. For a range of reports on a single case, see Cohen, "Pillars of Salt," pp. 366–73 and 377–78; also see chapters 8 and 9 below; Tebbel, *History of Book Publishing*, vol. 1, p. 563.

128. Michael McKeon describes a somewhat analogous resolution to the destabilization of social and spiritual status in early modern England: "In the absence of the once-authoritative guides—tacit social sanction, priestly absolution—nobility and salvation became problematic categories whose stabilization required not just the inner conviction of the individual but community accreditation, a validating social consensus by which the reputation of the individual and the coherence of the category itself were constituted" (*Origins of the English Novel*, p. 194).

129. See Cohen, "Pillars of Salt," chapter 8.

130. On the one-sidedness of the Salem witch trials, see David H. Flaherty, "Criminal Practice in Provincial Massachusetts," in *Law in Colonial Massachusetts 1630–1800* (Boston: Colonial Society of Massachusetts, 1984), p. 241; Edwin Powers, *Crime and Punishment in Early Massachusetts, 1620–1692* (Boston: Beacon Press, 1966), pp. 438 and 477. For contemporary trial reports of several of the witchcraft cases, see C. Mather, *Wonders of the Invisible World*, pp. 120–59. On criminal trials in seventeenth-century England, see J. M. Beattie, *Crime and the Courts in England, 1660–1800* (Princeton: Princeton University Press, 1986), pp. 314–56; John H. Langbein, "The Criminal Trial Before the Lawyers," *University of Chicago Law Review* 45 (Winter 1978): 263–316.

131. See the piracy trial reports cited in note 61 above. On the restriction of defense lawyers to matters of law, see *Tryal of Quelch*, pp. 4–5 and 12, and *Trials of Five Persons*, p. 12; however, judging from those trial reports, along with *Trials of Eight Persons*, that restriction does not seem to have been tightly enforced. On the apparent absence of cross-examination by counsel, see the three reports just cited. On those same points, also see Ritchie, *Captain Kidd*, pp. 212 and 214. Ironically, the cross-examination of prosecution witnesses was to become the "main responsibility" of early criminal defense lawyers in eighteenth-century England; see John H. Langbein, "Shaping the Eighteenth-Century Criminal Trial: A View from the Ryder Sources," *University of Chicago Law Review* 50 (Winter 1983): 129. Although the special admiralty courts did not use juries, and although at least one defense lawyer claimed that civil law should therefore apply, they seem to have operated under common-law procedures; see *Tryal of Quelch*, pp. 5–6 and 13–14. The parliamentary statute establishing the special admiralty courts is somewhat ambiguous on the question of civil-law versus common-law procedures; see Pickering, *Statutes at Large*, vol. 10, pp. 321 and

324. While practices in the special courts of admiralty were certainly not identical to procedures normally followed in other colonial criminal trials, there is little reason to believe that they were entirely exceptional; in that regard, it should be noted that both John Valentine and Robert Auchmuty, attorneys for pirates, were also prominent practitioners—particularly in criminal cases—before the regular provincial courts; see Cohen, "Pillars of Salt," pp. 336–39 and 341–42; Flaherty, "Criminal Practice," pp. 194–201.

132. See John Hodgson, reporter, *The Trial of William Wemms [et al.]* (Boston: J. Fleeming, 1770); for a modern account of the trial, see Hiller B. Zobel, *The Boston Massacre* (New York: W. W. Norton, 1970), 267–94.

133. On the routine appointment of defense counsel by the court in capital cases in Massachusetts by the 1780s, see, for example, SJC, Recs., 1783, fols. 82–83; 1784, fols. 230, 232, 338–39; June–Nov. 1785, fols. 81–83. Although evidence is sparse, a few modern scholars suggest that the practice actually began before the Revolution; see William E. Nelson, "Emerging Notions of Modern Criminal Law in the Revolutionary Era: An Historical Perspective," *New York University Law Review* 42 (May 1967): 480; L. Kinvin Wroth and Hiller B. Zobel, eds., *Legal Papers of John Adams*, 2 vols. (Cambridge: Harvard University Press, 1965), vol. 1, pp. li–lii; vol. 2, pp. 402–3 fn. 40; also see Powers, *Crime and Punishment*, pp. 438–39.

134. For detailed accounts of such criminal trials, see chapters 8 and 9 below.

135. See Erwin C. Surrency, "Law Reports in the United States," *American Journal of Legal History* 25 (Jan. 1981): 48–66; Alan V. Briceland, "Ephraim Kirby: Pioneer of American Law Reporting, 1789," *American Journal of Legal History* 16 (Oct. 1972): 297–319; Charles Currier Beale, "Little Visits to the Homes of Eminent Stenographers. No. 1, William Sampson," *Proceedings of the New York State Stenographer's Association* (Albany: 1906), pp. 20–42.

136. See my discussion of William Coleman's *Report of the Trial of Levi Weeks* in "Pillars of Salt," chapter 8; also see T. Lloyd and Geo. Caines, reporters, *Trial of Thomas O. Selfridge* (Boston: Russell and Cutler, [1806]), taken in shorthand by the reporter of Congress and the former reporter for New York State; also Beale, "Little Visits," pp. 32–41.

137. See Lloyd and Caines, *Trial of Thomas O. Selfridge*, t.p. and p. [3].

138. See works cited below in chapter 5, note 47.

139. On the maturation of the legal profession in Massachusetts, see Gerard W. Gawalt, *The Promise of Power: The Emergence of the Legal Profession in Massachusetts 1760–1840* (Westport, Conn.: Greenwood Press, 1979).

140. See *Report of the Trial of Jason Fairbanks*, 4th ed. (Boston: Russell and Cutler, 1801), p. [4]; Lloyd and Caines, *Trial of Thomas O. Selfridge*, t.p. and p. [3]; and *Trial of Stephen and Jesse Boorn* (Rutland, Vt.: Fay and Burt, [1820]), p. 27.

141. Otis defended Jason Fairbanks (1801); Mellen defended David Lynn et al. (1809) and Moses Adams (1815); Shaw defended Henry Phillips (1817); Webster defended Levi and Laban Kenniston (1817); and Choate twice defended Albert Tirrell (1846–47). See *Report of the Trial of Jason Fairbanks*; John Merrick, reporter, *Trial of David Lynn [et al.]* (Hallowell, Me.: E. Goodale, 1810); John Bulfinch, reporter, *The Trial of Moses Adams* (Boston: E. B. Tileston, 1815); *Report of the Trial of Henry Phillips* (Boston: Russell, Cutler, 1817); *Report of the Evidence and Arguments of Counsel at the Trial of Levi and Laban Kenniston* (Boston: J. T. Buckingham, 1817); J. E. P. Weeks, reporter, *Trial of Albert John Tirrell for the Murder of Mary Ann*

Bickford (Boston: "Times" Office, 1846); *The Trial of Albert J. Tirrell . . . on the Charge of Arson* (Boston: 1847).

142. David Lynn et al., Moses Adams, and Levi and Laban Kenniston were all acquitted; see citations in note 141.

143. On the ethnic homogeneity of colonial New England, see Michael Zuckerman, "The Social Context of Democracy in Massachusetts" (1968), in Stanley N. Katz and John M. Murrin, eds., *Colonial America: Essays in Politics and Social Development*, 3d edition (New York: Alfred A. Knopf, 1983), p. 388.

144. See *Report of the Trial of Dominic Daley and James Halligan* (Northampton, Mass.: S. & E. Butler, [1806]), pp. 32–35; for recent ramifications, see Joe Quinlan, "Governor's Pardon 178 Years Later in Holyoke," *Boston Globe*, March 19, 1984, p. 16.

145. See Lloyd and Caines, *Trial of Thomas O. Selfridge*; for a modern account of the same case in its political context, see Charles Warren, *Jacobin and Junto* (1931; rpt. New York: AMS Press, 1970), pp. 183–214.

146. See Merrick, *Trial of David Lynn*. For a scholarly discussion of the case in its social-historical context, see Alan Taylor, *Liberty Men and Great Proprietors: The Revolutionary Settlement on the Maine Frontier, 1760–1820* (Chapel Hill: University of North Carolina Press, 1990), pp. 202–5.

147. See contemporary works on the Avery/Cornell case cited in *McDade*, nos. 33–53; for scholarly accounts, see David Richard Kasserman, *Fall River Outrage: Life, Murder, and Justice in Early Industrial New England* (Philadelphia: University of Pennsylvania Press, 1986); William G. McLoughlin, "Untangling the Tiverton Tragedy: The Social Meaning of the Terrible Haystack Murder of 1833," *Journal of American Culture* 7 (Winter 1984): 75–84.

148. Brown, "Afterword," p. 307, quoted.

149. See Clark, "Public Prints"; Mott, *American Journalism*, pp. 11–213; Bleyer, *Main Currents*, pp. 43–153.

150. For early examples of piracy coverage, see *News-Letter*, May 29, 1704, pp. 1–2; June 5, 1704, pp. 1–2; June 12, 1704, p. 2; June 19, 1704, p. 2; June 26, 1704, pp. 1–2; July 3, 1704, p. 2. For early examples of counterfeiting coverage, see *News-Letter*, Aug. 14, 1704, p. 2; June 4, 1705, p. 2; June 11, 1705, p. 2; June 18, 1705, p. 2. For additional evidence of the extensive coverage given by eighteenth-century newspapers to counterfeiting, see Kenneth Scott, *Counterfeiting in Colonial Connecticut* (New York: American Numismatic Society, 1957), pp. 53–54, 61–68, 136–39, and passim.

151. See David Ray Papke, *Framing the Criminal: Crime, Cultural Work, and the Loss of Critical Perspective, 1830–1900* (Hamden, Conn.: Archon Books, 1987), pp. 33–74; Dan Schiller, *Objectivity and the News: The Public and the Rise of Commercial Journalism* (Philadelphia: University of Pennsylvania Press, 1981), pp. 12–75; Michael Schudson, *Discovering the News: A Social History of American Newspapers* (New York: Basic Books, 1978), pp. 12–60; Frank Luther Mott, *The News in America* (Cambridge: Harvard University Press, 1952), pp. 50–51; Mott, *American Journalism*, pp. 215–52; Bleyer, *Main Currents*, pp. 155–84.

152. For a thorough discussion of newspaper coverage of one major mid-nineteenth-century case, see chapter 9 below.

153. See chapters 8 and 9 below.

154. Literary scholars formulate the relationship between sentimentalism and romanticism in a variety of ways, some very different from the one offered here. My

generalizations concerning literary sentimentalism apply to the earliest sentimental novels and related discourse, not to the "women's novels" published after 1820 and described by scholars like Nina Baym, Jane Tompkins, and Susan K. Harris; on the distinction between the two types, see Baym, *Woman's Fiction: A Guide to Novels by and about Women in America, 1820–1870* (Ithaca: Cornell University Press, 1978), pp. 25–26 and 29; also see Susan K. Harris, *Nineteenth-Century American Women's Novels: Interpretive Strategies* (Cambridge, Eng.: Cambridge University Press, 1990), pp. 1–59, passim.

155. See James D. Hart, *The Popular Book: A History of America's Literary Taste* (New York: Oxford University Press, 1950), pp. 51–52; Alexander Cowie, *The Rise of the American Novel* (New York: American Book, 1948), pp. 4 and 9; Frank Luther Mott, *Golden Multitudes: The Story of Best Sellers in the United States* (New York: Macmillan, 1947), pp. 35–37; Lyon N. Richardson, *A History of Early American Magazines 1741–1789* (1931; rpt. New York: Octagon, 1966), pp. 211–36 and 351–61; Herbert R. Brown, "Elements of Sensibility in *The Massachusetts Magazine*," *American Literature* 1 (1929–30): 286–96; Bertha M. Stearns, "Early New England Magazines for Ladies," *New England Quarterly* 2 (July 1929): 420–28. For a recent scholarly analysis of the first American novel, see Cathy N. Davidson, *Revolution and the Word: The Rise of the Novel in America* (New York: Oxford University Press, 1986), pp. 83–109.

156. See Davidson, *Revolution*, pp. 27–29; Herbert Ross Brown, *The Sentimental Novel in America 1789–1860* (1940; rpt. New York: Pageant Books, 1959), pp. 3–27; Hart, *Popular Book*, pp. 51–66, quoted at p. 52; Cowie, *Rise of the American Novel*, p. 8.

157. For citations of the two last speeches mentioned by Tyler, both published during the 1770s, see *Ritz*, nos. 5.02(27) and 5.02(32)(e).

158. Royall Tyler, *The Algerine Captive*, excerpted in Robert E. Spiller, ed., *The American Literary Revolution 1783–1837*, pp. [21]–23; also quoted in Brown, *Sentimental Novel*, pp. 15–16. For the timing of Underhill's absence and captivity, see Royall Tyler, *The Algerine Captive*, 2 vols. (Walpole, N.H.: D. Carlisle, Jr., 1797), vol. 1, pp. 186 and 205; vol. 2, p. 239.

159. For recent findings suggesting that Tyler's account overstated the speed and completeness with which the new print culture conquered rural New England, see Robert A. Gross, "Much Instruction from Little Reading: Books and Libraries in Thoreau's Concord," *Proceedings of the American Antiquarian Society* 97 (April 1987): 129–188, esp. 152; Jack Larkin, "The Merriams of Brookfield: Printing in the Economy and Culture of Rural Massachusetts in the Early Nineteenth Century," *Proceedings of the American Antiquarian Society* 96 (April 1986): 39–73, esp. 68. But also see my own discussion of those findings at the end of chapter 8 below.

160. See Hall, "Introduction," pp. 20–38 and passim; also see Hall, "Literacy, Religion and the Plain Style," in Jonathan L. Fairbanks and Robert F. Trent, eds., *New England Begins: The Seventeenth Century* (Boston: Museum of Fine Arts, 1982), vol. 2, pp. 102–12; Hall, "The World of Print and Collective Mentality in Seventeenth-Century New England," in John Higham and Paul K. Conkin, eds., *New Directions in American Intellectual History* (Baltimore: Johns Hopkins University Press, 1979), pp. 166–80.

161. On the rapid introduction of fiction reading to the Upper Connecticut River Valley of northern New England (and also to a town in rural Massachusetts) during the 1790s, see Gilmore, *Reading Becomes a Necessity*, pp. 26, 172, and 208; Gilmore

concludes: "The novel, tale, and story engulfed the district after their rather sudden appearance among lists of popular sellers during the 1790s" (p. 208). Also see works cited in notes 155 and 156 above; Hall, "Introduction," pp. 1–2 and 38–47; Brown, "Afterword," pp. 300–9; Russel Blaine Nye, *Society and Culture in America 1830–1860* (New York: Harper & Row, 1974), pp. 75–76. On the widespread rise of literacy rates during the first forty years of the nineteenth century, see Lee Soltow and Edward Stevens, *The Rise of Literacy and the Common School in the United States: A Socioeconomic Analysis to 1870* (Chicago: University of Chicago Press, 1981). For more specific data on rural New England, see William J. Gilmore, "Elementary Literacy on the Eve of the Industrial Revolution: Trends in Rural New England, 1760–1830," *Proceedings of the American Antiquarian Society* 92 (April 1982): 87–171. For useful overviews of technological innovation in book production during the first half of the nineteenth century, see Ronald J. Zboray, "Antebellum Reading and the Ironies of Technological Innovation," *American Quarterly* 40 (March 1988): 65–82; Tebbel, *History of Book Publishing*, vol. 1, pp. 257–62. For an overview of antebellum book distribution methods, see Ronald J. Zboray, "Book Distribution and American Culture: A 150-Year Perspective," *Book Research Quarterly* 3 (Fall 1987): 37–59.

162. Tebbel, *History of Book Publishing*, vol. 1, p. 224.

163. For reference to a similar perception in England during the 1790s, see Margaret Anne Doody, "'Those Eyes Are Made So Killing': Eighteenth-Century Murderesses and the Law," *Princeton University Library Chronicle* 46 (Autumn 1984): 80.

164. See Mrs. [Susanna] Rowson, *The Inquisitor; or, The Invisible Rambler*, 2d American ed. (1788; rpt. Philadelphia: M. Carey, 1794), pp. 62–64, quoted at 63 (I am very grateful to Michael L. Nicholls for first bringing a reprint of that passage in a Virginia newspaper to my attention). It is curious to note that Tyler linked last speeches to a rural readership, while Rowson linked them to a wealthy urban "lounger"; if those characterizations are at all indicative of actual distribution, last speeches must have enjoyed a wide and socially diverse readership.

165. Although execution broadsides remained extremely popular in Great Britain through the mid-nineteenth century (and were still sometimes formulaically titled "last speeches"), they rarely took the form of first-person autobiographical narratives of the type so popular during the eighteenth century.

166. See such works cited in chapters 8 and 9 below.

167. Some recent scholarship suggests that older patterns of "intensive" reading actually persisted well into the nineteenth century in some cases; see, for example, Harris, *Nineteenth-Century American Women's Novels*, p. 31.

168. According to literary theorist Mikhail Bakhtin, such a "variety of individual voices" in a single work is characteristic of novelistic prose; see Bakhtin, *The Dialogic Imagination*, ed. Michael Holquist, trans. Caryl Emerson and Michael Holquist (Austin: University of Texas Press, 1981), p. 264.

169. On the connection between news genres and the development of the novel, see Lennard J. Davis, *Factual Fictions: The Origins of the English Novel* (New York: Columbia University Press, 1983); Ian Watt, *The Rise of the Novel: Studies in Defoe, Richardson, and Fielding* (Berkeley: University of California Press, 1957), p. 35. On the importance of trial coverage in the rise of popular newspapers, see Bleyer, *Main Currents*, pp. 154–84; also see Schiller, *Objectivity and the News*, pp. 55–70; Mott, *American Journalism*, pp. 222–23, 233, and 238–40. For comparisons of novelistic detail and courtroom testimony, see Watt, *Rise of the Novel*, pp. 31–34 and 57. On the prevalence of criminal themes in early novels, see John Bender, *Imagining the Peniten-*

tiary: Fiction and the Architecture of Mind in Eighteenth-Century England (Chicago: University of Chicago Press, 1987), p. 11; Davis, *Factual Fictions*, pp. 123–37; J. M. S. Tompkins, *The Popular Novel in England* (London: Methuen, 1932), p. 61.

170. I am grateful to Karen Halttunen for heightening my awareness of the porno-graphic emphasis on female mutilation in nineteenth-century crime literature.

171. One of the rare bits of direct evidence as to readership of a nineteenth-century trial report actually appears in the trial report of another case. On a Sunday morning in June 1833, Mr. Chauncey Cochran sat in the front room of his house in Pembroke, New Hampshire, engrossed in a trial report that he had borrowed on the recent case of Ephraim Avery, a Methodist minister accused of impregnating and then murdering a Fall River factory worker. When a young hired laborer who lived in his household came into the room and told him that his wife wanted him to go out with her to pick some strawberries, Cochran declined. The laborer then accompanied Sally Cochran to a secluded field, where he clubbed her to death with a wooden stake. Although a defense lawyer claimed that the Avery report had induced his client to murder the woman while in a somnambulistic fit, the prosecutor pointed out that there was no evidence that the laborer had ever read the pamphlet. The miscreant was convicted and executed. See *Report of the Trial of Abraham Prescott* (Concord, N.H.: M. G. Atwood, and Currier and Hall, 1834), pp. 9, 54, 115, 126, 138, 140, and passim; I am grateful to Karen Halttunen for bringing this case to my attention.

172. [Catharine Williams], *Fall River: An Authentic Narrative* (Boston: Lilly, Wait, 1834), p. 58.

173. On the attendance of women at public executions, see *Biography of Mr. Jason Fairbanks and Miss Eliza Fales*. On the attendance of women at antebellum capital trials, see *Trial of Dr. Valorous P. Coolidge, for the Murder of Edward Mathews* ([Boston]: Boston Daily Times, [1848]), p. 2. On the patrons of the wax museum, see Nathaniel Hawthorne, *American Notebooks*, ed. Claude M. Simpson (Columbus: Ohio State University Press, 1972), pp. 176–78; cited in Patricia Cline Cohen, "The Helen Jewett Murder: Violence, Gender, and Sexual Licentiousness in Antebellum America," *NWSA Journal* 2 (Summer 1990): 377 fn. 9. On the readers of "shocking murder" stories in newspapers, see "The Fascination of Crime," *Yankee Blade*, July 10, 1852, p. 2, quoted in Ronald J. Zboray, "A Fictive People: Antebellum Economic Development and the Reading Public for American Novels: 1837–1857" (Ph.D. diss., New York University, 1984), p. 283. On the reading habits of the factory girls, see *City Crier* 1, no. 2 (April 1846): 1. On the readership of English street literature, see Mayhew, *London Labour*, vol. 1, pp. 222–23, 228, and 234; also see Altick, *Victorian Studies*, pp. 42–43. It might also be noted that a modern survey of British true-crime magazines (which specialized in cases of sexual violence) conducted during the 1980s indicated that over 85 percent of their readers were women, mostly in their forties and fifties; see Deborah Cameron and Elizabeth Frazer, *The Lust to Kill* (New York: New York University Press, 1987), pp. 44–52.

174. See *The Eventful Lives of Helen and Charlotte Lenoxa, the Twin Sisters of Philadelphia* (Memphis, Richmond, Baltimore, and Philadelphia: A. R. Orton, 1853). The copy with the owner's inscription is in my possession. On the reading of crime literature around the family circle, one of the English street peddlers interviewed by Mayhew gave the following account: "Not long after Rush was hung [in 1849], he saw, one evening after dark, through the uncurtained cottage window, eleven persons, young and old, gathered round a scanty fire, which was made to blaze by being fed with a few sticks. An old man was reading, to an attentive audience, a broad-sheet of

Rush's execution, which my informant had sold to him"; Mayhew, *London Labour*, vol. 1, pp. 280–81.

175. On the technological innovations, see Zboray, "Antebellum Reading"; Tebbel, *History of Book Publishing*, vol. 1, pp. 257–62.

176. See Tebbel, *History of Book Publishing*, vol. 1, p. 221.

177. *Bangor Daily Whig and Courier*, November 17, 1845, p. 2, quoted; *City Crier and Country Advertiser*, April 1846, p. 1, quoted. On the accessibility of cheap antebellum literature to working-class readers, see discussion in text and notes of chapter 9 below.

178. *Boston Daily Times*, February 2, 1850, p. 2, quoted. The *Times* editor may be referring here specifically to the *National Police Gazette*, established in 1845; see Schiller, *Objectivity and the News*, pp. 96–178. On bookstore clerks and newsboys, see *Uncle Sam*, May 9, 1846, p. 3.

179. For documentation of most of the claims made in this paragraph, see text and notes in chapter 9 below. On the population of Boston during the mid-nineteenth century, see Oscar Handlin, *Boston's Immigrants: A Study in Acculturation*, rev. and enlarged ed. (Cambridge: Harvard University Press, 1979), p. 239. It should be noted that the population of the metropolitan area as a whole was above two hundred thousand by 1850.

180. For a similar assessment of the mass audience for crime literature in Victorian England, see Altick, *Victorian Studies*, p. 43.

181. As Simon Lesser has observed: "We read because we are beset by anxieties, guilt feelings and ungratified needs." Simon O. Lesser, *Fiction and the Unconscious* (Boston: Beacon Press, 1957), p. 39.

Chapter 2. *Pillars of Salt and Monuments of Grace*

1. For an extensive bibliography and discussion of English crime publications of the late sixteenth and early seventeenth centuries, see Joseph H. Marshburn, *Murder and Witchcraft in England, 1550–1640* (Norman: University of Oklahoma Press, 1971). For a perceptive discussion of English rogue biographies and criminal conversion narratives of the seventeenth and eighteenth centuries, see Lincoln B. Faller, *Turned to Account: The Forms and Functions of Criminal Biography in Late Seventeenth- and Early Eighteenth-Century England* (Cambridge, Eng.: Cambridge University Press, 1987). For useful overviews of the literary output and marketplace of early modern England, see H. S. Bennett, *English Books and Readers, 1558 to 1603* (Cambridge, Eng.: Cambridge University Press, 1965); Bennett, *English Books and Readers, 1603 to 1640* (Cambridge, Eng.: Cambridge University Press, 1970); M. A. Schaaber, *Some Forerunners of the Newspaper in England 1476–1622* (1929; rpt. New York: Octagon Books, 1966); Charles C. Mish, "Best Sellers in Seventeenth-Century Fiction," *Papers of the Bibliographical Society of America* 47 (1953): 356–73; Charles C. Mish, "English Short Fiction in the Seventeenth Century," *Studies in Short Fiction* 6 (Spring 1969): 233–330.

2. See Clyde Augustus Duniway, *The Development of Freedom of the Press in Massachusetts* (Cambridge: Harvard University Press, 1906), pp. 22–82.

3. For the general absence of imports of such popular English crime genres as hanging ballads, murder plays, and rogue biographies (as well as crime accounts and trial reports), see Worthington Chauncey Ford, *The Boston Book Market 1679–1700*

(1917; rpt. New York: Burt Franklin, 1972), pp. 88–182; for an apparent exception—two imported copies of a rogue biography—see p. 89; note, however, that those volumes came in a shipment sent by a London dealer on his own initiative; they were not ordered by a Boston bookseller.

4. See chapter 1 above at notes 6 and 7.

5. It should also be noted that Cotton Mather, one of the chief producers of early New England crime accounts (including several with strong conversion themes), has been credited by a modern scholarly biographer with "an excellent record for accuracy as a factual reporter"; see David Levin, *Cotton Mather: The Young Life of the Lord's Remembrancer, 1663–1703* (Cambridge: Harvard University Press, 1978), p. 126, quoted. In fact, David P. Nord has recently argued that the roots of modern American journalism lie in the spiritual reportage of Puritan ministers like Cotton Mather; see Nord, "Teleology and News: The Religious Roots of American Journalism, 1630–1730," *Journal of American History* 77 (June 1990): 9–38.

6. See [Giuseppe Blondo], *A Relation of the Death, of the Most Illustrious Lord, Sigr. Troilo Savelli, a Baron of Rome*, trans. Sir Tobie Matthew ([Saint Omer, France]: 1620), t.p. and pp. 7–8, 13–14, 220–21, 252–55. On the activities of the gangs of aristocratic bandits who terrorized the Italian countryside during the late sixteenth century, see Henry Kamen, *The Iron Century: Social Change in Europe, 1550–1660* (London: Weidenfeld and Nicholson, 1971), pp. 341–44.

7. See [Blondo], *Relation*, pp. 45–48, 64–66, and passim. For a recent scholarly discussion of such fraternities in Renaissance Italy, see Samuel Y. Edgerton, Jr., *Pictures and Punishment* (Ithaca: Cornell University Press, 1985), pp. 165–80.

8. See Blondo, *Relation*, passim, quoted at pp. 29–31 and 226.

9. For biographical information on Giuseppe Blondo (whose last name is also variously spelled Biondi, Blondus, and Biondo), see entry in *Dizionario biografico degli Italiani*, 32 vols. [ongoing] (Rome: Instituto della Enciclopedia Italiana, 1968-), vol. 10, pp. 531–33. For Sir Tobie Matthews's assessment of the purpose of Blondo's account, see [Blondo], *Relation*, p. 49.

10. See Blondo, *Relation*, pp. 1–3. For other discussions or citations relating to the diffusion of Blondo's narrative, see *Dizionario*, p. 533; Carlos Sommervogel, *Bibliothéque de la Compagnie de Jesus*, new ed., 11 vols. (Brusells: O. Schepens and Paris: A. Picard, 1890–1932), vol. 1, pp. 1546–47; Ministére de L'Instruction Publique et des Beaux-Arts, *Catalogue général des livres imprimés de la Bibliotéque Nationale*, 231 vols. (Paris: Imprimerie Nationale, 1897–1981), vol. 14, p. 398; *National Union Catalog*, 754 vols. (Mansell, 1968–81), vol. 61, p. 546; *Catalog of Printed Books of the Folger Shakespeare Library*, 28 vols. (Boston: G. K. Hall, 1970) [cited hereafter as *Folger Catalog*], vol. 3, p. 174.

11. Although no place of publication is indicated on the title page of Matthew's translation, it has been widely attributed to a press in Saint Omer; see, for example, *Folger Catalog*, vol. 3, p. 174.

12. See Blondo, *Relation*, pp. 3–4.

13. For a perceptive scholarly discussion of that broader complex of devotional practice and literary expression, see Charles E. Hambrick-Stowe, *The Practice of Piety: Puritan Devotional Disciplines in Seventeenth-Century New England* (Chapel Hill: University of North Carolina Press, 1982), pp. [vii]–ix, 23–36, and passim. Natalie Zemon Davis finds themes of repentance in French crime pamphlets of the sixteenth and early seventeenth centuries, and she particularly notes a criminal conversion narrative produced by French Protestants in 1566; see Davis, *Fiction in the Ar-*

chives: Pardon Tales and Their Tellers in Sixteenth-Century France (Stanford, Calif.: Stanford University Press, 1987), pp. 60–61, 64, and 87. For an earlier use of the term "penitent sinner," see Daniel E. Williams, "'Behold a Tragic Scene Strangely Changed Into a Theater of Mercy': The Structure and Significance of Criminal Conversion Narratives in Early New England," *American Quarterly* 38 (Winter 1986): 844.

14. See Blondo, *Relation*, pp. 45–49. For a recent scholarly discussion of those Italian confraternities, see Edgerton, *Pictures*, pp. 165–80.

15. See Samuel Clark [often spelled Clarke], *The Marrow of Ecclesiastical History* (London: R. White for W. Roybould, 1654), p. 851.

16. See Clark, *Marrow*, pp. 852–53.

17. See [Arthur Golding], *A Brief Discourse of the Late Murther of Master George Saunders* (London: H. Bunneman, 1573), passim, quoted at sig. leaves C1 and C3; Gilbert Dugdale, *A True Discourse of the Practises of Elizabeth Caldwell* (London: J. Roberts for J. Busbie, 1604), sig. leaf B2; Charles Courtney, *The Life, Apprehension, and Execution of Charles Courtney* (London: E. Merchant, 1612), t.p. and passim; Henry Goodcole, *A True Declaration of the Happy Conversion, Contrition, and Christian Preparation of Francis Robinson* (London: E. All-de, 1618), t.p. and passim.

18. In regard to hanging ballads, see W. Chappell and J. Woodfall Ebsworth, eds., *The Roxburghe Ballads*, 8 vols. (1869–1901; rpt. New York: AMS Press, 1966), vol. 1, pp. 33–34, 555–58, and 580; in regard to rogue biographies, see John Leon Lievsay, "Newgate Penitents: Further Aspects of Elizabethan Sensationalism," *Huntington Library Quarterly* 7 (Nov. 1943): 47–69.

19. Nicholas Barnard, *The Penitent Death of a Woefull Sinner* (Dublin: Society of Stationers, 1641), treating the case of John Atherton; [Robert Boreman], *A Mirrour of Mercy and Judgement* (London: T. Dring, 1655), treating the case of Freeman Sonds; Randolph Yearwood, *The Penitent Murderer* (London: T. Newcomb for J. Rathwell, 1657), treating the case of Nathaniel Butler; [Richard Alleine], *A Murderer Punished and Pardoned* (London: 1668), treating the case of Thomas Savage; *The Murtherer Turned True Penitent* ([London]: P. Brooksby, [1680]), also treating the case of Thomas Savage. See also Faller, *Turned to Account*, chapters 4 and 5; J. A. Sharpe, "'Last Dying Speeches': Religion, Ideology and Public Execution in Seventeenth-Century England," *Past and Present*, no. 107 (May 1985): 144–67. On the broader genre of spiritual (auto)biography, see Owen C. Watkins, *The Puritan Experience: Studies in Spiritual Autobiography* (New York: Schocken Books, 1972); Paul Delany, *British Autobiography in the Seventeenth Century* (London: Routledge & Kegan Paul, 1969), pp. 27–104; G. A. Starr, *Defoe and Spiritual Autobiography* (Princeton: Princeton University Press, 1965), pp. 3–50. On that genre in early America, see Cecilia Tichi, "Spiritual Biography and the 'Lords Remembrancers,' " in Sacvan Bercovitch, ed., *The American Puritan Imagination* (London: Cambridge University Press, 1974), pp. 56–73; Daniel B. Shea, Jr., *Spiritual Autobiography in Early America* (Princeton: Princeton University Press, 1968).

20. See primary sources cited in note 19, passim. For the sermon transcripts, see Barnard, *Penitent Death*, pp. 79–179; [Alleine], *Murderer Punished*, pp. 49–72.

21. See *The Penitent Prisoner* (London: John Williams, 1675), t.p. and passim, quoted at 1.

22. See [Boreman], *Mirror of Mercy*, p. 14; [Alleine], *Murderer Punished*. The title page of the latter work lists five nonconformist ministers—Robert Franklin, Thomas Doolitel, Thomas Vincent, James Janeway, Hugh Baker—as authors; however, Wing lists the author as another nonconformist minister, Richard Alleine; see

Wing, no. 996. See also Yearwood, *Penitent Murderer*, pp. [81]ff., with the names of the eighteen ministers listed on the last (unnumbered) page. Butler was even proselytized in prison by Catholic priests; see Yearwood, *Penitent Murderer*, pp. [90–91].

23. Two examples: Robert Boreman, the author of *Mirrour of Mercy*, was an Anglican royalist divine; see *DNB*, vol. 2, pp. 856–57; Robert Tichborne, mayor of London during the 1650s, was a regicide (involved in the execution of Charles I) who collaborated in the production of Yearwood, *Penitent Murderer*; see *DNB*, vol. 19, pp. 857–59. For an interesting note on the authorship of English criminal conversion narratives, see Faller, *Turned to Account*, pp. 246–47 n. 15; Faller suggests that "the form was largely invented by Calvinists and then coopted by more moderate, mainstream Church of England types." I would question that particular formulation, arguing that the literary form—and the devotional practices on which it was based—were embraced concurrently by English adherents to a wide spectrum of religious affiliations, including Catholics (note the Savelli narrative), Anglicans, and various nonconformists.

24. See Barnard, *Penitent Death*, pp. 28–32; for a listing of the three editions, see *Wing*, nos. 2014–16.

25. See *BMC*, vol. 262, pp. 147–48; *Wing*, nos. 996–97; Faller, *Turned to Account*, pp. 219–20; according to Faller, another pamphlet on the Savage case reached a twenty-second edition by 1710 and was reprinted at least twice again thereafter.

26. See discussion in note 23 above. Once transferred to America, the tradition of criminal proselytization was no more the monopoly of any single denomination than it had been in England. In 1715, for example, an axe murderer from Providence, Rhode Island, was proselytized by a Congregational minister, an Anglican clergyman, an elderly Baptist, and some Quakers; see Nathaniel Clap, *Sinners Directed to Hear & Fear* (Boston: J. Allen for N. Boone, 1715), p. xii.

27. N. Partridge and J. Sharp, *Blood for Blood, or Justice Executed for Innocent Blood-Shed* (London: F. Smith and D. Newman, 1670); J[ohn] Q[uick], *Hell Open'd, or The Infernal Sin of Murther Punished* (London: F. Eglesfield, 1676); *A Warning to Young Men; or, A Man of Bloods* (London: T. Parkhurst, 1680). However, the first two of those also featured prominent themes of repentance and redemption. Conversely, even conversion narratives sometimes stressed themes of warning. One such account on the case of Nathaniel Butler included a joint statement by eighteen London ministers bemoaning the sinfulness of their city. "Oh! the Scarlet sins that swarm in *London*, even in *London*!" the clergymen wailed. "Tis a wonder *London* is not made as *Sodom*" (Yearwood, *Penitent Murderer*, p. [86]).

28. See Quick, *Hell Open'd*, pp. 85 and 91, quoted.

29. See Richard D. Brown, *Knowledge Is Power: The Diffusion of Information in Early America, 1700–1865* (New York: Oxford University Press, 1989), pp. 16–17; for a somewhat different assessment, see Darrett B. Rutman, *Winthrop's Boston: A Portrait of a Puritan Town, 1630–1649* (1965; rpt. New York: W. W. Norton, 1972), pp. 274–79.

30. See Duniway, *Development of Freedom of the Press*, pp. 22–62.

31. John Noble, ed., *Records of the Court of Assistants of the Colony of the Massachusetts Bay, 1630–1692*, 3 vols. (Boston: County of Suffolk, 1901–1928), vol. 1, pp. 10–11.

32. See *Sprague*, vol. 1, pp. 138–41, quoted at 139.

33. In fact, Johnson's reconciliation with the Puritan authorities would soon be registered by the General Court's granting of his petition to be allowed to move his press from Cambridge to Boston (as it turned out, Johnson died shortly thereafter,

before issuing any Boston imprints); on the shifting, sometimes troubled, relations between Johnson and the Puritan authorities, see Duniway, *Development of Freedom of the Press*, pp. 44–57; for more general discussions of Johnson's career and output, see Benjamin Franklin V, ed., *Boston Printers, Publishers, and Booksellers: 1640–1800* (Boston: G. K. Hall, 1980), pp. 303–9, quoted at 308; George Emery Littlefield, *The Early Massachusetts Press, 1638–1711*, 2 vols. (Boston: Club of Odd Volumes, 1907), vol. 1, pp. 209–69.

34. S[amuel] D[anforth], *The Cry of Sodom Enquired Into* (Cambridge, Mass.: M. Johnson, 1674), p. [iv]. On the three ministers, John Sherman, Urian Oakes, and Thomas Shepard, as censors (or licensers) of the press, see Duniway, *Development of Freedom of the Press*, p. 58 fn. 1.

35. See ibid., pp. 2–5 and 18–22, quoted at 21–22.

36. See Noble, *Records*, vol. 1, p. 30. For the defendants' contradictory claims concerning who had delivered the fatal blow, see Increase Mather, *The Wicked Man's Portion* (Boston: J. Foster, 1675), p. 24.

37. See I. Mather, *Wicked Man's Portion*; Thomas James Holmes, *Increase Mather: A Bibliography of His Works*, 2 vols. (Cleveland: n.p., 1931), vol. 2, pp. 622–28; *Evans*, vol. 1, p. 39. On Foster and his relationship with Mather, see Michael G. Hall, *The Last American Puritan: The Life of Increase Mather, 1639–1723* (Middletown, Conn.: Wesleyan University Press, 1988), pp. 135–36 and 158–65; Franklin, *Boston Printers*, pp. 178–80; Littlefield, *The Early Massachusetts Press*, vol. 2, pp. 3–13.

38. See I. Mather, *Wicked Man's Portion*, pp. 16–17.

39. Ibid., p. 17.

40. For scholarly discussions of the Puritan jeremiad, see Perry Miller, *The New England Mind: From Colony to Province* (1953; rpt. Boston: Beacon Press, 1968) [cited hereafter as *Colony to Province*], pp. 27–39, quoted at 28; Perry Miller, *Errand Into the Wilderness* (1956; rpt. Cambridge: Harvard University Press, 1978), pp. 1–15; David Minter, "The Puritan Jeremiad as a Literary Form," in Sacvan Bercovitch, ed., *American Puritan Imagination*, pp. 45–55; Bercovitch, *The American Jeremiad* (Madison: University of Wisconsin Press, 1978), pp. xi–92; Harry S. Stout, *The New England Soul: Preaching and Religious Culture in Colonial New England* (New York: Oxford University Press, 1986), pp. 62–63, 74–77, 108–11, 142–44, and passim.

41. See, for example, William Williams, *The Serious Consideration* (Boston: T. Fleet, 1738), p. 17; Chauncy Graham, *God Will Trouble the Troublers of His People* (New York: H. Gaine, 1759), pp. 13–14; Henry Trevett Channing, *God Admonishing His People of Their Duty* (New London: T. Green, 1786), p. 17.

42. See Ronald A. Bosco, "Lectures at the Pillory: The Early American Execution Sermon," *American Quarterly* 30 (Summer 1978): 156–76.

43. Those generalizations are based on my readings of all surviving execution sermons published in New England between 1674 and 1740, as located through a page-by-page scan of *Evans*. For a comprehensive listing of those sermons, see *Ritz*, pp. 249–61 and cross-references.

44. That generalization is based on my reading of all surviving execution sermons published in New England between 1741 and 1825, as located through a page-by-page scan of *Evans, Shaw and Shoemaker*, and *American Imprints*. For a comprehensive listing of those sermons published before 1801, see *Ritz*, pp. 249–61 and cross-references.

45. For an example of motifs of warning carried over into a mid-nineteenth-

century trial report, see *The Trial of Albert John Tirrell, for the Murder of Maria A. Bickford* (Boston: H. B. Skinner, 1846), t.p. and pp. 7–8.

46. See Ct. Files, no. 2385, papers 4 and 6. For Morgan's approximate age, see Increase Mather, *A Sermon Occasioned by the Execution of a Man Found Guilty of Murder*, 2d ed. (Boston: R. P[ierce], 1687), p. 117. To minimize confusion, all subsequent citations to I. Mather, *Sermon Occasioned* will also be to the second edition; it should be noted, however, that there are numerous small differences in typeface, capitalization, and punctuation between the two editions. For a very perceptive scholarly treatment of the Morgan case, see David Levin, *Cotton Mather: The Young Life of the Lord's Remembrancer, 1663–1703* (Cambridge: Harvard University Press, 1978), pp. 119–27.

47. See Ct. Files, no. 2385, papers 3 and 5–6. On the disreputable character of the boardinghouse, see I. Mather, *Sermon Occasioned*, p. 36.

48. See Ct. Files, no. 2362; no. 2383; no. 2385, papers 3 and 6–7; Noble, *Records*, vol. 1, pp. 294–95; Samuel Sewall, *The Diary*, ed. M. Halsey Thomas, 2 vols. (New York: Farrar, Straus and Giroux, 1973), vol. 1, p. 97.

49. See Ct. Files, no. 2385, paper 2.

50. I. Mather, *Sermon Occasioned*, pp. 30–31, 76, [84], [114], and 120.

51. See ibid., pp. 22–23, 38, 76, [84], [115]–24; John Dunton, *Letters Written from New-England* (1867; rpt. New York: Burt Franklin, [1966]), pp. 118–36; Sewall, *Diary*, vol. 1, pp. 99–100.

52. I. Mather, *Sermon Occasioned*, pp. 1–35, quoted at 33.

53. Ibid., pp. 35–36.

54. Ibid., pp. 37–113.

55. The assumption that the Morgan volume was the inspiration of John Dunton is based largely on Dunton's own account; however, it should be noted that Dunton is not a reliable source; see Chester Noyes Greenough, "John Dunton's Letters from New England," *Publications of the Colonial Society of Massachusetts*, no. 14 (Boston: The Society, 1913), pp. 213–57.

56. See Thomas J. Holmes, *Cotton Mather: A Bibliography of His Works*, 3 vols. (Cambridge: Harvard University Press, 1940), vol. 1, pp. 109–13; Thomas J. Holmes, *Increase Mather: A Bibliography of His Works*, 2 vols. (Cleveland: 1931), vol. 2, pp. 479–87. On Dunton, Brunning, and Pierce, see Franklin, *Boston Printers*, pp. 59–60, 115–16, and 412–14; Littlefield, *Early Massachusetts Press*, vol. 2, pp. 43–47; Littlefield, *Early Boston Booksellers, 1642–1711* (Boston: Club of Odd Volumes, 1900), pp. 120–22 and 139–43. On Pierce's marriage into the Mather family, see Hall, *Last American Puritan*, p. 174.

57. I. Mather, *Sermon Occasioned*, pp. [114]–124, quoted at [114].

58. Ibid., pp. [115]–124, quoted at [115], 122, and 124.

59. Ibid., pp. [iii] and 35–36.

60. Ibid., pp. 42, 82, 113.

61. Ibid., pp. [114]–124, quoted at 124.

62. See *The Wonders of Free Grace* (London: J. Dunton, 1690); Holmes, *Increase Mather*, pp. 482–86; for earlier publications dealing with Atherton, Butler, and Savage, see works cited in note 19 above.

63. For a listing of those volumes of sermons, see *Ritz*, pp. 250–58 and cross-references.

64. For a scholarly discussion of the crime of infanticide in early modern England

and New England, see Peter C. Hoffer and N. E. H. Hull, *Murdering Mothers: Infanticide in England and New England, 1558–1803* (New York: New York University Press, 1984).

65. Cotton Mather, *Warnings from the Dead* (Boston: B. Green for S. Phillips, 1693); Samuel Willard, *Impenitent Sinners Warned of Their Misery and Summoned to Judgment* (Boston: B. Green and J. Allen, 1698); Cotton Mather, *Pillars of Salt* (Boston: B. Green and J. Allen for S. Phillips, 1699); Increase Mather, *The Folly of Sinning* (Boston: B. Green and J. Allen for M. Perry, 1699); and John Williams, *Warnings to the Unclean* (Boston: B. Green and J. Allen for M. Perry, 1699).

66. C. Mather, *Pillars of Salt*, t.p..

67. Ibid.; the execution volume on Hugh Stone was C. Mather, *Speedy Repentance Urged* (Boston: S. Green [for] J. Browning and B. Harris, 1690).

68. See Faller, *Turned to Account*, pp. 73 and 233 n. 2; William P. Bowser, "Murder by the Book: A Survey of the Criminal Calendar," *American Book Collector* 21 (Sept. 1970): 11.

69. See *Wonders*, t.p. and passim; C. Mather, *Pillars of Salt*, t.p. and passim.

70. See Ford, *Boston Book Market*, pp. 48–50 and 57–64.

71. See David D. Hall, *Worlds of Wonder, Days of Judgment: Popular Religious Belief in Early New England* (New York: Alfred A. Knopf, 1989), pp. 43–61, esp. 52–55, quoted at 53.

72. See Hall, *Last American Puritan*, pp. 300–301.

73. One loyal Puritan printer, John Foster, went so far as to remember the two Mathers, along with a third local minister, in his will; see Hall, *Last American Puritan*, pp. 161–64.

74. On Foster, see Hall, *Last American Puritan*, pp. 161–64; Thomas C. Simonds, *History of South Boston* (1857; rpt. New York: Arno Press, 1974), pp. 33–39, elegy quoted at 38; on Green, see obituary in *Boston News-Letter*, Jan. 4, 1733, p. 2.

75. See, for example, Cotton Mather, *The Wonders of the Invisible World* ([1692, postdated] 1693; rpt. London: J. R. Smith, 1862), pp. 120–59; C. Mather, *Pillars of Salt*, passim.

76. See note 3 above.

77. On the apparent absence of separately published English execution sermons during the seventeenth century, see chapter 1 above at notes 6 and 7.

78. See Ford, *Boston Book Market*, pp. 163–82; the copies of I. Mather's execution sermon are listed on pp. 174 and 182; twenty copies of another execution sermon by John Williams are listed on p. 178; the two romances cited by Hall are listed on pp. 170–71; for Hall's mention of those chivalric tales, see Hall, *Worlds of Wonder*, p. 54 (he erroneously cites *Seven Wise Masters of Rome* as *The Seven Wise Champions of Christendom*).

79. See Ford, *Boston Book Market*, p. 64. Of 133 books known to have been published in Boston between 1682 and 1698, 95 (or 71 percent) were sermons or other religious works; see Tebbel, *History of Book Publishing*, vol. 1, p. 30. On a related issue, Stephen Foster points out that, contrary to a common assumption, English imports (whatever their content) served only as a minor supplement to domestic presses largely dominated by the output of local ministers; see Foster, "The Godly in Transit: English Popular Protestantism and the Creation of a Puritan Establishment in America," in *Seventeenth-Century New England* (Boston: Colonial Society of Massachusetts, 1984), pp. 219–31.

Chapter 3. *Toward a Great Awakening*

1. For a very perceptive scholarly analysis of the New England conversion narratives, marred only by the author's apparent lack of familiarity with the similar English and European literature (discussed above in chapter 2), see Daniel E. Williams, "'Behold a Tragic Scene Strangely Changed Into a Theater of Mercy': The Structure and Significance of Criminal Conversion Narratives in Early New England," *American Quarterly* 38 (Winter 1986): 827–47. Williams claims that eighteen of twenty-seven crime publications produced in New England between 1700 and 1740 depicted offenders as "penitent" and twelve of those described "successful conversions" (p. 829).

2. See John Rogers, *Death the Certain Wages of Sin* (Boston: B. Green and J. Allen for S. Phillips, 1701); on the lack of relation between John Rogers and Esther Rodgers, see p. [ix].

3. Ibid., pp. [iii]-[xii], quoted at [iv] and [viii]-[ix].

4. Ibid., passim.

5. Ibid., pp. 118–20, quoted at 118.

6. Ibid., pp. 119–20.

7. For basic information on the seven ministers, see Frederick Lewis Weis, *The Colonial Clergy and the Colonial Churches of New England* (Lancaster, Mass.: 1936), pp. 30–31 (Samuel Belcher), 91 (Joseph Gerrish), 112–13 (William Hubbard), 153 (Nicholas Noyes), 160 (Edward Payson), 176 (John Rogers), and 233 (John Wise). More detailed biographical information on all of those men can be obtained from the appropriate volumes in *Sibley*. For evidence of the professional and social interactions of several of the North Shore ministers, see S. P. Fowler, ed., "Diary of Rev. Joseph Green, of Salem Village," *Historical Collections of the Essex Institute*, vol. 8 (1868; rpt. New York: Johnson Reprint Corporation, 1971), pp. 215–24, passim.

8. See Rogers, *Death*, pp. 121–53, quoted at 122.

9. Ibid., pp. 123–24.

10. Ibid., pp. 124–31, quoted at 127, 129, and 131.

11. Ibid., pp. 136–43, quoted at 136–37 and 143.

12. Ibid., pp. 143–45.

13. Ibid., pp. 146–51, quoted at 146 and 148.

14. Ibid., pp. 151–52.

15. Ibid., p. 153; for a local clergyman's characterization of Rodgers's dying conversion as a form of theater, see ibid., p. 118.

16. Ibid., p. [v]; for the accounts of Butler, Savage, and others, see chapter 2 above.

17. Ibid., pp. [viii]-[ix], 119–25, 127–28, 131, 138–43, 145, and 151–52, quoted at 119.

18. For a modern sociological discussion of the role of confession in symbolically (or actually) reintegrating deviant members into the community, see Mike Hepworth and Bryan S. Turner, *Confession: Studies in Deviance and Religion* (London: Routledge & Kegan Paul, 1982), pp. 14, 22, 35, 37, 43, 132, 159, and passim.

19. On the Puritan model of conversion, see Edmund S. Morgan, *Visible Saints: The History of a Puritan Idea* (1963; rpt. Ithaca: Cornell University Press, 1974), pp. 67–72; Norman Pettit, *The Heart Prepared: Grace and Conversion in Puritan Spiritual Life*, 2d ed. (Middletown, Conn.: Wesleyan University Press, 1989); Patricia Caldwell,

The Puritan Conversion Narrative (Cambridge, Eng.: Cambridge University Press, 1983); Charles Lloyd Cohen, *God's Caress: The Psychology of Puritan Religious Experience* (New York: Oxford University Press, 1986). Cohen differs with Morgan as to whether saints were supposed to have persistent doubts concerning their spiritual state (compare Morgan, p. 67, to Cohen, pp. 100–101); the confidence displayed by Esther Rodgers seems more consistent with Cohen's formulation.

20. See Hepworth and Turner, *Confession*, pp. 129 and 159.

21. As in most other aspects of published conversion accounts, it is impossible to verify that the first-person narrative of Rodgers really did represent her own voice (on related issues, see discussion near the beginning of chapter 2 above, and discussions of the authorship and reliability of criminal confessions and last speeches in chapters 1 above and 6 below, passim). But whether authentic or not, the narrative of Esther Rodgers (and those of other criminal converts) helped create an expectation among New England readers of access to the confessions and autobiographies of condemned criminals, an expectation that would be realized with increasing regularity over the course of the eighteenth century.

22. Rogers, *Death*, p. 119. On the tendency of Puritan spirituality to minimize gender distinctions, see Laurel Thatcher Ulrich, "Vertuous Women Found: New England Ministerial Literature, 1668–1735," *American Quarterly* 28 (Spring 1976): 20–40; for a very different interpretation of Puritan gender ideology, see Lyle Koehler, *A Search for Power* (Urbana: University of Illinois Press, 1980).

23. See David Grayson Allen, *In English Ways: The Movements of Societies and the Transferal of English Local Law and Custom to Massachusetts Bay in the Seventeenth Century* (Chapel Hill: University of North Carolina Press, 1981), pp. 82–116, 180–84, and 215–18, passim.

24. See Allen, *In English Ways*, pp. 117–60 and 184–204, passim. As Christine L. Heyrman has demonstrated, there was no necessary contradiction on the North Shore of Massachusetts between a commercial orientation and a thriving spiritual life; see Heyrman, *Commerce and Culture: The Maritime Communities of Colonial Massachusetts, 1690–1750* (New York: W. W. Norton, 1984).

25. See *Sibley*, vol. 4, pp. 113–17, quoted at 116.

26. See *Sibley*, vol. 3, p. 276.

27. See Marcus Rediker, "'Under the Banner of King Death': The Social World of Anglo-American Pirates, 1716 to 1726," *William and Mary Quarterly*, 3d ser., 38 (April 1981): 203–27; Hugh F. Rankin, *The Golden Age of Piracy* (Williamsburg, Va.: Colonial Williamsburg, 1969); George Francis Dow and John Henry Edmonds, *The Pirates of the New England Coast, 1630–1730* (Salem, Mass.: Marine Research Society, 1923).

28. For a listing of those volumes of execution sermons, see *Ritz*, pp. 253–58 and cross-references.

29. Thus in 1724 Mather wrote in his *Diary*: "One of the first Things which the Pyrates, who are now so much the *Terror of them that haunt the Sea*, impose on their poor Captives, is; *To curse Dr M——*." C. Mather, *Diary*, 2 vols. (New York: Frederick Ungar, n.d.), vol. 2, p. 729.

30. C. Mather, *Faithful Warnings to Prevent Fearful Judgments* (Boston: T. Green, 1704); C. Mather, *The Converted Sinner* (Boston: N. Belknap, 1724).

31. See [C. Mather], *Useful Remarks* (New London: T. Green, 1723), pp. 29–45; C. Mather, *The Converted Sinner* (Boston: N. Belknap, 1724), pp. 31–49.

32. See citations in note 31 and C. Mather, *The Sad Effects of Sin* (Boston: J. Allen for N. Boone, 1713), pp. [i]–14; [C. Mather], *Instructions to the Living, from the Condition of the Dead* (Boston: J. Allen, for N. Boone, 1717), pp. 3–38.

33. See *An Account of the Behaviour and Last Dying Speeches of the Six Pirates, That Were Executed* (Boston: N. Boone, 1704), p. [ii]; [C. Mather], *Instructions*, pp. 37–38.

34. For a perceptive discussion of William Fly and his relationship with Cotton Mather, see Daniel E. Williams, "Puritans and Pirates: A Confrontation Between Cotton Mather and William Fly in 1726," *Early American Literature* 22 (1987): 233–51.

35. See C. Mather, *The Vial Poured Out upon the Sea* (Boston: T. Fleet for N. Belknap, 1726), pp. 6–27, quoted at 15–16 and 21.

36. See ibid., pp. 47–48.

37. See John Deane Potter, *The Fatal Gallows Tree* (London: Elek Books, 1965), pp. 50–60; Michael Ignatieff, *A Just Measure of Pain: The Penitentiary in the Industrial Revolution, 1750–1850* (New York: Pantheon Books, 1978), pp. 22–23; J. A. Sharpe, "'Last Dying Speeches': Religion, Ideology and Public Execution in Seventeenth-Century England," *Past and Present*, no. 107 (May 1985): 165.

38. See Lincoln B. Faller, *Turned to Account: The Forms and Functions of Criminal Biography in Late Seventeenth- and Early Eighteenth-Century England* (Cambridge, Eng.: Cambridge University Press, 1987), pp. 125–93, passim.

39. See C. Mather, *Vial*, p. 47.

40. See C. Mather, *Instructions*, pp. 37–38; C. Mather, *Vial*, pp. 5 and 47.

41. It should be noted that the dialogue between Mather and Morgan was incorporated into the second edition of the Morgan anthology.

42. See C. Mather, *Vial*, pp. 21 and 44–45.

43. See C. Mather, *Vial*, pp. 16–17; *Account*, p. [ii].

44. Samuel Moodey [but generally spelled Moody], *Summary Account of the Life and Death of Joseph Quasson, Indian* (Boston: S. Gerrish, 1726).

45. See ibid., t.p. and pp. 2–5, 21, and 28. Information on the present-day location of Monamoy provided by Ruth Friedman of Lawrence University.

46. See *Sibley*, vol. 4, pp. 356–65; Charles E. Clark, *The Eastern Frontier* (New York: Alfred A. Knopf, 1970), pp. 82–89.

47. On Moody's birthplace, see citations in note 46; on the efforts of others in Quasson's behalf, see Moodey, *Summary Account*, pp. 9–10, 14, 18, 22–23, 28–29, and passim.

48. See Moodey, *Summary Account*, pp. 5–7, 9–10, 14, 33, and passim, quoted at 9–10. On the practice of "intensive" reading in early New England, see David D. Hall, "Introduction: The Uses Of Literacy in New England, 1600–1850," in William L. Joyce et al., eds., *Printing and Society in Early America* (Worcester: American Antiquarian Society, 1983), pp. 23–24 and 28–35.

49. See Moodey, *Summary Account*, pp. 10 and 28–29.

50. J[ohn] Q[uick], *Hell Open'd, or, The Infernal Sin of Murther Punished* (London: F. Eglesfield, 1676), p. 58.

51. See Moodey, *Summary Account*, pp. 6–12, 17, 19, and passim, quoted at 7, 9, 12, and 17.

52. See ibid., pp. 20, 23–27, and 39; *Boston News-Letter*, Nov. 24, 1726, p. 2; my characterization of Gerrish's business orientation at the time is based on a scan of his advertisements in the *Boston News-Letter* for 1726 and 1727.

53. See Samuel Moody and Joseph Moody, *A Faithful Narrative of the Wicked Life and Remarkable Conversion of Patience Boston* (Boston: S. Kneeland and T. Green, 1738), quoted at p. 29.

54. The spellings differ in the two narratives, but the place is undoubtedly the same; see Moodey, *Summary Account*, p. 2 (spelled Monamoy); Moody and Moody, *Faithful Narrative*, p. 1 (spelled Menomey).

55. See Moody and Moody, *Faithful Narrative*, pp. 1–3.

56. Ibid., p. 3.

57. Ibid., p. 4. For an example of a scholar who sharply distinguishes between oral and print culture in eighteenth-century America, see Harry S. Stout, "Religion, Communications, and the Ideological Origins of the American Revolution," *William and Mary Quarterly*, 3d ser., 34 (Oct. 1977): 519–41, esp. 530–40. For a broad theoretical analysis of the distinction between oral and print cultures, see Walter J. Ong, *Orality and Literacy: The Technologizing of the Word* (London: Methuen, 1982).

58. Ibid., pp. 4–7.

59. Ibid., pp. 7–8. For the date of the murder, see extended title of pamphlet cited in *Ritz*, no. 5.02(10)(a).

60. See Moody and Moody, *Faithful Narrative*, pp. 8–33, especially 8–9, 12, and 16–19, quoted at 17–19. The reference to Mather's "church history" is to his *Magnalia Christi Americana* (London: T. Parkhurst, 1702); Book 6, Chapter 5 of that compilation consists of criminal narratives.

61. For her responses to passages from sermon and Scripture, see ibid., pp. 12, 14, 16–18, 21–24, 28, and 33.

62. Ibid., pp. 10–13, 29–31, and passim.

63. Ibid., pp. 10–13.

64. On the somewhat similar use of light imagery in the language of the great revivalist Jonathan Edwards, see Harry S. Stout, *The New England Soul: Preaching and Religious Culture in Colonial New England* (New York: Oxford University Press, 1986), pp. 230–31.

65. See Moody and Moody, *Faithful Narrative*, pp. 12–29 and 31–32, quoted at 27.

66. For a perceptive discussion of Boston's altered attitude toward her surviving child, see Williams, "Behold a Tragic Scene," p. 841.

67. See Moody and Moody, *Faithful Narrative*, pp. 32–34.

68. Ibid., pp. 34–35.

69. Ibid., pp. [ii] and 29–33, quoted at [ii].

70. Ibid., p. [ii].

71. *Boston News-Letter*, May 25, 1738, p. 2.

72. The similarity of the titles is noted by Williams, "Behold a Tragic Scene," p. 846 n. 31; on the many printings of Edwards's tract, see Clarence H. Faust and Thomas H. Johnson, *Jonathan Edwards: Representative Selections* (1935; rpt. New York: Hill and Wang, 1962), p. 420.

73. On the support offered by Rogers and Moody to the revivalists of the Great Awakening, see *Sibley*. vol. 3, p. 276 (on Rogers); vol. 4, p. 362–63 (on Moody); Clark, *Eastern Frontier*, p. 85 (on Moody). Daniel E. Williams also suggests a linkage between the criminal conversion narratives and the evangelicalism of the Great Awakening; see Williams, "Behold a Tragic Scene," pp. 829 and 845 n. 3.

74. On the increasingly secular (auto)biographical literature that emerged during the 1730s and thereafter, see chapter 1 above and chapters 6–9 below.

75. See chapters cited in note 74.

76. On the changing conceptions of salvation, see Conrad Wright, *The Beginnings of Unitarianism in America* (Boston: Starr King Press, 1955), pp. 115–34, esp. 132–34; Joseph Haroutunian, *Piety Versus Moralism: The Passing of the New England Theology* (New York: Henry Holt, 1932), pp. 43–71; also see David D. Hall, *Worlds of Wonder, Days of Judgment: Popular Religious Belief in Early New England* (New York: Alfred A. Knopf, 1989), p. 244; Richard Rabinowitz, *The Spiritual Self in Everyday Life: The Transformation of Personal Religious Experience in Nineteenth-Century New England* (Boston: Northeastern University Press, 1989), p. 218. For traces of the new understanding of spiritual development in a New England execution sermon, see Peres Fobes, *The Paradise of God Opened to a Penitent Thief* (Providence: B. Wheeler, [1784]), pp. 24–25.

77. On the early movement against the death penalty, see text and notes in chapters 4 and 5 below.

78. See, for example, M. M. Knappen, *Tudor Puritanism: A Chapter in the History of Idealism* (1939; rpt. Chicago: University of Chicago Press, 1965), pp. 434–36.

79. That conclusion is strongly reinforced by the findings of Charles E. Hambrick-Stowe, based on a completely different body of devotional practices and materials; see Hambrick-Stowe, *The Practice of Piety: Puritan Devotional Disciplines in Seventeenth-Century New England* (Chapel Hill: University of North Carolina Press, 1982), pp. viii–ix, 23–39, and passim.

80. See Carlos Sommervogel, *Bibliothque de la Compagnie de Jesus*, new ed., 11 vols. (Brusells: O. Schepens and Paris: A. Picard, 1890–1932), vol. 1, p. 1547.

81. See Edmund Fortis, *The Last Words and Dying Speech* (n.p.: [1794]), broadside; the same work was also published as a pamphlet in Exeter, New Hampshire, in 1795. For another example of the criminal conversion motif emerging in an execution broadside, see *The Execution Hymn* ([Boston]: E. Russell, [1773]).

82. This list accurately suggests the disproportionate presence of members of "outsider" social groups (especially racial or ethnic minorities) on the gallows of early eighteenth-century New England. For a similar pattern, see chapter 6.

83. See Michael Warner, *The Letters of the Republic: Publication and the Public Sphere in Eighteenth-Century America* (Cambridge: Harvard University Press, 1990), pp. 11–17 and 48–49.

Chapter 4. *The Road to the Scaffold*

1. My analysis of ministerial ideology in parts 1 and 2 seeks to mediate between the traditional view that the Calvinist worldview disintegrated over the course of the eighteenth century and the revisionist view that it largely persisted through the Revolutionary period; for those competing viewpoints, see Joseph Haroutunian, *Piety Versus Moralism: The Passing of the New England Theology* (New York: Henry Holt, 1932); Harry S. Stout, *The New England Soul: Preaching and Religious Culture in Colonial New England* (New York: Oxford University Press, 1986).

2. S[amuel] D[anforth], *The Cry of Sodom Enquired Into* (Cambridge, Mass.: M. Johnson, 1674), p. 11. For another study of attitudes concerning the causes of crime in colonial New England, based largely on early execution sermons, see Eli Faber, "The Evil That Men Do: Crime and Transgression in Colonial Massachusetts" (Ph.D. diss., Columbia University, 1974), pp. 126–73. For some discussion of the

etiology of crime as presented in a mid-nineteenth-century crime periodical, see Dan Schiller, *Objectivity and the News: The Public and the Rise of Commercial Journalism* (Philadelphia: University of Pennsylvania Press, 1981), pp. 173–75.

3. See, for example, Increase Mather, *The Folly of Sinning, Opened and Applyed* (Boston: B. Green and J. Allen, 1699), p. 51; John Rogers, *Death the Certain Wages of Sin* (Boston: B. Green and J. Allen, 1701), p. 94; Cotton Mather, *The Curbed Sinner* (Boston: J. Allen, 1713), pp. 16–17; Benjamin Colman, *The Hainous Nature of the Sin of Murder* (Boston: J. Allen, 1713), p. 16; Cotton Mather, *The Converted Sinner* (Boston: N. Belknap, 1724), pp. 39–40.

4. Nathaniel Clap, *The Lord's Voice, Crying to His People* (Boston: B. Green, 1715), p. 35.

5. For a similar point, see Daniel E. Williams, "'Behold a Tragic Scene Strangely Changed into a Theater of Mercy': The Structure and Significance of Criminal Conversion Narratives in Early New England," *American Quarterly* 38 (Winter 1986): 830.

6. Thomas Foxcroft, *Lessons of Caution to Young Sinners* (Boston: S. Kneeland and T. Green, 1733), p. 60.

7. C. Mather, *Curbed Sinner*, t.p. and pp. 6–16.

8. C. Mather, *Pillars of Salt* (Boston: B. Green and J. Allen, 1699), p. 17.

9. It also appeared in pious English crime pamphlets of the seventeenth century; see, for example, J[ohn] Q[uick], *Hell Open'd, or, The Infernal Sin of Murther Punished* (London: F. Eglesfield, 1676), p. 91.

10. I. Mather, *The Wicked Man's Portion* (Boston: J. Foster, 1675), p. 21.

11. Clap, *Lord's Voice*, p. 48.

12. C. Mather, *A Sorrowful Spectacle*, (Boston: T. Fleet and T. Crump, 1715), p. 22.

13. C. Mather, *Pillars*, pp. 6 and 14–18.

14. Ibid., pp. 19–29.

15. Ibid., pp. 42–43.

16. Clap, *Lord's Voice*, pp. 19–23.

17. C. Mather, *Pillars*, pp. 12–13.

18. On the spiritual voluntarism and democratic ethos of American Protestantism by the early nineteenth century, see Nathan O. Hatch, *The Democratization of American Christianity* (New Haven: Yale University Press, 1989); Gordon Wood, "Evangelical America and Early Mormonism," *New York History* 61 (Oct. 1980): 374–75 and passim.

19. See Kai T. Erikson, *Wayward Puritans: A Study in the Sociology of Deviance* (New York: John Wiley & Sons, 1966), p. 40.

20. The last reference to the doctrine I have found is in C. Mather, *Curbed Sinner*, p. 18.

21. Danforth, *Cry of Sodom*, pp. 21–22.

22. On sin as a downhill fall, see Eliphalet Adams, *A Sermon Preached on the Occasion of the Execution of Katherine Garret* (New London: T. Green, 1738), p. 29; Aaron Hutchinson, *Iniquity Purged by Mercy and Truth* (Boston: T. and J. Fleet, 1769), p. 28; Ezra Witter, *A Discourse* (Springfield: H. Brewer, [1805]), p. 10. On sin as a habit, see Rogers, *Death*, pp. 104–5; Noah Hobart, *Excessive Wickedness, the Way to an Untimely Death* (New Haven: T. and S. Green, [1768]), pp. 16–17. On sin as an appetite, see Hobart, *Excessive Wickedness*, p. 16. On sin as a spark, see Witter, *Discourse*, p. 15.

23. Joshua Moody, *Exhortation to A Condemned Malefactor* (Boston: R. P.[ierce], 1687) [bound with Increase Mather, *A Sermon Occasioned by the Execution of a Man Found Guilty of Murder*, 2d ed.], p. 107.

24. Adams, *Sermon*, p. 29.

25. Danforth, *Cry of Sodom*, pp. 3–5 and 18–23; I. Mather, *Sermon*, 15–19.

26. C. Mather, *Speedy Repentance Urged* (Boston: S. Green, 1690), pp. 71–72; C. Mather, *Tremenda. The Dreadful Sound with Which the Wicked Are to Be Thunderstruck* (Boston: B. Green, 1721), p. 34; C. Mather, *The Vial Poured Out upon the Sea* (Boston: T. Fleet, 1726), p. 10.

27. For examples of recalcitrant offenders, see C. Mather, *Tremenda*, pp. 39–40; C. Mather, *Vial*, pp. 8–22.

28. C. Mather, *Instructions to the Living, from the Condition of the Dead* (Boston: J. Allen, 1717), p. 23.

29. I. Mather, *Sermon*, p. 24. On Mather's ongoing campaign against drunkenness, see Michael G. Hall, *The Last American Puritan: The Life of Increase Mather, 1639–1723* (Middletown, Conn.: Wesleyan University Press, 1988), pp. 100, 108, 113, 122–23, 130, and 199.

30. I. Mather, *Sermon,* pp. 24–25.

31. Samuel Danforth (the younger), *The Woful Effect of Drunkenness* (Boston: B. Green, 1710), t.p. and pp. 1–2 and 6.

32. Ibid., pp. 8–10.

33. Ibid., pp. 11–29.

34. For biographical information on Arthur Browne, see *Sprague*, vol. 5, pp. 76–82.

35. Arthur Browne, *Religious Education of Children Recommended* (Boston: S. Kneeland and T. Green, 1739), pp. 5–7.

36. Ibid., pp. 10 and 13.

37. For biographical information on Henry Channing, see *Dexter*, vol. 4, pp. 183–86; *Sprague*, vol. 8, p. 361 fn.

38. Henry Channing, *God Admonishing His People of Their Duty, as Parents and Masters* (New London: T. Green, 1786), t.p. and pp. 25 and 30.

39. Ibid., p. 12. Compare to John Locke, quoted in Jay Fliegelman, *Prodigals and Pilgrims: The American Revolution Against Patriarchal Authority, 1750–1800* (Cambridge, Eng.: Cambridge University Press, 1982), p. 59; also see p. 12.

40. Channing, *God Admonishing*, pp. 13–18, quoted at 13.

41. See ibid., pp. 6, 9, and 29, quoted at 9.

42. See *Sprague*, vol. 8, p. 361 fn. Channing would later be dismissed from the New London church, partly on account of his Unitarian views; see *Dexter*, vol. 4, pp. 184–85.

43. For biographical information on Aaron Bancroft, see *Sprague*, vol. 8, pp. 132–40.

44. Aaron Bancroft, *The Importance of a Religious Education* (Worcester: I. Thomas, 1793), t.p. and p. 22. For details of the case, see *The Confession and Dying Words of Samuel Frost* (Worcester: I. Thomas, [1793]), broadside.

45. Bancroft, *Importance*, pp. 16–19.

46. For biographical information on Jonathan Going, see *Sprague*, vol. 6, pp. 591–95; William Lincoln, *History of Worcester* (Worcester: C. Hersey, 1862), pp. 178–79.

47. Jonathan Going, *A Discourse Delivered at Worcester* (Worcester: W. Manning, 1825), t.p. and pp. 5–8.

48. Ibid., pp. 6, 15–16, and 19–21.

49. On the declining belief in natural depravity and other Calvinist doctrines in eighteenth-century New England, see Conrad Wright, *The Beginnings of Unitarianism in America* (Boston: Starr King Press, 1955), esp. pp. 59–90; Haroutunian, *Piety Versus Moralism*, esp. pp. 22–23.

50. See Fliegelman, *Prodigals*, pp. 1–10, 14, 36–37, 67–89, and passim, quoted at 5 and 14.

51. See David Hackett Fischer, *Growing Old in America*, expanded ed. (Oxford: Oxford University Press, 1978), pp. 77–112 and passim.

52. See Fliegelman, *Prodigals*, pp. 86–87; Nina Baym, *Woman's Fiction: A Guide to Novels by and about Women in America, 1820–1870* (Ithaca: Cornell University Press, 1978), p. 37.

53. Bancroft, *Importance*, p. 17; Going, *Discourse*, p. 5.

54. For biographical information on Thaddeus MacCarty, see *Sprague*, vol. 1, pp. 423–25.

55. Thaddeus MacCarty, *The Guilt of Innocent Blood Put Away* (Norwich: J. Trumbull, 1778), pp. 19 and 25. For more information on the case, see *The Last Words and Dying Speech of Ezra Ross, James Buchanan and William Brooks* (n.p.: [1778]), broadside (this work appeared in a number of variant broadside and pamphlet editions).

56. MacCarty, *Guilt*, pp. 19 and 26.

57. For biographical information on Enoch Huntington, see *Dexter*, vol. 2, pp. 594–97; *Sprague*, vol. 1, pp. 606–7.

58. Enoch Huntington, *A Sermon Preached at Haddam* (Middletown: M. H. Woodward, [1797]), pp. [23–24].

59. For biographical information on Nathan Strong, see *Dexter*, vol. 3, pp. 357–63; *Sprague*, vol. 2, pp. 34–41.

60. Nathan Strong, *A Sermon, Preached in Hartford* (Hartford: E. Babcock, 1797), pp. 17–19.

61. On the rise of romantic conceptions of love in American culture during the second half of the eighteenth century, see Ellen K. Rothman, *Hands and Hearts: A History of Courtship in America* (New York: Basic Books, 1984), p. 31; Fliegelman, *Prodigals*, p. 137; Nancy F. Cott, "Eighteenth-Century Family and Social Life Revealed in Massachusetts Divorce Records," in Cott and Elizabeth H. Pleck, eds., *A Heritage of Her Own* (New York: Simon and Schuster, 1979), pp. 122–23.

62. See Bancroft, *Importance*, pp. 8–9; Going, *Discourse*, p. 15. On Going's advocacy of improved common schools, see *Sprague*, vol. 6, pp. 592 and 595. At least one modern scholar has argued that the widely perceived link between illiteracy and criminality was a "myth"; see Harvey J. Graff, *The Labyrinths of Literacy: Reflections on Literacy Past and Present* (London: Falmer Press, 1987), pp. 187–213; Graff, *The Literacy Myth: Literacy and Social Structure in the Nineteenth-Century City* (New York: Academic Press, 1979), pp. 235–67.

63. See W. J. Rorabaugh, *The Alcoholic Republic: An American Tradition* (New York: Oxford University Press, 1979).

64. See Ian R. Tyrrell, *Sobering Up: From Temperance to Prohibition in Antebellum America, 1800–1860* (Westport, Conn.: Greenwood Press, 1979), pp. 33–53; Donald M. Scott, *From Office to Profession: The New England Ministry, 1750–1850* (Philadelphia: University of Pennsylvania Press, 1978), pp. 29–35; Joseph R. Gusfield, *Symbolic Crusade: Status Politics and the American Temperance Movement* (Urbana: University of Illinois Press, 1963), pp. 36–44.

65. See Strong, *Sermon*, pp. 12 and 20.

66. For biographical information on David D. Field, see *Dexter*, vol. 5, pp. 488–91.

67. David D. Field, *Warning Against Drunkenness* (Middletown, Conn.: S. Richards, 1816), p. 8.

68. See ibid., pp. 16–19. The Massachusetts Society for the Suppression of Intemperance and the Connecticut Society for the Reformation of Morals had actually been founded three years earlier; however, they do not seem to have pursued a program quite as aggressive or comprehensive as the one envisioned by Field; see Tyrrell, *Sobering Up*, pp. 33–53; Gusfield, *Symbolic Crusade*, p. 41.

69. For biographical information on Ezra Witter, see *Dexter*, vol. 5, pp. 94–95.

70. See Ezra Witter, *A Discourse Delivered in Wilbraham* (Springfield: H. Brewer, [1805]), pp. 12–14.

71. For biographical information on William Andrews, see *Sprague*, vol. 2, p. 237 fn.; *The Two-Hundredth Anniversary of the Organization of the Congregational Church in Windham, Conn.* (Willimantic, Conn.: Hall & Bill, 1901), pp. 35–36; James M. Bailey, *History of Danbury, Conn., 1684–1896*, comp. Susan B. Hill (New York: Burr, 1896), p. 292.

72. See William Andrews, *A Sermon, Delivered at Danbury* (New Haven: T. G. Woodward, 1817), pp. 14–15.

73. See ibid.

74. See Louis P. Masur, *Rites of Execution: Capital Punishment and the Transformation of American Culture, 1776–1865* (New York: Oxford University Press, 1989), pp. 66–69.

75. See David Brion Davis, "The Movement to Abolish Capital Punishment in America, 1787–1861," *American Historical Review* 63 (Oct. 1957): 29–31.

76. See Masur, *Rites of Execution*, pp. 76–79; Michael Ignatieff, *A Just Measure of Pain: The Penitentiary in the Industrial Revolution, 1750–1850* (New York: Pantheon Books, 1978), pp. 66–67; Davis, "Movement to Abolish Capital Punishment," pp. 24–25 and 31; David Brion Davis, *Homicide in American Fiction, 1798–1860: A Study in Social Values* (Ithaca: Cornell University Press, 1957), pp. 294–95 and 299.

77. See Masur, *Rites of Execution*; Michael Meranze, "The Penitential Ideal in Late Eighteenth-Century Philadelphia," *Pennsylvania Magazine of History and Biography* 108 (October 1984): 419–50; Philip English Mackey, *Hanging in the Balance: The Anti–Capital Punishment Movement in New York State, 1776–1861* (New York: Garland, 1982); David J. Rothman, *The Discovery of the Asylum: Social Order and Disorder in the New Republic* (Boston: Little, Brown, 1971), pp. 57–108; Davis, "Movement to Abolish Capital Punishment."

Chapter 5. *In Defense of the Gallows*

1. Thomas Dunn English, "The Gallows-Goers," quoted in Philip English Mackey, *Hanging in the Balance: The Anti–Capital Punishment Movement in New York State, 1776–1861* (New York: Garland, 1982), pp. 184–85. Another version of this chapter has appeared as Daniel A. Cohen, "In Defense of the Gallows: Justifications of Capital Punishment in New England Execution Sermons, 1674–1825," *American Quarterly* 40 (June 1988): 147–64. My thanks to the editor of *American Quarterly* for permission to use material here that has already appeared in his journal.

2. For example, such perceptions are indicated in Peres Fobes, *The Paradise of God* (Providence: B. Wheeler, [1784]), "Appendix," p. 1.

3. Increase Mather, *A Sermon Occasioned by the Execution of a Man* (Boston: J. Brunning, 1686), pp. 1, 4, and 17. For biographical treatments of Increase Mather, see *Sibley*, vol. 1, pp. 410–70; Robert Middlekauff, *The Mathers: Three Generations of Puritan Intellectuals, 1596–1728* (New York: Oxford University Press, 1971), pp. 77–187.

4. S[amuel] D[anforth], *The Cry of Sodom Enquired Into* (Cambridge, Mass.: M. Johnson, 1674), p. 8. For a biographical sketch of Danforth, see *Sibley*, vol. 1, pp. 88–92.

5. On the efforts of religious reformers in England, see George Lee Haskins, *Law and Authority in Early Massachusetts* (New York: Macmillan, 1960), p. 145; Barbara Shapiro, "Law Reform in Seventeenth Century England," *American Journal of Legal History* 19 (Oct. 1975): 290, 296–97, and 311; Kathryn Preyer, "Penal Measures in the American Colonies: An Overview," *American Journal of Legal History* 26 (Oct. 1982): 332. On the early capital codes in Massachusetts, see Haskins, *Law and Authority*, pp. 145–54; Edwin Powers, *Crime and Punishment in Early Massachusetts 1620–1692* (Boston: Beacon Press, 1966), pp. 252–72; and Preyer, "Penal Measures," pp. 332–33.

6. See Haskins, *Law and Authority*, pp. 145–47; Powers, *Crime and Punishment*, pp. 254–69.

7. See Haskins, *Law and Authority*, pp. 147–52; Powers, *Crime and Punishment*, pp. 252–53.

8. Danforth, *Cry of Sodom*, pp. 8–9.

9. Ibid., pp. 8–9. On the Puritan jeremiad, see Perry Miller, *Errand into the Wilderness* (Cambridge: Harvard University Press, 1956), pp. 1–15; David Minter, "The Puritan Jeremiad as a Literary Form," in Sacvan Bercovitch, ed., *The American Puritan Imagination* (London: Cambridge University Press, 1974), pp. 45–55; Sacvan Bercovitch, *The American Jeremiad* (Madison: University of Wisconsin Press, 1978), pp. xi–92; Harry S. Stout, *The New England Soul: Preaching and Religious Culture in Colonial New England* (New York: Oxford University Press, 1986), pp. 62–63, 74–82, 108–11, 142–44, and passim.

10. I. Mather, *The Wicked Man's Portion* (Boston: J. Foster, 1675), p. 12.

11. For sermon texts condemning capital crimes, see Eliphalet Adams, *A Sermon* (New London: T. Green, 1738), p. 1; Charles Chauncy, *The Horrid Nature and Enormous Guilt of Murder* (Boston: T. Fleet, 1754), p. 5; Timothy Pitkin, *A Sermon Preached at Litchfield* (Hartford: Green and Watson, 1768), p. [3].

12. See Benjamin Colman, *The Hainous Nature of the Sin of Murder* (Boston: J. Allen, 1713) [published in volume with Cotton Mather, *The Sad Effects of Sin*], p. 14; Samuel Checkley, *Murder a Great and Crying Sin* (Boston: T. Fleet, 1733), pp. 14–15; Chauncy, *Horrid Nature*, p. 21.

13. On the early Enlightenment's love of balance, see David Lundberg and Henry F. May, "The Enlightened Reader in America," *American Quarterly* 28 (Summer 1976): 265; Henry F. May, *The Enlightenment in America* (New York: Oxford University Press, 1976), pp. 1–101. For biographical treatments of Colman, Checkley, and Chauncy, see *Sibley*, vol. 5, pp. 120–37; vol. 6, pp. 74–78 and 439–67; Charles Burke Giles, "Benjamin Colman: A Study of the Movement Toward Reasonable Religion in the 17th Century" (Ph.D. diss., University of California, 1963); Edward M. Griffin, *Old Brick: Charles Chauncy of Boston, 1705–1787* (Minneapolis: University of Minnesota Press, 1980); Charles H. Lippy, *Seasonable Revolutionary: The Mind of Charles*

Chauncy (Chicago: Nelson-Hall, 1981). Similar arguments also appear in Nathaniel Clap, *Sinners Directed to Hear & Fear* (Boston: J. Allen for N. Boone, 1715), pp. 39–40.

14. Colman, *Hainous Nature*, p. 14; Checkley, *Murder*, pp. 14–16; Chauncy, *Horrid Nature*, p. 17.

15. See Colman, *Hainous Nature*, pp. 6–14; Checkley, *Murder*, pp. 8, 14–15, and 23; Chauncy, *Horrid Nature*, pp. 5, 10, 16–17, and 21.

16. Colman, *Hainous Nature*, p. 13; Checkley, *Murder*, p. 3; Chauncy, *Horrid Nature*, p. 12. Similar arguments had appeared earlier in I. Mather, *Sermon*, pp. 9–11.

17. Colman, *Hainous Nature*, pp. 10–11; Checkley, *Murder*, pp. 14–16; Chauncy, *Horrid Nature*, pp. 14–15 and 21.

18. See Powers, *Crime and Punishment*, pp. 269–72 and 303–8; Preyer, "Penal Measures," pp. 333–34, 342, and 348.

19. On the process of anglicization, see John M. Murrin, "Anglicizing an American Colony" (Ph.D. diss., Yale University, 1966).

20. *The Charters and General Laws of the Colony and Province of Massachusetts Bay* (Boston: T. B. Wait, 1814), pp. 239, 392–93, and 406–7; Powers, *Crime and Punishment*, pp. 303–8; Preyer, "Penal Measures," p. 342.

21. The emergence of a secular component in the ministers' arguments within execution discourses was also paralleled by the introduction in New England of more secular crime genres independent of the sermon form, such as trial reports and last-speech broadsides.

22. On the gradual demise of Calvinist theocentrism in eighteenth-century New England, see Joseph Haroutunian, *Piety Versus Moralism: The Passing of the New England Theology* (New York: Henry Holt, 1932), pp. 30–42, 86–87, 145, and passim.

23. On opposition to the execution of burglars, see above in this chapter; see also *Theft and Murder! A Poem* ([Boston]: [1773]), broadside.

24. For examples of the new secular orientation not included in the discussion here, see James Diman, *A Sermon* (Salem, Mass.: S. and E. Hall, 1772), p. 7 [execution for rape]; James Dana, *The Intent of Capital Punishment* (New Haven: T. and S. Green, [1790]), pp. 5–13 [rape]; Aaron Bancroft, *The Importance of a Religious Education* (Worcester: I. Thomas, 1793), pp. 22–23 [murder].

25. For a biographical sketch of Noah Hobart, see *Sibley*, vol. 7, pp. 359–68, quoted at 359.

26. On Frasier's crime spree, see *Account of the Life and Abominable Thefts of Isaac Frazier* (New Haven: S. Green, 1768).

27. See Noah Hobart, *Excessive Wickedness, the Way to an Untimely Death* (New Haven: T. and S. Green, [1768]), pp. 13–14 and 19.

28. See Hobart, *Excessive Wickedness*, p. 14.

29. Hobart, *Excessive Wickedness*, pp. 6 and 12.

30. Ibid., p. 13.

31. On Hobart as a leading voice of "Connecticut orthodoxy," see *Sibley*, vol. 7, p. 366.

32. Fobes, *Paradise*, "Appendix," p. 1, emphasis added. For a biographical sketch of Fobes, see *Sibley*, vol. 15, pp. 229–35.

33. Fobes, *Paradise*, "Appendix," pp. 2–7.

34. Ibid., "Appendix," pp. 7–8.

35. Ibid., "Appendix," pp. 11–12.

36. On the deployment of a sheriff's guard at the execution of Bly and Rose, see

Worcester Magazine, 2d week of December 1787, p. 139; on the broader historical context within which the execution took place, see David P. Szatmary, *Shays' Rebellion: The Making of an Agrarian Insurrection* (Amherst: University of Massachusetts Press, 1980), especially pp. 91–119. A sizeable sheriff's guard was also deployed at the execution of Dixson; see Fobes, *Paradise*, p. 26.

37. Stephen West, *A Sermon . . . at the Execution of John Bly, and Charles Rose* (Pittsfield, Mass.: E. Russell, 1787), pp. 4–8. For a biographical sketch of West, see *Dexter*, vol. 2, pp. 388–94.

38. On West's adherence to Hopkinsianism, see *Dexter*, vol. 2, p. 389. On the broad shift in New England theology, see Haroutunian, *Piety*, pp. 30–42, 86–87, 145, and passim.

39. West, *Sermon*, p. 6.

40. See William E. Nelson, "Emerging Notions of Modern Criminal Law in the Revolutionary Era: An Historical Perspective," *New York University Law Review* 42 (May 1967): 450–82; William E. Nelson, *Americanization of the Common Law* (Cambridge: Harvard University Press, 1975), pp. 117–21; David H. Flaherty, "Law and the Enforcement of Morals in Early America," *Perspectives in American History* 5 (1971): 245–48, quoted at 248; Michael Stephen Hindus, *Prison and Plantation: Crime, Justice, and Authority in Massachusetts and South Carolina, 1767–1878* (Chapel Hill: University of North Carolina Press, 1980), pp. 67–69; Richard Gaskins, "Changes in the Criminal Law in Eighteenth-Century Connecticut," *American Journal of Legal History* 25 (Oct. 1981): 309–11 and passim.

41. On one minister's weakening faith in the scriptural defense, see discussion of Fobes sermon in text above; on another's loss of faith in the effectiveness of capital punishment as a deterrent, see Thomas Baldwin, *The Danger of Living Without the Fear of God* (Boston: J. Loring, [1819]), p. 17.

42. See discussion of Welch sermon in text below; for the legal-procedural defense in a sermon on another such case—that of Jason Fairbanks—see Thomas Thacher, *The Danger of Despising the Divine Counsel* (Dedham: H. Mann, 1802), pp. 17–24, particularly 20 and 24.

43. Elements of the new defense had appeared earlier, in embryonic form, in Thaddeus MacCarty, *The Guilt of Innocent Blood Put Away* (Worcester: I. Thomas, 1778), p. 16; Fobes, *Paradise*, p. 8.

44. Enoch Huntington, *A Sermon* (Middletown, Conn.: M. H. Woodward, [1797]), pp. 15 and 17, emphasis added. For a biographical sketch of Huntington, see *Dexter*, vol. 2, pp. 594–97.

45. S[amuel] Blatchford, "Address," in Timothy Langdon, *A Sermon* (Danbury, Conn.: Douglas & Nichols, 1798), pp. 20–22. For a biographical sketch of Blatchford, see Samuel Orcutt, *A History of the Old Town of Stratford and the City of Bridgeport Connecticut* (New Haven: Fairfield County Historical Society, 1886), vol. 1, pp. 630–31.

46. Moses C. Welch, *The Gospel to Be Preached to All Men* (Windham, Conn.: J. Byrne, 1805), p. 16. For a biographical sketch of Welch, see *Dexter*, vol. 3, pp. 459–63.

47. On the increasingly law-oriented culture of America's early republic, see Alexis de Tocqueville, *Democracy in America*, ed. Richard D. Heffner (New York: Mentor, 1956), pp. 123–28; Perry Miller, *The Life of the Mind in America* (New York: Harcourt, Brace & World, 1965), pp. 96–265; Maxwell Bloomfield, *American Lawyers in a Changing Society, 1776–1876* (Cambridge: Harvard University Press, 1976), pp. 57–58; Gerard W. Gawalt, *The Promise of Power: The Emergence of the Legal Profes-*

sion in Massachusetts, 1760–1840 (Westport, Conn.: Greenwood Press, 1979), pp. 5, 117–18, and passim; Robert A. Ferguson, *Law and Letters in American Culture* (Cambridge: Harvard University Press, 1984), pp. 11–15 and 20; also, on increasing litigiousness in the early republic, see William E. Nelson, *Dispute and Conflict Resolution in Plymouth County, Massachusetts, 1725–1825* (Chapel Hill: University of North Carolina Press, 1981), pp. 76–152.

48. Several reports of criminal trials, particularly of piracy cases, were issued in New England during the eighteenth century; however, the trial-report genre does not seem to have become popular in the region until the first decade of the nineteenth century. For an early example of the newly popularized form, see *Report of the Trial of Jason Fairbanks*, 4th ed. (Boston: Russell and Cutler, 1801). Note the edition number as an indication of the new genre's public reception; clearly, lawyers could not have been the primary purchasers of so many editions of a single report.

49. On antigallows sentiment and penal reform in the early national period, see David J. Rothman, *The Discovery of the Asylum: Social Order and Disorder in the New Republic* (Boston: Little, Brown, 1971), pp. 57–62; Philip English Mackey, *Voices Against Death: American Opposition to Capital Punishment, 1787–1975* (New York: Burt Franklin, 1976), pp. xiv–xviii; Mackey, *Hanging*, pp. 36–97; Adam J. Hirsch, "From Pillory to Penitentiary: The Rise of Criminal Incarceration in Early Massachusetts," *Michigan Law Review* 80 (May 1982): 1246–62 and passim; Louis P. Masur, "The Culture of Executions and the Conflict over Capital Punishment in America, 1776–1860" (Ph.D. diss., Princeton University, 1985), pp. 57–148; Louis P. Masur, *Rites of Execution: Capital Punishment and the Transformation of American Culture, 1776–1865* (New York: Oxford University Press, 1989).

50. David Sutherland, *A Sermon . . . at the Execution* (Hanover, N.H.: M. Davis, 1806), pp. 5–6; William Andrews, *A Sermon* (New Haven: T. G. Woodward, 1817), p. 9; Charles Lowell, *A Discourse* (Boston: J. Eliot, 1817), p. [3]; Baldwin, *Danger*, p. 11.

51. Jonathan Going, *A Discourse Delivered at Worcester* (Worcester: W. Manning, 1825), p. 11. For a biographical sketch of Jonathan Going, see William Lincoln, *History of Worcester, Massachusetts* (Worcester: C. Hersey, 1862), pp. 178–79.

52. On clerical opposition to the movement for abolition of the death penalty, see Mackey, *Voices*, pp. xxiii–xxiv; Mackey, *Hanging*, pp. 125, 145, 154–63, 214–17, 280, 318, and passim; Masur, "Culture of Executions," pp. 234–44 and passim; Masur, *Rites of Execution*, pp. 141–59, passim. For detailed accounts of the abolition movement of the 1830s through 1850s, see David Brion Davis, "The Movement to Abolish Capital Punishment in America, 1787–1861," *American Historical Review* 63 (Oct. 1957): 29–46; Mackey, *Hanging*, pp. 112–319; Masur, "Culture of Executions," pp. 196–264; Masur, *Rites of Execution*, pp. 3–24 and 93–163. It should be noted that the movement for abolition of the death penalty was largely led by ministers of the unorthodox Universalist, Unitarian, and Quaker denominations; see Mackey, *Voices*, p. xxiii; Mackey, *Hanging*, pp. 214–16 and 318.

53. See William I. Budington, *Capital Punishment* (Boston: T. R. Marvin, 1843), pp. 7–11; Mackey, *Voices*, xxiii–xxiv; Mackey, *Hanging*, pp. 95 (fn. 16) and 156; Masur, "Culture of Executions," p. 237; Masur, *Rites of Execution*, pp. 147–48; for a rather different emphasis, see Davis, "Movement," pp. 38–40.

54. See Mackey, *Voices*, pp. xxiii–xxiv; Mackey, *Hanging*, pp. 95 (fn. 16), 136, and passim; Masur, "Culture of Executions," p. 230; Masur, *Rites of Execution*, pp. 142–43.

55. On the influence of revivalism, see Mackey, *Hanging*, p. 95 fn. 16. On the "bibliolatry" of nineteenth-century New England Calvinism, see Haroutunian, *Piety*, pp. 186–87.

56. On the transformation of the public role of New England clergymen, see Donald M. Scott, *From Office to Profession: The New England Ministry, 1750–1850* (Philadelphia: University of Pennsylvania Press, 1978), pp. 1–17, 148–55, and passim. Note particularly Scott's conclusion on p. 151: "The recovery of a clerical public voice in the 1850s built upon the distinction between the political and moral spheres of public culture. In the eighteenth century, the clergy had articulated the nature of public . . . authority. . . . [But by the 1850s, the] role of religion in sustaining the broader public culture consisted in laying out the Christian dimensions of public issues." On the clergy's self-image as scriptural specialists, see Mackey, *Hanging*, pp. 154–55.

57. For the clerical criticisms of public hangings, see Thacher, *Danger*, pp. 24–26; Going, *Discourse*, p. 11; on the abolition of such hangings, see Masur, *Rites of Execution*, pp. 93–116 (cites Going criticism of public hangings on p. 96); Mackey, *Voices*, pp. xx–xxi; Masur, "Culture of Executions," pp. 149–95. For an address, published outside of New England, that might be considered an execution sermon of sorts and that does implicitly condemn the death penalty, see Orestes A. Brownson, *An Address, Prepared at the Request of Guy C. Clark* (Ithaca, N.Y.: S. S. Chatterton, 1832).

Chapter 6. *A Fellowship of Thieves*

1. Those popular antiauthoritarian narratives will be examined at length in chapter 7 below. Another version of this chapter has been published as Daniel A. Cohen, "A Fellowship of Thieves: Property Criminals in Eighteenth-Century Massachusetts," *Journal of Social History* 22 (Fall 1988): 65–92. My thanks to the editor of the *Journal of Social History* for permission to use material here that has already appeared in his journal.

2. Those generalizations about the social status of executed criminals are based on my reading of all extant crime publications issued in New England between 1674 and 1800.

3. This chapter will be examining the property crimes of robbery, burglary, and larceny (or simple theft); it will not deal with such offenses as fraud, forgery, counterfeiting, and arson.

4. *The Charters and General Laws of the Colony and Province of Massachusetts Bay* (Boston: T. B. Wait, 1814), p. 56; Nathaniel B. Shurtleff, ed., *Records of the Governor and Company of the Massachusetts Bay in New England* (Boston: W. White, 1854), vol. 3, p. 244; vol. 4, p. 82; Carl Bridenbaugh, *Cities in the Wilderness: The First Century of Urban Life in America 1625–1742* (1938; rpt. New York: Oxford University Press, 1971), pp. 69–70.

5. Bridenbaugh, *Cities in the Wilderness*, pp. 69–73 and 220–21; David H. Flaherty, "Law and the Enforcement of Morals in Early America," *Perspectives in American History* 5 (1971): 235–36.

6. See SC, Recs., 1700–14, fols. 278v–279r.

7. Cotton Mather, *A True Survey & Report of the Road* (Boston: B. Green, 1712); C. Mather, *A Flying Roll* (Boston: B. Green, 1713); William R. Manierre II, ed., *The Diary of Cotton Mather D.D., F.R.S. for the Year 1712* (Charlottesville: University Press of Virginia, 1964), pp. 48–49 and 55. Mather's sermons on theft cited in Eli

Faber, "The Evil That Men Do: Crime and Transgression in Colonial Massachusetts" (Ph.D. diss., Columbia University, 1974), p. 35 n. 1; one also cited in Kenneth Silverman, *The Life and Times of Cotton Mather* (New York: Harper & Row, 1984), p. 452. Although it would otherwise appear quite likely that the group of thieves referred to in Mather's *Diary* was the same group tried before the Superior Court in November 1712 (see note 6), there is a problem with dates; Mather noted the arrest of the gang on July 6, but the last of the burglaries for which two of the thieves were indicted in November was not committed until July 10.

8. *A Report of the Record Commissioners of the City of Boston, Containing the Records of Boston Selectmen, 1701 to 1715* (Boston: Rockwell and Churchill, 1884), p. 221; Bridenbaugh, *Cities in the Wilderness*, p. 221.

9. *Charters and General Laws*, pp. 406–7.

10. Ibid., pp. 435, 509–10, 644, and 668–69.

11. See Adam J. Hirsch, "From Pillory to Penitentiary: The Rise of Criminal Incarceration in Early Massachusetts," *Michigan Law Review* 80 (1982): 1244–47.

12. *Boston Post-Boy & Advertiser* [cited hereafter as *Post-Boy*], Dec. 5, 1763, p. 2; Nov. 12, 1764, p. 3; Dec. 10, 1764, p. 3; Dec. 24, 1764, p. 2; Jan. 7, 1765, p. 3; Jan. 14, 1765, p. 3; Jan. 21, 1765, p. 3; Feb. 11, 1765, p. 2; and Feb. 18, 1765, p. 3; Dec. 7, 1767, p. 3; *Massachusetts Gazette and Boston News-Letter* [continuation of the *Boston News-Letter*, cited hereafter as *News-Letter*], March 10, 1768, p. 2; Jan. 4, 1770, p. 3; July 30, 1772, pp. 2 and 4 (advertisements); Aug. 13, 1772, p. 2; Bridenbaugh, *Cities in Revolt: Urban Life in America, 1743–1776* (1955; rpt. London: Oxford University Press, 1971), pp. 299–301; Hirsch, "From Pillory to Penitentiary," pp. 1229–31 and 1244–46. On the higher incidence of property crime during the winter months, see *Post-Boy*, Dec. 7, 1767, p. 3.

13. [Thomas Hutchinson], "Charge to the Grand Jury," in Josiah Quincy, *Reports of Cases Argued and Adjudged in the Superior Court of Judicature of the Province of Massachusetts Bay, Between 1761 and 1772* (Boston: Little, Brown, 1865), p. 223; [Thomas Hutchinson], "The Charge Given to the Grand Jury," in Quincy, *Reports of Cases*, p. 261; [Thomas Hutchinson], "A Message from His Honor the Lieutenant Governor," in *Journals of the House of Representatives of Massachusetts, 1770* (Boston: Massachusetts Historical Society, 1977), p. 108. Cited in Hirsch, "From Pillory to Penitentiary," p. 1229 n. 254; p. 1246 n. 340.

14. See Louis P. Masur, *Rites of Execution: Capital Punishment and the Transformation of American Culture, 1776–1865* (New York: Oxford University Press, 1989), pp. 59–60; Linda Kealey, "Patterns of Punishment: Massachusetts in the Eighteenth Century," *American Journal of Legal History* 30 (April 1986): 169; Hirsch, "From Pillory to Penitentiary," pp. 1229–31; Kealey, "Crime and Society in Massachusetts in the Second Half of the Eighteenth Century" (Ph.D. diss., University of Toronto, 1981), pp. v, 142, 199, 366–67, 372, 377, and 410.

15. *The Boston Gazette and the Country Journal* [cited hereafter as *Boston Gazette*], Oct. 20, 1783, p. 2; May 17, 1784, p. 3; May 24, 1784, p. 2; Sept. 27, 1784, p. 3; March 14, 1785, p. 3; *The Massachusetts Centinel and the Republican Journal* [cited hereafter as *Massachusetts Centinel*], Oct. 16, 1784, p. 1; SC, Recs., 1778–80, fol. 184; SJC, Recs., 1781–82, fol. 84; 1783, fols. 30–31 and 82–83; 1784, fols. 50–51, 88, 185, 227, 230–32, 263–264, 274, 316, 338–39, and 375.

16. The five executed offenders were Dirick Grout and Francis Coven (executed Oct. 28, 1784); John Dixson (Nov. 11, 1784); and Richard Barrick and John Sullivan (Nov. 18, 1784).

17. See Kealey, "Patterns of Punishment," p. 169; Kealey, "Crime and Society," pp. 142, 199, 367, 372, 377, and 410.

18. *Boston Gazette*, Feb. 6, 1797, p. 3; Feb. 13, 1797, p. 3; Feb. 20, 1797, p. 3; Feb. 27, 1797, pp. 1–3; March 6, 1797, pp. 2–3; March 13, 1797, p. 3; March 20, 1797, p. 3; April 3, 1797, p. 3; John Lathrop, *God Our Protector and Refuge in Danger and Trouble* (Boston: Manning & Loring, 1797), passim, quoted at pp. 28–29.

19. For an earlier eighteenth-century expression of fear of the strolling poor, see C. Mather, *Flying Roll*, p. 12. For scholarly discussions of the phenomenon of transiency in England during the sixteenth and seventeenth centuries, see A. L. Beier, *Masterless Men: The Vagrancy Problem in England 1560–1640* (London: Methuen, 1985); John H. Langbein, "The Historical Origins of the Sanction of Imprisonment for Serious Crime," *Journal of Legal Studies* 5 (Jan. 1976): 45–47; A. L. Beier, "Vagrants and the Social Order in Elizabethan England," *Past and Present*, no. 64 (Aug. 1974): 3–29; Paul A. Slack, "Vagrants and Vagrancy in England, 1598–1664," *Economic History Review*, 2d ser., 27 (Aug. 1974): 360–79. For scholarly discussions of the new era of penal reform, see Masur, *Rites of Execution*; Philip English Mackey, *Hanging in the Balance: The Anti–Capital Punishment Movement in New York State, 1776–1861* (New York: Garland, 1982); David J. Rothman, *The Discovery of the Asylum: Social Order and Disorder in the New Republic* (Boston: Little, Brown, 1971).

20. See Bridenbaugh, *Cities in the Wilderness*, pp. 68–78, 220–31, and 379–91; Bridenbaugh, *Cities in Revolt*, pp. 107–22 and 299–305.

21. See David H. Flaherty, "Crime and Social Control in Provincial Massachusetts," *Historical Journal* 24 (June 1981): 339–60, passim, quoted at 356.

22. See Masur, *Rites of Execution*, pp. 59–60; N. E. H. Hull, *Female Felons: Women and Serious Crime in Colonial Massachusetts* (Urbana: University of Illinois Press, 1987), appendix 3; Kealey, "Patterns of Punishment," p. 169; Hirsch, "From Pillory to Penitentiary," pp. 1228–35 and 1246; Kealey, "Crime and Society," pp. v, 142, 199, 367, 372, 377, and 410.

23. See James A. Henretta and Gregory H. Nobles, *Evolution and Revolution: American Society, 1600–1820* (Lexington, Mass.: D. C. Heath, 1987), p. 72; Hull, *Female Felons*, pp. 157–61; Gary B. Nash, *The Urban Crucible: Social Change, Political Consciousness, and the Origins of the American Revolution* (Cambridge: Harvard University Press, 1979), pp. 253–56, 325–38, and passim; Douglas Lamar Jones, "The Strolling Poor: Transiency in Eighteenth-Century Massachusetts," *Journal of Social History* 8 (Spring 1975): 28–54; and Allan Kulikoff, "The Progress of Inequality in Revolutionary Boston," *William and Mary Quarterly*, 3d ser., 28 (July 1971): 375–412.

24. See Hull, *Female Felons*, pp. 158–60.

25. On the rationalization of settlement and poor-relief laws during the 1790s, see Jones, "Strolling Poor," pp. 48–49.

26. On property crime in nineteenth-century American cities, see David R. Johnson, *Policing the Urban Underworld: The Impact of Crime on the Development of the American Police, 1800–1887* (Philadelphia: Temple University Press, 1979), pp. 12, 15–16, 41–89, and passim. For a somewhat different view, see Roger Lane, *Policing the City: Boston, 1822–1885* (New York: Atheneum, 1971), pp. 6, 54–57, 142–145, and passim; Roger Lane, "Crime and Criminal Statistics in Nineteenth-Century Massachusetts," *Journal of Social History* 2 (Winter 1968): 156–63. The application of the terms *epidemic* and *endemic* to patterns of property crime in eighteenth- and nineteenth-century Massachusetts was suggested to me by James A. Henretta. Given the paucity of scholarship on American property crime during the period 1800–30, any conclusions

concerning the transition from eighteenth- to nineteenth-century patterns must be highly speculative.

27. *Charters and General Laws*, p. 56.

28. For citations of eighteenth-century Massachusetts execution broadsides, see *Ritz*, pp. 192–220, passim.

29. See Peter Linebaugh, "The Ordinary of Newgate and His *Account*," in J. S. Cockburn, ed., *Crime in England, 1550–1800* (Princeton: Princeton University Press, 1977), pp. 246–69; Peter Linebaugh, "Tyburn: A Study of Crime and the Labouring Poor in London During the First Half of the Eighteenth Century" (Ph.D. diss., University of Warwick, 1975), pp. 256–325; John H. Langbein, *Prosecuting Crime in the Renaissance* (Cambridge: Harvard University Press, 1974), pp. 45–47; and A. D. J. MacFarlane, *Witchcraft in Tudor and Stuart England* (New York: Harper & Row, 1970), p. 85.

30. That claim is based on my own study of the early records and files of the Massachusetts Superior Court of Judicature and of its successor, the Supreme Judicial Court. I have located court files or entries in the court records for crimes referred to in the last speeches or other autobiographical narratives of all but one of the twenty-five property criminals in my sample; for citations to many of those, see passim in notes below.

31. For a more complete discussion of execution broadsides and related genres, see chapter 1 above. For more skeptical assessments of the reliability of last-speech broadsides and similar pamphlets as social-historical sources, see Masur, *Rites of Execution*, pp. 33–34; Faber, "The Evil That Men Do," pp. 241–46.

32. William Welch, *The Last Speech & Dying Words* ([Boston]: [1754]); William Linsey, *The Dying Speech and Confession* (Boston: 1770).

33. See, for example, Matthew Cushing, *The Declaration & Confession* ([Boston]: [1734]); Welch, *Last Speech*, quoted; Isaac Frasier, *A Brief Account of the Life and Abominable Thefts* (New London: T. Green, [1768]), p. 3; Johnson Green, *The Life and Confession* (Worcester: [I. Thomas], [1786]).

34. John Sheehan, *Life, Last Words and Dying Speech* (Boston: E. Russell, [1787]; Rachel Wall, *Life, Last Words and Dying Confession* ([Boston]: [1789]).

35. Burglars and robbers probably represented about 40 percent of all men and women hanged in Massachusetts between 1730 and 1799; that crude estimate is based largely on data obtained from M. Watt Espy and John Ortiz Smykla, *Executions in the United States, 1608–1987: The Espy File* (Ann Arbor, Mich.: ICPSR, 1988–89); I am grateful to Patterson Smith for providing the relevant data.

36. The broadsides are Matthew Cushing, *The Declaration & Confession* ([Boston]: [1734]); Hugh Henderson, *The Confession and Dying Warning* (Boston: [Kneeland & Green], [1737]); William Welch, *The Last Speech & Dying Words* ([Boston]: [1754]); John Shearman, *The Last Words and Dying Speech* (Boston: R. and S. Draper, [1764]); Joseph Lightly, *The Last Words and Dying Speech* ([Boston], [1765]); Arthur, a Negro Man [*sic*], *The Life, and Dying Speech* (Boston: [1768]); William Linsey, *The Dying Speech and Confession* (Boston: 1770); Levi Ames, *The Last Words and Dying Speech* (Boston, [1773]); Daniel Wilson, *The Life and Confession* ([Providence?]: [1774]); William Huggins and John Mansfield, *The Last Words* (Worcester: [I. Thomas], [1783]); Dirick Grout and Francis Coven, *The Life, Last Words and Dying Speech* ([Boston?]: [1784]); Johnson Green, *The Life and Confession* (Worcester: [I. Thomas], [1786]); John Sheehan, *Life, Last Words and Dying Speech* (Boston: E. Russell, [1787]); Rachel Wall, *Life, Last Words and Dying Confession* ([Boston]: [1789]); John Bailey, *Life, Last*

Words and Dying Confession (Boston: E. Russell, [1790]); John Stewart, *The Confession, Last Words, and Dying Speech* ([Boston]: [1797]); Stephen Smith, *Life, Last Words and Dying Speech* ([Boston], [1797]); Samuel Smith, *Last Words and Dying Speech* (Concord: R. Bryant, [1799]). The longer narratives are Isaac Frasier [or Frazier], *A Brief Account of the Life, and Abominable Thefts* (New London: T. Green, [1768]); Richard Barrick and John Sullivan, *The Lives and Dying Confessions* (Worcester: [1784]); Thomas Mount, *The Confession* (Portsmouth: J. Melcher, [1791]); Henry Tufts, *A Narrative of the Life, Adventures, Travels and Sufferings* (Dover, N.H.: S. Bragg, Jun., 1807). All of the above works are cited hereafter by the criminal's name only. The sample includes two men executed for rape and two executed for murder; however, all four of those offenders had also committed property crimes; for a list of the twenty-five thieves, see table in text.

37. This table is drawn from the publications cited in note 36 above. The birthplace and year of birth of John Shearman were drawn from his examination, March 1, 1764, Ct. Files, no. 100375, paper 15; on the unreliability of Shearman's testimony, see note 40 below. Although Joseph Lightly's *Last Words* claimed that he had been born in 1739, a contemporary newspaper report said that he gave a birthdate of 1736; however, both accounts gave his birthplace as Newcastle, England. The newspaper report also suggested that the name Joseph Lightly was an alias; see *Boston Evening-Post*, Nov. 25, 1765, p. 3. Another newspaper lists his birthdate as 1739, suggesting that the *Post*'s report may simply be a misprint; see *Massachusetts Gazette*, Nov. 21, 1765, p. 3. The names Huggins and Mansfield were also aliases. On Stephen Smith's year of birth, see note 49 below.

38. See J. A. Sharpe, *Crime in Early Modern England 1550–1750* (London: Longman, 1984), pp. 108–9; Sharpe, *Crime in Seventeenth-Century England* (Cambridge, Eng.: Cambridge University Press, 1983), pp. 107–8; Julius R. Ruff, *Crime, Justice and Public Order in Old Regime France* (London: Croom Helm, 1984), pp. 132–33; and Antoinette Wills, *Crime and Punishment in Revolutionary Paris* (Westport, Conn.: Greenwood Press, 1981), pp. 110 and 113–15. The preponderance of men in their twenties is even more striking in the Massachusetts sample than it is in the European studies.

39. Ames.

40. It should be noted, however, that John Shearman's claim to have been born in Rochester, Massachusetts, is suspect because it was made in the context of other testimony about his identity that was false; see the examination of John Shearman, March 1, 1764, Ct. Files, no. 100375, paper 15. Some support for Shearman's claim may be found in the vital records of Rochester, Massachusetts, which list the birth of one "John Sherman" on July 27, 1721; see *Vital Records of Rochester, Massachusetts*, 2 vols. (Boston: New England Historic Genealogical Society, 1914), vol. 1, p. 266. For the birthplaces of the other criminals in the sample, see the various publications listed in note 36 above.

41. On the "wider criminal underworld" of the second half of the eighteenth century, see Bridenbaugh, *Cities in Revolt*, p. 300.

42. The four blacks were Arthur, Johnson Green, John Bailey, and Stephen Smith; the Irishmen were Matthew Cushing, Hugh Henderson, William Welch, Richard Barrick, John Sullivan, John Sheehan, and John Stewart. The approximate percentage of blacks in the population of Massachusetts during the last two-thirds of the eighteenth century fluctuated between 1.2 and 2.2 percent; see Lorenzo Johnston Greene, *The Negro in Colonial New England* (New York: Atheneum, 1971), p. 81. The percent-

age of Irish in the population of Massachusetts in 1790 has been estimated at 3.9 percent; see Richard B. Morris, ed., *Encyclopedia of American History*, enlarged and updated (New York: Harper & Row, 1970), p. 470. Those percentages for both blacks and Irish are obviously much lower than their representation in the sample of thieves, 16 percent of whom were black and 28 percent of whom were Irish.

43. On economic discrimination against blacks in colonial New England, see Greene, *Negro in Colonial New England*, pp. 304 and 332. For a recent assessment of discrimination against blacks in the court system of colonial Massachusetts, see Hull, *Female Felons*, pp. 106–7.

44. For a provocative discussion of negative stereotypes of blacks in early New England crime literature, see Richard Slotkin, "Narratives of Negro Crime in New England, 1675–1800," *American Quarterly* 25 (March 1973): 3–31; on negative images of the Irish, see ibid., p. 27. On the perceived association of blacks with property crime in late eighteenth-century Philadelphia, see G. S. Rowe, "Black Offenders, Criminal Courts, and Philadelphia Society in the Late Eighteenth Century," *Journal of Social History* 22 (Summer 1989): 685–712, passim. On the association of blacks and Irish with criminality in nineteenth-century Boston, see Oscar Handlin, *Boston's Immigrants*, rev. and enlarged ed. (New York: Atheneum, 1975), p. 121.

45. *Boston News-Letter*, quoted in Charles E. Clark, "The Public Prints: The Origins of the Anglo-American Newspaper, 1665–1750" (unpublished manuscript, University of New Hampshire, ca. 1989), pp. 35–36.

46. See William Andrews, *A Sermon, Delivered at Danbury* (New Haven: T. G. Woodward, 1817), pp. 14–15, quoted at 14.

47. See Barrick and Sullivan, p. [3].

48. Welch; Barrick and Sullivan, pp. [3]–4; also see Henderson.

49. Frasier, pp. 3–4; Steven Smith. Although Smith's last speech implies that he had been born in 1769 or 1770, local parish records suggest that he was actually born several years earlier, in 1764; see Gertrude R. B. Richards, ed., *Register of Albermarle Parish, Surry and Sussex Counties 1739–1778* (Richmond: National Society of Colonial Dames of America in the Commonwealth of Virginia, 1953), p. 349. I am grateful to Kevin P. Kelly for bringing that citation to my attention.

50. Ames; Huggins and Mansfield; Grout and Coven.

51. See Cushing; Lightly; Sheehan; Stewart; Linsey; Green; Samuel Smith; Grout and Coven; Tufts, pp. [9]–11; Huggins and Mansfield; Wall; Bailey.

52. Cushing; Arthur; Wall; Mount, p. [3]; Stewart. For other early turns to crime, see Tufts, pp. 10–15; Ames; Green.

53. Wilson; Stewart; for other examples of the corrupting influence of associates, see Cushing; Bailey.

54. For a somewhat similar view of the motives of British offenders, see John H. Langbein, "*Albion's* Fatal Flaws," *Past and Present*, no. 98 (Feb. 1983): 100.

55. Lightly.

56. Grout and Coven; Green; Huggins and Mansfield.

57. For an exception, see Mount, p. 4.

58. Lightly; SC, Recs., 1764–65, fol. 342; Ct. Files, nos. 147270 and 147371; *Post-Boy*, Feb. 11, 1765, p. 2.

59. Grout and Coven; SJC, Recs., 1784, fol. 230; Ct. Files, no. 103472, no. 106011, papers 25–27; *Boston Gazette*, Nov. 1, 1784, p. 3. The precise chronological relationship of Grout's search for employment and his criminal activities is not entirely clear.

60. Huggins and Mansfield.

61. Ibid.

62. Ibid.; SJC, Recs., 1783, fols. 82v–83; Ct. Files, no. 153329; *Boston Gazette*, June 23, 1783, p. 3.

63. SC, Recs., 1753–54, fol. 185 (Welch).

64. See Peter Lawson, "Property Crime and Hard Times in England, 1559–1624," *Law and History Review* 4 (Spring 1986): 114–17; J. M. Beattie, *Crime and the Courts in England 1680–1800* (Princeton: Princeton University Press, 1986), pp. 213–35; Douglas Hay, "War, Dearth and Theft in the Eighteenth Century," *Past and Present*, no. 95 (May 1982): 117–60; Michael Ignatieff, *A Just Measure of Pain: The Penitentiary in the Industrial Revolution, 1750–1850* (New York: Pantheon Books, 1978), pp. 44, 82, 103, and 154; J. J. Tobias, *Crime and Industrial Society in the Nineteenth Century* (New York: Schocken Books, 1967), pp. 40–41.

65. See Kealey, "Crime and Society," pp. 156–59.

66. See, for example, Cushing; Henderson; Ames; Wall.

67. See, for example, Henderson; Ames; Mount, p. 3.

68. Cushing; Ames. Ames's statement even included a brief conversion account.

69. For evidence that John Shearman may have been a professional thief who performed no honest labor, see testimony in deposition of Elizabeth Erving, March 6, 1764, Ct. Files, no. 100375, paper 16. Yet Shearman identified himself as a shipwright; see examination of John Shearman, March 1, 1764, Ct. Files, no. 100375, paper 15; on the unreliability of his testimony, see note 40 above.

70. See examination of John Shearman, March 1, 1764, Ct. Files, no. 100375, paper 15 (shipwright); Wilson; Ct. Files, no. 102252d (Wilson, housewright); Grout and Coven (Grout, bricklayer). On the unreliability of Shearman's testimony, see note 40 above.

71. See Sheehan; Bailey.

72. See Ames; Tufts, pp. 33–35 and 54.

73. See SC, Recs., 1700–14, fol. 278v; 1730–33, fols. 211v–12; SJC, Recs., June–Nov. 1785, fols. 81v–83r (Mount); 1787, fol. 214 (Sheehan). Also see Ct. Files, no. 40162; no. 100375, papers 17–21 (Shearman); no. 100391 (Shearman); no. 103483 (Coven); no. 103879 (Mount); no. 104770 (Sheehan). Also see *News-Letter*, May 8, 1735, p. 2; *Post-Boy*, Oct. 29, 1764, p. 3; March 4, 1765, p. 3; *Boston Gazette*, Oct. 13, 1783, p. 3; July 5, 1784, p. 2; March 13, 1797, p. 3. Also see Frasier, pp. 6–7, 11, and 15; Linsey; Barrick and Sullivan, pp. 5 and 11; Mount, pp. 4, 7–10, and 12–14; and Tufts, pp. 33–36 and 54.

74. SC, Recs., 1769, fols. 128v–129v; Ct. Files, no. 152410.

75. SC, Recs., 1770, fol. 176; Ct. Files, no. 152512. For other similarly modest yields of under twenty pounds, see SJC, Recs., 1784, fol. 228 (Coven); June–Nov. 1785, fol. 83 (Wall); Feb.–June 1786, fols. 181v–82r (Green); 1794, fols. 119v–20r (Tufts). Also see Ct. Files, no. 44640 (Henderson); no. 44647 (Henderson); no. 103472, papers 2 and 4 (Grout); no. 103477 (Coven); no. 134593 (Tufts); no. 154711 (Green); no. 154717 (Green). Also see citations in notes 78–79 below.

76. Stolen property might be sold to local receivers, shipped for safe resale to networks of accomplices in other colonial towns, or taken out into the country to be hawked to rural consumers; see Welch; *Post-Boy*, Nov. 13, 1769, p. 3; *News-Letter*, Aug. 13, 1772, p. 2.

77. See Kealey, "Crime and Society," pp. 156–59 and 205–6.

78. Arthur.

79. Tufts, pp. 53, 61, 126–28, and 181; Green.

80. Barrick and Sullivan, pp. 6 and 12; Wall (she claimed to be innocent); SJC, Recs., 1784, fols. 338–39; May–Nov. 1789, fols. 257–58; Ct. Files, no. 106011, paper 90 (Wall); no. 149055 (Barrick and Sullivan); *Boston Gazette*, July 26, 1784, p. 3. For other cases of robbery reported in contemporary newspapers, see *News-Letter*, March 18, 1736, p. 2; Nov. 25, 1736, p. 2; *Post-Boy*, Dec. 5, 1763, p. 2; May 14, 1764, p. 3; *Boston Gazette*, Sept. 29, 1783, p. 2; Oct. 13, 1783, p. 2; May 24, 1784, p. 3; Oct. 25, 1784, p. 3; Nov. 22, 1784, p. 2; and May 1, 1797, p. 3.

81. For an exception, see Mount, p. 5.

82. Arthur; Wall; Tufts, passim; Green.

83. Sheehan; Bailey.

84. Flaherty, "Crime and Social Control," p. 356. It should be stressed that Flaherty's study addresses the issue of crime during the provincial period only.

85. Henderson; Welch.

86. Frasier, passim, quoted at p. 15; on Frasier and Arthur's joint crime spree, see text above.

87. Linsey; Green.

88. Mount; Tufts, pp. 11–15, 53–54 (quoted), 331, and passim; Samuel Smith. According to his *Narrative*, Tufts's capital conviction occurred in 1793 (see p. 286); however, court records indicate that the year was 1794 (see SJC, Recs., 1794, fols. 119–20). On the occasional resort to exaggeration or invention by Tufts (or his ghostwriter), see Daniel E. Williams, "Doctor, Preacher, Soldier, Thief: A New World of Possibilities in the Rogue Narrative of Henry Tufts," *Early American Literature* 19 (Spring 1984): 3–20; Edmund Pearson, ed., *The Autobiography of a Criminal: Henry Tufts* (New York: Duffield, 1930), pp. 347–57; Thomas Wentworth Higginson, "A New England Vagabond," *Harper's Magazine* 76 (March 1888): 611.

89. Frasier, passim; Green; Mount, passim; Linsey; Tufts, pp. 63–64, 109–12, 114, 156–57, 218–19, 240–41, and passim; Samuel Smith; SJC, Recs., Feb.–July 1788, fol. 367 (Samuel Smith); Ct. Files, no. 149877 (Samuel Smith).

90. Frasier, passim; Green.

91. Mount, pp. 9, 11, and passim; Tufts, passim.

92. *Charters and General Laws*, pp. 200, 334–38, 525–34, 669–70; *The Laws of the Commonwealth of Massachusetts* (Boston: Thomas & Andrews and Manning & Loring, June, 1807), vol. 1, pp. 411–13; vol. 2, pp. 812–14; vol. 3, pp. 78–80. Also see Jones, "Strolling Poor." For discussions of transiency in early modern England, see works by Beier, Langbein, and Slack, cited in note 19 above.

93. On the frequency of private settlements of property crimes in early modern Europe, see Sharpe, *Crime in Seventeenth-Century England*, p. 177; Alfred Soman, "Deviance and Criminal Justice in Western Europe, 1300–1800," *Criminal Justice History* 1 (1980): 11.

94. Hutchinson, "Charge to the Grand Jury," in Quincy, *Reports of Cases*, p. 223; Frasier, pp. 5–6, 8, and 14–15.

95. Arthur; Linsey; Ames; Wilson; Tufts, pp. 43–44, 120, 137, 164, 243, and 262.

96. For an exception, see Barrick and Sullivan, pp. 5–6.

97. On the general inadequacy of jails in colonial America, see Rothman, *Discovery*, p. 56; Kenneth Scott, *Counterfeiting in Colonial America* (New York: Oxford University Press, 1957), pp. 9, 140, 209, 263, and passim. On the similar situation in eighteenth-century France, see Ruff, *Crime, Justice and Public Order*, pp. 52 and 160.

98. See *New-England Courant*, Jan. 21, 1723, p. 2; *News-Letter*, July 21, 1726, p. 2; Oct. 19, 1732, p. 2; May 17, 1733, p. 2; March 3, 1737, p. 2; Aug. 20, 1772, p. 3; Apr. 8, 1773, p. 3; *Post-Boy*, May 9, 1763, p. 3; Apr. 9, 1764, p. 4; *Boston Gazette*, Oct. 18, 1784, p. 2.

99. See, for example, SJC, Recs., 1783, fol. 133; 1784, fols. 88, 130, 231, 373–74; 1785, fols. 267–68.

100. Edwin Powers, *Crime and Punishment in Early Massachusetts 1620–1692* (Boston: Beacon Press, 1966), pp. 241–42.

101. Frasier, pp. 4, 7, and 9–12. On Frasier's burning down of the Fairfield jail in an unsuccessful escape attempt, see Frasier, *Brief Account*, pp. 11–12, confirmed in Richard Gaskins, "Changes in the Criminal Law in Eighteenth-Century Connecticut," *American Journal of Legal History* 25 (Oct. 1981): 329 n. 84.

102. Mount, pp. 5–6, 8–10, and 12–13; Tufts, pp. 38–41, 56–60, 134–36, 137, 141–50, 199–204, 211–13, 220–23, 283–86, and 321–22.

103. Arthur; Wilson; Grout and Coven; Green; Samuel Smith; Ct. Files, no. 106786, paper 1.

104. Mount, p. 6; *Massachusetts Centinel*, Sept. 22, 1784, p. 1, quoted; also see Oct. 16, 1784, p. 1. On the similar disillusionment with whipping as a criminal sanction in late eighteenth-century England, see Ignatieff, *Just Measure of Pain*, p. 90.

105. Tufts, p. 165; *Massachusetts Centinel*, Oct. 16, 1784, p. 1; Hirsch, "From Pillory to Penitentiary," pp. 1231–32.

106. See, for example, Frasier, p. 8.

107. On the shift to the penalty of incarceration during the last decades of the eighteenth century, see Hirsch, "From Pillory to Penitentiary"; Kealey, "Patterns of Punishment." On the origins of the same shift in Europe, see Beattie, *Crime and the Courts*, pp. 548–82 and 601–37; Langbein, "Historical Origins of the Sanction of Imprisonment." On the insecurity of the facility on Castle Island, see Powers, *Crime and Punishment*, pp. 241–42.

108. [Litchfield, Conn.] *Weekly Monitor*, Oct. 25, 1790, p. 2; cited in Masur, *Rites of Execution*, pp. 60 and 177 n. 27.

109. Tufts, pp. 44–46, 61, and 188.

110. See Bridenbaugh, *Cities in the Wilderness*, p. 70; *News-Letter*, Jan. 17, 1715, p. 2; Sept. 2, 1773, p. 3; *Post-Boy*, Dec. 12, 1763, p. 3; Nov. 13, 1769, p. 3; *Boston Gazette*, Aug. 25, 1783, p. 2; Oct. 20, 1783, p. 2; May 17, 1784, p. 3. On the similar organization of property criminals into small gangs (typically of between two and five members) in early modern Europe, see Beattie, *Crime and the Courts*, pp. 256–58; John L. McMullan, *The Canting Crew: London's Criminal Underworld 1550–1700* (New Brunswick: Rutgers University Press, 1984), pp. 110–11; Pieter Spierenburg, *The Spectacle of Suffering: Executions and the Evolution of Repression* (Cambridge, Eng.: Cambridge University Press, 1984), p. 138.

111. See discussion of those cases in text above; on Barrick and Sullivan's accomplice, see Barrick and Sullivan, pp. 6 and 12.

112. Tufts, pp. 32, 53, and 188; SC, Recs., 1778–80, fol. 64r (Dennis); SJC, Recs., 1783, fol. 133v (Dennis); 1784, fols. 231v (Dennis) and 231v–232r (Smith); June–Nov. 1785, fol. 78v (Dennis); Feb.–June 1786, fol. 77 (Dennis); 1794, fol. 287 (Sanborn); Ct. Files, no. 102623 (Dennis); no. 103484 (Dennis); no. 103485 (Smith); no. 103660 (Smith); no. 103855 (Dennis); no. 104113 (Dennis); no. 104848b (Smith); no. 106011, paper 35 (Dennis); no. 132922 (Dennis); no. 134651 (Sanborn).

113. Mount, passim (Millar and Taylor mentioned on pp. 7–8); SJC, Recs., June–

Nov. 1785, fols. 81v–83r (Mount and Miller); Feb.–July 1788, fol. 356 (Taylor); Ct. Files, no. 104888 (Taylor).

114. See Scott, *Counterfeiting*, pp. 10, 23–26, 35, 123–25, 157, 220, 222, 225, 227, 229, 235–36, 262, and passim.

115. See Bridenbaugh, *Cities in Revolt*, p. 300.

116. *Post-Boy*, Dec. 12, 1763, p. 3; Jan. 16, 1764, p. 3; Nov. 13, 1769, p. 3; Tufts, p. 196.

117. Mount, pp. [2] and 19–21.

118. Tufts, p. 315.

119. Cushing; Henderson; Welch.

120. Green; Tufts, pp. 36–37 and 54–56; Mount, pp. 16–17.

121. For a brief discussion of Massachusetts property criminals in comparative perspective (with accompanying citations), see Cohen, "Fellowship of Thieves," p. 65.

122. Mount, p. 17.

123. See Lightly (in his case, some bitterness is apparent); Sheehan; Wall.

124. In fact, Levi Ames's *Last Words* actually included a brief conversion account.

Chapter 7. *Injured Innocents*

1. *Theft and Murder! A Poem on the Execution of Levi Ames* ([Boston?: 1773]), broadside.

2. I have borrowed the phrase "critical perspective" from David Ray Papke; see Papke, *Framing the Criminal: Crime, Cultural Work, and the Loss of Critical Perspective* (Hamden, Conn.: Archon, 1987), pp. xvi–xvii and passim.

3. See Peter A. Tasch, *The Dramatic Cobbler: The Life and Works of Isaac Bickerstaff* (Lewisburg, Pa.: Bucknell University Press, 1971), pp. 178–81 and passim.

4. See ibid., pp. 178–81; *NUC*, vol. 52, pp. 582–83; *BMC*, vol. 94, p. 989. Toybooks were small pamphlets, usually published for children.

5. See *Evans*, nos. 18505–6, 19695, 28294, 33418, and 37561; *Bristol*, nos. B5493, B5868, and B10717; *Shaw and Shoemaker*, 1807, no. 12919; 1812, no. 24867; 1815, no. 34116; *NUC*, vol. 52, pp. 582–83. A copy of the New York City edition of 1836 is in my possession.

6. See [Isaac Bickerstaffe or Bickerstaff], *The Life and Adventures of Ambrose Gwinett* [cited hereafter as *Gwinett*] (1768; rpt. n.p.: Printed for the Travelling Booksellers, 1798) , pp. 2–11. Unless otherwise indicated, all subsequent citations of *Gwinett* are to this edition.

7. *Gwinett*, pp. 11–23.

8. See title pages of *Evans*, no. 18505–6.

9. See title pages of indicated editions, listed in *Evans*, no. 19695, 28294, and 37561; *Shaw and Shoemaker*, no. 34116.

10. See *Gwinett* (Boston: J. White, 1800), p. [iii].

11. See *Report of the Trial of Dominic Daley and James Halligan* (Northampton: S. & E. Butler, [1806]) [cited hereafter as *Trial of Daley and Halligan*], pp. 28–65 and passim. For biographical information on Francis Blake, see William T. Davis, *Bench and Bar of the Commonwealth of Massachusetts* (1895; rpt. New York: Da Capo Press, 1974), vol. 1, p. 286; vol. 2, p. 357.

12. See *Trial of Daley and Halligan*, pp. 28–65, quoted at 59.

13. For contemporary newspaper stories on the execution, see *Pennsylvania Packet, and Daily Advertiser*, Jan. 12, 1786, p. 3; *Pennsylvania Mercury and Universal Advertiser*, Jan. 13, 1786, p. 3; *Carlisle Gazette*, Jan. 25, 1786, p. 3.

14. See *Ritz*, no. 5.07(9); *McDade*, no. 1106; *Evans*, nos. 19635–39; *Bristol*, nos. B6279 and B6364; *NUC*, vol. 166, p. 64; also, for information on unlocated editions, see *Evans Microprint*.

15. *A Faithful Narrative of Elizabeth Wilson* (Hudson: A. Stoddard, 1786), pp. 4–9, quoted at 5.

16. Ibid., p. 5.

17. Ibid., pp. 5–8, quoted at 7–8.

18. Ibid., pp. 3–4 and 9–13.

19. For a recent scholarly discussion of some early American novels that sought to expose society's sexual double standard, see Cathy N. Davidson, *Revolution and the Word: The Rise of the Novel in America* (New York: Oxford University Press, 1986), pp. 110–50.

20. *The Victim of Seduction!* (Boston: J. Wilkey, [1822]).

21. Ibid., p. 9.

22. Ibid., pp. 10–11.

23. *The Sweets of Solitude!* (Boston: J. Wilkey, 1822).

24. For citations, see *NUC*, vol. 666, p. 373.

25. See Whiting Sweeting, *The Narrative of Whiting Sweeting* (1791; rpt. Providence: B. Wheeler, [1792]), pp. 3–6, 17, and 45–47. Unless otherwise indicated, all subsequent citations of Sweeting's *Narrative* are to that Providence edition. For a contemporary newspaper story on the killing, see *Albany Gazette*, January 6, 1791, p. 2. For the date of Wilson's execution, see *Faithful Narrative*, p. [1].

26. See Whiting Sweeting, *The Narrative of Whiting Sweeting* (Lansingburgh: S. Tiffany, 1791), p. [2]; *Albany Register*, Aug. 8, 1791, p. 2; Aug. 29, 1791, p. 3; *American Spy*, Aug. 26, 1791, p. 2; Sept. 2, 1791, p. 2; *Albany Gazette*, Sept. 22, 1791, p. 1; American Antiquarian Society catalog cards for *The Narrative of Whiting Sweeting* ([Albany?: John Barber?, 1791?]).

27. The rival printer was John Barber, publisher of the *Albany Register*. See citations in previous note and *Albany Register*, Sept. 19, 1791, p. 3; Sept. 26, 1791, p. 3.

28. For citations of the various editions and related information, see *Ritz*, no. 5.05(13); *McDade*, no. 960; "Report of the Librarian," *Proceedings of the American Antiquarian Society*, new ser., 43 (Oct. 1933): 293–94; *Evans*, nos. 23814–15, 24836, 24838, 26237–38, 27767–68, 32899, and corresponding microcards in *Evans Microprint*; *Bristol*, no. B7835, B9715, and corresponding microcards in *Evans Microprint*; *NUC*, vol. 579, pp. 23–24.

29. See *Ritz*, no. 5.05(13); *McDade*, no. 960; "Report," p. 294; *Evans*, no. 24837, 29598, and corresponding microcards in *Evans Microprint*; American Antiquarian Society catalog cards cited in note 26 above.

30. See Sweeting, *Narrative*. As with many such works, the exact process by which Sweeting's narrative made its way into print is somewhat unclear. According to the appended account by William Carter, Sweeting had written his narrative with much physical difficulty while chained in jail following his condemnation and had asked Carter to transcribe it for him (pp. 62–63). According to a contemporary account in the *Albany Register*, "Mr. *Carter*" was "the gentleman whom Sweeting appointed to see his Narrative published" (*Albany Register*, Sept. 19, 1791, p. 3). According to the librarian of the American Antiquarian Society, Carter was "doubtless a local clergyman" ("Report," p.

294); I have been unable to confirm that. According to the first U. S. census, a man named William Carter was living in 1790 in Rensselaerwick, not far from Albany and Stephentown; see *Heads of Families at the First Census of the United States Taken in the Year 1790: New York* (1908; rpt. Baltimore: Genealogical Publishing, 1966), p. 38. Silvester Tiffany, the printer of the first authorized edition, indicated that he had dealt with Sweeting directly; in a notice inserted into his edition he wrote: "The unfortunate *Whiting Sweeting*, having confidence in my promise, left with me his narrative, for publication; his injunctions have been strictly adhered to, as will appear on comparing with the copy. No other person has had his writings, nor an opportunity of transcribing therefrom" (Sweeting, *Narrative* [Lansingburgh, 1791], p. [2]). Whatever the roles of Carter and Tiffany in transcribing and/or editing the work, there is no firm reason to doubt that the narrative was initially written by Sweeting in jail.

31. See Sweeting, *Narrative*, pp. 3–6, 17, and 45–47, quoted at 5.

32. See ibid., pp. 6–11 and 45–49.

33. See ibid., pp. 59–63.

34. See Henry Peterson, *The Canons of Dort: A Study Guide* (Grand Rapids, Mich.: Baker Book House, 1968), pp. 93–100; *The Judgement of the Synode Holden at Dort* (1619; rpt. Amsterdam and Norwood, N.J.: Walter J. Johnson, 1974) [cited hereafter as *Synode*], pp. 3–17; for brief overviews of the Synod of Dort, see Samuel Macauley Jackson and George William Gilmore et al., eds., *New Schaff-Herzog Encyclopedia of Religious Knowledge*, 13 vols. (New York: Funk and Wagnalls, 1908–14), vol. 3, pp. 494–95; *Encyclopaedia Britannica*, 32 vols. (New York: Encyclopaedia Britannica, 1910–11), vol. 8, pp. 436–37. Of course, the Canons of Dort are simply a convenient reification of an extraordinarily complex and varied belief system.

35. See Sweeting, *Narrative*, pp. 49–50, 52–54, and 56, quoted at 52.

36. See Peterson, *Canons*, pp. 100–103; *Synode*, pp. 18–24.

37. See Sweeting, *Narrative*, pp. 22–23, 27–28, 31, 37, 49–50, and 54, quoted at 23, 27–28, and 49.

38. See Peterson, *Canons*, pp. 103–9, quoted at 104; *Synode*, pp. 25–40.

39. See Carl Bangs, *Arminius: A Study in the Dutch Reformation*, 2d ed. (Grand Rapids, Mich.: Francis Asbury Press, 1985), pp. 212–13; for the use of that distinction in American execution sermons, see chapter 4 above.

40. See Sweeting, *Narrative*, pp. 50–52.

41. See Peterson, *Canons*, pp. 103–9; *Synode*, pp. 25–40.

42. See Sweeting, *Narrative*, pp. 22–23, 25, 28, 51, 53, quoted at 51 and 53.

43. See Peterson, *Canons*, pp. 109–15; *Synode*, pp. 41–53.

44. See Sweeting, *Narrative*, pp. 56–58.

45. Ibid., p. 28.

46. Ibid., p. 32.

47. Ibid., p. 41.

48. See ibid., pp. 60–63, quoted at 62.

49. On the doctrines of Arminius and his followers, see Bangs, *Arminius*; Peterson, *Canons*, p. 9; *Encyclopaedia Britannica*, vol. 2, pp. 576–77; vol. 23, p. 82; James Hastings, ed., *Encyclopaedia of Religion and Ethics*, 12 vols. (New York: Charles Scribner's Sons, 1928), vol. 1, pp. 807–16; Jackson and Gilmore et al., *New Schaff-Herzog Encyclopedia*, vol. 9, pp. 481–83. It should be noted that there actually were a few explicit discussions of Arminian doctrines published in late eighteenth-century New England; see, for example, *The Articles of Belief Professed By the Followers of*

Calvin, Luther, and Arminius (Norwich, Conn.: Green & Spooner, [1774]), pp. 9–14; *A Sketch of the Life of James Arminius* (Providence: B. Wheeler, 1793), pp. 11–12.

50. On that larger religious ferment, see Stephen A. Marini, *Radical Sects of Revolutionary New England* (Cambridge: Harvard University Press, 1982); C. C. Goen, *Revivalism and Separatism in New England, 1740–1800* (New Haven: Yale University Press, 1962), passim; Norman Allen Baxter, *History of the Freewill Baptists* (Rochester, N.Y.: American Baptist Historical Society, 1957), pp. 1–64; Whitney R. Cross, *The Burned-Over District: The Social and Intellectual History of Enthusiastic Religion in Western New York, 1800–1850* (New York: Harper & Row, 1950), pp. 1–51.

51. See George Baker Anderson, *Landmarks of Rensselaer County, New York* (Syracuse, N.Y.: D. Mason, 1897), pp. 487–88 and 498–99; J. M. Brewster, "The Freewill Baptists," in Brewster et al., *The Centennial Record of Freewill Baptists, 1780–1880* (Dover, N.H.: Printing Establishment, 1881), pp. 31–32; Stephen Wright, *History of the Shaftsbury Baptist Association* (Troy, N.Y.: A. G. Johnson, 1853), pp. 18–19 and 320. Three of the first five meetings of the theologically orthodox Shaftsbury Baptist Association (encompassing congregations in Massachusetts, New York, and Vermont) were held at Stephentown; see Wright, *History*, p. 18.

52. See Anderson, *Landmarks*, pp. 498–99.

53. See Brewster, "Freewill Baptists," pp. 31–32; on the Freewill Baptists then spreading throughout northern New England, see Marini, *Radical Sects*, passim; Baxter, *History*, pp. 1–64; I[saac] D. Stewart, *The History of the Freewill Baptists* (Dover, N.H.: Freewill Baptist Printing Establishment, 1862).

54. On the theology of the Freewill Baptists, see Marini, *Radical Sects*, pp. 139–44 and passim; Baxter, *History*, pp. 114–37; Brewster, "Freewill Baptists," pp. 18–19; Stewart, *History*, pp. 27–28. It should be noted, however, that the fit between Sweeting's doctrines and those of the Freewill Baptists may not have been perfect. According to Marini (citing the writings of the Canadian proto–Freewill Baptist, Henry Alline), the Freewill Baptists did not believe that Jesus had died to appease the vindictive wrath of God (see *Radical Sects*, p. 141); by contrast, Sweeting affirmed that Christ had died "to satisfy the vindictive justice of God" (see *Narrative*, p. 53).

55. Sweeting's father had been born in Rehoboth, Massachusetts, and Sweeting's mother and Whiting himself had been born in Norton, Massachusetts; both of those towns are in southeastern Massachusetts, not far from the Rhode Island border. The parents, along with other family members, also moved to upstate New York. See George Langford, *Genealogy of Langford and the Allied Families of Sweeting, Robertson, Bell* (Joliet, Ill.: unpublished manuscript, September 1936), pp. 52–54, and information provided to me by the Stephentown Historical Society.

56. On the paucity of early published statements of anti-Calvinist evangelical doctrine, see Marini, *Radical Sects*, pp. 139, 144, and 148; Baxter, *History*, p. 114; I. D. Stewart, "Publications," in Brewster et al., *Centennial Record*, pp. 203–4.

57. On the shattering of the spiritual hegemony of Calvinism in late eighteenth-century New England, see Marini, *Radical Sects*, pp. 1–7 and passim.

58. Two defective copies of the Sweeting narrative in my possession match that general description; most copies in institutional hands seem to be similarly worn and soiled; on that point, see *Evans Microprint*, nos. 23814–15, 26237–38, 27767–68, 32899, and 46293. A copy of the Gwinett pamphlet in my possession is also worn and mended. By contrast, many surviving execution sermons are in nearly pristine condition.

59. See *Evans*, no. 33478. Although I do not agree with them on every point, the

following discussion of the *Memoirs* of Stephen Burroughs was greatly enriched by my reading of Robert A. Gross, "The Confidence Man and the Preacher: The Cultural Politics of Shays's Rebellion" (unpublished paper, College of William and Mary, Nov. 1989) and a draft of John L. Brooke, "Alchymical Experiments," chapter 2 of *Joseph Smith, Early American Occult Traditions, and the Origins of Mormonism* (Cambridge, Eng.: Cambridge University Press, forthcoming), both of which were kindly made available to me by their authors.

60. Stephen Burroughs, *Memoirs*, [vol. 1] (Hanover, N.H.: B. True, 1798) and vol. 2 (Boston: E. Lincoln for C. Bingham, 1804). Two manuscript letters written by Burroughs from jail, surviving in early court files, suggest that he was in fact sufficiently literate to have written his own *Memoirs*, although he may have required some editorial assistance, particularly in regard to punctuation and capitalization; see Ct. Files, no. 155603, paper 4; no. 155604, paper 2.

61. Stephen Burroughs, *Memoirs*, 2 vols. (Albany: R. Packard for B. D. Packard, 1811). Unless otherwise indicated, all subsequent citations to the *Memoirs* are to this edition. A surprisingly large number of copies of this edition survive, suggesting that Packard either produced one extremely large printing or several printings of the same edition. Some copies of this edition were apparently issued in two separate volumes; others were published as two volumes in one; all seem to have been bound in full leather.

62. See *Shaw and Shoemaker*, 1809, no. 17129; 1810, nos. 19690–91; 1811, no. 22446; 1812, nos. 25002–3; 1813, no. 28051; 1814, nos. 31043–44; 1818, no. 43498; *NUC*, vol. 86, p. 358.

63. *NUC*, vol. 86, pp. 357–58. The new edition is Stephen Burroughs, *Memoirs of the Notorious Stephen Burroughs*, with a foreword by Philip F. Gura (Boston: Northeastern University Press, 1988).

64. See Robert A. Gross, "Confidence Man," pp. 7 and 22.

65. *NUC*, vol. 86, pp. 357–58, lists Burroughs's birthdate as 1765, a date that can also be extrapolated from the account in his *Memoirs* of his abortive military enlistment in 1779 at the age of fourteen (see Burroughs, *Memoirs*, I, 11–16). However, at least one local history lists his birthdate as 1766; see George F. Daniels, *History of the Town of Oxford, Massachusetts* (Oxford: Published by the Author, 1892), p. 467. The probable birthplace of South Killingly, Connecticut, is inferred from the fact that his father was settled at a church there between 1760 and 1771, before his removal to Hanover, New Hampshire; for biographical information about Eden Burroughs, see *Dexter*, vol. 2, pp. 454–56; Frederick Chase, *A History of Dartmouth College and the Town of Hanover New Hamphshire*, ed. John K. Lord, 2d ed. (Brattleboro: Vermont Printing, 1928), pp. 190–216 (cited in Brooke, "Alchymical Experiments," p. 67 n. 47). One source (probably mistakenly) lists Stephen Burroughs's birthplace as Hanover, New Hampshire; see James Grant Wilson and John Fiske, *Appletons' Cyclopaedia of American Biography*, 11 vols. (New York: D. Appleton, 1891–1928), vol. 1, p. 470.

66. See Burroughs, *Memoirs*, vol. 1, pp. [5]–7.

67. See ibid., pp. 11–33. For biographical information about the Reverend Joseph Huntington, see *Dexter*, vol. 2, pp. 750–55; *Sprague*, vol. 1, pp. 602–7; E. B. Huntington, *A Genealogical Memoir of the Huntington Family* (Stamford, Conn.: Published by the Author, 1863), pp. 117–22.

68. See Burroughs, *Memoirs*, vol. 1, pp. 38–51, quoted at 47.

69. See ibid., pp. 51–95. For the date of his arrest and details of the charges against him, see Ct. Files, no. 158700.

70. See Ct. Files, no. 158700; Burroughs, *Memoirs*, vol. 1, pp. 95–186.

71. See Burroughs, *Memoirs*, vol. 1, pp. 188–224; Ct. Files, nos. 155602–5. On the town of Charlton during the late eighteenth century, see Peter Whitney, *The History of the County of Worcester* (1793; rpt. Worcester: Isaiah Thomas Books & Prints, 1983), pp. 221–25. On Burroughs's marriage to his cousin Sally (or Sarah) Davis, see *Vital Records of Charlton, Massachusetts* (Worcester: F. P. Rice, 1905), p. 147. For biographical information on Burroughs's uncle, Ebenezer Davis, see Anson Titus, Jr., "Reminiscences of Early American Universalism—First Paper," *Universalist Quarterly and General Review*, new ser., 18 (Oct. 1881): 437–39 (cited in Brooke, "Alchymical Experiments," p. 67 n. 47); Anson Titus, Jr., *Charlton Historical Sketches* (Southbridge, Mass.: G. M. Whitaker, 1877), p. 12; Holmes Ammidown, *Historical Collections*, 2d ed. (New York: Published for the Author, 1877), pp. 219–20; George Davis, *A Historical Sketch of Sturbridge and Southbridge* (West Brookfield, Mass.: O. S. Cooke, 1856), pp. 115–18.

72. For biographical information on Aaron Woolworth, see Dexter, *Biographical Sketches*, vol. 4, pp. 372–74; Sprague, *Annals*, vol. 3, pp. 468–72; Nathaniel S. Prime, *A History of Long Island* (New York: R. Carter, 1845), pp. 201–8.

73. See Burroughs, *Memoirs*, vol. 2, pp. [3]–102 for material covered in this paragraph.

74. See ibid., 102–36. Local records confirm that Burroughs was formally appointed rector of the academy at Washington, Georgia, on August 25, 1794; see Minutes of the Board of Commissioners of the Academy at Washington, Georgia, 1784–1808, William R. Perkins Library, Duke University, unpaginated. The information about his management of his father's farm and their subsequent falling out, along with details concerning his various business ventures in the South, are actually contained in a "Sequel" and an "Appendix" to the 1811 edition; see Burroughs, *Memoirs*, vol. 2, pp. 137–48.

75. See Burroughs, *Memoirs*, vol. 2, p. 147; Stephen Burroughs, *Sketch of the Life of the Notorious Stephen Burroughs* ([1809]; rpt. Philadelphia: D. Hogan, 1812), pp. 106–8; Abby Maria Hemenway, *The Vermont Historical Gazetteer*, 5 vols. (Burlington, Vt.: Published by Mrs. A. M. Hemenway, 1867–91), vol. 2, pp. 831–32 (citation provided by John L. Brooke); Brooke, "Alchymical Experiments," pp. 23–24.

76. See Burroughs, *Memoirs*, vol. 2, p. 148.

77. See Burroughs, *Memoirs* (Amherst, Ma.: M. N. Spear, 1858), pp. 350–52, quoted at 351. For brief references to Burroughs as a schoolmaster and a convert to Catholicism, see Francess G. Halpenny, ed., *Dictionary of Canadian Biography*, 11 vols. (Toronto: University of Toronto Press, 1961-), vol. 6, p. 592; vol. 8, p. 406.

78. Burroughs, *Memoirs*, vol. 1, p. 162; vol. 2, p. 59.

79. See ibid., vol. 1, pp. 71–72, 92–93, and 126; vol. 2, pp. 94 and 107–8. Charles Brockden Brown's contemporary fictional hero, Arthur Mervyn, made strikingly similar claims concerning the purity of his intentions; see Daniel A. Cohen, "Arthur Mervyn and His Elders: The Ambivalence of Youth in the Early Republic," *William and Mary Quarterly*, 3d ser., 43 (July 1986): 375–77.

80. For perceptions of the world as characterized by deception, delusion, and/or prejudice, see Burroughs, *Memoirs*, vol. 1, pp. 47, 67, 84, 97, 100, 134, 160–161, 218, 229, 233–37, and 244; vol. 2, pp. 33–35, 46, and 98–99. In much of his fiction, Charles Brockden Brown also described a social world pervaded by deception and delusion; see Cohen, "Arthur Mervyn," p. 376.

81. Burroughs, *Memoirs*, vol. 1, pp. 71–72.

82. See ibid., vol. 1, pp. 95–104, quoted at 97 and 103; for official information about the case, see Ct. Files, no. 158700. For the reprint of an article generally matching Burroughs's description, datelined "Springfield, April 19," see *Boston Gazette*, May 2, 1785, p. 3; although Burroughs implies that the article appeared *after* his arrest, it actually seems to have appeared several months *prior* to his arrest, and it does not identify Burroughs by name.

83. See Burroughs, *Memoirs*, vol. 1, pp. 202–31; vol. 2, pp. 8–10; quoted at vol. 1, pp. 219 and 222. For official information about the case, see Ct. Files, nos. 155602–5. There are only slight discrepancies between Burroughs's account and the information contained in the files. The man who had allegedly trumped up the charges against Burroughs was Israel Waters; for contemporary mention of Waters as a prominent citizen of Charlton, see Whitney, *History of Worcester*, p. 224. Another person who testified against Burroughs was Eli Wheelock, who is also mentioned by Whitney as a prominent local citizen; see ibid. Philip Gura identifies the elderly lawyer as Robert Treat Paine, one of the judges at Burroughs's trial; see Burroughs, *Memoirs* (1988), p. xvi.

84. See Burroughs, *Memoirs*, vol. 2, pp. 76–85; for the reprint of an article matching Burroughs's description, datelined "Springfield, June 25," see *Salem Gazette*, July 2, 1793, p. 3.

85. See Burroughs, *Memoirs*, vol. 2, pp. 85–89, quoted at 85.

86. See ibid., vol. 1, pp. 104–5, 124–25, 135–38, and 186–88; quoted at 124 and 187. The characterization of prisons as "schools of vice" was an eighteenth-century Anglo-American cliché; see Michael Ignatieff, *A Just Measure of Pain: The Penitentiary in the Industrial Revolution, 1750–1850* (New York: Pantheon Books, 1978), p. 52; Michael Meranze, "The Penitential Ideal in Late Eighteenth-Century Philadelphia," *Pennsylvania Magazine of History and Biography* 108 (Oct. 1984): 442.

87. Burroughs, *Memoirs*, vol. 1, p. 229; see William E. Nelson, *Americanization of the Common Law* (Cambridge: Harvard University Press, 1975), pp. 97–101; William E. Nelson, "Emerging Notions of Modern Criminal Law in the Revolutionary Era: An Historical Perspective," *New York University Law Review* 42 (May 1967): 477–81.

88. See Burroughs, *Memoirs*, vol. 1, pp. 7–11, esp. 9, and 137–38.

89. See discussion in chapter 4 above; Jay Fliegelman, *Prodigals and Pilgrims: The American Revolution Against Patriarchal Authority, 1750–1800* (Cambridge, Eng.: Cambridge University Press, 1982); David H. Fischer, *Growing Old in America*, expanded ed. (Oxford: Oxford University Press, 1978), pp. 77–112.

90. Again and again throughout his *Memoirs*, Burroughs alluded to the importance of friendship; see vol. 1, pp. 45, 64, 82, 92–93, 107, 148, 185, 209, 212, 216–17, 232–33, and 240; vol. 2, pp. 6 and 62.

91. Ibid., vol. 1, p. 239.

92. On the shift from a "vertical" to a "horizontal" social order in the early republic, see Karen Halttunen, *Confidence Men and Painted Women: A Study of Middleclass Culture in America, 1830–1870* (New Haven: Yale University Press, 1982), pp. 12–13 and 20–21.

93. On Burroughs's pose as a cosmopolitan Enlightenment figure, see Gross, "Confidence Man," p. 26.

94. Burroughs, *Memoirs*, vol. 2, p. 42.

95. See ibid., pp. 23–24 and 46. See *Frothingham's Long Island Herald*, May 10, 1791, p. 1; June 21, 1791, pp. 1–2; July 12, 1791, p. 2; July 26, 1791, p. 3; Aug. 9, 1791, p. 1; Aug. 30, 1791, p. 3; Sept. 13, 1791, p. 2. On that newspaper, see Beatrice

Diamond, *An Episode in American Journalism: A History of David Frothingham and His* Long Island Herald (Port Washington, N.Y.: Kennikat Press, 1964).

96. Burroughs, *Memoirs*, vol. 2, p. 46. Again and again throughout his *Memoirs*, Burroughs (and other characters) stressed the importance of benevolence; see vol. 1, pp. 93, 114, 138, 178, 211, and 216; vol. 2, pp. 12, 14, 47, 100, 109, 124, 138, and 146. For a philosophical discussion of the concept of benevolence during the eighteenth century, see Tom A. Roberts, *The Concept of Benevolence* (London: Macmillan, 1973).

97. See Burroughs, *Memoirs*, vol. 2, pp. 52–69, esp. 59–60.

98. Ibid., vol. 1, pp. 7 and 82; vol. 2, pp. 51, 102, and 134–35.

99. Stephen Burroughs, *Stephen Burroughs's Sermon Delivered in Rutland, on a Hay-Mow* ([1798?]; rpt. Boston: Printed for the Publisher, 1832), p. [2] (cited in Gross, "Confidence Man," pp. 26–27). The *Sermon* was a short satirical piece, first published at about the same time as the first volume of his *Memoirs*.

100. For Burroughs as an injured innocent, note the following exchange between an enemy (Hedges) and a supporter (Halsey) on Long Island: "'Dare you, Mr. Halsey,' said Deacon Hedges, 'take the part of that villain?' 'I dare,' replied Mr. Halsey, 'advocate the cause of injured innocence, wherever I find it, let the power of the oppressor be ever so great' " (Burroughs, *Memoirs*, vol. 2, p. 70).

101. M. R. Werner, *Brigham Young* (New York: Harcourt, Brace, 1925), p. 21; E. W. Vanderhoof, *Historical Sketches of Western New York* (1907; rpt. New York: AMS Press, 1972), p. 141. It should be noted that those sources are hostile toward Smith and that the claim that he read Burroughs may have been fabricated to discredit him.

102. Two modern scholars have also explored Burroughs's family links to radical traditions of Protestant dissent; see Gross, "Confidence Man," pp. 22–24; Brooke, "Alchymical Experiments," pp. 35–37.

103. I am inferring that they were intensely (and intensively) read and painstakingly preserved by the ragged and yet mended condition of surviving copies; see discussion in this chapter and in note 58 above.

Chapter 8. *The Story of Jason Fairbanks*

1. Although arguably a popular crime genre of sorts, the polemical literature of penal reform is not considered here because it did not generally address specific criminal cases. For scholarly discussions of that literature, see Louis P. Masur, *Rites of Execution: Capital Punishment and the Transformation of American Culture, 1776–1865* (New York: Oxford University Press, 1989), passim; Philip English Mackey, *Hanging in the Balance: The Anti–Capital Punishment Movement in New York State, 1776–1861* (New York: Garland, 1982), passim; David Brion Davis, "The Movement to Abolish Capital Punishment in America, 1787–1861," *American Historical Review* 63 (Oct. 1957): 29–46.

2. For citations of publications on other highly publicized criminal cases of the first half of the nineteenth century revolving around issues of gender, courtship, illicit sex, and sexual violence, see *McDade*, nos. 33–53 (Avery/Cornell, 1833), 80–89 (Beauchamp/Sharp, 1826), 812–22 (Robinson/Jewett, 1836), 881–89 (Smith/Carson, 1816), and 932–43 (Strang/Whipple, 1827). On such themes in contemporary fiction, see David Brion Davis, *Homicide in American Fiction, 1798–1860* (Ithaca: Cornell University Press, 1957), pp. 147–236. In addition to murder cases with a sexual angle,

sensational cases of adultery and divorce also received much coverage in the popular press.

3. See Cathy N. Davidson, *Revolution and the Word: The Rise of the Novel in America* (New York: Oxford University Press, 1986), p. 106 and passim; Herbert Ross Brown, *The Sentimental Novel in America, 1789–1860* (New York: Pageant Books, 1959), pp. 28–51; James D. Hart, *The Popular Book: A History of America's Literary Taste* (New York: Oxford University Press, 1950), pp. 51–57; Alexander Cowie, *The Rise of the American Novel* (New York: American Book, 1948), pp. 11–17; Frank Luther Mott, *Golden Multitudes: The Story of Best Sellers in the United States* (New York: Macmillan, 1947), pp. 35–40.

4. J. M. S. Tompkins, *The Popular Novel in England 1770–1800* (London: Methuen, 1932), p. 61.

5. Herbert R. Brown, "Elements of Sensibility in *The Massachusetts Magazine*," *American Literature* 1 (1929–30): 289, quoted, and passim.

6. See Davidson, *Revolution and the Word*, pp. 83–109; Brown, *Sentimental Novel*, pp. 44–45; Cowie, *Rise of the American Novel*, pp. 9–12.

7. See Davidson, *Revolution and the Word*, pp. 110–50; Brown, *Sentimental Novel*, pp. 50–51; Hart, *Popular Book*, pp. 63–64; Cowie, *Rise of the American Novel*, pp. 12–17; Mott, *Golden Multitudes*, pp. 39–40.

8. See Emily Pendleton and Milton Ellis, *Philenia: The Life and Works of Sarah Wentworth Morton 1759–1846* (Orono, Me.: University Press, 1931), pp. 32–39; Cowie, *Rise of the American Novel*, p. 11.

9. See Mott, *Golden Multitudes*, pp. 39–40.

10. See Charles Knowles Bolton, *The Elizabeth Whitman Mystery* (Peabody, Mass.: Peabody Historical Society, 1912), pp. 33–37, 57–63, and passim; Brown, *Sentimental Novel*, pp. 50–51.

11. See Terence Martin, *The Instructed Vision: Scottish Common Sense Philosophy and the Origins of American Fiction* (Bloomington: Indiana University Press, 1961), p. 70; Brown, *Sentimental Novel*, pp. 9–12; G. Harrison Orians, "Censure of Fiction in American Romances and Magazines 1789–1810," *Publications of the Modern Language Association of America* 52 (March 1937): 204; Tremaine McDowell, "Sensibility in the Eighteenth-Century American Novel," *Studies in Philology* 24 (July 1927): 401. As late as 1839, one of the definitions of the word *novel* offered by *The Moral Encyclopaedia* was "a lie"; quoted in Ronald J. Zboray, "A Fictive People: Antebellum Economic Development and the Reading Public for American Novels: 1837–1857" (Ph.D. diss., New York University, 1984), p. 291.

12. See Ellen K. Rothman, *Hands and Hearts: A History of Courtship in America* (New York: Basic Books, 1984), pp. 45–46 and passim; Janet Wilson James, *Changing Ideas About Women in the United States, 1776–1825* (New York: Garland, 1981), pp. 128–29 and 135–38, quoted at 138; Linda K. Kerber, *Women of the Republic: Intellect and Ideology in Revolutionary America* (Chapel Hill: University of North Carolina Press, 1980), p. 245; Mary Beth Norton, *Liberty's Daughters: The Revolutionary Experience of American Women, 1750–1800* (Boston: Little, Brown, 1980), p. 55; Robert V. Wells, "Illegitimacy and Bridal Pregnancy in Colonial America," in Peter Laslett, Karla Oosterveen, and Richard M. Smith, eds., *Bastardy and its Comparative History* (Cambridge: Harvard University Press, 1980), pp. 353–55; Daniel Scott Smith, "The Long Cycle in American Illegitimacy and Prenuptial Pregnancy," in Laslett et al, *Bastardy*, pp. 363 and 369–70; Daniel Scott Smith and Michael S. Hindus, "Premarital Pregnancy in America 1640–1971: An Overview and Interpretation," *Journal of Inter-*

disciplinary History 5 (Spring 1975): 537–38, 553–57, 561–62, and passim; Brown, "Elements of Sensibility," p. 287; McDowell, "Sensibility," pp. 401–2.

13. See Kerber, *Women of the Republic*, pp. 239–46; Brown, *Sentimental Novel*, pp. 4–9, quoted at 7–8; Hart, *Popular Book*, pp. 53–54; Cowie, *Rise of the American Novel*, pp. 5–6; Orians, "Censure of Fiction," pp. 195–214, quoted at 198.

14. See Jack Larkin, *The Reshaping of Everyday Life, 1790–1840* (New York: Harper & Row, 1988), p. 193; Rothman, *Hands and Hearts*, pp. 45–46; Kerber, *Women of the Republic*, p. 245; Norton, *Liberty's Daughters*, p. 55; Smith, "Long Cycle," pp. 363 and 369–70; Smith and Hindus, "Premarital Pregnancy," pp. 537–38, 553–57, 561–62, and passim.

15. See Smith, "Long Cycle," pp. 363–64; Smith and Hindus, "Premarital Pregnancy," pp. 553–57; Edward M. Cook, Jr., "Social Behavior and Changing Values in Dedham, Massachusetts, 1700 to 1775," *William and Mary Quarterly*, 3d ser., 27 (Oct. 1970): 548–53, 580, and passim. For controversial discussions of the trend in sexual behavior in a comparative/European context, see the following works by Edward Shorter: *The Making of the Modern Family* (New York: Basic Books, 1975), pp. 79–119 and passim; "Female Emancipation, Birth Control and Fertility in European History," *American Historical Review* 78 (June 1973): 605–40; "Capitalism, Culture, and Sexuality: Some Competing Models," *Social Science Quarterly* 53 (Sept. 1972): 338–56; "Illegitimacy, Sexual Revolution, and Social Change in Modern Europe," *Journal of Interdisciplinary History* 2 (Autumn 1971): 237–72. For a refutation of Shorter's thesis, see Joan W. Scott and Louise A. Tilly, "Women's Work and the Family in Nineteenth Century Europe," in Charles E. Rosenberg, ed., *The Family in History* (Philadelphia: University of Pennsylvania Press, 1975), p. 168 fn. 71.

16. See Jay Fliegelman, *Prodigals and Pilgrims: The American Revolution Against Patriarchal Authority, 1750–1800* (Cambridge, Eng.: Cambridge University Press, 1982), pp. 86–87; Kerber, *Women of the Republic*, p. 245; Herman R. Lantz et al., "Pre-Industrial Patterns in the Colonial Family in America: A Content Analysis of Colonial Magazines," *American Sociological Review* 33 (June 1968): 413–26; Brown, *Sentimental Novel*, pp. 34–38.

17. See Rothman, *Hands and Hearts*, p. 31; Nancy F. Cott, "Eighteenth-Century Family and Social Life Revealed in Massachusetts Divorce Records," in Cott and Elizabeth H. Pleck, *A Heritage of Her Own* (New York: Simon and Schuster, 1979), pp. 122–27; Lantz, "Pre-Industrial Patterns."

18. For a provocative discussion of that broader development, see Stephen Watts, *The Republic Reborn: War and the Making of Liberal America, 1790–1820* (Baltimore: Johns Hopkins University Press, 1987).

19. This irony was suggested to me by a comment from David D. Hall.

20. See Larkin, *Reshaping of Everyday Life*, pp. 199–200; Rothman, *Hands and Hearts*, pp. 48–55; Smith, "Long Cycle," pp. 370 and 373–75; Smith and Hindus, "Premarital Pregnancy," pp. 537–38, 549–52, and passim.

21. See Rothman, *Hands and Hearts*, pp. 57–58.

22. For other modern accounts of the Fairbanks/Fales case, see Robert Brand Hanson, *Dedham, Massachusetts 1635–1890* (Dedham: Dedham Historical Society, 1976), pp. 176–89; Edward Rowe Snow, *Piracy, Mutiny and Murder* (New York: Dodd, Mead, 1959), pp. 80–94; Ferris Greenslet, *The Lowells and Their Seven Worlds* (Boston: Houghton Mifflin, 1946), pp. 95–111; Charles Warren, *Jacobin and Junto or Early American Politics as Viewed in the Diary of Dr. Nathaniel Ames 1758–1822* (Cambridge: Harvard University Press, 1931), pp. 127–45. In regard to my own treat-

ment of the case, I would like to thank Robert B. Hanson of the Dedham Historical Society for kindly sharing his wealth of knowledge on the subject.

23. On the founding of Dedham and its early history, see Kenneth A. Lockridge, *A New England Town: The First Hundred Years*, expanded ed. (New York: W. W. Norton, 1985); on the gradual shift from communal to individualistic behavior and values in Dedham during the first three-quarters of the eighteenth century, see Cook, "Social Behavior and Changing Values"; on Dedham during the early nineteenth century, with discussions of political and religious contention, see Warren, *Jacobin and Junto*; Erastus Worthington, *The History of Dedham* (Boston: Dutton and Wentworth, 1827). For evidence of the local contention aroused by the Fairbanks case, see Warren, *Jacobin and Junto*, pp. 127–45, esp. 133–34 and 144–45.

24. *Columbian Minerva* [cited hereafter as *Minerva*], May 19, 1801, p. 3.

25. See ibid.

26. *A Mournful Tragedy* (n.p., [1801]), broadside. This broadside appeared in at least two editions.

27. See *Minerva*, May 23, 1801, p. 2; May 26, 1801, p. 4; Nathaniel Ames, Manuscript Diary, Dedham Historical Society, entries for May 20 and May 21, 1801; *Report of the Trial of Jason Fairbanks, on an Indictment for the Murder of Miss Elizabeth Fales*, 4th ed. (Boston: Russell and Cutler, 1801) [cited hereafter as *Fairbanks Report*], pp. 27–28 and 33.

28. [Boston] *Columbian Centinel* [cited hereafter as *Centinel*], Aug. 8, 1801, p. 2; *Minerva*, Aug. 11, 1801, p. 3.

29. *Fairbanks Report*, p. [5]. For biographical information on Sullivan, see *DAB*, vol. 18, pp. 190–91; Thomas C. Amory, *Life of James Sullivan: With Selections from his Writings*, 2 vols. (Boston: Phillips, Sampson, 1859); on Otis, see Samuel Eliot Morison, *Harrison Gray Otis, 1765–1848: The Urbane Federalist* (Boston: Houghton Mifflin, 1969); *DAB*, vol. 14, pp. 98–100; on Lowell, see Greenslet, *Lowells*, pp. 88–111 and passim; *DAB*, vol. 11, pp. 465–66.

30. On the young Federalists, see David Hackett Fischer, *The Revolution of American Conservatism: The Federalist Party in the Era of Jeffersonian Democracy* (New York: Harper & Row, 1965); on Otis and Lowell in particular, see Fischer, *Revolution*, pp. 38–41 and 268.

31. *Fairbanks Report*, pp. [5]–36.

32. Ibid., pp. 15–36, passim.

33. Ibid., pp. 18 and 25. The document was a certificate of "publishment."

34. See ibid., pp. 16–17 and 20–22; on the plot of *Julia Mandeville*, see Greenslet, *Lowells*, pp. 101–2.

35. See *Fairbanks Report*, pp. 12–18.

36. See ibid., pp. 11–12, 14–15, 18–20, 28–30, and 33.

37. See ibid., pp. 15, 19, 21, 25–27, 30–31, and 33–36.

38. Ibid., pp. 37–80; *Minerva*, Aug. 11, 1801, p. 3.

39. See *Fairbanks Report*, pp. 43–47. Although Otis is not identified by name as having given the closing argument for the defense recorded in the published report, both Greenslet and Morison agree that it was delivered by Otis rather than Lowell; see Greenslet, *Lowells*, p. 105; Morison, *Harrison Gray Otis*, pp. 54 and 528.

40. *Fairbanks Report*, pp. 47–48.

41. Ibid., p. 56.

42. Ibid., pp. 7, 69–71, and 75, quoted at 69 and 75. For a discussion of the idea of the "progress of vice," see chapter 4 above.

43. See, for example, Mrs. Althorpe's characterization of Arthur Mervyn in Charles Brockden Brown, *Arthur Mervyn, or Memoirs of the Year 1793*, ed. Warner Berthoff (New York: Holt, Rinehart and Winston, 1962), pp. 219–26.

44. *Fairbanks Report*, p. 66.

45. Ibid., pp. 73–74.

46. Ibid., p. 73.

47. Ibid., pp. 81–82.

48. See ibid., pp. 82–83; *Boston Gazette* [cited hereafter as *Gazette*], Aug. 10, 1801, p. 3, quoted, emphasis added; *Minerva*, Aug. 11, 1801, p. 3, quoted.

49. *Independent Chronicle* [cited hereafter as *Chronicle*], Aug. 10, 1801, pp. 2–3; *Mercury and New-England Palladium* [cited hereafter as *Palladium*], Aug. 11, 1801, p. 2; *Centinel*, Aug. 12, 1801, p. 1.

50. *A Correct and Concise Account of the Interesting Trial of Jason Fairbanks* (Boston: [1801]); *A Deed of Horror! Trial of Jason Fairbanks* (Salem: W. Carlton, [1801]).

51. For examples of mid-nineteenth-century trial pamphlets based on newspaper reports, see *The Trial of Albert J. Tirrell, Charged with the Murder of Mrs. Maria A. Bickford* (Boston: Daily Mail Report, [1846]); J. E. P. Weeks, reporter, *Trial of Albert John Tirrell for the Murder of Mary Ann Bickford* (Boston: "Times" Office, 1846).

52. For an account of how the Fairbanks case became entangled in the political passions of the day, see Warren, *Jacobin and Junto*, pp. 127–45.

53. See *Chronicle*, Sept. 10, 1801, p. 3; Sept. 14, 1801, p. 2; *Palladium*, Sept. 11, 1801, p. 2; *Centinel*, Sept. 12, 1801, p. 2; *Gazette*, Sept. 14, 1801, p. 2; *Minerva*, Sept. 15, 1801, p. 3; *Fairbanks Report*, p. 85; Warren, *Jacobin and Junto*, p. 134; Hanson, *Dedham*, pp. 186–87.

54. *Palladium*, Sept. 11, 1801, p. 2; *Centinel*, Sept. 12, 1801, p. 2; *Chronicle*, Sept. 14, 1801, p. 2; *Gazette*, Sept. 14, 1801, p. 2; *Minerva*, Sept. 15, 1801, p. 3, quoted.

55. *Minerva*, Sept. 8, 1801, p. 3; Sept. 15, 1801, p. 3; Oct. 6, 1801, p. 1; *Chronicle*, Sept. 10, 1801, p. 3; *Centinel*, Sept. 12, 1801, p. 3; Sept. 19, 1801, p. 3; *Gazette*, Sept. 14, 1801, p. 3; *Palladium*, Sept. 15, 1801, p. 1; *Fairbanks Report*.

56. See *Fairbanks Report*.

57. Ibid., pp. [3–4].

58. See *Chronicle*, Sept. 10, 1801, p. 3; *Palladium*, Sept. 15, 1801, p. 1; *Fairbanks Report*, pp. 37–38; Otis claimed to have borrowed the characterization from the attorney general, although it does not appear in the report of his opening argument (see *Fairbanks Report*, pp. 7–11).

59. *A Poem on Jason Fairbanks* ([Dedham?]: 1801), broadside, quoted; *Lines Composed on the Execution of Jason Fairbanks* ([Dedham?]: 1801); broadside; copies of those broadsides in the collection of the Dedham Historical Society are printed on a single oblong sheet. The subtitle of *Poem* indicates that it was to be sold on the day of execution. As in the advertisements for Russell and Cutler's trial report, one of the poems also contained an explicit denial (and implicit affirmation) of its relationship to sentimental literature: "And as you read these lines as true,/(For they are no romantic tales)/Detest—yet deign to pity too/The Murd'rer of ELIZA FALES."

60. . . . *Biography of Mr. Jason Fairbanks and Miss Eliza Fales* (Boston: Printed and sold in Russell-Street, [1801]), broadside (there is a copy of this early [first?] edition at the Houghton Library, Harvard University); *Biography of Mr. Jason Fairbanks and Miss Eliza Fales* (Boston: Pandamonium Press, [1801]), broadside (variant editions located at the Boston Athenaeum and the Massachusetts Historical Society).

All three editions will be cited below and will be identified parenthetically by institutions at which they are located. The attribution to Nathaniel Coverly, Jr., is made by R. W. G. Vail in the "Report of the Librarian," *Proceedings of the American Antiquarian Society*, new ser., 48 (Oct. 1938): p. 237, on the basis of the Russell Street address; that attribution is strengthened by the fact that the work was advertised by Coverly's father in a Salem newspaper; see *Salem Impartial Register*, Sept. 17, 1801, p. 3.

61. See Benjamin Franklin V, *Boston Printers, Publishers, and Booksellers: 1640–1800* (Boston: G. K. Hall, 1980), pp. 76–80.

62. See *Biography* (Houghton).

63. See ibid.; on the reception of Goethe's Werther in American culture of the late eighteenth and nineteenth centuries, see O. W. Long, "Werther in America," in *Studies in Honor of John Albrecht Walz* (Lancaster, Pa.: 1941), pp. 86–116.

64. See *Biography* (Houghton); compare it to the trial account in the *Chronicle*, Aug. 10, 1801, pp. 2–3.

65. See *Biography* (Houghton). On the defense counsel's characterization of the tragedy, see comment in note 58 above.

66. See *Biography* (Athenaeum; Mass. His. Soc.).

67. That structure was accentuated in the elder Coverly's advertisement for the work; see *Salem Impartial Register*, Sept. 17, 1801, p. 3.

68. See *Biography* (Athenaeum; Mass. His. Soc.).

69. It should also be noted that one of the only surviving copies of that version has the early owner's inscription of a woman from West Roxbury; see *Biography* (Athenaeum).

70. I am grateful to Patricia Cline Cohen for suggesting the possibility of an intended audience of young men.

71. Cathy N. Davidson argues that the implied readers of "the early American sentimental novel" were American women who were "young, white, of good New England stock, and for the most part unmarried"; in regard to actual readership, she notes that women's signatures outnumber men's by about two to one in the more than one thousand extant copies of early American novels she examined; see Davidson, *Revolution and the Word*, pp. 8, 45, and 112, quoted.

72. *Biography* (Athenaeum; Mass. His. Soc.). Although the account of a thronged printer's office may well be fanciful, the fact that the broadside appeared in at least three editions within a period of only a week or two suggests that it was indeed avidly received. In addition, Ebenezer Fairbanks, Jr., referred to the broadside as having been "exposed for sale in every corner of the country"; see Ebenezer Fairbanks, Jr., comp., *The Solemn Declaration of the Late Unfortunate Jason Fairbanks*, 2d ed. (Dedham: H. Mann, 1801), p. 36.

73. As Michael McKeon has brilliantly demonstrated, the problematic quality of gentility (or nobility or honor) was characteristic of the broader "destabilization of social categories" that generated the early English novel; see McKeon, *The Origins of the English Novel, 1600–1740* (Baltimore: John Hopkins University Press, 1987), part 2.

74. See *Biography* (Athenaeum). On the theme of male duplicity in fiction of the period, Cathy Davidson notes that the first American novel, *The Power of Sympathy* (1789), exposes the victimization of women "by the verbal chicanery of men"; Davidson, *Revolution and the Word*, p. 111; also see p. 105.

75. See *Biography* (Athenaeum). On the abolition of public executions during the 1830s, see Louis P. Masur, *Rites of Execution: Capital Punishment and the Transforma-*

tion of American Culture, 1776–1865 (New York: Oxford University Press, 1989), pp. 5 and 93–116. On the antebellum culture of middle-class gentility, see Karen Halttunen, *Confidence Men and Painted Women: A Study of Middle-class Culture in America, 1830–1870* (New Haven: Yale University Press, 1982). I am grateful to Robert A. Gross for suggesting the significance of revulsion at the executed man's physical contortions in light of the emerging cultural emphasis on physical self-control.

76. For a definition and discussion of "epistemological" texts, see Thomas Kent, *Interpretation and Genre: The Role of Generic Perception in the Study of Narrative Texts* (Lewisburg: Bucknell University Press, 1986), pp. 79, 126–27, and 142. It should be noted that Kent applies the label to works of much greater literary sophistication than the broadside under examination here.

77. See *Biography* (Mass. His. Soc.); *Biography* (Athenaeum). The imprint may have also extended the broadside's implied ridicule of the traditional fixation in New England crime literature on the spiritual afterlives of criminals and their victims; recall the apparently satirical accounts of Eliza's ascent to Paradise and Jason's descent to Pandemonium (i.e., hell).

78. On the literary judgments of Rowson and Tyler, see discussion in chapter 1 above. Although several execution broadsides with familiar formulaic titles were published during the first decades of the nineteenth century, their tone and content actually differed significantly from the spare, first-person autobiographical narratives contained in conventional last speeches of the previous century. Few if any of the old type were published in New England after 1799. For examples of early nineteenth-century broadsides with similar titles but very different tone and content, see *The Last Words of Ebenezer Mason* (Boston: [1802]); *The Last Words of Samuel Tully* ([Boston]: T. Longlive [pseudonym?], [1812]); *Declaration and Dying Speech of Henry Phillips* ([Boston?]: [1817]).

79. See Thaddeus Mason Harris, *A Sermon Preached in the First Parish in Dedham, September 13, 1801* (Dedham: H. Mann, 1801), pp. [7]–9, 21, and 24–25.

80. See Thomas Thacher, *The Danger of Despising the Divine Counsel: Exhibited in a Discourse* (Dedham: H. Mann, 1802), pp. 19–22 and passim, quoted at 19. On Thacher, see Frank Smith, *A History of Dedham, Massachusetts* (Dedham: Transcript Press, 1936), pp. 110–11. There is at least a bit of evidence that Thacher maintained good relations with the Fairbanks family; many years after Jason's hanging, his brother Ebenezer acquired a pamphlet containing two of Thacher's sermons; see Fairbanks's inscription on Thomas Thacher, *Two Discourses* (Dedham: H. Mann, 1809), p. [1], copy in my possession.

81. Thacher, *Danger of Despising*, pp. 24–26. It may be worth noting that the two attacks on public hangings evoked by the Fairbanks case predate the movement against public executions described by Louis P. Masur by more than twenty years; see Masur, *Rites of Execution*, pp. 95–96.

82. Harris, *Sermon*, p. [5].

83. *Minerva*, Sept. 29, 1801, p. 3; Oct. 6, 1801, p. 3.

84. See Harris, *Sermon*, t.p.; *Minerva*, Dec. 1, 1801, p. 3; Jan. 26, 1802, p. 1 (notice dated Jan. 16).

85. On the changing roles of ministers in late eighteenth-century and early nineteenth-century America, see Donald M. Scott, *From Office to Profession: The New England Ministry, 1750–1850* (Philadelphia: University of Pennsylvania Press, 1978); Ann Douglas, *The Feminization of American Culture* (New York: Alfred A. Knopf, 1978), pp. 17–43, 80–164, and passim.

86. See *Minerva*, Jan. 26, 1802, p. 1.

87. See *Minerva*, Dec. 8, 1801, p. 3; Dec. 29, 1801, p. 3; Jan. 5, 1802, p. 1; on the actual date of issue, see entry in Nathaniel Ames's diary, excerpted in Hanson, *Dedham*, p. 187; Fairbanks, *Solemn Declaration*.

88. It should be noted that Thacher's sermon on the Fairbanks case was also decorated with the same funereal vase.

89. For the third edition, published in 1802, see *Shaw and Shoemaker*, 1802, no. 2208. In regard to the popular reception of the work, it should be noted that at least two contemporary responses were extremely hostile; see Hanson, *Dedham*, p. 187; Charles Grenfill Washburn, ed., "Letters of Thomas Boylston Adams to William Smith Shaw, 1799–1823," *Proceedings of the American Antiquarian Society*, new ser., 27 (April 1917): 161.

90. See Fairbanks, *Solemn Declaration*, pp. [3]–6.

91. Ibid., pp. 6–8.

92. On that transition, see discussion in text, and sources cited in note 20, above.

93. Fairbanks, *Solemn Declaration,* pp. 10–11 and 36–37, quoted at 36.

94. Ibid., pp. 13–17, quoted at 13.

95. Ibid., pp. 14–17.

96. Ibid., pp. 19–20.

97. Ibid., pp. 18–19.

98. See *Fairbanks Report*, p. 20; Harris, *Sermon*, p. 21, quoted.

99. See Fairbanks, *Solemn Declaration*, p. 55; Washburn, "Letters of Thomas Boylston Adams," p. 161.

100. "Remarkable Trials. Case of Jason Fairbanks for the Murder of Elizabeth Fales," undated newspaper clipping in Jason Fairbanks file at Dedham Historical Society (ca. 1868).

101. See Pendleton and Ellis, *Philenia*, pp. 26, 29, 89, and passim.

102. On Otis's conviction that Fairbanks was innocent, see Morison, *Harrison Gray Otis*, p. 54; on Mrs. Morton's tendency to befriend and patronize young persons, see Pendleton and Ellis, *Philenia*, p. 76.

103. Sara Wentworth Morton, *My Mind and Its Thoughts, in Sketches, Fragments, and Essays* (1823; rpt. Delmar, N.Y.: Scholars' Facsimiles & Reprints, 1975), p. 281; also see Pendleton and Ellis, *Philenia*, pp. 31, 79–80, 90–91.

104. See Pendleton and Ellis, *Philenia*, pp. 32–39.

105. See [Lucius M. Sargent], *Dealings with the Dead*, 2 vols. (Boston: Dutton and Wentworth, 1856), vol. 1, p. 191; Amory, *Life of James Sullivan*, vol. 1, pp. 35–36.

106. The work is mentioned without citation in Warren, *Jacobin and Junto*, p. 142, perhaps on the basis of a newspaper advertisement; I have been able to find no further information on the book. Ferris Greenslet reports that the case also inspired a popular French novel; see Greenslet, *Lowells*, pp. 110–11.

107. See, for example, the works of Silas Estabrook and Osgood Bradbury, cited in chapter 9 below.

108. See *Palladium*, Oct. 13, 1801, p. 2; excerpted and attributed to Fisher Ames in Frank Luther Mott, *The News in America* (Cambridge: Harvard University Press, 1952), pp. 50–51, and Willard Grosvenor Bleyer, *Main Currents in the History of American Journalism* (Boston: Houghton Mifflin, 1927), pp. 136–37; for Ames's earlier complaint over the local hysteria aroused by the Fairbanks affair, see Fisher Ames, quoted in Hanson, *Dedham*, p. 186 fn. 10.

109. For examples of early national and antebellum crime publications that com-

bined trial reports with criminal (auto)biographies, see *McDade*, nos. 67, 108, 146, 210, 236, 252, 259, 289, 319, 327, 431, 436, 473, 487, 526, 540, 686–87, 738, 806, 813, 939, 971–72, 1019, 1050–51, 1096, and 1105. A great majority of those examples were issued in midatlantic or midwestern states; New England publishers evidently preferred to keep their genres formally distinct.

110. Amory, *Life of James Sullivan*, vol. 1, p. 36.

111. For a somewhat analogous assessment of the start of the nineteenth century as a "decisive transition" in the history of French popular literature, see James Smith Allen, *Popular French Romanticism: Authors, Readers, and Books in the Nineteenth Century* (Syracuse, N.Y.: Syracuse University Press, 1981), pp. 29–34.

112. See Hart, *Popular Book*, pp. 3–21; Jesse H. Shera, *Foundations of the Public Library: The Origins of the Public Library Movement in New England 1629–1855* (Chicago: University of Chicago Press, 1949), pp. 119–21 and 148–53; Brown, *Sentimental Novel*, pp. 3–27; Lillie Deming Loshe, *The Early American Novel, 1789–1830* (1907; rpt. New York: Frederick Ungar, 1958), pp. 2–3; I am grateful to David D. Hall for pointing out to me that Tyler was not a disinterested observer. For some recent findings that also tend to support Tyler's account, see William J. Gilmore, *Reading Becomes a Necessity of Life: Material and Cultural Life in Rural New England, 1780–1835* (Knoxville: University of Tennessee Press, 1989), pp. 26, 172, 208, and 220.

113. See Jack Larkin, "The Merriams of Brookfield: Printing in the Economy and Culture of Rural Massachusetts in the Early Nineteenth Century," *Proceedings of the American Antiquarian Society* 96 (April 1986): 39–73, quoted at 68.

114. See Robert A. Gross, "Much Instruction from Little Reading: Books and Libraries in Thoreau's Concord," *Proceedings of the American Antiquarian Society* 97 (April 1987): 129–88, quoted at 152.

115. See discussion in text above and *Fairbanks Report*, pp. 16–17 and 20; on the plot of the novel, see Greenslet, *Lowells*, pp. 101–102.

116. See discussion in text above and *Fairbanks Report*, pp. 43 and 47–48; Fairbanks, *Solemn Declaration*, p. 19.

117. See discussion in text above and *Minerva*, May 19, 1801, p. 3.

118. See discussion of and citations to various works in text and notes above, particularly *Mournful Tragedy*; *Biography*; and *Solemn Declaration*.

119. See discussion in text above and *Fairbanks Report*, pp. 47–48, 56, 66, and 71–74.

120. Along similar lines, Kenneth Silverman has described the earlier infiltration of sentimentalism into revolutionary political discourse; see Silverman, *A Cultural History of the American Revolution* (New York: Thomas Y. Crowell, 1976), pp. 82–87.

121. See Shera, *Foundations*, pp. 127–55.

122. See Larkin, "Merriams of Brookfield," pp. 68–69. Larkin notes that "one of the novel-buying apprentices later lamented his fiction reading, believing that it had permanently injured his powers of factual retention and concentration."

123. See Gross, "Much Instruction," pp. 148–49. It would be interesting to know whether Van Schalkwyck and her friends were among the social circle of Concord ladies addressed by the anonymous author of the *Biography of Mr. Jason Fairbanks and Miss Eliza Fales*.

124. On the similar appeal of novels to the youth of the Upper Connecticut River Valley of northern New England, see Gilmore, *Reading Becomes a Necessity*, p. 220.

125. On the adoption of new political tactics by young Federalists like Harrison Gray Otis, see David H. Fischer, *The Revolution of American Conservatism: The Federalist Party in the Era of Jeffersonian Democracy* (New York: Harper & Row, 1965).

126. On the rise of sentimental literature as a cultural insurgency of the socially subordinate, see Davidson, *Revolution and the Word*, pp. 38–54.

127. See Warren, *Jacobin and Junto*, p. 128.

128. See Greenslet, *Lowells*, p. 111.

129. Lawrence M. Friedman, "Law, Lawyers, and Popular Culture," *Yale Law Journal* 98 (July 1989): 1595.

130. On Gramsci's concept of "spontaneous philosophy," see T. J. Jackson Lears, "The Concept of Cultural Hegemony: Problems and Possibilities," *American Historical Review* 90 (June 1985): 570.

Chapter 9. *The Prostitute and the Somnambulist*

1. For other modern accounts of the Bickford/Tirrell affair, see Daniel A. Cohen, "The Murder of Maria Bickford: Fashion, Passion, and the Birth of a Consumer Culture," *American Studies* 31 (Fall 1990): 5–30; Barbara Hobson, "A Murder in the Moral and Religious City of Boston," *Boston Bar Journal* 22 (Nov. 1978): 9–21; Marjorie Carleton, "'Maria Met a Gentleman': The Bickford Case," in John N. Makris, ed., *Boston Murders* (New York: Duell, Sloan and Pearce, 1948), pp. 15–39.

2. For Boston population figures, see Oscar Handlin, *Boston's Immigrants: A Study in Acculturation* (Cambridge: Harvard University Press, 1979), p. 239. On the "urbanization" of "rural" Massachusetts in a slightly earlier period, see Richard D. Brown, "The Emergence of Urban Society in Rural Massachusetts, 1760–1820," *Journal of American History* 61 (June 1974): 29–51. Though much of the population growth in Boston was due to foreign immigration, a substantial amount also resulted from migration from rural New England; see Peter R. Knights, *The Plain People of Boston, 1830–1860: A Study in City Growth* (New York: Oxford University Press, 1971), pp. 33–47.

3. Barbara Meil Hobson, *Uneasy Virtue: The Politics of Prostitution and the American Reform Tradition* (New York: Basic Books, 1987), p. 42. On Boston's long-standing reputation as a "center of prostitution," see David J. Pivar, *Purity Crusade: Sexual Morality and Social Control, 1868–1900* (Westport, Conn.: Greenwood Press, 1973), pp. 21–23.

4. See William W. Sanger, *The History of Prostitution* (1859; rpt. New York: Arno Press, 1972), p. 454.

5. See *Friend of Virtue*, Dec. 1, 1846, p. 362.

6. On the wide range of settings for commercial sex in an antebellum city, see Sanger, *History of Prostitution*, pp. 549–74; for two other types of sexual commodification in antebellum cities, see *Boston Daily Times* [cited hereafter as *Times*], Feb. 24, 1846, p. 2 ("Obscene Books"); July 21, 1846, p. 2 ("Nude Daguerreotypes"). For a modern scholarly overview, see John D'Emilio and Estelle B. Freedman, *Intimate Matters: A History of Sexuality in America* (New York: Harper & Row, 1988), pp. 130–38.

7. For biographies of Rufus Choate, see Jean V. Matthews, *Rufus Choate: The Law and Civic Virtue* (Philadelphia: Temple University Press, 1980); C[laude] M.

F[uess], "Choate, Rufus," in *DAB*, vol. 4, pp. 86–90; Fuess, *Rufus Choate: The Wizard of the Law* (New York: Minton, Balch, 1928); Edwin Percy Whipple, *Recollections of Eminent Men* (Boston: Ticknor, 1886), pp. 1–76; Joseph Neilson, *Memories of Rufus Choate* (Boston: Houghton, Mifflin, 1884); Samuel Gilman Brown, *The Works of Rufus Choate with a Memoir of His Life*, 2 vols. (Boston: Little, Brown and Company, 1862), vol. 1; Edward G. Parker, *Reminiscences of Rufus Choate, The Great American Advocate* (New York: Mason Brothers, 1860). On Choate's relationship with Daniel Webster, see Matthews, *Rufus Choate*, pp. 61–62 and 204–12; Whipple, *Recollections*, pp. 31–37; Parker, *Reminiscences*, p. 64.

8. See Matthews, *Rufus Choate*, pp. 7–11; Brown, *Works*, vol. 1, pp. 203–4.

9. See Matthews, *Rufus Choate*, pp. 12–13; Fuess, *Rufus Choate*, pp. 39–40; Brown, *Works*, vol. 1, pp. 10–11.

10. See Brown, *Works*, vol. 1, p. 507. For contemporary newspaper coverage of the Jackman trial, see *Salem Gazette*, May 5, 1818, p. 3; *Essex Register*, May 6, 1818, p. 2.

11. On Webster's earlier defense of Jackman's alleged accomplices, see Joseph Jackman, *The Sham-Robbery, Committed by Elijah Putnam Goodridge on His Own Person* (Concord, N.H.: Printed for the Author, 1819), pp. 27–97.

12. On Choate's use of those techniques, see John W. Black, "Rufus Choate," in William Norwood Brigance, ed., *A History and Criticism of American Public Address* (New York: Russell & Russell, 1960), pp. 444–45 and 448–51; also see passim in text below.

13. Whipple, *Recollections*, p. 4. On Choate's legal training and early practice, see Matthews, *Rufus Choate*, pp. 16–42; Fuess, *Rufus Choate*, pp. 43–64; Parker, *Reminiscences*, pp. 30–49.

14. See Matthews, *Rufus Choate*, p. 23; Fuess, "Choate," pp. 86–87; Fuess, *Rufus Choate*, pp. 53–57; Neilson, *Memories*, pp. 6–7; Brown, *Works*, vol. 1, pp. 21–25.

15. See Matthews, *Rufus Choate*, p. 28; Fuess, "Choate," p. 87; Fuess, *Rufus Choate*, pp. 65–122; George S. Boutwell, *The Lawyer, The Statesman, and The Soldier* (New York: D. Appleton, 1887), p. 24.

16. For descriptions of Choate's courtroom performances, see Matthews, *Rufus Choate*, pp. 22–23; Fuess, *Rufus Choate*, p. 92; Brown, *Works*, vol. 1, pp. 22–25, 42–43, 251–52, 286–87, and passim; Parker, *Reminiscences*, pp. 127–230, 321–488, and passim; "Hon. Rufus Choate," *American Review* 5 (Jan. 1847): 63–71.

17. See Black, "Rufus Choate," pp. 440–53.

18. "Hon. Rufus Choate," p. 70.

19. Whipple, *Recollections*, pp. 1, 13–14, and 52–53.

20. On Choate's leadership of the Boston bar during the 1840s, see Matthews, *Rufus Choate*, pp. 41–42.

21. See, for example, *Times*, Oct. 4, 1845, p. 2; Nov. 29, 1845, p. 2; June 24, 1846, p. 2.

22. *Times*, June 24, 1846, p. 2.

23. See Fuess, *Rufus Choate*, pp. 150–51; Whipple, *Recollections*, pp. 34–35; Parker, *Reminiscences*, p. 212.

24. See William T. Davis, *Bench and Bar of the Commonwealth of Massachusetts*, 2 vols. (1895; rpt. New York: Da Capo Press, 1974), vol. 1, p. 429; "Samuel Dunn Parker," *Boston Daily Globe*, July 30, 1873, p. 5; "Sketches of Public Characters. No. 3. Samuel Dunn Parker, Esq., Prosecuting Officer of the Municipal Court," *City Crier and Country Advertiser* 1 no. 2 (April 1846): 2; Horatio Woodman, ed., *Reports of*

Criminal Cases Tried in the Municipal Court of the City of Boston (Boston: Little and Brown, 1845), pp. 1–9, 19–24, 67–69, 112–15, 132–37, 180–86, 202–11, 267–70, and 277–80. For Parker's defense of two accused murderers, see *Columbian Centinel*, Dec. 4, 1824, p. 2.

25. *Times*, Oct. 6, 1845, p. 2.

26. See *Times*, Oct. 1, 1845, p. 2.

27. *Times*, Oct. 6, 1845, p. 2.

28. *Daily Evening Transcript* [cited hereafter as *Transcript*], Sept. 29, 1845, p. 2; *Times*, Sept. 30, 1845, p. 2; *Boston Daily Mail* [cited hereafter as *Mail*], Sept. 30, 1845, p. 2. On Colonel Hatch, see *City Crier and Country Advertiser* 1, no. 2 (April 1846): 2. On the circulation of the *Times* and the *Mail*, see *Times*, May 23, 1846, p. 2; *Mail*, Oct. 30, 1846, p. 1, masthead.

29. *Boston Post* [cited hereafter as *Post*], Sept. 30, 1845, p. 2.

30. See J. E. P. Weeks, reporter, *Trial of Albert John Tirrell for the Murder of Mary Ann Bickford* (Boston: "Times" Office, 1846) [cited hereafter as *Times Report*], pp. 6–7. Cedar Lane was also known as Mount Vernon Avenue and Pinckney Lane.

31. *Mail*, Oct. 27, 1845, p. 4; Oct. 28, 1845, p. 2.

32. *Mail*, Oct. 28, 1845, p. 2.

33. *Times*, Oct. 29, 1845, p. 2; *Mail*, Oct. 29, 1845, p. 2; *Boston Courier* [cited hereafter as *Courier*], Oct. 29, 1845, p. 2; [Silas Estabrook?], *Eccentricities & Anecdotes of Albert John Tirrell* (Boston: 1846), pp. 44–48, quoted at p. 46.

34. *Mail*, Oct. 29, 1845, p. 2, and other sources cited in note 33.

35. For rumors concerning Tirrell's whereabouts, see *Times*, Nov. 5, 1845, pp. 2 and 4; Nov. 12, 1845, p. 2; Nov. 15, 1845, p. 2; Dec. 2, 1845, p. 4; *Mail*, Oct. 30, 1845, p. 2; Nov. 4, 1845, p. 4; Nov. 29, 1845, p. 2; *Transcript*, Oct. 30, 1845, p. 2; Nov. 4, 1845, p. 2; *Daily American Eagle* [cited hereafter as *Eagle*], Nov. 5, 1845, pp. 2 and 4; *Boston Daily Whig* [cited hereafter as *Whig*], Dec. 1, 1845, p. 4.

36. *Mail*, Oct. 31, 1845, p. 2. It was probably at least partly in response to this fanciful report that the *Bangor Daily Whig* noted that "Some of the Boston editors are disposed to romance a little on the history of Mrs. Bickford"; see *Bangor Daily Whig*, Nov. 3, 1845, p. 2.

37. *Mail*, Oct. 31, 1845, p. 2. For somewhat more detailed analysis of this and related coverage, see Cohen, "Murder of Maria Bickford," pp. 12–14.

38. *Post*, Nov. 10, 1845, p. 1.

39. Because I have not been able to locate any copy of the November 1, 1845, edition of the *Whig*, I have based my discussion of the *Whig*'s report on a reprint appearing in the *National Police Gazette* [cited hereafter as *Police Gazette*], Nov. 8, 1845, p. 93. Excerpts or synopses of the article also appeared in the *Boston Daily Bee* [cited hereafter as *Bee*], Nov. 12, 1845, p. 2; *Post*, Dec. 1, 1845, p. 2; *Times*, Dec. 2, 1845, p. 2; *Mail*, Dec. 2, 1845, p. 4.

40. See Barbara Meil Hobson, *Uneasy Virtue: The Politics of Prostitution and the American Reform Tradition* (New York: Basic Books, 1987), pp. 70–72; Hobson, "Sex in the Marketplace: Prostitution in an American City, Boston, 1820–1880" (Ph.D. diss., Boston University, 1982), pp. xxi and 90–91; William G. McLoughlin, "Untangling the Tiverton Tragedy: The Social Meaning of the Terrible Haystack Murder of 1833," *Journal of American Culture* 7 (Winter 1984): 81; David Brion Davis, *Homicide in American Fiction, 1798–1860: A Study in Social Values* (1957; rpt. Ithaca: Cornell University Press, 1968), pp. 165–70 and 201–9. As Peter Gay has observed, "no century depicted woman as vampire, as castrator, as killer so consistently, so program-

matically, and so nakedly as the nineteenth"; see Gay, *The Bourgeois Experience: Victoria to Freud*, vol. 1, *Education of the Senses* (New York: Oxford University Press, 1984), p. 207.

41. *Christian Reflector*, Nov. 13, 1845, p. 182.

42. *Mail*, Dec. 6, 1845, p. 2.

43. Ibid.

44. *Post*, Dec. 1, 1845, pp. 1–2; for reprints, see *Times*, Dec. 2, 1845, pp. 1–2; *Mail*, Dec. 2, 1845, p. 4; Dec. 6, 1845, p. 2 (advertisement for *Weekly Mail*); *Police Gazette*, Dec. 6, 1845, p. 123; *Hangman*, Dec. 17, 1845, p. [149]; *Friend of Virtue*, Feb. 1, 1846, pp. 35–38. The town records of Brewer, Maine, indicate that James Bickford married Mary Ann Dunn in March, *1840*; see Brewer, Maine, Vital Records, Marriages and Intentions of [Marriage], Book 2, 1839–54, p. 1 (Maine State Archives, reel 90). The subsequently published *Authentic Life*, also linked to James Bickford (and discussed below), got the year right and correctly placed her marriage at Brewer. I have not been able to find any record of Dunn's birth.

45. *Post*, Dec. 1, 1845, p. 1.

46. Ibid.

47. Ibid., pp. 1–2.

48. Ibid., p. 2.

49. See *Times*, Oct. 29, 1845, p. 2; *Police Gazette*, Dec. 13, 1845, p. 132.

50. [Silas Estabrook?], *The Life and Death of Mrs. Maria Bickford*, 4th ed. (Boston: 1846); *Times*, Dec. 9, 1845, p. 2; *Mail*, Dec. 9, 1845, p. 2; *Bee*, Dec. 9, 1845, p. 2.

51. [Estabrook?], *Life and Death*, t.p. On Estabrook's occupation and change in residence, see *Longworth's American Almanac, New-York Register, and City Directory* (New York: T. Longworth & Son, 1842), p. 228; *The New-York City Directory, for 1844 & 1845* (New York: J. Doggett, Jr., 1844), p. 219; *Adams's Boston Directory . . . 1847–1848* (Boston: J. French, 1847), p. 98. Estabrook edited a weekly periodical called *Rough and Ready* in Boston between 1847 and 1849.

52. [Estabrook?], *Life and Death*, p. 25.

53. See [Estabrook?], *Life and Death*, front wrapper. According to Ronald J. Zboray, most hardcover books sold for between 75 cents and $1.25 during the antebellum period, while the "usual minimum price" for paperbacks was 38 cents and the "most common price" was 50 cents; only "a handful of paperbacks sold for as low as $12\frac{1}{2}$ cents"; see Zboray, "Antebellum Reading and the Ironies of Technological Innovation," *American Quarterly* 40 (March 1988): 74–75. Zboray's formulation probably underestimates the rich vitality of the cheap end of the price spectrum, especially during the 1840s and 1850s; see Tebbel, *History of Book Publishing*, vol. 1, pp. 240–51. To provide some sense of context, it should be noted that, during the mid-1840s, an average Massachusetts laborer might expect to receive between about 80 and 95 cents a day; see U. S. Bureau of Labor Statistics, *History of Wages in the United States from Colonial Times to 1928* (1934; rpt. Detroit: Gale Research Company, 1966), p. 253. The cost of a $12\frac{1}{2}$-cent pamphlet was thus approximately 14 percent of a worker's daily wage, just a bit more than the cost of a $4.95 paperback to an unskilled laborer working an eight hour day at about $5.00 an hour in the 1990s. Obviously, that is a very crude analogy, given changes in the relative costs of food, housing, health care, and so forth. Still, those rough calculations do suggest that cheap pamphlets may have been about as accessible to antebellum working-class readers as cheap paperbacks are to working-class readers today. (It should also be noted that several other pamphlets on the Bickford case, discussed below, sold for only $6\frac{1}{4}$ cents!)

54. [Estabrook?], *The Early Love Letters, and Later Literary Remains of Maria Bickford* (Boston: 1846) [cited hereafter as *Love Letters*], p. 6.

55. [Estabrook?], *Life and Death*, pp. 1–13.

56. Ibid., pp. 10–13.

57. Ibid., pp. 13–16.

58. On Augustus, see Hobson, *Uneasy Virtue*, p. 132; Hobson, "Sex in the Marketplace," pp. 238–41; Charles Lionel Chute and Marjorie Bell, *Crime, Courts, and Probation* (New York: Macmillan, 1956), pp. 31–52; *John Augustus: First Probation Officer* (1939; rpt. Montclair, N.J.: Patterson Smith, 1972); *Letter Concerning the Labors of Mr. John Augustus, the Well-Known Philanthropist* (Boston: Published for Private Circulation, Dec. 1858); [John Augustus], *A Report of the Labors of Mr. John Augustus, for the Last Ten Years, In Aid of the Unfortunate* (Boston: Wright & Hasty, 1852).

59. [Estabrook?], *Life and Death*, pp. 17–21.

60. Ibid., pp. 21–22.

61. Ibid., pp. 22–23.

62. Ibid., pp. 23–32.

63. *Bee*, Dec. 9, 1845, p. 2.

64. *Times*, Jan. 28, 1846, p. 2; *Mail*, Jan. 29, 1846, p. 2; [Estabrook?], *Eccentricities*, pp. 5–14.

65. [Estabrook?], *Eccentricities*, pp. 14–48.

66. Ibid., pp. 24–25.

67. See [Estabrook?], *Love Letters*, pp. [5]–6.

68. *Times*, March 2, 1846, p. 3.

69. Compare letters in [Estabrook?], *Love Letters*, pp. 21–22, to letters printed in the *Post*, Dec. 1, 1845, pp. 1–2.

70. [Estabrook?], *Love Letters*, p. [5].

71. Ibid., p. 24.

72. Ibid., pp. 8, 26, and 32–33.

73. Ibid., pp. 23, 27–29, and 30–31.

74. Ibid., p. [5].

75. Ibid., pp. 26–27.

76. On the antebellum literature of "subversive reform," see David S. Reynolds, *Beneath the American Renaissance: The Subversive Imagination in the Age of Emerson and Melville* (New York: Alfred A. Knopf, 1988), pp. 54–91 and passim.

77. *Mail*, Dec. 13, 1845, p. 2.

78. On the price of the novel, see *Mail*, Jan. 2, 1846, pp. [2–3]. For a discussion of typical antebellum book prices, see note 53 above.

79. For biographical information on Bradbury, see obituaries in *Portland Advertiser*, Nov. 29, 1886; *Transcript*, Nov. 30, 1886, p. 1. For listings of Bradbury as a "counsellor," see *Stimpson's Boston Directory* (Boston: C. Stimpson, 1845), p. 96; *Adams's Boston Directory . . . 1847–1848* (Boston: J. French [and] C. Stimpson, 1847), p. 59. For the characterizations of Bradbury's legal practice (certainly inaccurate), see *Yankee*, Feb. 7, 1846, p. 3; Feb. 21, 1846, p. 4. Bradbury is not even listed in William T. Davis's *Bench and Bar of the Commonwealth of Massachusetts*.

80. See Mary Noel, *Villains Galore . . . The Heyday of the Popular Story Weekly* (New York: Macmillan, 1954), pp. 18–27 and passim; *Portland Advertiser*, Nov. 29, 1886. For listings of Bradbury's novels, see Lyle H. Wright, *American Fiction, 1774–1850*, 2d rev. ed. (San Marino, Calif.: Huntington Library, 1969), pp. 52–56; Wright,

American Fiction, 1851–1875 (San Marino, Calif.: Huntington Library, 1957), pp. 47–49.

81. On Ingraham, see Robert W. Weathersby II, *J. H. Ingraham* (Boston: Twayne, 1980); Wright, *American Fiction 1774–1850*, pp. 172–85; Lyle H. Wright, "A Statistical Survey of American Fiction, 1774–1850," *Huntington Library Quarterly* 2 (April 1939): pp. 312–13.

82. See Noel, *Villains Galore*, pp. 18–27 and passim; Longfellow misquoted at 18, periodical quoted at 300; Weathersby, *J. H. Ingraham*, p. 71; Andrew Hilen, ed., *The Letters of Henry Wadsworth Longfellow*, 4 vols. (Cambridge: Harvard University Press, 1966), vol. 2, p. 108, quoted. For characterizations of cheap fiction as an "industrial" product in France during the same period, see James Smith Allen, *Popular French Romanticism: Authors, Readers, and Books in the 19th Century* (Syracuse, N.Y.: Syracuse University Press, 1981), pp. 93 and 151.

83. See Wright, *American Fiction 1774–1850*, p. 56. On the broader genre of "city-mysteries," see Reynolds, *Beneath the American Renaissance*, pp. 82–84; Adrienne Siegel, *The Image of the American City in Popular Literature, 1820–1870* (Port Washington, N.Y.: Kennikat Press, 1981), pp. 36–46; Louis James, *Fiction for the Working Man, 1830–1850* (London: Oxford University Press, 1963), pp. 140–41 and 165.

84. For examples of Osgood Bradbury's penchant for resolving his plots with violent deaths, see *The Empress of Beauty* (Boston: J. N. Bradley, 1844), pp. 60–64; *The Eastern Belle: or, The Betrayed One!* (Boston: H. L. Williams, 1845), p. 56; *Henriette* ([Boston]: H. L. Williams, 1845); *Julia Bicknell: or, Love and Murder!* (Boston: H. L. Williams, 1845), pp. 69–72; *The Belle of the Bowery* (Boston: H. L. Williams, 1846); *Isabelle: or, The Emigrant's Daughter* (Boston: F. Gleason, 1848), p. 100.

85. *Yankee*, Feb. 7, 1846, p. 3.

86. Bradbury, *Julia Bicknell*, passim.

87. Ibid.

88. Ibid., pp. 23–65, quoted at 28.

89. Ibid., pp. 65–72, quoted at 72.

90. Such a conservative stance was somewhat similar to those typically adopted by the later mass-circulation "story papers"; see Noel, *Villains Galore*, pp. 247–53 and passim.

91. A rare surviving number of the English reprint seems to have been discovered about thirty years ago by a researcher amid the squalor of a condemned East End building belonging to a retired waste-paper collector. It was found among massive piles of damp and dusty Victorian serials and periodicals assembled in a dark sitting room. The earnest young scholar, after poring through the steamy account of Frederick Searsmont and Julia Bicknell, pronounced it "licentious in the extreme." See James, *Fiction for the Working Man*, pp. xiii (quoted), 12–44, 129–45, 184, 194, and 211, esp. 25–26 and 134–35; also see Richard D. Altick, *The English Common Reader: A Social History of the Mass Reading Public, 1800–1900* (1957; rpt. Chicago: University of Chicago Press, 1983), pp. 267–93 and 332–47.

92. *Uncle Sam*, May 9, 1846, p. 3.

93. See *Times Report*, pp. [7] and 13–16; *Times*, Oct. 30, 1845, p. 2; Dec. 20, 1845, p. 3; Dec. 30, 1845, p. 4.

94. See *Times*, Oct. 31, 1845, pp. 2 and 4; Nov. 4, 1845, p. 2; Nov. 6, 1845, p. 2, quoted. On the illness and death of Boston's mayor, see *Times*, Nov. 14, 1845, p. 2; Nov. 24, 1845, p. 2.

95. On the rumored sightings and arrests of Tirrell, see citations in note 35 above. A few of those newspaper stories labeled the fugitive "Tirrell, the Murderer"; for a squib that even seemed to presuppose his eventual execution, see *Mail*, Nov. 4, 1845, p. 4.

96. See *Mail*, Dec. 20, 1845, p. 2; *Courier*, Dec. 20, 1845, p. 2; *Times*, Dec. 20, 1845, p. 3; Dec. 24, 1845, p. 4; Dec. 30, 1845, p. 4; Jan. 15, 1846, p. 2; Feb. 5, 1846, p. 2; Feb. 6, 1846, p. 2.

97. *Times*, Feb. 7, 1846, p. 2; *Times*, Feb. 13, 1846, p. 2. On Annis and Amos B. Merrill, see Davis, *Bench and Bar*, p. 419.

98. See Parker, *Reminiscences*, p. 226.

99. *Times*, Feb. 17, 1846, p. 2; also see *Prisoner's Friend*, Feb. 25, 1846, p. 30.

100. *Mail*, March 25, 1846, p. 2; also see *Transcript*, March 24, 1846, p. 2.

101. Compare *Times Report*, pp. 4–8, to *The Trial of Albert J. Tirrell, Charged with the Murder of Mrs. Maria Bickford* (Boston: Daily Mail, [1846]) [cited herafter as *Mail Report*], pp. 4–8. There were at least two variant editions of the *Mail Report*, one thirty-two pages in length and the other thirty-seven; all subsequent citations are to the longer edition.

102. See *Times Report*, pp. 4–8; *Mail Report*, pp. 4–8.

103. See *Times Report*, pp. 8–16; *Mail Report*, pp. 8–15.

104. See *Times Report*, pp. 9–12 and 14–15; *Mail Report*, pp. 8–13; *The Trial of Albert John Tirrell for the Murder of Maria A. Bickford* (Boston: H. B. Skinner, 1846) [cited hereafter as *Skinner Report*], p. 25 (for reference to Moriarty's testimony).

105. See *Mail*, March 27, 1846, p. 2.

106. *Times Report*, pp. 16–17; *Mail Report*, pp. 15–16.

107. See *Times Report*, pp. 18–20; *Mail Report*, pp. 16–17.

108. See *Times Report*, pp. 18–20; *Mail Report*, pp. 16–18.

109. See *Times Report*, pp. 18–20, quoted at 19–20; *Mail Report*, pp. 17–18.

110. See *Times Report*, pp. 20–22, quoted at 20; *Mail Report*, pp. 18–21.

111. See *Times Report*, pp. 22–23, quoted at 22; *Mail Report*, p. 21. On the antebellum movement against capital punishment, see Louis P. Masur, *Rites of Execution: Capital Punishment and the Transformation of American Culture, 1776–1865* (New York: Oxford University Press, 1989), pp. 3–24 and 93–163; Louis P. Masur, "The Culture of Executions and the Conflict Over Capital Punishment in America, 1776–1860," (Ph.D. diss., Princeton University, 1985), pp. 149–278; Philip English Mackey, *Hanging in the Balance: The Anti–Capital Punishment Movement in New York State, 1776–1861* (New York: Garland, 1982), pp. 112–319; David Brion Davis, "The Movement to Abolish Capital Punishment in America, 1787–1861," *American Historical Review* 63 (Oct. 1957): 29–46. For contemporary evidence of active anti–death penalty agitation in Boston and elsewhere at about the time of Tirrell's murder trial, see *Times*, Jan. 14, 1846, p. 2; Jan. 28, 1846, p. 2; Feb. 5, 1846, p. 2; Feb. 6, 1846, p. 2; Feb. 10, 1846, p. 2; Feb. 13, 1840, p. 2; Feb. 16, 1846, p. 2; Feb. 17, 1846, p. 2; Feb. 23, 1846, p. 2; Feb. 27, 1846, p. 2; March 10, 1846, p. 2; April 1, 1846, p. 2; April 8, 1846, p. 2; May 7, 1846, p. 2.

112. *Mail Report*, pp. 21–22, quoted at 21; *Times Report*, p. 23. Albert's daughter was actually only three years old.

113. See Robert Wilson Tirrell, *The Tirrell, Tirrill-Terrill, Tyrell Book*, 2d ed. (Englewood, N.J.: 1969) [cited hereafter as *Tirrell Book*], p. 200.

114. See *Times Report*, pp. 23–28; *Mail Report*, pp. 22–25.

115. See *Times Report*, pp. 24–27; *Mail Report*, pp. 22–25; *Skinner Report*, pp. 17–20.

116. See *Times Report*, p. 28; *Mail Report*, pp. 25–26, quoted at 25.

117. See *Times Report*, pp. 28–30; *Mail Report*, pp. 26–27. For biographical information on Walter Channing, see *DAB*, vol. 4, pp. 3–4; on Samuel Woodward, see *DAB*, vol. 20, p. 511.

118. *Times Report*, pp. 30–31; *Mail Report*, p. 28; *Eagle*, March 28, 1846, p. 2; *Bee*, March 28, 1846, p. 2.

119. *Mail Report*, p. 28.

120. *Times Report*, pp. 31–35; *Mail Report*, pp. 28–32; *Bee*, March 28, 1846, p. 2; *Transcript*, March 28, 1846, p. 2. Estimates of the duration of Choate's address varied.

121. Compare the very different versions provided by the pamphlet compilations: *Times Report*, pp. 31–35; *Mail Report*, pp. 28–32; *Skinner Report*, pp. 23–27.

122. Fuess, *Rufus Choate*, pp. 187–88; Parker, *Reminiscences*, pp. 179–80.

123. See Whipple, *Recollections*, pp. 53 and 75; also see Boutwell, *Lawyer*, p. 17.

124. Boutwell, *Lawyer*, p. 32.

125. See *Mail Report*, pp. 28 and 30; *Times Report*, p. 31.

126. See *Skinner Report*, p. 23; *Mail Report*, pp. 28–29; *Times Report*, p. 31. For the quoted article itself, see "The Punishment of Death," *North American Review* 62 (Jan. 1846): 40–70.

127. *Bee*, March 28, 1846, p. 2; *Skinner Report*, p. 24.

128. *Times Report*, p. 31.

129. See *Skinner Report*, pp. 24–25, quoted at 24; *Mail Report*, pp. 29–30; *Times Report*, pp. 31–32 and 34.

130. See *Skinner Report*, pp. 25–27, quoted at 25; *Mail Report*, pp. 30–31, quoted at p. 30; *Times Report*, pp. 32–33, quoted at 32.

131. See *Times Report*, pp. 32–33; *Mail Report*, pp. 30–31; *Skinner Report*, p. 26, quoted.

132. See *Skinner Report*, pp. 26–27, quoted; *Times Report*, pp. 32–34, quoted at 32; *Mail Report*, pp. 30–31.

133. See *Bee*, March 28, 1846, p. 2, quoted; *Times Report*, pp. 34–35; *Mail Report*, pp. 31–32; *Skinner Report*, p. 27.

134. *Transcript*, March 28, 1846, p. 2.

135. *Times Report*, pp. 34–35.

136. On Choate's advocacy of historical novels, see Rufus Choate, "The Importance of Illustrating New-England History by a Series of Romances like the Waverley Novels" (1833), in Choate, *Addresses and Orations* (Boston: Little, Brown, 1878), pp. 1–39.

137. For the characterization of Choate's address as "splendid," see *Mail Report*, p. 32.

138. *Skinner Report*, p. 28, quoted; for a somewhat different enumeration of Parker's points, see *Times Report*, p. 35.

139. *Times Report*, p. 36.

140. *Mail Report*, p. 33; *Skinner Report*, p. 30.

141. *Times Report*, p. 37.

142. Ibid.

143. *Times Report*, pp. 37–39, quoted at 38; *Mail Report*, pp. 34–35; *Skinner Report*, pp. 30–32.

144. See *Stimpson's Boston Directory* (1845), pp. 192 and 254; *Stimpson's Boston Directory* (Boston: C. Stimpson, 1846), pp. 63, 120, 359, 363, and 423. For a somewhat different enumeration of juror occupations, see Black, "Rufus Choate," p. 454.

145. *Boston Daily Advertiser* [cited hereafter as *Advertiser*], March 30, 1846, p. 1; *Whig*, March 30, 1846, p. 2; *Post*, March 30, 1846, p. 2, quoted; *Mail Report*, pp. 35–36; *Times Report*, p. 39.

146. *Post*, March 30, 1846, p. 2; *Times Report*, p. 39; Whipple, *Recollections*, p. 10, quoted.

147. *Times*, March 21, 1846, p. 2; March 25, 1846, p. 2.

148. For examples of extensive coverage aside from the *Times*, see relevant issues of the *Mail*, *Eagle*, *Post*, *Bee*, and *Advertiser*.

149. See *Eagle*, March 28, 1846, p. 2 (advertisement for *Tocsin*); *Times*, April 2, 1846, p. 3 (advertisement for *Boston Notion*).

150. *Times*, March 26, 1846, p. 2; *Mail*, March 27, 1846, p. 2. During the mid-nineteenth century, an edition of only ten thousand indicated that a book was "a decided hit" (see Zboray, "Antebellum Reading," pp. 65–66).

151. See *Times Report*; *Mail Report*; *Times*, March 30, 1846, p. 2; *Mail*, March 30, 1846, p. 2; *Eagle*, March 30, 1846, p. 3 (advertisement probably refers to *Mail Report*).

152. *Mail*, April 16, 1846, p. 2; the American Antiquarian Society at Worcester owns two variant printings of the *Times Report*.

153. *Skinner Report*.

154. For example, it is unclear whether the advertisement in the *Eagle*, March 30, 1846, p. 2, refers to one of the three versions already described, or to a fourth pamphlet that has not survived.

155. On the pricing of the reports at $6\frac{1}{4}$ cents per copy, see *Times*, March 26, 1846, p. 2; *Mail*, March 30, 1846, p. 2; *Daily American Eagle*, March 30, 1846, p. 2; for a Tirrell trial report priced at $12\frac{1}{2}$ cents, see *Skinner Report*, t.p. For a comparative discussion of antebellum book and paperback prices, see note 53 above. Note that the *Mail* report was advertised in March 1846 as appearing in an edition of twenty thousand; in October of that year, a note on the *Mail*'s masthead began to claim that the newspaper itself enjoyed a circulation of twenty thousand (see *Mail*, Oct. 30, 1846, p. 1). Meanwhile, in May 1846 the *Times*, the *Mail*'s chief rival, claimed a circulation of more than eighteen thousand (see *Times*, May 23, 1846, p. 2). Of course, all circulation claims, whether of newspapers or trial reports, were subject to exaggeration.

156. *Mail*, March 27, 1846, p. 2, emphasis added.

157. Ibid.

158. See chapter 1 above.

159. *Times Report*, back wrapper; the Ingraham novels based on recent murder cases were *Herman De Ruyter* (Rogers) and *Frank Rivers* (Jewett); see Weathersby, *J. H. Ingraham*, pp. 79–80; Wright, *American Fiction 1774–1850*, pp. 173–74 and 177–78; in addition, *The Beautiful Cigar Girl*, also listed on the back wrapper of the *Times Report*, is probably *La Bonita Cigarera; or, The Beautiful Cigar-Vender!* (Rogers), described by Weathersby and Wright on some of the same pages.

160. On the relationship of Poe's story to the case of Mary Rogers, see John Walsh, *Poe the Detective: The Curious Circumstances Behind the Mystery of Marie Roget* (New Brunswick: Rutgers University Press, 1968); Edmund Pearson, *Instigation of the Devil* (New York: Charles Scribner's Sons, 1930), pp. 177–85 and 351–52.

161. For a brilliant survey of that broader literary complex, see Reynolds, *Beneath*

the American Renaissance. For a richly perceptive and evocative study of murder in American fiction of the early national and antebellum periods, see Davis, *Homicide in American Fiction.* On the significance of Poe's short stories in the development of modern detective fiction, see Julian Symons, *Mortal Consequences: A History—From the Detective Story to the Crime Novel* (1972; rpt. New York: Schocken, 1973), pp. 17 and 27–36.

162. See *Times,* Dec. 29, 1845, p. 2, quoted. Although the main issue in dispute related to the impact of pretrial crime coverage on the jury selection process, the *Times* editor implied that Shaw was displeased by trial reportage as well.

163. See *Transcript,* April 1, 1846, p. 2; April 3, 1846, p. 2; April 7, 1846, p. 2; April 8, 1846, p. 4; April 9, 1846, p. 4; April 14, 1846, p. 2; April 16, 1846, p. 2; April 30, 1846, p. 2; May 5, 1846, p. 2; *Times,* March 30, 1846, p. 2; March 31, 1846, p. 2; April 2, 1846, p. 2; April 8, 1846, p. 2, quoted; April 15, 1846, p. 2; May 2, 1846, p. 2; May 6, 1846, p. 2; May 11, 1846, p. 2.

164. Additional evidence of popular misogyny in connection with the case—and of resistance to it—is provided by the following excerpt from a satirical column, ostensibly by a rural Yankee, in a cheap literary periodical: "Wot maiks me mad is, I heer sum peepel argy that Turrel had orter be let augph becox the woman he killed wos a bad woman, and her lyfe of no akkownt to noboddy. I don't want to hav this rool established; for if awl the bad peepil air to hav thare throte's cut, the lord ony nose hoo wil be suffered to liv. I shoodent feel saif in my bed msyelf. Besyde, whoos to say whoos good and whoo bad?" *Uncle Sam,* May 9, 1846, p. 3.

165. See, for example, *Mail,* March 30, 1846, p. 2; *Courier,* March 31, 1846, p. 2; April 1, 1846, p. 2; *Boston Journal* [cited herafter as *Journal*], April 3, 1846, p. 2; April 4, 1846, p. 2.

166. For excerpts (or examples) of editorial opinion from other parts of the country, see *Transcript,* April 1, 1846, p. 2; April 14, 1846, p. 2; *Times,* April 15, 1846, p. 2; *Police Gazette,* April 4, 1846, pp. 260–61 and 264; April 11, 1846, p. 268.

167. *Eagle,* April 1, 1846, p. 2; *Times,* April 1, 1846, p. 2; *Police Gazette,* April 11, 1846, p. 267.

168. *Times,* May 19, 1846, p. 2; June 17, 1846, p. 2; *Prisoner's Friend,* May 27, 1846, p. 83; *Post,* June 17, 1846, p. 2.

169. See *The Authentic Life of Mrs. Mary Ann Bickford* (Boston: Published by the Compiler, 1846), p. [2]; *Times,* June 9, 1846, p. 3; *Mail,* June 9, 1846, p. 3; *Bee,* June 9, 1846, p. 3; *Post,* June 10, 1846, p. 2.

170. *Mail,* June 9, 1846, p. 3; *Times,* June 9, 1846, p. 3; *Bee,* June 9, 1846, p. 3; *Post,* June 10, 1846, p. 2.

171. *Authentic Life,* passim. On the details confirmed by local records, see note 44 above and accompanying text; the relevant details appear in the *Authentic Life* on p. 3. Compare the Tirrell letters in *Authentic Life,* pp. 29 and 33–34, with the letters inserted into the trial record by Samuel Parker; see *Times Report,* p. 15.

172. *Authentic Life,* pp. 3–4.

173. Ibid., p. 17.

174. Ibid., p. 20.

175. See *Times,* June 11, 1846, p. 2; June 16, 1846, pp. [2–3].

176. See William W. Sanger, *The History of Prostitution* (1859; rpt. New York: Arno Press, 1972), pp. 563–64.

177. See *Bangor Daily Whig,* Jan. 19, 1847, p. 2. The *Whig* reporter or editor thought Bickford was "making a fool of himself."

178. See *Times*, Dec. 28, 1846, p. 2; *Mail*, Dec. 28, 1846, p. 3; *Chronotype* (Boston), Jan. 11, 1847, p. 2.

179. On the heterogeneous audiences for antebellum wax museums, see Nathaniel Hawthorne, *The American Notebooks*, ed. Claude M. Simpson (Columbus: Ohio State University Press, 1972), pp. 177–78; cited in Patricia Cline Cohen, "The Helen Jewett Murder: Violence, Gender, and Sexual Licentiousness in Antebellum America," *NWSA Journal* 2 (Summer 1990): 377 n. 9.

180. For a more elaborate statement of that claim, see Cohen, "Murder of Maria Bickford." For another discussion of the development of a consumer culture in mid-nineteenth-century America, see Stuart M. Blumin, "The Hypothesis of Middle-Class Formation in Nineteenth-Century America: A Critique and Some Proposals," *American Historical Review* 90 (April 1985): 318–32.

181. *Times*, Jan. 11, 1847, p. 2; Jan. 13, 1847, p. 2; *Chronotype*, Jan. 13, 1847, p. 1.

182. For examples of meager trial coverage, see Jan. 12–20 issues of the *Chronotype*, *Courier*, and *Boston Daily Atlas*.

183. *The Trial of Albert J. Tirrell . . . on the Charge of Arson* (Boston: 1847) [cited hereafter as *Arson Report*].

184. See *Arson Report*, pp. 10–11 and 34; *Post*, Jan. 13, 1847, p. 2; *Daily Evening Traveller* (cited hereafter as *Traveller*], Jan. 13, 1847, p. 2; Jan. 19, 1847, p. 2 (on Judge Shaw's use of Warren's testimony to discredit Lawrence); *Advertiser*, Jan. 14, 1847, p. 2;

185. See *Arson Report*, pp. 17–18; *Traveller*, Jan. 13, 1847, p. 2; *Post*, Jan. 14, 1847, p. 2; *Advertiser*, Jan. 14, 1847, p. 2.

186. See *Arson Report*, pp. 24 and 35; *Traveller*, Jan. 14, 1847, p. 2; *Post*, Jan. 15, 1847, p. 2; *Mail*, Jan. 19, 1847, p. 2 (for Choate's hypothesis that an unknown person might have entered the house and committed the murder).

187. See *Arson Report*, pp. 18–19 and 25–32, quoted at 28.

188. See *Arson Report*, pp. 32–36; *Times*, Jan. 19, 1847, p. 2, quoted; *Mail*, Jan. 19, 1847, pp. 1–2, quoted; *Advertiser*, Jan. 19, 1847, p. 2, quoted.

189. *Times*, Jan. 19, 1847, p. 2.

190. *Arson Report*, p. 34.

191. *Mail*, Jan. 19, 1847, p. 2.

192. *Arson Report*, p. 36; *Transcript*, Jan. 18, p. 2, quoted; *Times*, Jan. 19, 1847, p. 2; *Post*, Jan. 19, 1847, p. 2; *Chronotype*, Jan. 20, 1847, p. 2.

193. See *Mail*, Jan. 19, 1847, p. 2, quoted; *Advertiser*, Jan. 19, 1847, p. 2, quoted; *Times*, Jan. 19, 1847, p. 2, quoted; *Advertiser*, Jan. 20, 1847, p. 2.

194. *Mail*, Jan. 19, 1847, p. 2.

195. See *Arson Report*, pp. 37–40; *Advertiser*, Jan. 20, 1847, p. 2; *Times*, Jan. 20, 1847, p. 2; *Journal*, Jan. 20, 1847, p. 2: *Post*, Jan. 20, 1847, p. 2.

196. See *Mail*, Jan. 22, 1847, p. 2, quoted; *Bee*, Jan. 22, 1847, p. 2; *Post*, Jan. 22, 1847, p. 2; *Times*, Jan. 22, 1847, p. 2.

197. See citations in note 196 above; *Mail* quoted.

198. *Times*, Feb. 27, 1847, p. 2.

199. See *Mail*, Feb. 27, 1847, p. 3. The advertisement on that page, indicating that the exhibition was in its last week, had run in the *Mail* for the previous ten days; the wax museum was not advertised subsequently, leading to the inference that it had in fact closed on February 27.

200. See, for example, *Mail*, Jan. 12, 1850, p. 2; Jan. 21, 1850, p. 2; Feb. 5, 1850, p. 4; Feb. 6, 1850, p. 4. On pardon appeals, see *Mail*, Feb. 6, 1850, p. 4.

201. See *Tirrell Book*, p. 197. On his residence in the home of his father-in-law, see U. S. Census, 1850, M-432, roll 329, pp. 267v–268r.

202. See *Tirrell Book*, p. 197; U. S. Census, 1850, M-432, Roll 329, pp. 267–268; 1860, M-653, roll 514, p. 334; 1870, M-593, Roll 637, p. 447; 1880, T-9, roll 549, p. 378; Massachusetts Census, 1855, reel 21, vol. 28, pagination illegible; 1865, reel 24, vol. 27, unpaginated; *Weymouth Gazette*, Sept. 17, 1880, p. 2; Pamela Blevins, "The Trial and Verdict," *Weymouth News*, Sept. 25, 1980, p. 19. On the Weymouth shoe industry, see Bates Torrey, *The Shoe Industry of Weymouth* (Weymouth: Weymouth Historical Society, 1933); Gilbert Nash, *Historical Sketch of the Town of Weymouth, Massachusetts* (Weymouth: Weymouth Historical Society, 1885), pp. 150–51; on the role of the Tirrell family as founders and leading participants in that industry, see *Tirrell Book*, p. 74; Torrey, *Shoe Industry*, passim.

203. See U. S. Census, 1860, M-653, roll 514, p. 334; 1870, M-593, roll 637, p. 447. The same page of the 1870 census lists two young factory workers in their twenties who also owned one hundred dollars in personal estate. On the failure of the daughters to marry, see *Tirrell Book*, p. 294.

204. In addition to the census records cited earlier, see U. S. Census, 1900, T-623, roll 672, e.d. 1084, sheet 3; *Tirrell Book*, p. 294; *Weymouth Gazette*, April 20, 1883, p. 3; April 26, 1912, p. 3; Aug. 3, 1917, p. 4, quoted.

205. See Brown, *Works*, vol. 1, pp. 187, 274, and 289; Parker, *Reminiscences*, p. 53; Neilson, *Memories*, p. 8.

206. See Fuess, *Rufus Choate*, pp. 270–71; George S. Boutwell, *Lawyer*, pp. 6–8; Wendell Philips, *Speeches, Lectures, and Letters* (Boston: Walker, Wise, 1863), pp. 251–54, quoted at 254; Parker, *Reminiscences*, pp. 216–18, 225, and 228–30.

207. See Benjamin R. Curtis, "Address," in Brown, *Works*, vol. 1, pp. 257–64, quoted at 259; an excerpt from the same address, including the quoted passage, also appears in Parker, *Reminiscences*, pp. 228–30.

208. Ibid.

209. See Parker, *Reminiscences*, pp. 191–92; Whipple, *Recollections*, p. 1; Brown, *Works*, vol. 1, pp. 110 and 251–54.

210. See Russell Blaine Nye, *Society and Culture in America 1830–1860* (New York: Harper & Row, 1974), pp. 136–46.

211. See Robert A. Ferguson, *Law and Letters in American Culture* (Cambridge: Harvard University Press, 1984), pp. 230, 265–66, and 286–87; Nye, *Society and Culture*, pp. 145–46; Parker, *The Golden Age of American Oratory* (Boston: Whittemore, Niles, and Hall, 1857), pp. 1–13. That development in the field of oratory, forensic and otherwise, was roughly analogous to—and contemporaneous with—the broader "chastening of American prose style," a process that would accelerate during and after the Civil War; see Edmund Wilson, *Patriotic Gore: Studies in the Literature of the American Civil War* (New York: Oxford University Press, 1962), pp. 635–54.

212. Parker, *Golden Age*, p. 10; Parker, *Reminiscences*, p. 28; "Remarks of Richard H. Dana, Jr., Esq.," in Brown, *Works*, vol. 1, p. 253.

213. See Ferguson, *Law and Letters*, quoted at p. 5. For a complementary study of the next generation of American authors, see Brook Thomas, *Cross-Examinations of Law and Literature: Cooper, Hawthorne, Stowe, and Melville* (Cambridge, Eng.: Cambridge University Press, 1987).

214. See Ferguson, *Law and Letters*, pp. 26–27, 78–79, 82–84, and 287; Thomas, *Cross-Examinations*, pp. 1–3 and 12.

215. See David Ray Papke, *Framing the Criminal: Crime, Cultural Work, and the*

Loss of Critical Perspective, 1830–1900 (Hamden, Conn.: Archon Books, 1987), pp. 33–53; Dan Schiller, *Objectivity and the News: The Public and the Rise of Commercial Journalism* (Philadelphia: University of Pennsylvania Press, 1981), pp. 47–75 and 96–178.

216. See, for example, [Estabrook], *Eccentricities*, pp. 24–25 and discussion in text above.

217. See *Times*, June 9, 1846, p. 3 and discussion in text above.

218. For the *Times*'s sustained defense of the verdict, see *Times*, March 30, 1846, p. 2; March 31, 1846, p. 2; April 2, 1846, p. 2; April 8, 1846, p. 2; April 15, 1846, p. 2.

219. See *Mail*, Oct. 28, 1845, p. 2; Oct. 31, 1845, p. 2; Dec. 6, 1845, p. 2.

Chapter 10. *Conclusion*

1. The function of crime nonfiction as a cathartic release for forbidden impulses is probably quite similar to that of fiction, as described by Simon O. Lesser: "Fiction makes restitution to us for some of our instinctual deprivations. It emphasizes 'sex' to augment the meager satisfactions available through sanctioned channels and to allay our guilt feelings about our frequent transgressions of those sanctions, either in deed or in desire. It gives expression and outlet to aggressive tendencies which we are expected to hold in strict leash though they are covertly encouraged by our competitive culture." Lesser, *Fiction and the Unconscious* (Boston: Beacon Press, 1957), pp. 82 (quoted), 238–68, and passim.

2. When Robert Calef, critic of the Salem witchcraft prosecutions, decided to publish an attack on the proceedings in 1698, he was apparently forced to bypass local printers and send his manuscript to London for publication; see David Levin, *Cotton Mather: The Young Life of the Lord's Remembrancer, 1663–1703* (Cambridge: Harvard University Press, 1978), p. 287.

3. On "naive empiricism" and related concepts, see Michael McKeon, *The Origins of the English Novel, 1600–1740* (Baltimore: Johns Hopkins University Press, 1987), pp. 25–128 and 316. On early modern "philosophical realism," see Ian Watt, *The Rise of the Novel: Studies in Defoe, Richardson, and Fielding* (Berkeley: University of California Press, 1957), pp. 11–13, 27–28, and 31–33. On the long-standing faith in the veracity of statements by dying men and women, see discussion and citations in chapter 1 above; on the sanctioning of that faith by Anglo-American legal practice, see Hiller B. Zobel, *The Boston Massacre* (New York: W. W. Norton, 1970), p. 286.

4. On the concept of "cultural hegemony," see T. J. Jackson Lears, "The Concept of Cultural Hegemony: Problems and Possibilities," *American Historical Review* 90 (June 1985): 567–93, esp. 573–74 on the concept of an "open" hegemony.

5. Classic detective stories also reflected the new epistemology.

6. The overall shift in New England crime literature from the late seventeenth to mid-nineteenth centuries, most broadly conceptualized as a transition from Puritan communalism to legal romanticism, may be seen as roughly analogous to the much debated transition in political economy from classical republicanism to bourgeois liberalism. For a number of key works in the vast literature on liberalism and republicanism, see Stephen Watts, *The Republic Reborn: War and the Making of Liberal America, 1790–1820* (Baltimore: Johns Hopkins University Press, 1987); Joyce O. Appleby, *Capitalism and a New Social Order* (New York: New York University Press, 1984);

Drew R. McCoy, *The Elusive Republic: Political Economy in Jeffersonian America* (1980; rpt. New York: W. W. Norton, 1982); Lance Banning, *The Jeffersonian Persuasion: Evolution of a Party Ideology* (Ithaca: Cornell University Press, 1978); J. G. A. Pocock, *The Machiavellian Moment: Florentine Political Thought and the Atlantic Republican Tradition* (Princeton: Princeton University Press, 1975); Bernard Bailyn, *The Ideological Origins of the American Revolution* (Cambridge: Harvard University Press, 1967).

7. Lawrence M. Friedman, "Law, Lawyers, and Popular Culture," *Yale Law Journal* 98 (June 1989): 1588.

8. Admittedly, this broad claim is asserted, not proved—but to prove it would require another book.

Index